W9-DAK-547

MY HAPPINESS
BEARS NO RELATION
TO HAPPINESS

MY HAPPINESS BEARS NO RELATION TO HAPPINESS

◆

A Poet's Life in the Palestinian Century

Adina Hoffman

Yale University Press ◆ New Haven & London

FEB 2 0 2009

Unless otherwise noted, all poems by Taha Muhammad Ali come from
So What: New & Selected Poems, 1971–2005, English translation
© 2000, 2006 by Peter Cole, Yahya Hijazi, and Gabriel Levin.
Reproduced by permission of Copper Canyon Press.

Grateful acknowledgment is made for permission to reprint excerpts from
The World of Rashid Hussein: A Palestinian Poet in Exile © 1979
by Kamal Boullata and Mirène Ghossein, editors, published
by the Association of Arab-American University Graduates.

Designed by Sonia Shannon
Set in Fairfield type by Integrated Publishing Solutions, Grand Rapids, Michigan.
Printed in the United States of America by Sheridan Books, Ann Arbor, Michigan.

Library of Congress Cataloging-in-Publication Data
Hoffman, Adina.
My happiness bears no relation to happiness : a poet's life in the Palestinian
century / Adina Hoffman.
p.   cm.
Includes bibliographical references and index.
ISBN 978-0-300-14150-4 (cloth : alk. paper)
1. 'Ali, Taha Muhammad.   2. Poets, Palestinian Arab—Biography.   I. Title.

PJ812.T34Z69 2009
892.7'16—dc22
[B]   2008037298

A catalogue record for this book is available from the British Library.

This paper meets the requirements of ANSI/NISO Z39.48-1992
(Permanence of Paper).
It contains 30 percent postconsumer waste (PCW)
and is certified by the Forest Stewardship Council (FSC).

10 9 8 7 6 5 4 3 2 1

For Yusra

CONTENTS

To think that the sun rose in the east—that men and women were
        flexible, real, alive—that every thing was alive,
To think that you and I did not see, feel, think, nor bear our part,
To think that we are now here and bear our part.

                              Walt Whitman, "To Think of Time"

◆

THE HOUSE IS DARK IN THE FEBRUARY DAMP, but when she opens the door to let me in, Imm Nizar is laughing. It seems to tickle her that I got lost on my way to the home she almost never leaves, and that—after driving in confused loops around a dingy Nazareth neighborhood where teenagers tinker with half-stripped cars and packs of chickens scuttle—I gave up, pulled to the side, and called to ask for help.

In fact, Imm Nizar appears to be giggling or at least grinning much of the time, the still-girlish planes of her grandmotherly face opened out into a permanent, amused high beam. And though she's sneezing and coughing today as she greets me in her long terry-cloth robe and two cardigan sweaters, her head swathed in a loosely knotted wool scarf, she waves me over the threshold and into the chill of the large living room with such insistent good cheer—"Ahlein, ahlein," the standard welcome transformed in her full-throated delivery into a kind of credo—I feel like a traveler returning home after a long and arduous journey.

Never mind that my trip is really just beginning. This morning I packed myself and my new tape recorder into a shiny rental car and trundled westward then north from Jerusalem, past the year's first almond blossoms and toward this frigid room in Bir el-Amir, the Well of the Prince, the Nazareth neighborhood where Taha Muhammad Ali and his family have lived for more than twenty years.

The approach to this house always entails a subtle recalibration, a gentle, almost unconscious readjustment of one's pulse and gaze. In this case, the gnawing drive I've just taken through the traffic-clogged center of the country and into congested downtown Nazareth began to fall away when I at last regained my bearings and turned down the steep hill that leads into the neighborhood. Not that the scene there is in any way pastoral or uplifting: the entry is marked by an ugly clot of concrete apartment buildings painted in fading shades—tan, cream, sickly yellowish and gray, one with a pink, confectionary stripe around the side, and each with laundry flapping. Despite the obvious crowding that this knot of structures implies, the place is always oddly quiet. Olive trees and vegetable gardens interrupt the cement at sudden intervals, and several forgotten-looking construction sites have themselves become prolific beds of plush grass and wildflower. For all the years I have known Taha, the space across the street from his house has been dominated by the skeleton of a massive apartment-building-to-be, and this unfinished monstrosity, with its abandoned cement mixers and heaps of litter-strewn dirt, has by now almost come to seem a natural feature of the landscape, like a cliff face or ancient boulder.

Taha's own house is something else altogether—in the context of this dreary block, the first sign that one is now in the proximity of serious imagination. Invisible from the road, the driveway leads into the heart of a thick grove (really a small forest) of fruit trees—orange, lemon, grapefruit, olive, pomegranate, fig, pecan and tangerine, pomella and almond and more olive, all planted close. Prickly pear, rose, jasmine, oleander, geranium, potato vine, chicory, daisy, and narcissus also cram the plot—as do swarms of apparently ecstatic blackbirds and sparrows. Though I knew from past visits that this lush and singular orchard awaited me, Emerald City–like, at the end of my drive, all the foliage and sweet scent and birdsong surprised me today nonetheless: the effect was at once stirring and calming.

I would be content to sit in this thicket of color all day, but it is Taha who I've come to see, and after making my way up the bougainvillea-drenched staircase to the second-floor entrance and being whisked indoors by the laughing Imm Nizar, Taha's wife (like most Palestinian women, she is known to all as the mother, Imm, of her oldest son, while in traditional contexts Taha is referred to as Abu Nizar, the father of Nizar), I am ushered without much pomp into the bedroom—the only heated space in the house—where Taha is lying down.

And now it is my turn to laugh—at the sight of him, prone in a puffy, full-length quilted robe of gold-tinted synthetic leopard skin, with long purple tassels and a two-inch-thick calico lining. "My children call it Gorbachev," Taha announces a bit cryptically, then explains with mock grandeur that the garment is "Circassian," a gift from a friend after Taha tripped and broke his leg in the living room a few months earlier and the doctor ordered him, after an operation, to stay warm. He wears it today over an old running suit and with his usual black pancake cap tilted at a rakish angle, and though his outfit is absolutely ridiculous, it does, in its peculiar way, suit him—equal parts clown and king.

◆

I am here today for a complicated web of reasons, some plain to me, others more obscure, but all of which amount to the fact that I have decided—or, in point of fact, felt myself weirdly compelled—to try and write the life and times of this man, the Palestinian poet Taha Muhammad Ali.

The choice may seem peculiar. Taha is hardly a well-known personality in the West; he is, in his own proud terminology, "a peasant, the son of a peasant!" and is, moreover, a latecomer to poetry: his first book was published when he was fifty-two years old. He's a writer with a relatively small oeuvre (five collections of poems and a book of short stories) and a mostly underground reputation in the Arab literary world—where, it should be said, poetry has always been a highly public medium. One eleventh-century North African commentator described the fuss surrounding a poet's emergence in the years before Muhammad: "Feasts would be declared, and the women would gather together playing on lutes, as people do at weddings; men and boys alike would exchange the good news. For the poet was a defense to [the tribe's] honor, a protection for their good repute; he immortalized their deeds of glory and published their eternal fame." The centrality of verse is perhaps even more pronounced in the modern Palestinian context, where for much of the past century certain contemporary poets have been—and even in the era of the satellite dish

still are—treated as nothing less than national heroes and where poetry has been *the* medium of popular choice for both literary and
political expression.

Taha Muhammad Ali is, meanwhile, nobody's national poet. An
autodidact, he has operated a souvenir shop near Nazareth's Church
of the Annunciation for more than fifty years. Although his store has
for much of that time served as a modest magnet for poets, intellectuals, teachers, and ordinary people of all Arabic-speaking stripes and
camps, his perspective on modern Palestinian history and literature
has remained unusually private. He has never edited an important literary journal or run for office or published a fiery political manifesto—
all of which other writers, including many of Taha's shop guests and
good friends, have done with gusto in the extremely dynamic Palestinian cultural scene of the last half century.

Taha was born and grew up in Saffuriyya, a Galilee village that Israel destroyed in the wake of the 1948 war, and most of his poems well
up from the hard ground of that setting. Cunningly combining a
plainspoken register with an idiosyncratic (sometimes biting, sometimes mournful) storytelling sense, these are quietly sophisticated
lyrics, many of them populated by "simple" characters like the trusting and doomed peasant-everyman Abd el-Hadi—"In his life / he neither wrote nor read. / In his life he / didn't cut down a single tree, /
didn't slit the throat / of a single calf. / In his life he did not speak / of
the *New York Times* / behind its back . . ." These poems are engaged
and political in the deepest sense—the word, after all, comes from
the Greek *politikos,* "of a citizen"—though they eschew the direct approach to the so-called Struggle that is the hallmark of the "poetry of
resistance" written by many of Taha's peers and by the next, most acclaimed generation of Palestinian poets. Younger than Taha, Mahmoud Darwish and Samih al-Qasim, for instance, began to write much
earlier and came to widespread fame almost as soon as they did. Taha
has often likened his own poetic method to what he calls in English
"bill-i-ar-des": the word has four syllables when he says it. "You aim
over here—" a long, gnarled, yet delicately mottled farmer's finger
points to the right—"to strike over there." The finger bends sharply
to the left.

If one adds to this apparently odd selection of biographical subject my own oblique angle of approach to all things Palestinian, the

undertaking may sound, at best, surprising. An American-born Jew who has lived in Jerusalem for much of her adult life—assuming a sort of bifocal nationality in the process—I carry two passports, American and Israeli, and am someone who arrived in the Middle East knowing not a word of Arabic and bearing no particular affinity for Palestinian culture.

But that soon changed in ways that I could never have foreseen. The month my first book was published in the United States in 2000, Israel descended into one of the more brutal periods in its history: the dubious theatrics at Camp David gave way to the al-Aqsa Intifada, as it became known, which marked a new low in the relations between Palestinians and Israelis—and, indeed, between Jewish and Palestinian Israelis. (Twenty percent of Israeli citizens are Arab, Taha among them.)

And although my own life in Jerusalem was not dramatically affected by the violence escalating so close by—like all Israelis, I had the luxury that Palestinians in the West Bank and Gaza Strip did not, to come and go as I chose, without curfews, closures, or roadblocks— a gradual shift began to take place both within and around me. Like so many people I knew, I found myself shrinking inward, less eager than ever to venture out into the increasingly depressed, Jewish west of the city, where bombs were exploding with scary regularity. We felt them in our chest cavities when they went off downtown, then we waited to hear the sirens. After a friend—Anna, a plucky free spirit, avid reader, and lifelong peacenik—was killed by a Palestinian suicide bomber on a bus, I stopped taking public transportation. I also stopped talking politics with many Jewish friends, who had converted their own fear of such a violent demise into the most unapologetic racism. "The Arabs are animals," was now a phrase one heard almost daily, and "Death to the Arabs" became the literal writing on the wall, spray painted blackly all around town.

Neither during this time did I often cross the road right outside my own house and wander into Palestinian East Jerusalem, a change of pace to which I had once looked forward and which now filled me with a creeping sense of unease. This slowly spreading apprehension was, in many ways, the most demoralizing effect of the recent events: my brain had been colonized by new suspicions, new inhibitions, new categories of doubt. And when it came to my desire to wander the streets that I loved—by a host of grim new hesitations. As a writer whose primary concern has always been the detailed rendering of people and places, I found myself in the terrible position of not wanting to look hard at the very place where I'd chosen to live—or, worse still, to interact with many of its people.

Several years earlier, my husband, Peter Cole, and I had first come to know Taha Muhammad Ali, and Peter had begun, together with Yahya Hijazi and Gabriel Levin, to translate Taha's work into English. Within months of the start of that same Intifada, Ibis Editions, the small, nonprofit press that Peter, Gabriel, and I run together in Jerusalem, published a book of these translations. We must have known in some inchoate way then that bringing out such a book—of Arabic poems inspired by a bulldozed Palestinian village, translated by a trio of two Jews and a Muslim, all three of them Israeli citizens, as was the Palestinian poet himself—was, in its small way, an act of protest. ("Us [the Jews] here and them [the Arabs] there" had by then become the separatist slogan of many liberal Jewish Israelis.) But it was only later, as the situation around us worsened considerably and we grew to know Taha much better that I began to grasp the political, personal, and artistic implications of this alliance, this friendship.

By that time, Peter and I had begun to travel often with Taha around the United States, and as the two appeared together before a wide and welcoming range of audiences, a visceral bond evolved between them that exceeded even the typically close link between a poet and his translator. For all their obvious ethnic and generational differences, each, it seemed as they read together, was somehow communicating through the other. After all of our weeks spent, miles crossed, breakfasts eaten, and landscapes absorbed together, the trust among the three of us ran deep. The more time I spent with Taha and his poetry, the more I came to realize that he had something profound to tell me about the place that I'd recently had such difficulty staring in the face. I had, of course, been conscious before of the terrifically rich—and sometimes cruel—reality of Palestinian life, both before and after 1948, but I had never attempted to get too close or to ask the hardest questions about my connection, as a Jew, to that history. And for all my "knowledge" of this part of the world, I now realized I knew very little. "The limits of my language are the limits of my world," said the philosopher—and with this in mind, I was soon propelled to take on the serious study of both literary Arabic and the spoken Palestinian dialect; I also began at this point to consider the prospect of writing about Taha and his surroundings.

Among multiple things, I wanted to know how it was that an elderly Palestinian Muslim with four years of formal education, few teeth, and a literary obsession with a place where I myself have never been—and *could never go*—could "speak," as the idiom has it, so powerfully to my experience and to that of so many. Taha's frank, keen, off-kilter presence—both in person and on the page—has transformed Saffuriyya into something much larger than a single vanished village. Quite conscious of the difference in scale and notoriety, Taha has often, and not without irony, likened his Saffuriyya to Homer's Troy, a "lost" city whose mythic essence has fueled the imaginations of writers and readers for more than thirty centuries.

It also seemed to me then—and has only proven truer the more time I have spent with Taha—that his story is at once entirely singular (even eccentric) and completely representative of the sagas through which his people have lived. Born in 1931, Taha has witnessed enough history to fill several lifetimes, and I wanted, as I set out, not just to account for *what* he had seen but *how* he had seen it: to try, in other words, to convey the way such cataclysmic historical events look through the eyes of one exceptional man. As most everything in the Middle East inevitably is, the effort may be viewed as political—but it was inspired, first and foremost, by the far less absolute realm of art.

That said, Taha is hardly the only artist in this story. What follows is the tale of his own personal and poetic growth, but it is also a kind of group portrait. To the best of my knowledge, no one has ever written a biography of a Palestinian writer before, in any language (including Arabic), and that—together with the fact that most Western readers have little if any experience of that culture and literature—brings with it extra responsibility. To understand Taha and his place in Palestinian and indeed Arabic letters, it's crucial to be conscious of the range of personalities that have surrounded him over the years. Many of these poets and novelists are, it should be said, a good deal more famous than Taha, and there will be those who question my choice to focus on him. Where, they will ask, is Emile Habiby's biography? Mahmoud Darwish's? Samih al-Qasim's? Tawfiq Zayyad's? They are right to wonder, and I can only hope that those books will also be written one day. But these writers are here as well. Intellectuals everywhere draw sustenance, influence, and aggravation from their peers, and the situation is especially pronounced in Palestinian circles, which overlap to an uncommon degree and where everyone seems somehow linked to everyone else.

Similar imbrications and connections have also typified much of the rest of Taha's experience—and, as such, this book attempts to render both his life and his times. For while he is unique, Taha is not alone, and his story is laced through with the stories of many others, as it is with the story of Saffuriyya and its loss—and, by extension, Palestine and *its* loss. So that even when it is his "own" story I am relating, it may also belong to his society in a more collective sense. In Taha's 1984 poem "The Falcon," he writes of watching a songbird being attacked by a viper and seeing the terror explode in the bird's eyes: "Forests, moons, and lakes— / exile, streams, / and pastures the eye can't hold— / all were heaped around its neck / . . . / Massacres and cities / were gathered there in its gaze." This makes him realize how "That small bird's fear / cannot possibly be / its alone! / . . . / The fear of that small bird / . . . / cannot be fathomed except / as the fear of the flock as a whole."

◆

The idea of a Jew like me writing about, and expressing a tacit identification with, an Arab like Taha may provoke suspicion in some readers. For this very reason, when I'd first considered the project, I'd shied away, reluctant to set out across the narrative minefield of Palestinian-Israeli history. Before putting a single word on paper, I could already hear a chorus of readerly complaints: I'd be damned by some indignant partisan no matter what I wrote. But the closer Peter and I have become to Taha and, ironically enough, the darker the political skies over all our heads have grown—a recent survey shows that 41 percent of Israeli Jews support the separation of Arabs and Jews in places of entertainment, 46 percent would be unwilling to have an Arab visit their home, and 68 percent object to an Arab living in their apartment building—the more such hesitations have fallen away and the more I've come to appreciate Taha's undogmatic and ebulliently independent example. "Taking sides" is not the point here, because I do not consider myself and Taha—or Jews and Arabs, Israelis and Palestinians, for that matter—to be by nature on different "sides" at all; if anything, more joins than separates us.

One of the questions that I'm eager to answer as I grapple with Taha's life and its times concerns his unlikely exuberance. I have seen so many people on both sides of the ostensible Palestinian-Israeli divide become sour, depressed, shrill, stunted. ("A land that devours its inhabitants" is the eerily dead-on biblical diagnosis.) How, I have wondered, despite everything that Taha has endured, does he manage to remain so alert and joyful? If he has been angry—and his poetry acknowledges that at times he has—he has not let this anger flare into hatred but has turned it into an art and a generosity of feeling that seem almost to defy history. And maybe geography as well: his poetry has come to embody the essence of this place—addressing as it does the most difficult and painful dimensions of what is known as "the conflict"; at the same time, it also reaches far beyond these borders to speak both to those who know the land intimately and to those on the opposite ends of the earth. It is profoundly local—and utterly universal. As Taha himself once explained, "In my poetry, there is no Palestine, no Israel. But [there are] suffering, sadness, longing, fear, and [these] together, make . . . Palestine and Israel."

And so here I am, sitting by the side of Taha's bed with my notebook and tape recorder ready. Imm Nizar has plied me with tea and a large wedge of frosted cake. "It is ver-y sweet," Taha warns me, without further comment. The air is close: as cold as it is outside this room, it's hot and stuffy in here, and the paint on the walls is peeling. Other than the wardrobe with the large television on top, the bed, a chair, and a small dresser, cluttered with family photographs and untouched-looking perfume bottles, there is little in here besides Taha's books.

His untidy heaps of English and Arabic volumes have taken over his side of the room, and under an etched portrait of Beethoven and a reproduction of his favorite van Gogh—*Old Man in Sorrow*—spill the *Oxford Book of American Verse,* a selected William Carlos Williams (a recent gift from a friend), a volume by al-Jahiz, the eighth-century Basra-born man of letters, Sartre's *The Wall,* several copies of Taha's own books in Arabic, his battered and beloved *Webster's* English dic-

tionary, Tolstoy, Maupassant, Dante, an anthology of English translations of Sanskrit poems, another from the Chinese, stories by the
Egyptian modernist Yusuf Idris, a treatise by the twelfth-century grammarian Ibn al-Anbari, Robert Penn Warren and Cleanth Brooks's
Understanding Poetry, which, after lively and protracted bargaining,
Taha bought for just two dollars on a sidewalk near New York's Washington Square, and too much more to absorb in one glance—all of it
piled crookedly or backwards or upside down. Next to the bed are two
radios—the first, a boom box that Taha explains is tuned at all times
to the Voice of Music, Israel's only classical station; the second, a
small white transistor, is always set to the BBC Arabic Service, "Big
Ben," as he calls it, for the hourly chiming of those somber bells. On
the nightstand are multiple cardboard pill packets and Erskine Caldwell's *A Woman in the House* in a 1950s dimestore paperback edition,
with a slightly tawdry, pin-up girl–styled cover and Taha's bookmark
inside. Three or four flowered polyester blankets are piled around him
on the bed, and from beyond the closed window, I can hear the constant clucking, sometimes crowing, of the roosters next door.

SAFFURIYYA I

◆

MAP OF A VANISHED TOWN

◆

WITH A TITLE AS HAUNTED AND HAUNTING as its subject
matter, *All That Remains* is a monumental reference book, in which
the distinguished historian Walid Khalidi and a team of researchers
set out to chronicle the 418 Palestinian villages that Israel effectively
erased in 1948. A painstakingly compiled document that is all the
more moving for its matter-of-factness, the book offers photographs
and brief, businesslike descriptions of each of these villages—before
'48, during the war, and today—and in doing so it attempts to preserve on paper what has disappeared from the earth: "Now and then
a few crumbled houses are left standing, a neglected mosque or
church, collapsing walls along the ghost of a village lane, but in the
vast majority of cases, all that remains is a scattering of stones across
a forgotten landscape." The book is, says the preface, "an attempt to
record that lost world."

There is in this effort an air both of urgency and of futility: if these
facts aren't set down now, the authors seem to be saying, they will be
gone forever; on the other hand, it is clear—as it is clear to anyone
who has spent time trying to account in words for a way of life that
no longer exists—that the book cannot ever be more than "an attempt." Too many traces have already been destroyed or washed away;
too much time has passed; too many witnesses have sunken into silence, forgotten, or died. . . . Venturing to reconstruct the years
of Taha's childhood and adolescence, or to imagine Saffuriyya in all
its vanished richness and complication, is of course a similar task,
and as I work (interviewing, translating and transcribing those inter-

views, sifting through archival files, combing footnotes and card catalogues, Xeroxing, looping microfilm onto spools, poring through old
journals and newspapers) I sometimes feel myself an archaeologist,
entrusted with an especially precious—but partial and vulnerable-to-
the-elements—mound of chipped relics and fragmented memories,
each of which must be examined and gingerly placed in a pattern that
makes some kind of sense.

There are obstacles. "Arkhas hibr, afdal min idh-dhikr" (the cheapest ink is better than memory), as Amin, Taha's then-seventy-year-old
and youngest brother, once told me, explaining his own passionate
work as amateur historian and president of the Saffuriyya Heritage
Society, a cultural-political group he founded with several friends in
1993. Among the society's goals is to salvage the remnants of the material and human past of Saffuriyya and other obliterated villages like
it, through the preservation of oral history and the collection of daily
objects. One floor of Amin's Nazareth house is home to the society's
offices and a remarkable, single-room museum. This is a generic, almost corporate space with fluorescent lights, fiberglass ceilings, and
shiny tile floors—filled almost to bursting with the incongruously
preindustrial and heartbreakingly modest paraphernalia of pre-1948
Galilee village life: baskets and mortars, shaving kits and wooden dowry
boxes, a gauzy woman's headscarf, trimmed with a dainty, handmade
menagerie of silk-thread birds and flowers. Amin has, it seems, paid
for much of this collection out of his own pocket, and driven himself
into debt in the process. When he sees an old Palestinian object, he
must have it for the museum—rescue it, as it were, from near-certain
oblivion and so somehow restore it to its proper place in the order of
things. (He himself doesn't talk in such cosmic terms but does admit
to the slightly obsessive nature of his collecting.) He has also single-
handedly performed a kind of oral-history triage, as he realized that
he had to act right away or else the older people would take with them
to the grave irreplaceable information about the village—the popular
names, for instance, for the different parts of town. Almost every plot
in Saffuriyya was known to the villagers by a name based on its past or
present owners (Khallet ish-Sheikh Hassan, Sheikh Hassan's Knoll),
what grew there (Juret iz-za'tar, Hyssop Gulley), or some more mysterious association (Balatet il-hayyeh, the Stone of the Snake).

At some point in the 1990s, Amin told me, he realized that "the old people are dying, and those names will disappear. I told myself I have no choice. I'll ask them: What do you remember of the names from the village? I'll write it down. From here ten names, from there twenty names, from there thirty, from there fifteen. . . . Then I'd go back and say, okay, we're in Saffuri, we want to go to Shafa ʿAmr [the next large village]—what is the name of the first block? The first parcel of land, what's it called? And what's after it? And after that? And after? And how big was this one? And this? It wasn't exact. But how much, approximately? I worked on this list for maybe two years. And the names I didn't write down are gone." In a similar inch-by-inch way, he went from house to house around Nazareth—where today some fifteen thousand of the city's sixty thousand residents count themselves as Saffuriyyans, or descendants of Saffuriyyans—and transcribed what the older people remembered of the names and owners of the village thoroughbreds, the names of the teachers in the village school. . . . As he worked, word of his fascination with the town's history spread, and aging former villagers sought him out and presented him with priceless documents: one man had been responsible in the early 1940s for water distribution in the orchards and had kept a detailed notebook, listing the sizes and owners of the various plots. When the Israeli army occupied Saffuriyya in 1948, the man fled to Nazareth, but in the days immediately following the conquest, he managed to sneak back into his house and rescue the notebook, whose previously humdrum subject matter (irrigation) had been transformed in the course of that fateful week into the most valuable sort of written proof—sentimental proof of an eclipsed way of life but also potentially legal proof of land ownership. Now, almost fifty years after Saffuriyya was leveled, he handed the notebook over for safekeeping to Amin—that is, to posterity.

But as Amin is the first to admit, such systematically kept written records were the exception in the village and not the rule. Saffuriyya was an almost entirely oral place, and written documentation of the village—of the sort biographers tend to take for granted when constructing timelines and portraits of their subjects—simply does not exist. The village had no local newspaper, no records office, no medical files, no school yearbook. None of Taha's relatives or friends kept date books or diaries or wrote newsy letters to out-of-town aunts; his mother hung no smiling wedding pictures from her walls, and she did

not memorialize her children's growth in a scrapbook or photo album. And whatever private papers of Taha's that might once have
existed—his report cards, his first attempts at writing, the single photograph taken of him as a child—were destroyed when the village was
destroyed.

"We have a problem. Our problem is that our people aren't historians. We depend on listening. You hear a story, and you tell it, and
distort it. You add to it, you take away from it," says Amin, and aside
from the information and old photographs that he himself has
valiantly gathered and that the Saffuriyya Heritage Society printed in
two glossy magazines and a wall calendar, the written vestiges of the
village are sketchy in the extreme: recently a former villager published
a catch-all collection of Saffuriyya history and lore—which includes
folk songs, family names, pictures of ancient coins and oil lamps
found in the village, a chronicle of "Saffuriyya during the Crusader
Aggression," lists of local birds, the "martyrs" killed in 1948, herbal
medicine prescriptions, wedding customs, and so on. And another
slender memorial volume was compiled in Syria by two refugees who
live there and whose work is apparently unknown to their former
neighbors, the Saffuriyyans in Israel. (I stumbled on a copy while
browsing in the stacks of a large American university library.)

Beyond that, the only paper trail left by the village is a thin, fascinating, and distinctly misleading one—which passes through
archives now housed in Israel and England. (The British controlled
Palestine from 1917 until 1948—the period known now simply as the
Mandate—and when they decamped in the chaos of that last year,
they took some files with them, burned some, and left others behind,
in uncharacteristically pell-mell fashion.) These records provide a
glimpse into the life of the village that is, on the one hand, mar-
velously concrete—not precarious and shifting like memory and so
an exciting discovery for someone trying to rebuild the village, as it
were, on the page. The tabletop-sized Mandate-era Nazareth police
station logs that have survived the years, for instance, offer the most
tangible facts about the people and pulse of the village—who bullied
who, who cheated who, who beaned who with a rock at exactly what
hour on what day. . . . But as these few examples indicate, and as logic
dictates, the only sort of events that are preserved in the law enforcement files are the grumbling, ugly ones: this is merely a story of grievances and arrests. And though the tale told by these records is no

doubt true—and important to account for, somehow, as one tries to conjure the village—it also leaves out the contented, day-in-day-out, uncomplaining side of Saffuriyya. And according to the people who lived there, *this* was the place they knew and loved.

The villagers entered the written record only when they were dealing with the outside world, which is to say, when something went wrong. Besides the fistfights and robberies recorded in the police logs, various "crimes" are set down there that seem, in retrospect, to implicate the English authorities more than the villagers. The strict legalism of the Mandatory system grated against the villagers' traditional way of life, so that, for instance, the police could often be found charging the people of Saffuriyya with "harvesting and threshing wheat without a permit" and "picking olives before the date appointed by the Administrative Office." In one case, a charge of "Illegal Celebration of a Marriage" is noted, followed by a brief, cryptic explanation: "Secret information that 4 girls were married under age in Saffourieh. All X-rayed, found to be under 15 years old."

Other loaded interactions are preserved in innocuous-sounding files like the one called "Saffuria Roads," now housed in the Israel State Archive. There one finds the lengthy correspondence between the Saffuriyya local council and the British high commissioner about the urgent need to pave the single road that connected Saffuriyya with the towns nearby—with, in other words, that very outside world. This exchange kicks off with a respectful 1935 letter, written in literary Arabic and translated by a Mandatory clerk into slightly stilted English:

> During your last visit to Saffuriya, Your Excellency noted how large is our village with its numerous inhabitants, large areas of lands [sic] sufficient water and vast gardens. On your return to Jerusalem Your Excellency have [sic] kindly ordered your local representatives to expend a certain amount on leveling the road to our village. Whereas we have important commercial relations with the towns of Haifa, Acre, Nazareth, and Tiberias to which our vegetables, fruits and animals are exhibited for sale, therefore we have no easy connection with the said towns in view of the fact that the licensed busses of our village are unable to pass the said road which is now muddy from rains.

After their request was summarily rejected by the district commissioner on what appear to be financial grounds, the bus owners themselves began to complain, since their business was suffering during the rainy season, and by 1937 the town's mayor, Sheikh Saleh Salim Sulayman, and the council were driven to write another—much testier, and surprisingly political—letter to His Excellency:

> We suggest that because we are native landlords, the Public Works Department did not take an interest in this matter, while for the interest of the Jews a road from Ginesar to Nahalal is being constructed which will cost Government twenty two thousand pounds and another road from Afula to Shatta which will also cost double the expenses of the other roads. . . . Seeing this injustice, we humbly complain to Your Excellency against the action of the Public Works Department.

More than a decade after the council's first letter on the subject had been delivered to Jerusalem, the road was still washing out, complaints were registered that doctors couldn't get through to the village, and the district commissioner finally wound around to recommending a loan to the council for the long-awaited pavement. His reasoning, though, is startling in its steeliness. After admitting that the village is indeed "one of the principal suppliers for the vegetable markets of Haifa and [that] a considerable amount of commercial traffic proceeds in and out of the local council area daily," he gets down to what's really on his mind:

> I would also add that in the event of a recrudescence of disorders on the Arab Side, Saffuriyya would undoubtedly be the chief center in the Nazareth area of organised resistance to Government, and the existence of a fast asphalted approach road would be of considerable assistance to the forces of law and order.

Even the logic of so-called security didn't win out, though: the loan was declined, 1948 soon arrived, and it seems the village never got its asphalt.

Sheikh Saleh and the council make frequent appearances in the files. They were, after all, the village's official representatives before the Powers That Were. In only a few instances do the people of Saffuriyya speak for themselves. Aside from several appeals on behalf of prisoners and the desperate letter of a father about the disappearance of his two boys—one of whom is preserved forever in epistolary amber as a fourteen-year-old, "wearing khaki trousers and a shirt under a yellow kumbaz [robe]" when he was last seen—there is, as far as I can tell, a single file that contains letters from ordinary citizens. Though it should be said here that the archives themselves are vast haystacks containing who-knows-how-many-needles: the Israel State Archive in particular holds a treasure trove of Mandate-era documents—everything from files called Maronite Monks to Field Mice, Erection of Electric Poles, Bomb Outrages, Nutrition in the Colonial Empire, Enumeration of Goats, Lunatics, Playing Cards, Stamp Vendors, Alleged Discovery of Gold in Palestine, Preservation of Public Morality, Search for Buried Treasures, and Manufacture and Sale of Whipped Cream.

But at the time of my work there, the archive lacked a centralized cataloguing system, and to find any trace of the village at all one had to pore over long, irregular, and often incorrectly typed or scribbled (half-Hebrew, half-English) lists under an assortment of headings and flip through unalphabetized, handwritten card catalogues in search of the place, spelled variably as Saffuriyya, Saffuriya, Safuriya, Safuriyeh, Saffurieh, Saffourieh, Safourieh, Safuria, Saffuria, and by its Hebrew name, Tzippori, Tsippori, Zippori—not to be confused with a different village, in the Jaffa District, called Safiriyya or Safiriya. Each file had to be ordered up from the vaults, at which point one would inevitably be told that certain documents were "missing" or off-limits because of their fragile state. The folders that did arrive—their contents sometimes crumbling or preserved in the faintest carbon copy— had then to be sorted through carefully for clues. It seems almost certain that the archive contains other mentions of the village that I have not unearthed or been able to decipher.

Once in hand, that "Saffuria Village—General Correspondence" file itself is both fascinating and frustrating. If it is an encounter with the actual voices of the villagers one is looking for, one will not find it there. Because of the tonal and formal gaps between written and spoken Arabic, and because most of the people of Saffuriyya were illiterate, the letters that have survived in the files seem oddly filtered, or displaced. A few of the authors were educated and wrote in their own

words and hand. And here and there a letter does exist that blends literary and transliterated spoken Arabic in intriguing ways: these seem
to be letters written by the villagers without outside help. But the vast
majority of the petitioners must have relied on a kind of scribe or, really,

a translator, a person like one
of the local schoolteachers,
who would have listened patiently to whatever the particular complaint, offered up in
the thick village dialect and
probably in scrappy, conversational terms, then paused
for a moment before dipping
a pen in ink and recasting the
same thoughts in "proper" literary Arabic and in a register
that would have been "appro-
priate" for addressing a foreign figure of authority. When the letter
was complete, the complainant would stick a thumb into that same
ink pot and stamp the page in lieu of signing. Oddly, these smudged
fingerprints seem a more intimate link to the peasants than do any
number of the scribes' polished words.

Although the villagers' particular cadences may be lost forever,
the nature of their complaints is telling—and moving in its humble
scale. As one reads, it is difficult to keep from one's mind the tremendous losses that awaited the people of Saffuriyya in 1948 and that
would forever dwarf gripes like the one conveyed in a 1947 letter from
a man who writes to the Nazareth district commissioner to register
his dismay that his neighbor had been digging under a stone wall
that separated their two gardens, so rendering the divider dan-
gerously unstable. Or the letter from one Muhammad, whose son
Ibrahim died and left his children a cow. Muhammad's other son,
Lafi, meanwhile sold the cow to his father-in-law, but, argues
Muhammad, it still belongs to the children. He asks the help of the
assistant district commissioner in attempting to return the cow to its
rightful owners. . . .

The British archives, for their part, are almost parodic models of
efficiency, good cheer, and order. (Israel may have inherited harsh
methods of equestrian crowd-control and prisoner interrogation from

the British, but somehow the legacy of neat bookkeeping and gracious service got away at the end of the Mandate.) The papers that are preserved so conscientiously in London and in Oxford, though, tend to belong on a different—loftier, more abstract—plane than the cows, stone walls, and washed-out roads of the Israel State Archive files. The documents of the Colonial Office, for instance, now kept in the National Archives at Kew, concern matters of government policy and broader "security" trends, while the Foreign Office papers contain lengthy exchanges about such sweeping subjects as "Arab Political Activity in General." A village like Saffuriyya, not surprisingly, barely registers in this Whitehall-centered context.

At Oxford, where the private papers of various Mandatory clerks, ambassadors, army officers, missionaries, and teachers are held, the village turns up just a few times—as several high-ranking police officials preserved the records of two famous crimes that may or may not have involved Saffuriyyans. These crimes and their aftermath also account for the village's fleeting appearance in the newspapers of the period. Here and there mention is made in a less fraught framework, such as the 1943 *Palestine Post* article about how "a fine wolf was killed by British Police near Saffuriya and its very excellent skin adorns the canteen floor of the Mounted Police Striking Force" or the report from 1944 of a Saffuriyya flour mill gutted by a fire "believed to have been caused by an over-heated exhaust pipe."

Other archival sources of information about the village exist, though these belong to the more slippery—and menacing—category of "army intelligence." And here another point of view appears: throughout the 1940s, the pre-state intelligence branch of the Haganah, the precursor to the Israel Defense Forces (IDF), compiled "surveys" of some seven hundred Arab villages, towns, cities, and Bedouin encampments—whether for eventual operational purposes or, as one scholar has proposed, to prove the theory that was then being floated in certain Jewish circles (and still convinces some today) that the Arabs of Palestine were recent arrivals in the country, a random assortment of Egyptians and nomads with little claim on the land. According to one Jewish historian at the time who was eagerly urging the Jewish Agency to sponsor an investigation "in a scientific fashion" into the origins of each Arab village, "This [information] has great political worth."

Saffuriyya was one of the villages included in the survey, and the

1943 document that survives in the Haganah Archive is as interesting for what it gets wrong as what it gets right. These neatly typed six pages of Hebrew include more-or-less accurate information about the village's water sources, roads, livestock, lands, and agricultural production, as they manage to completely misrepresent the town's social fabric, scrambling the names and importance of the main families of the town, their precise origins, the *mukhtars* (family or village chiefs), the number of mosques and guesthouses. For reasons that remain unclear, the document also claims that 50 percent of the villagers could read—unlikely at a time when the literacy rate for Muslims throughout Palestine was probably less than half that.

The rest of the material put forth in the survey is hard to prove or disprove: lists of men who allegedly participated in the 1936–1939 revolt fought by Palestinian Arabs against British rule and Jewish settlement, an account of the weapons confiscated from the villagers, names of "troublemakers," and an estimate of the damages incurred during this period—whether inflicted by the government (house demolitions, for example) or by the rebels, who seized money and guns from the villagers. The village is described as a "nest" for the Young Men's Muslim Association (YMMA), and a place where "the Arab terrorists and murderers found shelter." In the sole first-person sentence in the whole document, its author—who was known to have been an Arab collaborator from the village of 'Anabta—declares: "I do not think there was a single young man in Saffuriyya who did not participate in the disturbances [the revolt], whether openly or secretly." Because of the complete absence of written accounts from the villagers' perspective about what went on in Saffuriyya during the revolt, these aspects of the report are hard to dispute—but not at all difficult to doubt, given the identity of their author and apparent purpose. The typed, tagged, and catalogued record is, it turns out, pace Amin, often just as dubious as half-recalled, even secondhand bits and pieces, recounted some sixty years on. That said, files of this tendentious "intelligence" sort, whether British or Zionist, also constitute the most systematically preserved body of firsthand documentation from the pre-1948 period; given the scarcity of real-time sources, anyone searching for Saffuriyya's traces simply cannot afford to dismiss them.

Another place one may turn to catch a glimpse of Saffuriyya and its people as they were then—and not as they're remembered now—is in the few photographs of the village that exist. A handful of these were taken by the gifted and prolific Eric Matson, Swedish-born photo-

grapher for the American Colony, the legendary messianic Christian commune and charitable enclave in Jerusalem, now the site of a famously posh hotel and the most elegant garden bar in all of Israel/Palestine. Between 1898 and 1946, Matson and his pictorially inclined predecessors and colleagues at the colony shot some twenty thousand photographs and lantern slides of, as they dubbed them, "Bible Lands etc." These were images whose subjects ranged widely, from the scriptural to the botanical to the documentary to the romantic. Matson's photographs of Saffuriyya are few but powerful, all dated from "c. 1940" and what must have been a single summertime outing to the village with his camera. These include several glowing shots of the threshing floors and water station—both bustling and alive as seen through Matson's lens. Given how vivid these few flashes are, one only wishes he had taken more pictures of the village.

Here and there other glimpses of the place surface. In 1932, a group of educational inspectors snapped photos of village children

throughout Palestine and placed the pictures in an album, which they planned to turn into a lantern-slide show "to be shown to the Fellahin [peasants] on our trips to the villages. The appeal that the projection of his life conditions on the screen will make to the Fel-

lah cannot be overestimated." The seven staged-looking photos of
Saffuriyya students in this album are labeled with captions that veer
from the sticky sweet ("School boys happy at their Dabkeh, a fine
native dance that should be preserved") to the paternalistic ("The
teacher explaining to the Fellahin [most of the villagers in the picture
are adults and probably farmers] how to prepare seedbeds for the
propagation of forest and fruit trees") to the presumptuously melodramatic: "The neglected future generation!"

A smattering of other pictures exist, with no photographer's name
attached. But to my mind one of the strangest and most telling visual
keyholes into Saffuriyya lies in the images shot by an archaeological
team that excavated in the village—the site of the ancient and illus-

trious town of Sepphoris—in the early
1930s. Perhaps these photos are so potent
because they weren't meant to "represent" the village at all, a notion that was
freighted from the moment cameras came
to Palestine in the second half of the
nineteenth century and Western photographers set about trying to capture for
the viewers back home "authentic biblical scenes" and the country's "timeless
landscapes." In a few instances the dig's
official photographer—Fadeel Sabba, a
Palestinian Arab himself, as it happens—
turned his camera directly to face the
people of Saffuriyya. The archaeological album contains several
posed portraits of the laborers and a single candid shot of the work
unfolding. But the vast majority of the excavation photographs are
meant to show off the relics that the crews were digging up: the villagers appear in these photos as no more than biped measuring sticks.
And while it is slightly unsettling to see the Saffuriyyans acting in this
objectlike way—standing stiff and blank faced beside some stone
column or at the end of a newly unearthed basilica—there they are,
in the flesh and in their own clothes, with their thoughts tucked a
bit mysteriously behind their impassive expressions. Cipherlike mes-
sengers from that now-vanished world, they have a ghostly presence

at the corners and edges of these pictures. Hovering there in the ruins-of-Sepphoris that were soon to become the ruins-of-Saffuriyya, they seem at once closer—and farther off—than ever.

And finally—a single map of the village exists. It is a carefully rendered English plan of the older parts of town, dated 1945, and though it does not contain the maniacally precise agricultural and architectural minutiae of other Mandatory maps from around the same time—whose colored keys include dainty symbols for such features as Mosque with Minaret, Coniferous Trees, and Limekiln, along with a sternly italicized proviso: "*N.B. The representation on this map of a Road, Track, or Footpath, is no evidence of the existence of a right of way*"—its cartographers did take pains to chart every building in Saffuriyya. Amin's museum boasts a blurry poster-sized copy-of-a-copy of this map, and one evening when I am in Nazareth he offers to bring it over to Taha's house so that the two of them can give me a "tour" of the village. First Imm Nizar makes the rounds with the usual nut-stuffed cookies and small cups of coffee, then she sits, exhausted as always after a full day's housework, talking, sighing, and giggling with Imm 'Arab, Amin's wife, who was also born in Saffuriyya but who

dresses and carries herself differently from Imm Nizar, like a city
woman. They are just a few years apart but belong somehow to two
distinct generations, as do Taha and Amin—whose four-year age
gap seems multiplied severalfold in both physical and psychological
terms. With his crooked lope, booming rasp of a voice, prodigious
wrinkles, and ability to take command of any room, Taha is not just
the older but an elder—a kind of born mukhtar. Amin, meanwhile,
though now gray-haired and fairly wrinkled himself, is very much the
younger brother. Sprier, itchier, more coiled to spring than Taha, he
seems thoroughly unconcerned with his appearance but cannot help
his own slightly down-at-the-heels handsomeness. Almost despite
himself and his polyester pants, he bears a rather uncanny resem-
blance to the aging Marcello Mastroianni.

    After all my time in the archives dowsing for some—any—trace
of the people of Saffuriyya, it is a relief to sit with Taha and Imm
Nizar, Amin and Imm 'Arab, sipping coffee in this familiar living room
with its worn couches, plush drapes, and brass bric-a-brac. Under the
gaze of a plastic wall clock, a large reproduction of the Mona Lisa,
and perhaps the most iconic photo of Saffuriyya that exists—a 1931
panorama of the village, shot by that same archaeological dig's unfa-
mous photographer—we huddle over the map of the lost town. Amin
ignores the women's soft laughter and begins to point and narrate in
intent Arabic, leading me from front door to front door—"This is the
house of H'ssein Ibrahim, and this is the house of Flefel. . . ." Taha
adds (in English), "the one with the goats." Amin: "Flefel . . . what's
his name?" Taha: "Salim." Amin: "Salim il-Flefel, Salim. Here's
'Brahim Abu Qasim." Taha: "He is a relative. . . ." Amin: "And here,
here's our house . . . here's the street . . . and here's the compound of
Sheikh Saleh Salim"—this name is offered in chorus, the two of them
singing it out. Taha: "He had many houses . . . for his brothers and
his three wives. . . . And here's 'Ali H'ssein—no! First it was Qasim
Mustafa." "No," says Amin. "You are right," says Taha. "And this is
Shantawi. . . . No, no, next to it—What's his name?" "Who?" "The
one with the books, the one who read many books, an educated one,"
says Taha. "Who do you mean, ya Taha? This here is Abu Ahmed's
house, next to it is, eh . . . Sa'id Amin. Near it is the house of il-
Imbadna—am I right, ya Taha?" and on into the night we go—with
Imm Nizar and Imm 'Arab gossiping animatedly and sometimes chip-

ping in the chortled nickname of a neighbor or store owner, at one
point even bursting out into a series of Saffuriyya wedding songs,
whose jubilantly simple refrains appear to have resurfaced suddenly
after more than fifty years underground: "Leina ya Saffuriyat, leina, /
farah jdid mbarak 'aleina" (O women of Saffuriyya, a new joy has
blessed us).

As they sing and talk I'm scribbling to set down whatever I can,
and the brothers are taking turns pressing their fingers into the tiny
cubes that indicate what once were houses on the map. The longer
we sit here, the more involved the two become in each other and in
their sometimes disparate visions of the village, which begins, nonetheless, to emerge in composite before me on the fuzzy Xerox. Their tone
veering from excitement to melancholy and back again, one will gently place a hand on the other's wrist to correct or argue or agree as now
they chuckle at some newly remembered detail and now fish in vain
for a name that has disappeared into the distance.

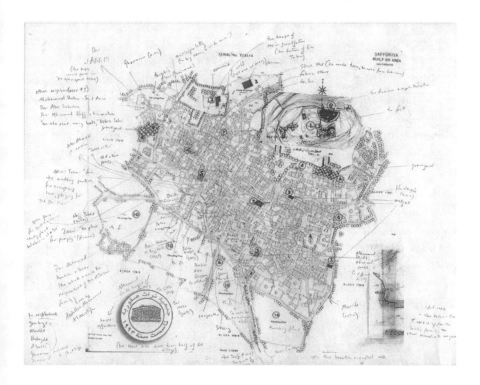

PREHISTORY

♦

EVEN BEFORE HE COULD SEE THE VILLAGE, he has said, the scent of it was overpowering—the thyme and the mint and the lemon trees, the broom and the wheat and the olives. The thorns themselves seemed to smell sweetly there, and though he couldn't say which perfume belonged to what plant—or explain how he knew the difference between the fragrance of a Nazareth sage bush and a sage bush with its roots in the soil of Saffuriyya—the boy was convinced that he could tell in his nose when he'd crossed the border, and as he made his way toward home through the *basatin*, as the orchards and vegetable gardens were known, the scents grew stronger and more complicated, more human. The fruit trees were everywhere, and at the Qastal spring he got a clean, cold whiff of the abundant water that made the village lands so rich (and, according to local lore, its people so strong-headed), then, getting closer, the smoky perfume of the cooking fires joined in with the savor from the packed plots of tomato, cabbage, parsley, cauliflower, scallion, cucumber, and his favorite, *mlukhiyyeh,* the dark green mallow that his mother would chop fine or spread out to dry and that they would eat as a stew. Thinking of it would make him hungry and eager for the other scents to come: the way the garlic she fried before adding the leaves would blend and merge with the piercing aroma of the basil planted in clay pots before the nearby houses.

Next came the spot they called Bab il-Matalleh, Prospect Gate, which marked the true entrance to the village: after meandering through the basatin, the dirt path swept downward then suddenly up and around to the left; the boy had walked this way hundreds, maybe thousands of times before, but the view that awaited him there always made his heart beat a bit faster. While it may have been the hike up the incline that speeded his breath, he liked to imagine that what caused him to inhale more deeply was that first—familiar yet forever tremendous—vision of Saffuri.

He called it Saffuri, as all the villagers did, though its official name was Saffuriyya. He didn't know then that the name came from the Syriac or Hebrew words for bird, *sefre* and *tzippor,* which were close to the word *'asfur* in Palestinian Arabic. (It had also been known in other eras as Sepphoris, Tzippori, and Le Sephorie.) Still, he might have understood instinctively what his ancient predecessors in the village had meant by such a title: that the town sat perched on its hill like some marvelous sky-bound creature. All the majesty and poverty, the confinement and expanse of the place were visible in that first eyeful, which included a sweeping view of the crowded older parts of town, built low and pale over the hill, and at the crest—protective or a bit aloof, depending on one's angle—the stately box of a citadel, the Qal'a. This structure had been rebuilt by the eighteenth-century Bedouin ruler of the Galilee atop the ruins of a Byzantine base whose cornerstones were Roman sarcophagi and which had also served as a Crusader watchtower—though again these dates and long-gone civilizations meant little to the boy. He knew simply that his village was very old. (There had been a settlement or city here on and off since the time of the Canaanites.) It was very distinguished. (Saffuriyya's illustrious Persian-Greek-Roman-Jewish-Byzantine-Crusader-Arab history was vague to him and he'd never heard of Josephus, who dubbed the town's first-century incarnation the "ornament of all

Galilee," but he understood that he lived in the largest and most important village in the Nazareth District of British Mandatory Palestine.) And it was the place where he belonged.

If he kept walking then, he'd reach the *bayader*, the threshing floors, which flanked the village to the south and which were crowded in the warm season with the pillowy geometries of the harvest: the great sunny mounds of wheat and barley, vetch and lentil, and the spheres trod around them by the donkeys and horses who dragged their stone-studded boards in

seemingly endless circles. Sometimes he would pause to watch and listen to the shouts and singing of the boys who'd been hired to prod the animals along—but when he was hungry he would begin to run as he reached the bayader, and he would keep running, all the way home.

The boy would have said to a stranger that his home was Saffuri, yet he would really have meant something at once smaller and larger. There was, first of all, the literal house—with its three adjacent rooms built of stone and whitewashed inside, its cement floors and blue-trimmed windows, its plain wooden door, the low wall that enclosed the little courtyard and his mother's vegetable patch. But then there was the wider human sphere—the concentric circles that began in this dwelling and radiated outward. His parents, siblings, uncles, cousins, his best friend, Qasim, Sheikh Saleh, the mayor and their next-door neighbor, Shantawi, the aging bachelor grocer, the *khatib*, or preacher, Hassan Halabo, who sometimes fell asleep as he taught the boys Qur'an . . . they were all planets in this solar system known as Saffuri, at the center of which was his house.

This is the story of the structure as he'd heard it: before the boy had even been born, his father was called Abu Taha—or the father of Taha. When Muhammad Ali 'Abd el-Mo'ti was still a child, during the time of the Turks, he had acquired this name. He looked, it was said, a bit like an uncle whose name was Taha, and so the moniker stuck. As an adult, Abu Taha was known to be judicious, clearheaded, and scrupulously honest. He was a slightly stern man, though one given to gales of deep, unstinting laughter. There is no way to know for sure, but one wonders if the other reason that such a young boy was assigned an older man's name was a certain gravity, tinged with dark wit, that characterized him already as a child and that was brought on in part by the polio he'd contracted when he was three: he woke one morning, found he couldn't walk, and spent the rest of his life severely hobbled and dependent on a cane. To move up the hill and into the center of town—or to get to school in the Qal'a—he relied on his brothers and friends to carry him on their backs. A black sense of humor was, it seems, a useful means of enduring his condition.

When Abu Taha was twenty-one, just a few years after the British had come to rule Palestine, his father—the extended family's mukhtar—arranged for him to marry a neighbor the young man had noticed and thought pretty, fifteen-year-old Fatima, known in the local dialect as Fatmeh. It was not unusual for females to marry at this age, though Fatmeh really was still a girl. Years later, an elderly neighbor who had been at the wedding described how Fatmeh's friends had spent their time before and after the ceremony, playing, shrieking, and running around while all the henna-handed bride could do was sit stiffly and look on in sorrow, trapped in her mature new role as wife. "In Palestine," one of her contemporaries explained to a visiting American woman who preserved her words in a 1930 book, advertised as the Story of a Peasant Woman of Palestine, "we don't congratulate a bride; we give her our sympathy and wish her many sons."

After the wedding, as was the custom, Fatmeh moved in right away with Abu Taha and his parents—and his brothers and their wives and several children. Though the whole family and its livestock occupied a single vaulted room, the newlyweds were shuttled off at nighttime (as was also the custom) to a small attic space for a few months of procreative privacy. And when Fatmeh gave birth to a baby boy there was much celebration. They named him Taha, of course, and she became Imm Taha—proud mother of a firstborn son. But after less than two years the child died, and Imm Taha went on in her mourning to get pregnant again, and again she gave birth to a son—

and again they named him Taha. But again the little Taha died—and again Imm Taha wailed and cried, and again she conceived . . . the familiar cycle of pregnancy, birth, and rapid death no doubt growing more fraught, more painful with each repetition. This time, the third time, one of the old women of the village gave some hushed advice to Abu Taha, whose nickname must have started to seem to him the cruelest of jokes. You have no choice, she said, but to change your wife's name. To trick the evil eye, you must from now on call her something else. Desperate for a living son, Abu Taha agreed and dubbed his distraught wife "Nijmeh," which means Star, and Nijmeh then became her name to everyone except her own mother and father, who announced that they, too, were changing her name—to "Jamileh," which means Beautiful. No doubt everyone's intentions were good. The bereaved teenage mother, though, was now faced not only with the loss of her children but also with the loss of her *self*. She no longer knew her own name.

Soon Fatmeh/Nijmeh/Jamileh gave birth to another son, Taha. But after some time the child died: she thought she'd go mad. What had she done? Were the jinn responsible? Was the evil eye? Was she? She knew she wasn't the first woman ever to lose a child—one of the graveyards in Saffuriyya was set aside for children, so many of them died—but that fact hardly lightened her grief. (Nijmeh couldn't read and didn't know English and so couldn't have fathomed the tidy charts published by the British Mandatory authorities, which put her anguish in the driest terms and showed that in 1928, for instance, 43 percent of Muslim male children in Palestine died before they were five, miscarriages not included.) In addition to the unthinkable prospect of a life without children, the growing threat to her marriage must also have crossed her frantic mind: it was not uncommon for a man whose spouse had not produced offspring to take a second wife.

But Abu Taha was not eager to marry again. He had, it seems, come to love her and did not blame her for what had happened. Perhaps his own limp made him more sympathetic to her suffering. And he was suffering, too—though, maybe also because of his limp, he was used to struggling forward. (His will, it was later said, was as strong as his right leg was weak.) The next time they found that she was pregnant, Abu Taha decided that the very name Taha must be the problem. If Nijmeh had a son, he resolved, they would name him something else altogether, his own childhood name be damned.

And so they did—but when the boy they called Milad, or Birth, died too, Abu Taha gritted his teeth and vowed that the next child would be another Taha. This name game wasn't working, and when the still-childless Nijmeh became pregnant for the fifth time in twice as many years, Abu Taha announced to her that he was going to build her a house. Perhaps if they moved away from the place where all these children had died, their luck would be different.

Abu Taha's father had died in the interim, bringing another wave of sorrow in his absence but also an inheritance. Of the thirteen small parcels of land that Abu Taha was bequeathed, he chose for the house a two-*dunam,* that is, half-acre, swatch at the foot of the hill, in the western, open part of the village. By the late 1920s, the old town was crammed to bursting, and new buildings were slowly appearing on these lower slopes and across the bayader to the south, in an area they called as-Sidr, or the Bosom, for the way the hill there swelled. There was air and light around Abu Taha's lot—perhaps he thought that just getting Nijmeh out of the cramped old town would do her good—and when he hired a mason from nearby Nazareth, he explained that he wanted something different from the traditional structure like the one in which he'd been born and grown up. These one-room homes were the rule in the old Saffuriyya, as they were then throughout rural Palestine. Whole large families lived with their animals in them, and while there was something comforting—and warm in the winter— about the extreme proximity of all that breath and life, he had another sort of house in mind, something more spacious and modern.

As the mason and his men laid the limestones row by row, Abu Taha sat on a low straw stool and watched: his limp made it impossible for him to work. While he sat, Nijmeh, now hardly a girl and used to carrying on with her daily chores as she also carried the weight of a child inside her, drew water for the workers, baked them bread, cooked them meals, and tried, one imagines, to hope for the best. (That 1930 chronicle of a Palestinian peasant woman's life put it plainly: "Life ceases; work never ceases.") She was by all accounts a kind, simple woman, small and a bit hard of hearing, but someone to whom everyone turned, nonetheless, with their woes. She would listen, nodding, as neighbors grumbled and gossiped, poured out their hearts, and her sympathetic silence made her popular. She herself, despite her trials, rarely complained. "She loves everyone," it was said, and she called them all "yama" or "habibi," honey or my dear.

She wore a black headscarf and prayed constantly, stopping her almost round-the-clock work to bow down five times a day. She also believed with a whole heart in the jinn. They were mentioned often in the Qur'an, after all, where it was written that they were created from smokeless fire. Jinn, she said, were just like people: there were good jinn and bad, and the latter congregated, in particular, on Friday nights around the graveyards, which were to be avoided, since those jinn—female demons with long black hair and unnaturally white eyes—liked to eat little children. . . . In her devotion—whether to Allah, her husband, or the power of those ghouls—she was like most of the women in the village, and while it may be tempting today to look back and feel sorry for Fatmeh/Nijmeh/Jamileh/Imm Taha in her illiteracy, her superstition, and her apparent servitude, there is no indication whatsoever that she felt the slightest pity for herself. (She said "Il-hamdu lillah"—Praise be to God!—in almost every fourth sentence.) The one thing she wanted and did not have was, it is clear, a child.

As the birth drew closer, the women pummeled Nijmeh with advice: don't drink too much water, drink more water, eat this, don't eat that, don't lift heavy things. . . . Everyone had a tip. She tried to listen and do what they said, though by now she must have started to feel somewhat helpless in the face of her impending motherhood. The house was finished in the meantime, and she and their family and friends built the roof themselves, as was always done, then they slaughtered a sheep and roasted it and ate it to celebrate the house's completion. She and Abu Taha moved their single small wooden wardrobe, mats and bedding, their clothes, pots, jugs, and baskets into the three newly painted rooms. There was nothing else now to do but wait.

♦

It was the summer of 1931. There was great excitement in Saffuriyya: in late June an archaeological team from the University of Michigan had descended on the town, rented rooms in a house on its outskirts, and hired some thirty men and boys to help them dig around the Qal'a. The building was then being used as the village *maktab* or *kuttab*, a Qur'anic elementary school for boys, so when the Ohio-born Bible scholar, archaeologist, and translator Leroy Waterman and his crew arrived—heavy with equipment and eager to apply what Waterman called "the scientific test of the spade" to "the site of the city that at the beginning of the first Christian century reared its brilliant acropolis, Sepphoris"—they had to wait for the start of summer vacation.

A devout Baptist and ordained minister, as well as an Oxford-trained Semitic language specialist and professor of religion, Waterman was drawn to the place, it seems, because of the legends that connected it to the birthplace of the Virgin Mary. Jesus' grandparents, Anna and Joachim, were alleged to have lived in Sepphoris—and Waterman wrote with excitement of the "presence and prime importance of Sepphoris as an outstanding factor in the early life of Jesus," as well as its "Jewish significance, both before and after the Christian century [which] was very considerable." (The Mishnah, the primary text of Jewish oral law, was redacted in Sepphoris in the early third century, when the town was a major center of Palestinian Jewry and the seat of the Sanhedrin, the ruling political and judicial council of all the Jews of the Roman Empire.) Like many of the archaeologists who worked in late-nineteenth and early twentieth-century Palestine, though, Waterman was mainly concerned with Jesus' possible connection to the place. He went on about it in pious, if slightly heavy-breathing, terms: "Is it any wonder that the Sermon on the Mount contains the proverb: 'A city that is set on a hill cannot be hid'? There must have been few days during the youth and early manhood of Jesus of Nazareth when this saying was not superbly illustrated for Him in Sepphoris."

Waterman was fresh from a dig at Seleucia on the Tigris, and from the first time he visited Saffuriyya—no doubt attracting the fascinated stares of the locals, with his pale pith helmet, pressed white cotton trousers, and proper Midwestern American tiepin—he was thrilled: "A detailed examination of the site revealed that probably over half of ancient Sepphoris lay beneath the sprawling Muhammedan village." And although he could not, of course, dig to

find what lay beneath the densely inhabited old town, he arranged
with the British Mandatory bureaucrats and with Abu Taha's good
friend Sheikh Saleh the mayor to work in the unpopulated area
around the citadel.

To celebrate the commencement of the dig, Waterman and his
bespectacled Syrian graduate-student assistant were invited to eat
with Sheikh Saleh. "Had 14 dishes and we were only guests with
Saleh & father," he scrawled in his diary, and at five the next morning, July 9, the laborers began laboring. ("The workmen at quitting
time threatened to strike for less hours & more pay," he noted
tersely—though that evening he reached an agreement with Sheikh
Saleh to increase wages slightly and reduce the workday to nine
hours.) By mid-August they had unearthed an impressive Greco-
Roman theater, "the first . . . to be discovered in Palestine," according to a report published that month in the *New York Times,* which
went so far as to speculate that as a carpenter in this part of the world,
Jesus would have been a "worker in both wood and stone" and that
perhaps the Christian messiah had actually helped to build the
theater. Modern scholarship has, alas, dispensed with this fanciful
theory.

They dug up, too, the Crusader foundations of the Qal'a, an an-
tique oil press, some cave tombs, and the remains of an extensive
Roman waterworks, along with dozens of ancient odds and ends: a
stone amulet, game pieces, kohl sticks, cooking pots, water jars,
drinking vessels, a bronze mirror, bone hairpins, a gold chain, glass

bangles, a bronze key ring, dice, spindle whorls, toggles, stoppers, weights, paste insets for rings "imitating precious or semiprecious stones," and a veritable mound of old coins. This once-commonplace, now-valuable horde of household and personal objects had belonged to the people who had called this place home in earlier generations— and the discovery of the mostly Roman-era assortment did as much as the four-thousand-seat theater to convince Waterman that they had indeed struck Christological pay dirt. Shoveling, sifting, stooping, lifting, and hauling in the hot light of the Palestinian summer, the workers—whose numbers had now grown to nearly eighty—also uncovered the remains of a building that Waterman, his expert adviser from Jerusalem's American School of Oriental Research, and his Odessa-born Jewish field manager first believed to be a church or a villa, then upgraded to the status of early Christian basilica, finally declaring to all the world that this was likely the original Church of the Annunciation, constructed on the very site where the angel Gabriel was said to have appeared to Mary. The *New York Times* reported this find as well and even published an editorial on the subject, enthusing about the new discoveries being made in the Galilee, since, "In that place history A.D. began to be written. Anything that throws more light on its beginnings will be welcomed by all Christendom."

Because of the sensation surrounding Waterman's findings, an unusually heavy stream of Christian visitors poured into Muslim Saffuriyya, which was home to an Italian convent and a small group of nuns but which hadn't, before now, much interested the crowds of Christian pilgrims who flocked regularly to Nazareth, just three miles away. But the summer of 1931 was different: curious to see what Waterman was up to, several contingents of priests from Jerusalem and Nazareth arrived, along with six American missionaries visiting from Korea; a group of Franciscans came from Nazareth and Damascus; and on the day of the church's discovery itself, Waterman played host, according to his diary, to "four Catholic priests in A.M. three more in P.M."

Meanwhile that summer, British census takers were busy counting heads throughout the country and gathering information from the local mukhtars, who kept track for the government authorities of births and deaths in their towns. Some four thousand clerks were

hired to do the work, and when the results were announced in November, it was declared that the population of Palestine was 1,035,154,
of which 73.4 percent were Muslim, 16.9 percent Jewish, and 8.6
percent Christian—though there is no way of knowing if that very
exact-sounding figure included the son born to Muhammad Ali 'Abd
el-Mo'ti and Nijmeh 'Abd Abu Shehadeh in their new house on the
western side of Saffuriyya, on July 27. The infant's name was—it almost goes without saying—Taha or, actually, Taha Muhammad Ali
'Abd el-Mo'ti 'Abd el-Qadar 'Isa Ibrahim 'Isa Sulayman Bakr Nijim,
though no one ever called him such an unwieldy thing. The huge
name given the tiny baby was, in fact, not meant to be used out loud
but to serve as a kind of oral chronicle, or sedimentary layering, of the
boy's lineage—for this one long title was nothing more complicated
than a string of the names of his father, grandfather, great-grandfather,
great-great-grandfather . . . and so on, extending some nine generations back to Nijim, who was known as the progenitor of his clan.

Would the boy live? Because Imm Taha's milk might, it was reasoned, be the problem, as an extra precaution this time around Abu
Taha employed the services of a wet nurse. Then Imm Taha did as
she'd done with all the previous Tahas and with Milad, rubbing the
baby in olive oil before swaddling him as tightly as a miniature mummy.
She sang to him ("Nam, habibi, nam," Sleep, my sweet, sleep), she
powdered his diaper with dried basil leaves, she rocked him in the
iron cradle that all the nearby neighbors shared, she hung a special
harazeh zarqa', a blue glass amulet, over his head, and, as she always
did, she prayed.

He lived. He lived longer than the other babies had, but only
when he was a few years old did Imm Taha begin to believe that he
might survive. By then she had planted fig trees and a garden around
the house—onion, garlic, parsley, radish, squash—and she was pregnant again, and when another son, Feisel, was born, she hardly dared
to imagine that *both* boys would grow up. . . . But he lived on too, and
after two more years a third son, Amin, was born, and he was strong,
and by now it seemed obvious to her that the house had been the answer, the cure, the source of their new good luck.

Many years later, Taha claimed to remember his brother Feisel's
birth, which took place when he himself was just two years old, in
1933. He recalled how an aunt, one of his father's sisters, had tried to

distract him, to pull him away from his mother and out of the house where the midwife and female relatives were hovering with gas lamps and jugs of water and rags: Come, she said, let's go hunt for a camel's hair! The little boy cried, and stopped only when he was reunited with his mother and saw the baby for the first time. They drank hot, sweet cinnamon water in celebration, and Imm Taha was fed a special fortifying meal of chicken with eggs and sugar.

There was in his mind's eye, too, another memory of another birth. This one happened when he was four years old, and describing it decades on his voice sinks almost to a whisper. The day after the arrival into the world of Amira, the daughter of one of Abu Taha's brothers, Abu Taha took his oldest son to see the baby who was now being rocked in the very same cradle in which Taha had been rocked a few years before and who, the man with the cane explained to his toddler son, had been chosen to be his eventual wife. And the little boy, peering down at his newborn cousin and bride-to-be, asked: If she's ours, why can't we take her with us now?

Letting out one of his big dusky laughs, Abu Taha explained that they would have to be patient and wait but that Amira would always be right here—just across the bayader in her father's house, growing up, getting ready. It had all been arranged.

IF NOT CAMELS

◆

THEY SLEPT TWO TO A BLANKET on straw mats in the same room: Abu Taha, Imm Taha, Taha, Feisel, Amin, and after another few years a little girl, Ghazaleh (pronounced RaZAAlly), whose name means Doe or Gazelle. Their bedroom also functioned as a pantry of sorts, and when Taha lay on his back in the dark he could see the outlines of the bottles of oil, cracked olives, *labneh*, or yogurt cheese, and salt-preserved cheese, the thin cotton sacks of wheat and bulgur and dried figs, the blocks of olive oil soap that his mother made from scratch in a big black cauldron, then poured, cooled, cut, and arranged in neat stacks on the shelves. Set into the thick walls, these shelves were lined with simple but delicate painted wooden scalloping. A movable ladder rested near the doorway.

The sense of contentment that Taha conveys when he describes the idyllic scene of his slumbering family, surrounded by all this bounty, is at odds, though, with other stories that he also tells—about their often desperate material situation and the ever-widening gap between Abu Taha's sorry financial state and his brothers' prosperity. Ahmed, the youngest, stayed on in their childhood house in the old part of town and opened a shop where he did well for himself, selling groceries, meat, and clothes. At the same time, their older brother Muhammad Sa'id took his inheritance and transformed it into a booming business, first earning money by working as a foreman in the fields of a nearby German Templar settlement called Bethlehem— not to be confused with the more famous town near Jerusalem.

40

The Templars were messianic Christians from the Swabian king-dom of Württemberg who had established, throughout the late nine-teenth and early twentieth centuries, rural farming communities and villagelike neighborhoods in the cities of Palestine. They established flour mills that ran on steam, irrigated their fields with the help of motors, and ran the first horse-drawn carriage service on the heavily trafficked pilgrimage route from the port of Jaffa to Jerusalem. The Templars also boasted the first flush toilet in Palestine. Perhaps in-spired by his Teutonic employers' forward-thinking approach to indus-try, Muhammad Sa'id built a complex of buildings in as-Sidr and bought a state-of-the-art, diesel-fueled olive press—imported from Germany—in which he processed oil for customers from Saffuriyya and the sur-rounding villages. He also founded two workshop-factories, one for white cheese and labneh, another for soap. Then with the proceeds from these various operations, he procured more land and eventually even a small truck—one of the only non-horse or donkey-driven ve-hicles in the village—for transporting goods to market in Nazareth and points farther off.

A member of the Saffuriyya local council, Muhammad Sa'id was a tall, handsome man who always dressed impeccably; his nephew, Taha's brother Amin, remembers that he never dirtied his hands or his robe with the soil itself but worked in the tidier capacity of command-giving boss. He was also president of the village's Young Men's Mus-lim Association, a group founded in 1932 with some 150 dues-paying members, and he owned one of the town's few radios, which ran on a car battery, since there was no electricity in Saffuriyya. His stables were filled with cows, goats, sheep, hens, and a glorious, dappled thoroughbred named il-Hadra, the Green One, after the horse ridden by the legendary warrior Dhiyab ibn Ghanim in the Bedouin saga of *Bani Hilal,* which the villagers loved to recount. Muhammad Sa'id's il-Hadra was treated with a coddling care unknown to the four work-horses that his children and employees harnessed to carry loads and to cultivate his various pieces of land. They would wash il-Hadra, brush her, and feed her the best grain, and the youngest and lightest of his sons would ride her in the races that took place in the bayader during village weddings. The prancing of this elegant creature—out-fitted with a good iron bit and leather saddle whose edges were decorated with tiny, handmade knots of colored wool—was the surest sign of all that Muhammad Sa'id had arrived and was now among the wealthiest and most important men in Saffuriyya.

Abu Taha, though, knew no other way to support himself and his wife but to sell off what he had. Because of his lame leg, he could not work the land, and in those ten long married years without children, he had no one but Nijmeh to help him. His brothers of course were eager to shower him with sacks of grain and jugs of oil, and they even designated the fruit of a particular fig tree the property of Abu Taha. But such fraternal charity was far from a long-term solution. The scattered plots he owned did not yield enough for him both to pay a laborer to work the land and to support a family. So bit by bit he parted with his possibilities. First he sold the bracelets and rings that had been Nijmeh's dowry—after two years of marriage she had no jewelry left—and after trying and failing several times to open a shop, he turned to his land. In what must have been a slightly humiliating reversal of fortunes, much of Abu Taha's property was purchased by his worker, one Saleh Dakakini, who now claimed ownership of the soil he had once tilled and sowed and harvested on Abu Taha's behalf. After his father's death, meanwhile, the honorary role of mukhtar had been passed on to one of Abu Taha's uncles: Muhammad Sa'id and Ahmed were too occupied with their businesses for such unprofitable formalities, and Abu Taha was, it was quietly agreed, not "active" enough for the job.

By the time Taha was born, almost half his father's holdings were gone, and though Abu Taha had resolved to cling to as much as he could, he had no other options. He continued to sell. As a young child Taha knew that sometimes there was not even enough flour in the house for his mother to bake bread and that to fill her children's empty stomachs she would roast a few lentils or chickpeas and pour extra cold water to drink. But he did not realize what was happening to his father's land. Later, however, he remembered the way, periodically and without warning, his father would appear with gifts for the whole family—new clothes and meat and chocolate. Although this was exciting for the children, it was also a sign that more land had been sold, and that soon the family would own nothing.

There is more than a touch of Tiny Tim—like pathos in the story of the crippled Abu Taha and his dwindling prospects, yet it seems that he did not act the victim. If anything, those who knew him make it clear that he was a major social and ethical force in Saffuriyya: while Muhammad Sa'id and Ahmed earned much more money than he did (their wives had gold bangles to wear on special occasions and their children ate meat often), it was Abu Taha to whom they themselves turned for insight and stories, for news and advice. His brothers were not alone in looking up to him. Men of all sorts—fieldworkers, nearby Bedouin, teachers, Saleh al-'Afifi, whose family had begun a business with some chairs and a mere truck bed and now ran the biggest bus company in the Galilee, Sheikh Saleh the mayor himself—sought him out and were eager to spend long hours in his company. Perhaps it was compensation for his gimp leg and for what he lacked in financial terms, but Abu Taha had, over the years, developed formidable gifts.

◆

When a seventy-something Taha Muhammad Ali was asked to choose a favorite poem to read at a 2004 European literary festival, he picked a snippet attributed to the great pre-Islamic bard Imru' al-Qays. Though this short lyric was composed in the Arabian desert nearly fifteen hundred years ago, it also sounds very much like an account of an unusually good year in the life of Taha's own family in British Mandatory Saffuriyya.

> If not camels, let it be goats,
>   with horns like staves.
> When first they're milked, they shout—
>   like someone announcing a death at dawn.
> Cheese and butter fill our home,
>   and food and drink are wealth enough.

His affinity for the verse of this legendary preliterate era is no coincidence. As the grown-up Taha describes his early childhood, he conjures an epoch that is, in a way, part of history but outside of ordinary clock-time. In retrospect, it is hard to fix specific dates for most of what happened in Saffuriyya, though the imperfect tense of the day-to-day remains clearly etched.

Around dawn, he says, his mother would be the first to wake.
She would rise in the half-light, then slip out and walk to the nearby
water station. This wasn't the picture-book, Rebecca-meets-Abraham's-
servant sort of well that still existed in some towns—in Nazareth, for
example—but a more modern stone structure with a generator and
pump, built recently with British help at the entrance to the village,
a few minutes from their house. After greeting the other women who
had already congregated there and were exchanging gossip in their
low morning tones, Imm Taha would fill a large clay jug from the
spigot, balance the weight of it on her head, then make her way home.
Now the path was almost empty, though later in the day, the same
trail from the spring would take on a theatrical aspect as the young,
unmarried women would mince by, bearing the jars, and the boys
would watch. The girls pretended not to notice who was staring at
them, and throughout the charged ritual the members of one sex
never exchanged a word with the other, but the route was well known
as the best place in the village for a young man to go looking (literally) for a wife. Many matches had been arranged as a result of this
coy parade. It may well be that Abu Taha first saw his future wife with
a jug of water perched on her pubescent head.

Once at home Imm Taha would pour a pitcher of the water and
assemble a plain breakfast of yesterday's bread and a bit of oil and
za'tar—crushed hyssop with sesame and salt—then rouse the boys

and help them wash, straighten the little belted and striped robe, the *qumbaz,* they each wore all day and also slept in. Every boy had two or three robes, and once a week they would rotate the qumbaz for laundering. In the years when they attended the municipal school, they exchanged this more traditional garb for button-down shirts and green or blue khaki shorts, in accordance with British regulations. Taha also owned a brightly embroidered skullcap of which he was very proud, and when she was old enough, Ghazaleh wore a flowered cotton dress with a high neck and square bodice.

The home was divided in the minds of its inhabitants into several strictly fixed zones. The courtyard was everyone's to share, even the chickens and the three goats, but the shelves of the supply room, the sitting room where they'd eat in the winter, the garden, and the small lean-to used as a kitchen—these belonged to the sovereign territory of Imm Taha. She would regularly venture out from the house to fetch water, bake bread in the neighborhood oven every midmorning, gather kindling, harvest olives, and help her friends and female neighbors with their work. (Every year, before the rainy season, all the women would come together to fix one another's roofs—patching the mud that covered the wood to keep the water from getting in.) Yet when she was home—which was much of the time—she confined her movements to the borders of this invisibly demarcated but distinct arena.

Abu Taha, meanwhile, spent almost all his waking hours in the third room in the house, his *madafeh.* In Saffuriyya, as in other Palestinian villages of the time, a madafeh—literally, a place for *dyuf,* guests—could mean any number of things. It might be a guesthouse for travelers: each clan would maintain its own, also sometimes called a *manzul,* and out-of-town visitors were welcome to spend the night there, free of charge. Or it might be a formal reception area where village dignitaries would receive their guests. Sheikh Saleh no doubt hosted the archaeologist Leroy Waterman in his own well-appointed madafeh, complete with its Western-styled armchairs, radio, and an attendant who made the coffee. (In his diary Waterman notes the purchase of a "phonograph and 3 records . . . for Sheikh Saleh.") Whenever government officials or British officers came to Saffuriyya on business, they and their translators were invited—but also expected—to pay a call and drink coffee with Sheikh Saleh, under the portrait of King George that he'd hung rather pointedly on the wall. At the other end of the spectrum, a madafeh might be nothing more than a humble room like the one where Abu Taha passed all of his days and most of his nights, together with a handful of friends.

But to call it "a humble room," or to detail its minimal contents— a few straw mats, several thin wool-stuffed mattresses, a low stool, the worn shoes of the men cast off by the door—is to do an injustice to the vast place this small square of plaster and stone occupied in the imagination of the young boy. It was—as his basically immobile father was—the sturdy pivot around which all his own wanderings through the village and orchards unfolded. It was the place where he first heard poetry and pre-Islamic legends, first encountered local history and world politics, first absorbed how men talked to one another, first learned how to listen. It was "the university of the *fallah*," as his brother Amin describes it, more than half a century later. The guests in the madafeh, he says, would constantly tell stories and talk and argue and laugh: the conversation never stopped. "They had knowledge of life, they had experience. And they had confidence in themselves."

The men came and went in twos and threes over the course of the day. Some, like Abu Taha, didn't work or worked sporadically; others would stop by at the end of a long day of labor and sit on the floor late into the night. In summertime—when, as Taha says, the "moon was high"—they would often move the proceedings outdoors, under the spreading fig tree. Sometimes they ate simple food there—fried eggs or labneh and oil with bread. (The boys would be called on to bring the meal and to wash the men's hands before and after the meal; Imm Taha never approached.) More often they smoked cigarettes and drank unsweetened black coffee, *sada,* served in little cups.

The preparation of the coffee itself was an elaborately prescribed way of passing the time in the madafeh, very different but no less intricate than a Japanese tea ceremony, and Abu Taha was acclaimed for his excellent brew: he had a small iron brazier filled with lit coals, over which he would first roast the greenish beans with a long-handled flat pan and spoon made for him by the gypsies who sometimes pitched camp in the bayader and were known for their metalwork. Then he'd transfer the hot beans to a small wooden scoop where they'd cool, then would move them again to a narrow-necked wooden mortar in which he'd pound them to a fine, aromatic dust. After trans-ferring the grounds to a bird-beaked pot, he would add the water from a jug, and when it had boiled, he would let the liquid sit and intensify, then move it to another, smaller pot, to which more water would be added. Again Abu Taha would boil the coffee and only then, after pouring it into the third and smallest pot, would the coffee be served in thimble-like cups, known as *abadi*, which contained just a few precious sips—the pungent essence of all that work, time, and concentration. No matter the number of guests, these vessels were always arrayed on the tray in odd numbers, three, seven, five, though no one in Abu Taha's day could recall the superstitious reason why.

Besides his good coffee, Abu Taha was known for his talk—and it was this, combined with his modesty, intelligence, and compassion, that brought such a varied cast of characters to sit in his madafeh. (When Taha is asked as an adult if he'd wanted already as a child to be a writer he says, "No. To speak like my father.") Abu Taha had, it seems, a profound ability to deal with the person before him on that person's own terms. As Amin recounts it: "If a shopkeeper was there, he knew how to talk about trade. . . . The same thing with the landowner. He could discuss the importance of tending your land, plowing it, sowing it, watering it. . . . He'd say: 'Whatever you give it, it will return.'"

Though he had received just a rudimentary education in the village school, learning to read the Qur'an and write simple Arabic as he absorbed some basic Turkish, he had also acquired over the years what amounted to an advanced degree at the university of the fallah. He was an expert storyteller and had at his extemporaneous disposal a serious store of legends. Some of these concerned the history of the Nijim clan, to which he and his family, as well as almost half of Saffuriyya, belonged; Nijim could trace its lineage back some five hundred years to a Bedouin tribe in what was known during Taha's childhood as Transjordan. Other tales were much older and more exotic, with origins in Abbasid Baghdad or pre-Islamic Mecca; Abu Taha and the other men who knew how would take turns reading these aloud from a book. Sometimes they would read from the Qur'an and the listeners would, out of respect, flick away their cigarettes. Still other stories were playful renderings of events in more recent history, happenings that he himself remembered. But Abu Taha also sometimes narrated a more severe sort of scenario, without funny frills.

There was no need to exaggerate or embellish, for instance, the near-biblical saga of the disease and starvation that had visited the village, as it had visited the whole region, around the time of the Great War: as if the devastating effects of overlapping typhoid and cholera epidemics hadn't been enough, drought struck, and a plague of locusts swarmed Palestine and killed off most of the crops. The people of Saffuriyya were so desperate for food, they stole into a nearby Turkish camp and picked grain from the dung of the horses, then cleaned it and ground it for flour. In Lebanon nearly a third of the population died of starvation during those years.

Meanwhile, the Turks had sided with the Germans in the war, and as they did so they cracked down on the draft. Now all Ottoman male citizens up to age sixty were obliged to serve the sultan. The young were sent off to fight, the older men forced to work in labor battalions, building roads and hauling water. The soldiers, everyone knew, were treated terribly. Their Turkish commanders barely fed them, and sometimes they had no choice but to kill their own camels and eat the meat. Many, understanding how slim were their chances of survival, tried to flee—but desertion was a risky business, and escapees were often hanged. As a precautionary measure, many new recruits were kept in shackles. Others were beaten. Besides hauling away most of the men of Saffuriyya, the army requisitioned the locals' crops and camels and hacked down the trees in the basatin for fuel. None of the villagers—that is, the women who'd been left behind to care for the land and support their families—resisted, since they'd heard terrible stories about what happened to those who tried.

Abu Taha's father the mukhtar, among many others, was conscripted. He was shipped off to a place with a mysterious name—Shalakala? Shanakala? the mellifluous array of Turkic consonants has been swallowed up by time—and since Abu Taha's brother Muhammad Sa'id was off working and Ahmed was still just a boy, Abu Taha became the man of the house. No more than fourteen years old, he received a summons to appear at the Casa Nova building in Nazareth. There a Turkish officer he identified later (correctly, it seems) as İsmet İnönü—who would go on to become the first prime minister of Turkey and to succeed Mustafa Kemal Atatürk as the president of that country—informed him that he was now the acting mukhtar of his clan. İnönü threw the official Ottoman stamp across the table and ordered the teenager to take charge. At first Abu Taha protested, saying he was too young, but in stern tones the future statesman made it clear that he had no choice in the matter. So Abu Taha served as mukhtar until the war's end and was responsible for registering all the births and deaths and taxes collected among this extended family of hungry village women.

◆

Although Abu Taha had remained in Saffuriyya throughout the war, some of the men who had traveled far to fight sat in his madafeh a few decades on and repeated stories about the atrocities they'd seen—stories whose grisly particulars made such an impression on Taha that he can still recount them almost seventy years later. One man named Shehadi described the battles with the British near the Suez Canal: he'd been fighting right beside a Syrian who was struck by a mortar and whose brains flew out and smacked Shehadi in the face. Shaken and weary, Shehadi and his fellow villagers were ordered to retreat toward Beersheba. They continued to fight for several years—many more of them died of disease than in actual combat—and when in the end those who'd survived began the long trek home on foot, they cast off their guns.

Were they aware as they trudged that the Ottoman Empire was now a thing of the past and that the British, their enemies in the war, were soon to rule Palestine? Stumbling, famished, toward Saffuriyya, had they heard of the Balfour Declaration, the promise made that year by the British foreign secretary to establish in Palestine a "national home for the Jewish people"? It is doubtful that the mostly illiterate peasant soldiers—many of whom arrived in Saffuriyya shoeless and nearly starved—had any idea of the implications of the war they'd just lost, but by the time Taha was old enough to hear their stories in his father's madafeh, the men knew all too well. And if they hadn't figured it out on their own, the Jaffa and Jerusalem newspapers that were sometimes read aloud in the madafeh apprised them in no uncertain terms. There the British Empire was called "deceitful" and London dubbed "the cause of the calamity." For his part, the six- or seven-year-old boy was less interested in such grand tectonic shifts of political power or high-flown journalistic accusations than in Shehadi's graphic account of the Syrian's splattered vitals.

But even without fathoming the forces that had realigned the structure of the entire Middle East some fourteen years before his birth, the young Taha understood from their tone that the men viewed the British victory as their own defeat. As cruel as the Turks had been to their soldiers and subjects, they were fellow Muslims, and the shame of having lost the war was compounded several times over by the stinging fact that Saffuriyya itself was now a part of the British Empire and that General Allenby—the very man responsible for defeating them in the south—had entered and taken the holy city of Jerusalem like some new Crusader. The men were quietly furious at the notion that an upper-crust Protestant sitting behind a desk in London felt he had the right to hand Palestine to the Jews. . . . Never mind that Lord Balfour's famous announcement of British intentions to "use their best endeavors to facilitate the achievement of [a 'national home for the Jewish people']" does include the assurance that "nothing shall be done which may prejudice the civil and religious rights of existing non-Jewish communities in Palestine." Such a crisp English aside, however well-intentioned, wouldn't have done much to calm the nerves of the men drinking coffee in Abu Taha's madafeh, who could only have seen the declaration as a threat. (Their *political* rights were not mentioned.) Though it seems they had not yet begun to imagine that their very existence in the land might be at risk, for now it was bad enough to think that the English were their masters and that boatloads of Jewish immigrants were arriving almost daily in Haifa. Since Hitler had come to power in Germany, the number of new Jewish arrivals in Palestine had skyrocketed, leaping from 9,553 in 1932 to 30,327 in 1933, according to British government estimates. By 1935, the number of newcomers had grown to some 65,000—and the Jewish population of Palestine had more than doubled in a mere four years.

Listening to an elderly Taha relating the stories that he himself heard related as a little boy, one feels oneself peering through layers of scrims. How much of his account is tinted by what happened in 1948? 1967? 2000? And before the events of such notorious years even enter the picture—to what degree were the madafeh memories of

World War I, such as Shehadi's, informed by all the interethnic acrimony that had accrued since those last battles?

Taha himself remembers little of the violence that reigned during this tumultuous period, whose events are known as the Great Revolt, the Arab Revolt, or the Disturbances: this is understandable. He was young—the revolt started when he was five and frittered out when he was eight—and while he did witness the often harsh curfews and roundups imposed by British soldiers who were searching Saffuriyya for armed rebels sympathetic to the assassinated Islamist revolutionary 'Izz al-Din al-Qassam, these memories have been rendered hazy by time and perhaps a bit of healthy repression. Whether these incidents affected him at a deeper, unconscious level is easy to speculate about but hard to say for sure. What does seem certain, however, is that the role that several men from Saffuriyya played in the revolt would have serious implications for the future of the whole village— and, by extension, for Taha.

BLACK HAND, WHITE PAPER

◆

THROUGHOUT PALESTINE MANY PEASANTS viewed the flamboyant Muslim preacher and social reformer 'Izz al-Din al-Qassam as their possible savior from the British and the Jews. A Syrian-born, religiously trained veteran of guerrilla warfare against the French in that country, al-Qassam liked to speak with a gun or a sword in his hand as he urged the peasants and poor—mostly vagrant, illiterate, young, male, village-born—Muslim workers of the cities to rise up against both foreign oppressors and the wealthy urban Palestinians who were, he insisted, also holding them down. He opened a night school in Haifa for the peasants who had come to live in the shantytowns there and taught the men to read, and he argued with Hajj Amin al-Husayni, the upper-class mufti of Jerusalem and official leader of Palestine's Muslims, about how money raised abroad ought to be used: the mufti was interested in renovating Jerusalem's mosques; al-Qassam wanted to buy arms. (The mufti won that particular debate and arranged to plate the formerly drab Dome of the Rock in gold.)

Al-Qassam's job as a traveling marriage registrar allowed him to move throughout the countryside, spreading his message and recruiting fighters, whom he organized into small, secretive bands of no more than five men each. He was, according to one Palestinian historian, "a dignified, charismatic and morally motivated puritanical Muslim cleric who had the uncanny ability to translate what he believed into steadfast commitment on the part of his followers." Among these followers were, she notes, men enlisted in Saffuriyya. Another historian (Israeli) writes, more bluntly, that "since 1929 [Saffuriyya] was the home of the most important rural terrorist cell of 'Izz al-Din al-Qassam's Black Hand organization." Because of such activity, he notes, Saffuriyya had "gone down in the annals of the Yishuv [Jewish community of pre-state Palestine] as a 'village of murderers.'"

Perception may matter more than reality here, since in 1948 Saffuriyya would be treated by the fledgling Israeli army according to the belief that its residents were, as one Israeli military account put it, "fierce warriors" or, in the words of a veteran Haganah intelligence officer, "a brutal people . . . fanatical Muslims." (He also dubs Saffuriyya "the most dangerous center of Arab nationalism," though tellingly in the same sentence he overestimates the population of the village by 250 percent: the official British 1944 census counted 4,330 people in Saffuriyya, while he claims there were 11,000.) But was Saffuriyya really a village of murderers? A small group of villagers was, there is little doubt, involved in violent activities: Jewish intelligence reports from the early 1930s describe secret military drills conducted by boy scout troops and members of Young Men's Muslim Associations from Saffuriyya and nearby villages, and when Taha was just a year old, at least one man from Saffuriyya snuck with a homemade bomb into the settlement of Nahalal—the first moshav, or collective farming community, in the land and the childhood home of the future one-eyed minister of defense Moshe Dayan—and murdered a Jewish farmer, Yosef Ya'akobi, and his nine-year-old son, David. The political killing was, according to the next day's *Palestine Post,* "an outrage which has deeply shaken the Emek [the Jezreel Valley, or Marj ibn 'Amr, where the moshav is located] and which has brought a warm message of sympathy from the High Commissioner [who spoke of] the 'calamity for Nahalal and sadness for everyone.'" More than a thousand people attended the funerals, and five men—from Saffuriyya and Haifa—were later charged with the crime: three were acquitted for lack of evidence, while two were condemned to death. In the end, the sentence of one of the convicted men (from Haifa) was commuted to fifteen years in prison, while the appeal of the other, Mustafa 'Ali Ahmed of Saffuriyya, was rejected. A newspaper story written at the time noted:

> There has been much comment on the fact that the villager who confessed and who appears to have been influenced by

the better educated Haifa accomplices should go to the gal-
lows while the latter's sentence should be commuted. The
view has been freely heard that the city man could hardly
be less responsible for his actions than the illiterate fallah.

Such fine class distinctions, though, were too little, too late to save
Mustafa 'Ali Ahmed, and he was hung. "In accordance with what appears the regular practice," the *Palestine Post* reported, "the body remained hanging for an hour after which it was delivered to the relatives of the deceased who took it for burial in his native village."

Whether the president of the Saffuriyya YMMA, Taha's uncle
Muhammad Sa'id, knew of the murderers' plans is not clear. Although
his organization was alleged in various press accounts and intelligence reports to be at the center of the bombing, he was not impli-
cated in the killings, and at the trial his testimony for the prosecution
bolstered the case against the accused. Taha remembers talk of how,
during this time, his uncle had been questioned by the police, who
suspected him of being among the leaders of al-Qassam's Black Hand
Band. In his possibly forced confession—one Palestinian history
book claims he was tortured—the condemned Mustafa 'Ali Ahmed
had named Muhammad Sa'id as being a member of a secret society
that existed "to defend our country from the Jews by killing them and
robbing them." When charges were brought against the men suspected of belonging to this society, however, Muhammad Sa'id was
not among the accused, and the case against the other men was eventually dropped. As the newspaper the day after their acquittal put it:
"The magistrate, while finding many suspicious circumstances in the
evidence tendered, . . . was not satisfied that it proved their member-
ship of an unlawful society or that the object was to kill Jews." Taha
insists that his uncle had nothing to do with such violent things ("He
was a businessman and he wasn't interested in politics. Maybe he
went to one meeting; that's all"), while Amin, for his part, announces
with pride that he is *sure* Muhammad Sa'id was "al-Qassam's representative in Saffuriyya." His uncle did not, says Amin, participate in
terrorist activities, nor did he hate Jews—but he was an unabashed
nationalist who believed in protecting his people's rights, and as a
wealthy and respected citizen, he would have been a logical choice as
the famous sheikh's man in the village. From this distance, and given

the dearth of firsthand evidence, we cannot, of course, know who is right—and neither is Muhammad Sa'id's ideological inner life central to our story. What concerns us here is how the brothers *tell* that story. As close as Taha and Amin are—to each other and to the spirit of Saffuriyya—their perspectives on the revolt and its latter-day echoes, on Palestinian politics and how best to remember the erased village, diverge radically.

The archival accounts of the legal proceedings contain, meanwhile, fairly convincing—if not, perhaps, trial-proof—indications that a branch of al-Qassam's stealth society did exist in Saffuriyya, whether on or under the radar of the YMMA. The members of this selective organization were said to swear loyalty and silence on a Qur'an—and a dagger or a pistol, according to some accounts—grow their beards long, and call one another "sheikh." After the killing in Nahalal, word of this underground spread, and its members became known as "al-Mashayikh," the Sheikhs, or "al-Darawish," the Dervishes—as if the armed struggle were part of an arcane Sufi rite.

At the same time, the files of the Haganah intelligence service include a 1933 report that predates the Nahalal trial and offers a glimpse at the murder's poisonous effects on the rest of the town: "The people of Saffuriyya say amongst themselves that the police suspect the people of their village of involvement in the killings in Nahalal. There are many undercover agents in the village and the townspeople are very afraid to deal with weapons and explosives. . . . Each one suspects that someone else will turn him in to the police." Still another Hebrew-language document from the same time would seem to support the villagers' worst fears: this mentions a proposal that was put forth within the Haganah—to send an Arabic-speaking Jew to live in Saffuriyya for a year to spy on the villagers. It is not clear if this plan was realized.

In 1935, al-Qassam was killed in an ambush by the British police, as legend has it, offering as his final words the call to his men to "Die as martyrs!"—a command that haunts the Palestinian national movement to this day, as does the figure of al-Qassam, whose mythic name has been affixed since his death to a range of havoc-wreaking rockets and Hamas brigades. His funeral drew thousands of angry mourners, and a series of bloody clashes between Jews and Arabs soon followed, prompting the declaration of a General Strike, which demanded a halt to Jewish immigration and land sales and proportional Arab representation in the government. It also led to the formation of the Arab Higher Committee—a group of urban aristocrats, whose president was Hajj Amin al-Husayni, the mufti, and which would soon come to dominate Palestinian politics. The strike paralyzed much of Palestine for half a year, and violent events connected with it brought about the deaths of some one thousand Arabs, eighty Jews, and thirty-seven British. But the economic effects of the strike were felt much more strongly in the cities than in the villages, where there were, political convictions or no, always crops to harvest and sheep to graze, goats to milk, wheat to plant or thresh. In Saffuriyya, people supported the idea of the strike, but by necessity daily life went on more or less as usual, which may account in part for Taha's dim memory of the period.

In the larger towns and throughout the countryside, though, the strike soon gave way to a genuine uprising. Rebel bands attacked British troops and Jewish civilians, burned crops, mined roads, blew up trains, cut phone lines, and sabotaged the main oil pipeline to Haifa, and at some point during 1936, several hundred foreign fighters entered Palestine. They were led by a Syrian-born professional soldier named Fawzi Qawuqji who would play a pivotal role in the later military history of Palestine, and, perhaps under his influence, the attacks were stepped up, as were the threats to Arabs who did not support the rebels' violent tactics. Dissenters were intimidated, forced to give money, even killed.

Many people in the villages did sympathize with the rebels, and Saffuriyya seems to have been generally welcoming to the men. According to one veteran historian of the events, seven Saffuriyyans were officers of the revolt, that is, "people with some responsibility." And though few of the villagers shared the fundamentalist theology of the shaggier rebels—the wild beards of the Qassamites had by then become something of a trademark—they still believed that these men were fighting for them, the underdogs, and gave them money, clothes, and food. That said, Sheikh Saleh the mayor, who'd been so proud to hang King George's portrait on his madafeh wall, took the occasion of this insurrection against British rule to leave for an extended vacation in Damascus.

Qawuqji was driven out of the country after just a few months, but the local rebels continued to launch attacks. At the same time, the British army adopted harsher new measures against villages that supported the *mujahidin*. These included house demolitions, a method the Israeli army borrowed and has used into the twenty-first century: "It is a quick and conclusive form of punishment and one that is understood by the Arab mind," according to a top-secret British report from 1936. On a more peaceful note, the government announced that it was establishing a royal commission "to ascertain whether . . . either the Arabs or the Jews have any legitimate grievances on account of the way in which the Mandate has been, or is being implemented." To prepare the people for the commission-to-come, the government dumped some 1.3 million leaflets from the air, "including a copy of His Excellency the High Commissioner's Speech [about the pending report] and a brief summary of the past careers of the members of the Royal Commission." What the vitae of these visiting British civil servants could possibly have meant to a peasant from Saffuriyya, plowing his field as the pamphlet-strewing RAF plane cruised overhead, is a good question. It is less difficult to imagine his reaction to the eventual publication of the commission's findings. In three languages, the members recommended the partition of Palestine. The division of the country into Arab, Jewish, and Mandatory states, they wrote, "offers a prospect . . . of obtaining the estimable boon of peace," though they qualified their admittedly imperfect plan with the proviso that "we see no such prospect in any other policy." The Galilee—and Saffuriyya within it—were slated for inclusion in the Jewish state.

Soon the rebels controlled much of the north of the country, though as their tactics grew more violent, their actions met even harsher British responses, and things came to a grisly head with the murder in the Nazareth market of the acting district commissioner of Galilee, Lewis Andrews, and his bodyguard, who, when "walking to evensong at the Anglican church," were, in the words of the then-classified British government account of the events, "set on in the narrow twisting road leading to the church by four Arab assassins." According to the flowery English-language press reports of the events, it was the bodyguard's last scheduled day in the country and the forty-first birthday of Andrews, an Australian who was "so gay in life, so ready in action, so downright in his candor, so humble and yet so confident." That the killing was political was obvious: Andrews was shot through the jugular at close range and had, in the minds of many Palestinian Arabs, two strikes against him as a pro-Zionist English official. His assassination prompted the posting of an unprecedentedly huge reward, ten thousand Palestinian pounds, and the expulsion to the Seychelles Islands of most of the members of the now-banned Arab Higher Committee as well as the mufti's incongruously Errol Flynn–like nighttime escape from Jerusalem. Disguised as a Bedouin—some accounts say a woman—he climbed down the walls of the Haram al-Sharif and was driven to Jaffa, from which he fled to Lebanon in a fishing boat.

Closer to home and so probably more strongly felt by the six-year-old Taha, the murder of Andrews, or "Indris," as his name was rendered in Palestinian dialect, also brought about the disappearance of his uncle Muhammad Sa'id and his father's friend, the bus-company owner Saleh al-'Afifi. In the immediate wake of the killing, a special guard was posted around the crime scene, all police stations throughout the country were alerted, search dogs were ordered from Jerusalem, a curfew was imposed on Nazareth—and "a party of police were dispatched to check the bad characters in Saffouriya village which was at first suspected."

A letter written after the murder by a high-ranking English official to the chief secretary in London states that, two weeks before he was shot, Andrews had told a colleague that "he was expecting an attack from Saffuriya village," and a Hebrew-language intelligence report from the same time claims that on the day before his death, Andrews had shown another officer a letter from a British source, warning him that "three Arabs from Saffuriyya had received an order from the Arab Higher Committee to kill Andrews at any cost." Because of these rumors, a group of Saffuriyya men were arrested, among them Muhammad Sa'id and Saleh al-'Afifi. At the same time, several hundred other men throughout the region—"political undesirables" in the terms of the British police—were also rounded up and sent to a newly built internment camp on the northern coast in Acre because of ostensible involvement in the killing. Given the extent of the sweep—640 men, all told, which was the absolute limit that the camp and nearby prison could hold (the jails were so crowded that the Mandatory files from that year contain bizarre calculations of how, for instance, a cell with 780 cubic yards of air would last the forty-seven men held there for sixteen and a half hours, "supposing it were hermetically sealed")—one wonders if the police truly suspected the two Saffuriyya businessmen of murder or if they simply wanted to make an example of them. "There was really little or nothing known against the majority of the people detained," one British police officer admitted in a report about a similar sweep, "but some reasonable excuse for detaining them had to be given for record purposes."

Whatever the rationale for his arrest, Saleh al-'Afifi tried while in prison to hang himself "because he suffered," in the 2005 words of his octogenarian nephew. "Because they tortured him," according to Taha. Saleh's suicide attempt failed, and he was eventually released without being charged. Muhammad Sa'id was, it seems, also set free at around the same time.

Although the killing itself is mentioned often in history books, no trace remains of a trial. According to Taha, Saffuriyya gossip held that the perpetrators were Bedouin. Who sent them on their mission remains a mystery.

◆

By now the struggle between the rebels and the government had become as intense as it was circular: killings and arrests and hangings and attacks followed in rapid succession, and the government beefed up its forces substantially, imposing military law, complete with countrywide curfews and severe travel restrictions. At around this time, permanent British army detachments were sent to occupy Saffuriyya, among numerous other towns in the center and north of the country. More attacks followed and more arrests. Soon the revolt unraveled. The leadership had been either deported or crushed, and with increasing frequency the rebels resorted to killing other Arabs—whether suspected collaborators or rivals for power, the chaotic results were the same.

And the army clamped down on those who were left—often in a brutal but "effective" manner. Until 1940, military courts had the power to order the execution of anyone caught carrying weapons, and in 1939 fifty-five people, all Arabs, were sentenced to death. Some six thousand Palestinian Arabs were imprisoned that year alone, many held without trial. The human toll the revolt took on the Arabs of Palestine was tremendous: one reliable source cites five thousand dead, fifteen thousand wounded—nearly a quarter of those killed by what the British government termed "gang and terrorist activities," that is, by other Arabs. Men like Taha's father, who had not actively participated but who had believed in the revolt in principle and even knew some of the fighters personally, were upset by what was happening and angry that the rebels had let their just cause fray into petty plots and killing.

There were, meanwhile, rumblings of war in far-off Europe, and the English, eager to garner Arab support against Hitler and convinced that the Jews had no choice but to side with the Allies, scrambled to take up a new tack. In 1939 they issued a white paper, which called for "the establishment within ten years of an independent Palestine State . . . in which Arabs and Jews share in government in such a way as to ensure that the essential interests of each community are safeguarded." The white paper also recommended substantial limits on Jewish immigration and, in certain parts of the country, the ban of land sales to Jews. The Zionists were furious, the Arabs less than thrilled, and soon the revolt was over. To the young Taha's chagrin, the men in his father's madafeh now talked more obsessively about politics and read fewer of Scheherazade's tales.

Even after the revolt was over, though, Saffuriyya's violent reputation remained, especially among the Jews who lived nearby. Why?

Saffuriyya was—it is clear from the inky evidence found in those surviving police station charge logs—a tumultuous town, and one where scores were often settled by violence. Charges of assault, "possessing a firearm without lawful authority and without a reasonable excuse," injuring or killing animals (cows stabbed, mares shot, a donkey burned to death), arson, theft (of chickens, olives, plows, gold pieces cut from a woman's hair while she was sleeping outside), damage to property (barley set alight, cauliflower uprooted), give way to more serious accusations of "wounding by knife," "carrying a dagger," attempted murder, and murder itself. The word "affray" also turns up often in the "description of offence" column, and the names, ages, and professions of the accused in these clashes between different clans or subclans are neatly listed in loopy English longhand, as are the weapons wielded in the course of each standoff—stones, sticks, the occasional knife, a rifle butt. This was entirely Arab-on-Arab, and in fact Saffuriyyan-on-Saffuriyyan, violence. Also common were the instances where brothers or cousins threatened each other and even came to blows. Fractured jaws and broken fingers are duly noted in the log; in another police document, a British official provides a not strictly medical diagnosis of "hot blood" to explain the cause of one misdemeanor: an olive orchard burned in retaliation for murder. This—like almost all the crimes committed in Saffuriyya in those years—had nothing whatsoever to do with the Jews. It was surely a backhanded compliment that Leroy Waterman paid Sheikh Saleh when, in the preface to his report on the 1931 dig at Sepphoris, he thanked the mayor for "preserving excellent order in a turbulent community."

Taha, for his part, laughs when asked about crime and punishment and neighborly relations: "Well, there was the west side of Saffuri, and there was the east, and this was exactly like the cold war between the United States and the Soviet Union. That was the cold war between the east and the west, and this cold war came and went without any fighting. But in Saffuri, the cold war erupted many times in real fighting." He remembers the groups of ten or fifteen men and boys—together with the occasional woman—who would pummel one another with stones and sticks and then make up at the *sulha*s, or reconciliation ceremonies, that usually followed.

At the same time, the tattered files of the British Criminal Investigation Department from those very years contain weekly intelligence summaries—in which the name Saffuriyya barely appears. When a 1938 plan was hatched by the British authorities to draw up registers of all the males, aged seventeen to fifty, in what were called in almost kindergarten terms "bad villages"—that is, villages from which the rebels came or where they were sheltered—Saffuriyya does not make the list.

One of the few references to Saffuriyya in the files is in fact a translation of an Arabic bulletin, written in Damascus in 1938 and "found posted on walls in Acre town," which describes how the British troops were alleged to have conducted a search in Saffuriyya and several other villages: "They shoot at old men, women, and children, demolish houses and villages out of revenge and satisfy their savage instincts." Taha has no memory of houses being destroyed, but the

Haganah's Hebrew-language intelligence reports from the 1940s clearly state that six Saffuriyya houses were blown up during what are referred to there as "the Disturbances." Their owners and the monetary value of the houses—a cumulative fifteen hundred Palestinian pounds —are listed matter of factly.

The charges in the Damascus bulletin may or may not be entirely true, but other documents make it clear that the British army did indeed maintain a thuggish presence in the village: a series of letters between officials at the Department of Antiquities and Lewis Andrews's harried-sounding replacement in Nazareth discuss the damage done around the Saffuriyya citadel by the troops who stayed there and pulled stones from the ancient theater walls to "build a car approach." The soldiers also destroyed a mosaic in the old monastery, broke and used drainage channels as toilets, and even took souvenirs: "The square stone bearing the Arabic inscription over the main entrance to the Castle was pulled off and taken by [a] Military Officer on 6th April, 1938."

One of Taha's only clear memories of this time involves the shooting of a seventeen-year-old Saffuriyya villager who was out picking green almonds when a curfew was announced. He didn't hear the town crier shouting at everyone to stay inside—and a British soldier killed him. (There is no way of tracking the date of this vividly recollected death, but the *Palestine Post* of December 11, 1938, reports that "on Wednesday night, a military patrol on [sic] the 1st Hampshire Regiment observed an Arab curfew breaker near Saffurieh, Galilee. They called on him to halt, and when he failed to do so, shot him dead.") Taha also remembers the armored cars that drove into the bayader during army roundups from which his father was exempt because of his leg. His mother, for her part, would have to go stand with the women while the children waited indoors. And he remembers other house searches: the British came to check his own house (they rifled through the family's clothes and food and, finding nothing suspicious, left), but he heard of others less fortunate. Their front doors were smashed down by the soldiers who ransacked storerooms in search of weapons, sometimes dumping an entire year's worth of food supplies all over the floor, mixing the oil with the corn and the wheat.

The boy scouts' military drills, the traumatic killing in Nahalal and the involvement of the small local network of fighters, together with the support of some of the villagers for the rebels—this is what appears to have won Saffuriyya its wicked reputation. To this day, when one mentions the village in the company of historically minded Israeli Jews, someone will trot out the standard line about the homicidal character of the people who lived there. The same two or three sources are always cited, which refer to the same two or three events—the killing at Nahalal, that symbol of Zionist idealism and initiative, central among them. The village's relatively high crime rate does not appear to have registered on the Jews who lived nearby. Neither do other, more conciliatory sorts of stories about Saffuriyya linger in the memory of most Israeli Jews: Amin and Taha both speak of the quietly warm relations that *also* existed between the villagers and nearby Jewish settlements—among them, amazingly, Nahalal. Once thirty cows were stolen from the moshav, and thieves from Saffuriyya were suspected. Two Jewish men came to speak to Sheikh Saleh about the problem, and he immediately summoned a tracker— "an artist of tracking" in Amin's words—who traced the prints of the herd to a different village, 'Iblin. The next morning, thirty men from Saffuriyya descended on 'Iblin—where, it seems, out-of-town thieves had been stashing their bovine loot—and demanded the cows be returned to their rightful Jewish owners. "The relations were good and human between the Jews and the Arabs," says Amin, "before the war [in 1948]. We were neighbors, friends."

Saffuriyya was, let us say then, a "village of murderers" in the sense that it was a village with murderers in it. Saffuriyya was, however, also a village of tinsmiths—and shoemakers, shepherds, teachers, teething babies, laborers, shopkeepers, new brides, barbers, folk poets, gravediggers, carpenters, landowners, teenage boys, builders, dyers, musicians, butchers, tailors, traveling salesmen, knife-sharpeners, old women, and a wandering ice-cream vendor who would appear on holidays and sell the children melting half-piaster scoops of their favorite flavor—chocolate, vanilla, or mint. It was a village of brilliant talkers, blubbering idiots, fat grocers, thin imams, of a kind Italian nun named Georgina, a fez-wearing Egyptian male nurse known as Sheikh 'Umar, and Abu Qasim the peripatetic ritual circumciser, who never went anywhere without his black doctor's bag and noisy motorcycle.

It was the village of Taha Muhammad Ali and his family and their neighbors and at least twenty other clans, divided into dozens of sub-groups, some of which were the best of friends and some of which had constant obscure scores to settle and whose squabbles would sometimes erupt into fist and stick fights, that is, a village of more than four thousand individual (cheerful, depressive, calm, anxious, bored, boisterous) human beings—of some twelve neighborhoods, thirty-five shops, three mosques, five graveyards, a town council building, ten oil presses, two religious schools, a municipal school for boys, a municipal school for girls, a convent-run orphanage where the nuns taught needlework, a modern mill, hundreds of community ovens, a bustling weekly animal market, a number of folk shrines draped with green fabric or surrounded by straw mats, and 747 houses the last time someone counted. It was a village of cooking pots, plows, mortars, wooden trunks, baskets, blankets, kerchiefs, pitchforks, coffee cups, water skins, bracelets, hammers, sieves, mirrors, slingshots, razor blades, buckets, cotton dresses, harnesses, clay jugs, cleavers, gas lamps, pestles, thimbles, combs, shears, Primus stoves, scythes, reed flutes, prayer beads, grindstones, saddlebags, cookie molds, serving platters, long robes, amulets, chalkboards, walking sticks, brooms, mousetraps, spinning wheels, and who knew how many buried cities' worth of smashed or whole or slightly cracked antiquities.

It was a village of the Qur'an, of epic tales and colored Damascene or Cairene prints of their heroes, as well as several oil-paint portraits (made in Jerusalem) of the mufti, and multiple calligraphed and framed verses from the Qur'an—the most popular of which read, "There is no god but He, the Living, the Everlasting. Slumber seizes Him not, neither sleep; to Him belongs all that is in the heavens and the earth." It was a village of goats, chickens, roosters, sheep, cows, donkeys, mules, racehorses, workhorses, and load-bearing camels; of wheelbarrows, carts, carriages, the 'Afifis' twelve buses, no more than three trucks; of stone walls, wood pens, hen coops, beehives, dirt paths, irrigation ditches, a Crusader church, a Roman amphitheater, a citadel, threshing floors, a famous spring, several radios, many outhouses, one telephone, 55,378 dunams of land that were planted with grains and olives and vegetables and which, in a good year, also yielded tens of thousands of perishable mounds of mulberries, quinces, black plums, apples, figs, lemons, grapefruits, tangerines, apricots, and the most sought-after pomegranates in the whole Galilee.

SAFFURIYYA II

◆

THE WINDOW IS OPEN

◆

"I WENT BAREFOOT THE FIRST TEN YEARS OF MY LIFE," says Khalid, the village boy at the center of Taha's remarkable 1996 short story "So What." A small but somehow tremendous tale (the late great American essayist Guy Davenport wrote that it seemed to him a cross between Kafka and Hans Christian Andersen), it recounts the agony and wonder of Khalid's first decade of barefootedness and the corresponding excitement and mortification that attend the purchase of his first pair of shoes. His parents have no money to pay for such things, and by the time they have scrounged the necessary twenty piasters,* the traveling Moroccan peddler on whose merchandise the boy has fixed his hopes has sold off his last proper pair. Determined nonetheless, Khalid buys what remains—two shoes for the right foot—and the results of his awkward, stubborn first walk in this mismatched pair are intensely painful, for him, for his parents, for the reader.

Before the boy even tries to put one right shoe in front of the other, though, the narrator has accounted for the whole intricate expanse of feeling, both physical and psychic, that comes from being barefoot—and, by extension, poor. The child's lack of shoes is not a symbol of poverty here so much as a smarting embodiment of all the shame and suffering that impoverishment brings. At the same time, that poverty is never merely a matter of corporeal discomfort but a magnified inner state. When he was still unshod, he explains, people would stare. The "looks from the children, in particular, struck with

---

* 1 piaster = 10 mils; 1,000 mils = 1 Palestinian pound

more power against my flesh and bones and blood, and burned more fiercely against my heart and spirit and nerves, than the hot embers of soil and sand beneath the soles of my feet in the scorching heat of summer."

At the same time, there were benefits. Khalid describes in vivid detail the games he would play in the winter, between rain showers, when he'd roll up his hem and plunge his feet in the water of the village irrigation canals, then make his way around the curves of the channel, his arms outstretched like wings: "I'd walk, stand, then walk in the water, which usually covered my calf, feeling against my bare legs and the flesh of my feet and the nerve-ends of my toes small pieces of metal, for the most part little coins with holes at their center, coins that had been lost by their owners and swept away by the water, or marbles, bullet casings, and old ladies' copper rings that had been thrown away by grandsons, and small keys, and sometimes bigger keys, in addition to crooked old nails, bent like the words of liars." He also managed to uncover colored Roman glass, crystal beads, and an old top which, when dried and painted with blue ink, looked, he says, brand-new.

Khalid's village is not named as Saffuriyya, but it seems—with its dirt paths, threshing floors, and Roman-glass-dotted water channels—very much like it; so, too, the boy's keen awareness of his family's poverty sounds familiar to the reader who knows something about the poet's life—all of which may lead one to ask if Khalid isn't in fact Taha. Are these literal memories that are being recorded or some more prismatic refraction of what really was?

Taha insists that he is not Khalid—that in fact he was inspired to write the story by seeing a snapshot of a group of children from Saffuriyya. In this 1925 picture, a cluster of kerchiefed young girls are standing close together, as though they'd been ordered to pose; the photographer must have been someone from out of town, since no one in Saffuriyya owned a camera. Off to one side is a little boy in a slightly ripped qumbaz, his head cocked quizzically to the right. He is squinting—at the camera? at the sun?—and he is barefoot. From this single image, says Taha, came the story of Khalid. He entered the character of the boy, he explains, the way an actor takes on a part: "I put myself in his shoes," or in this case, his lack of them.

Whatever the complex layering of mimetic and invented elements at work in this particular story, it's worth noting that Taha himself did not wear shoes until he was nine. And when he did finally buy a pair—red ones, with thick rubber soles—he did so only because barefoot children were not admitted to the municipal school in Saffuriyya. Those were the rules, and even after he'd gotten used to wearing the boxy weights on his feet he preferred to take them off and dash around without them: he felt freer that way.

When still shoeless, he had first attended Sheikh Hassan Halabo's maktab, the religious elementary school in the old part of town, and there he had learned to read. This is the beginning of the period Taha calls "my golden age"—and much of its glittering quality appears to have come from this newfound literacy and the world that it opened before him. At age seven, to hear him tell it, Taha suddenly popped into existence as a freestanding human being, a boy with a slightly loopy imagination, a serious work ethic, and a rich sense of all words could do. As he talks of himself in this era, it is possible for the first time to *see* him (there are no extant photographs of Taha before he was well into his twenties). A fair-haired, curly headed, blue-eyed child with a compact torso and long legs, he was terrible at team sports but loved to run races. He also adored school, even the strict and old-fashioned maktab taught by the drowsy, graying sheikh who would hit the boys with a stick and curse them when they answered his questions incorrectly: "Yilan kufrak!" Damn your blasphemy! he would shout at his stammering victim.

Taha was among the youngest and most eager students in a class whose male pupils ranged from ages six to thirteen and most of whom would come for just a year or two, then go back to work in the fields or herding flocks. On warm-weather days each student was expected to bring as "tuition" a flat loaf of bread for the turbaned Sheikh Hassan; in the winter the payment was a log. They sat in rows on straw mats on the floor with their handheld chalkboards, and the sheikh intoned the alphabet: "Alif, ba', ta', tha' . . ." And the boys imitated him, chanting in unison: "Alif, ba', ta', tha' . . ." When they'd memorized all twenty-eight letters, the sheikh began again from the letter *alif* and now added the vowels and their names to each consonant, bellowing the rhythmic "ba' fatha baa, ba' kasra bii, ba' damma buu . . ." And the boys called back in cacophonous singsong: "Ba' fatha baa, ba' kasra bii, ba' damma buu . . ." Over and over and over again.

Later on the letters formed words ("walad," boy) then arrayed themselves in short inflected sentences ("Dhahaba waladun," A boy went), then expanded into grammatical rules for the children to learn by rote ("Dhahaba fa'il madi mabni 'ala fatha," Went is a verb in the past tense, constructed with the "fatha" vowel). And from here they proceeded without much ado to the most famous phrases in the Arabic language, the opening sura of the Qur'an, "Bism'illah al-rahman al-rahim . . ."—In the name of God, the Merciful, the Compassionate—which Sheikh Hassan would half-sing and the children would echo, "Bism'illah al-rahman al-rahim . . ." and repeat until they knew the lines by heart. Then they inched through the rest of the verse, with the sheikh periodically yelling at one boy or another, "You! Read!" just as they were taught that the angel Gabriel had ordered the illiterate Prophet Muhammad: *Iqra!* Read!

Although Taha was elated at his newfound ability to decipher a book, Sheikh Hassan's educational repertoire was limited in the extreme: when he finished inculcating in his students the alphabet, the bare bones of Arabic grammar, a few Qur'anic suras, and the fundamentals of addition and subtraction, he circled around again to the beginning. "Alif, ba', ta', tha' . . ." After some two years in the maktab, it was time for Taha to leave. This was, after all, a kind of stopgap literacy the sheikh was instilling in the fallahin, and the boys who interrupted their plowing, planting, harvesting, threshing to come sit for a year on the dirt floor of his dank one-room classroom had no practical use for much more. Taha, though, was hungry to learn, and when he reached the age of nine, his father decided the moment had come to buy the boy his first pair of shoes and a set of those odd khaki shorts—and to transfer him to the municipal school.

But Taha's entry to this other institution meant much more than the acquisition of a funny British outfit: it marked the beginning of his fascination with the written—not the chanted, sung, or spoken—word and with the history and literature of the wider world. "You felt like a human being," he says now of the difference between the way his new teachers treated their students and the stern method practiced by Sheikh Hassan in the maktab. The school had been built recently on a hill in the open part of town, and it had "modern desks. Shelves for books and a nice wall with a blackboard, with windows." It was "a healthy place," hemmed by a flower and vegetable garden that was planted and maintained by the children. It was also expanding. The files of the Mandatory Department of Education contain detailed plans for building two extra wings, "latrines [which] are necessary," an improved playground, and "a covered verandah of light construction." The girls and the boys were kept apart, in separate buildings, so as, says Taha, "not to hear each other," and the children were divided into grades one through seven, according to their ages. (Taha was tested when he entered and placed ahead of many of the other nine-year-olds, in the rarefied air of the second grade.) Thirty-five pupils made up each class—a number of them traveling daily to Saffuriyya from the neighboring villages and Bedouin encampments—and each subject was taught by a special teacher. Some of these men had grown up in Saffuriyya, but many were temporary transplants from the cities and larger towns of Palestine—Nablus, Jaffa, Haifa, Nazareth—and their presence in the village very likely constituted Taha's first contact with urban, middle-class, "modern" Arabs; they wore the fez, as well as creased pants, jackets, and button-down shirts, and they spoke differently from the peasants.

Some of this difference could be chalked up to regional variation. But the strangeness of the teachers' speech, to the young Taha's ears, was also a subtler matter of class. The teachers at the municipal school were white-collar workers. They had studied for years and read many books: they spoke "correctly." In their tidy, well-lit classrooms in Saffuriyya they insisted that their pupils address them in *fusha* (pronounced foos-ha)—that is, literary or "pure" Arabic—a language Taha had heard from a young age, in the Qur'an and pre-Islamic poems and legends that filled the air of his father's madafeh, but which he had never before had occasion to shape into his own sentences. "It was hard," the grown-up Taha says tersely. He did not, he insists, truly learn to speak fusha until a good deal later, and then only after serious, extended study.

In the meantime, he was treated to history lessons about the Romans and Greeks, to math, geography, arts and crafts, and agricultural classes as well as physical education drills and Arabic-language instruction from a book called *The Garden*, by the poet, intellectual, and educator Muhammad Is'af al-Nashashibi, who was also a member of the illustrious Jerusalem family that had produced, among others, that city's one-time mayor. A collection of riddlelike rhymed snippets in quantitative meter and rhyme, culled from the classical Arabic tradition, the anthology didn't water things down for its young readers. Rather, it taught by sophisticated example, initiating its prepubescent, largely peasant audience into the unabashedly adult refinements of literature from medieval Baghdad and Damascus. In his introduction, the editor explains that he doesn't expect the pupils to understand all they read "on the day of memorization." True comprehension, he says, may come only "several years later."

Jasmine

Jasmine has already blossomed
    for one who can tell how it grows.
Like tufts of cotton combed—
    across an emerald robe.

Or:

Coffee

I am the dark beloved,
    within the cup unveiled.
My fragrance comes from India wood,
    to China I have sailed.

The natural world was a favorite subject of al-Nashashibi's quotations, and although the formal conventions employed by the long-dead poets might have seemed strange at first to the village boys, they were intimately familiar with most of the actual flora and fauna described in the sampler and so must have felt somehow at home with this book: they knew the rose, wallflower, stallion, workhorse, fox, dog, frog, jackal, fig, apple, almond blossom, olive tree, watermelon, narcissus, hoopoe, falcon, lark, partridge. Even the crop-devouring locusts deserved poetic mention. More abstract—and provocative—notions sometimes also emerged, such as "The Arabs" and "The Homeland," the rhymed glorification of which was, in ways the children themselves could not possibly have understood at the time, also central to the new teaching methods that were sweeping through Arabic-speaking Palestine during those years and that must also have informed the workings of the Saffuriyya municipal school.

Some two decades earlier, the educational reformer and Palestinian nationalist Khalil al-Sakakini had written of the need for schools that would "transmit to students the spirit of freedom, pride, independence, courage, truth, and other principles that would lift the nation from the depths of indifference and shake off the mantle of servitude that it has worn for many generations." By the time Taha donned shoes and entered the second grade, al-Sakakini's rather vatic plan had begun to take root: education was still not compulsory in Palestine during these years, but the number of students at village schools had more than tripled since the start of the Mandate, and many more schools now had classes that reached beyond the third grade. The literacy rate, though still low, had risen. In 1931, the year of Taha's birth, just 14 percent of Palestinian Muslims could read; by 1947, the rate had reached 27 percent. "Like an engine shifting from first gear straight to fourth" is how one historian has described the changes that this newfound literacy would ring on the culture at large: "Palestinian society moved within a brief historic moment [from the start of the century to the end of the Mandate] from near-complete illiteracy to massive reliance on the written word."

Meanwhile al-Nashashibi, al-Sakakini's colleague and friend in Jerusalem, explains in his introduction to *The Garden* that his reason for compiling a collection of the best poems from the tradition is so that, through their memorization, Arabic would enter the hearts of the young. The author and editor of numerous books in many genres, al-Nashashibi was by all accounts a man of tremendous learning and one for whom nationalism was a linguistic and cultural project as much as a political program. And though sometimes the poems the

children learned from his book preached patriotism, the more lasting
effect of this curriculum on a student like Taha was to instill in him
a deep love for the Arabic language and a taste for lines like these, by
the eleventh-century North African poet and critic Ibn Rashiq:

Poetry

Poetry is something noble,
    and in it there is no sin.
It's a cure for the soul—
    so teach it to your children.

The class's single copy of *The Garden* belonged to the teacher,
who would write the day's verse on the board, ask the boys to copy it
down, memorize it, then explain its grammar. (This technique may
sound dry, but it was effective: sixty-four years after committing these
words to memory and not, it seems, giving much thought to them
since, Taha can still jump in to complete a line I've started from the
textbook.) In order to hold in his hands a book of his "own," he had
to wait until Mondays—which were, he says, "like a holiday for me"—
when each student was allowed to choose a small volume to bring
home for the rest of the week. These were simplified, brightly illustrated Egyptian editions of classic works—funny stories about Juha
the joker, the didactic animal tales of *Kalila wa-Dimna*, Shakespeare's
Julius Caesar—and for Taha, they were as delicious as goat's milk
with a swirl of sugar, his favorite drink. He gulped down book after
book, and when he'd drained to the bottom of the entire set, he took
the few coins his father had given him as a gift on the last holiday and
he made his way—his heart pounding—to the house of il-Hajj Taher.
    A stooped, older man with a sharply defined civic sense, il-Hajj
Taher had a habit of leaning over to pick up and throw out any trash
that he saw in the street and a modest but profound vision of his fellow villagers' intellectual potential: he wanted people to read. The
conscientious Hajj lived near Taha's family, and he owned a small
library—really a single shelf with a few worn books . . . but what books!
For a mere ten-piaster deposit, Taha could borrow a volume of *Sirat
'Antar*, the extraordinary rhymed-prose epic about the exploits of the
pre-Islamic poet and warrior 'Antara ibn Shaddad. The real, sixth-

century 'Antara had composed one of the *mu'allaqat,* the suspended or golden odes that once hung on the Ka'ba in Mecca, but the apocryphal 'Antar and hero of the eleventh- or twelfth-century epic was a fighter, the bastard son of an Arabian tribal chief and a black Abyssinian slave. He was renowned for his courage, his desperate struggle to overcome his humble background, his magnanimity, his unswerving love for his cousin 'Abla, and his merciless, superhero-styled assaults on those who would harm his tribe or compromise the honor of its women.

The gleefully explicit gore and sheer motion of all 'Antar's adventures would, of course, have appealed to most young boys. Even as a child, 'Antar possesses rather alarming powers: "When a camel would stray away, he would cry out and make it stop . . . and when he seized one by the tail, he tore it off." As he grows older, 'Antar comes to disembowel scores of lions, to rescue 'Abla from countless virtue-threatening abductions, and to find himself slaughtering, single-handedly, five thousand men in one battle. But he isn't just a vicious killer; he is also a poet and a gentleman, and to hear Taha tell it, this former trait—his literary calling—was what drew him to the hero as a child. "My father liked him because he was brave and generous," he explains. "I liked him because he was a poet." In the epic, verse spills as freely as blood: the characters often halt the narrative to offer up emotion-intensifying rhymed and metered poems.

Sirat 'Antar filled ten volumes in il-Hajj Taher's edition—it had a red leather cover and yellowed pages—and Taha would read to the end of one book, then run right back to the Hajj's house to borrow the next. The story cycle was a favorite in his father's madafeh (it was a saga that was meant to be read aloud or even performed by a professional reciter, or *'Antari,* as it was in the cities) so Taha already knew many of the tales and poems recounted there. It was, in fact, probably the first poetry he ever encountered.

But to hold the book open in his own lap and read it quietly to himself was, for him, even more stirring than hearing it. He loved being able to start and stop and reread and slow down and speed up as he pleased. The words became *his* somehow, through these rhythms—and he even began to spin variations on 'Antar's adventures. Sometimes he related these to his friends at school. A boy once asked him, "How long was 'Antar's mustache?" and the ten- or eleven-year-old

Taha explained with great authority and a demonstration that 'Antar's mustache was so long he could knot it behind his head. Other times he sat alone or lay under a tree and imagined these improvisations, telling no one.

When he'd finished reading *Sirat 'Antar* he was tempted to go back and read it again, from the beginning—but instead he chose to slip from il-Hajj Taher's shelf and crack open the first volume of a very different book of stories that he already knew well and loved, *A Thousand and One Nights*, whose supernatural yet richly tactile medieval settings were as far from 'Antar's wide, brutal deserts as they were from his own Saffuriyya. In a short time, Taha had galloped through all four volumes of that masterpiece of courtly fantasy and narrative filigree—sometimes reading aloud to his father, who would correct his pronunciation of words that were written in Arabic letters but must have seemed thrillingly foreign to the boy. "Zabar Jaj," sounded out the young Taha as two separate parts. "Zabarjaj," said his father softly—it was one word: peridot.

◆

Abu Taha was pleased with his oldest son's quick mind and with his newfound interest in books: he imagined important things for Taha in the future. Perhaps he would study for a few years outside Saffuriyya; maybe he would return as a teacher. Still, instructing the boy in the names of obscure semiprecious stones might have struck him as a little absurd, considering that in those days a mere half-pound note was a fortune for the family.

By the time Taha enrolled in the municipal school, Abu Taha had sold off all his land except three subsistence-level parcels. Along with the plot where their house stood, he held on to two small patches of soil—the first planted with olives, the second with wheat. The yield from this land was wholly insufficient, though, to feed the family, which continued to grow. Imm Taha had just given birth to another boy, Yusuf, and now Abu Taha would, it seemed, need to part with these last few dunams—and with them, his last hope of providing for his children.

"Need teaches," explains Taha plainly, decades later, when asked how he understood—years before his voice cracked and his first mustache sprouted—that he must become his family's breadwinner. Following the lead of two older neighbors—Ahmed and Hussein, a couple of brothers in their thirties—the enterprising third-grader started collecting eggs from the village women and selling them at a profit to a merchant in Haifa. After school and on Fridays, when there was no class, he made his rounds through the dusty streets of town, armed with a straw basket and a little black book in which he inscribed the money paid and owed to each of his suppliers. Every week he collected some 250 eggs, and every week he transferred this delicate, feather-flecked treasure into a wooden box filled with hay, then he loaded it onto the back of the truck that Ahmed and Hussein used to transport their own 8,000 or 10,000 eggs to market. And every week, with the same sense of purpose and a faint flutter in his stomach, he jumped up onto the bed of the truck and nestled his small frame between the crates of fragile merchandise—then hung on tight all the way to the wholesale market at Haifa's Hanatir Square.

Not only did Taha earn a very respectable sum from this operation (he bought each egg for a piaster and sold it for a piaster and a half), he got to venture into the big city—that is, to see the world. The world had, it was true, already started to trickle into Saffuriyya and so into Taha's consciousness: traveling salesmen passed through the village, peddling clay pots, spices, handwoven baskets, Lebanese fabric, fish. They'd cry, "Samak! Ba'du bil'ab is-samak!!" Fish! So fresh it's still flapping!! And the gypsies sometimes arrived in town with their trained monkeys, metalwork, and the fine stud horses they'd breed with the local mares for a modest sum. A wandering troupe from the Caucasus also appeared every now and then to "sing foreign songs," dance, bang the drum, and walk upside down on a small tightrope; their star was a blonde named Latifa with "beautiful eyes," who wore bright-colored outfits "like a doll." Foreign tourists, English and Americans especially, would appear in the town on occasion and walk up the hill to the Qal'a, where a guard named Taha Toubi would unlock the door, let them in, and allow them to view the old building.

Egyptian preachers also turned up, urging people to fast and pray and make the pilgrimage to Mecca, and eventually they prompted a minor religious revival. One year, apparently under the influence of these roaming, al-Azhar–trained sheikhs, a contingent of several hundred people from Saffuriyya took loans and advances on future crops in order to fund the hajj they performed en masse. Taha's uncle Ahmed went on the trip, and in preparation for his return the family painted the doorframe of his house with indigo, hung palm branches, and slaughtered a sheep. When he and the other villagers arrived home, he came bearing stories of the far-off Sinai and the ship they had sailed through the Suez Canal, along with gifts of henna, worry beads, religious books, and a flask of well water from Mecca.

There was even a small-time impresario who circled the streets of the town, hawking what Taha calls a "cinema substitute." "A man used to come with a bench for five people, and a box with holes. We looked inside at small pictures of 'Antar and Abu Zayd [the trickster hero of the Bedouin saga of Bani Hilal], his horse and sword and mustache . . . with colors—beautiful!"

Still more exciting were the summertime evenings when the British authorities arranged for the real thing, a free, twenty-four-frames-per-second movie on the threshing floors. All the villagers would flock to see the Egyptian musicals they showed outdoors on a makeshift screen with the help of a generator. The more religious women, Taha remembers, would click their tongues, shake their heads, and denounce the "immorality" of these films, which had titles like *Dancing Together* and *Swimming Together*. . . . But they would always stay to watch till the last word of the final credits.

He had visited Nazareth a few times before, and that had been plenty exhilarating—even if it was really just a larger version of Saffuriyya, an old town surrounded by orchards and threshing floors. On the other hand, there was more bustle in Nazareth—along with Christian Arabs and British soldiers, hospitals and electricity, a cinema, two cigarette factories, pink painted houses with stained-glass windows and red-tiled roofs, and a daily market, as well as women in calf-length skirts and plenty of teenage tamarind-juice sellers who poured the sour-sweet drink from tinkly, gewgawed copper contraptions slung over their shoulders. . . . But still, it was familiar—and Saffuriyya was so close to Nazareth that a peasant venturing into the larger town from the smaller one would have felt somehow at home.

He had also caught a glimpse of the world beyond—albeit a very different world—when a delegation from the Bedouin tribe to which his family was related, the Beni Sakhr, visited Saffuriyya from their home near Irbid, as they had been doing for centuries. In years of little rainfall and food scarcities, they would lead a caravan of forty camels loaded with salt across the border and exchange the cargo for corn and wheat. When Taha was seven, they arrived and made a strong impression: the chief of the Ligtha clan, called Sa'id Saleh, was a friend of both Abu Taha and the emir (later king) 'Abdullah. He stayed in the madafeh in Taha's own house when he came to Saffuriyya, while his retinue of black attendants slept with the camels in the bayader. After unloading the salt and tending to the camels, these attendants, Shanhcr, Fankher, and Jakhsh al-Hamar—whose name brought peals of laughter to Taha and his friends, because it means Young Donkey—would talk late into the night, drinking coffee, smoking cigarettes, and telling stories about other Bedouin sheikhs and tribes, their alliances and feuds. Taha would sit up and listen. He was also listening when Sa'id Saleh announced to Abu Taha that he wanted to take the boy home with him to Transjordan—and though Taha was thrilled at the prospect of a faraway desert adventure, his father was not: What do you want from me? he half-snapped at Sa'id Saleh, and that was the end of that.

From the books he'd read and these various visits, Taha understood that a huge and fascinating human expanse existed beyond the borders of Saffuriyya. But he was still quite sheltered (he did not use a telephone or receive a letter until the 1950s), and the first time he contemplated with his own five senses the marvelous concretion and

multitudinousness of Haifa, he was, he says, "amazed." This was not
just a big town but a bona fide city, with cars and streetlights and
boulevards and fancy shops and factories and all kinds of people, not
to mention the sea. He saw many men there who dressed as his teachers at school did, in Western suits and ties—doctors and lawyers and
merchants and clerks—and he noticed Arabs talking calmly with
Jews. He'd already caught his first glimpse of this legendary people—
a favorite source of rueful mumbling in his father's madafeh—when
a school group from a nearby kibbutz had once traipsed through Saffuriyya, on their way to visit a village tomb that the Jews believed held
one of their ancient rabbis and that the local people maintained belonged to a *wali*, or saint. Taha's first reaction to this suntanned crew
had been one of wonder—even incredulity—since the boys and girls
were walking and talking together, and the girls were wearing shorts!
He had never in his life witnessed anything like it or glimpsed genuine female kneecaps.

But here in Haifa, coed bare legs were the least of it: he saw men
in straw hats and women in high heels, and some of them strolled arm
in arm and laughed and others sat in cafés together or by themselves
and read the newspaper or checked their pocket watches or drank
coffee (he'd never seen anyone drinking coffee alone, not to mention
paying good money for that weird privilege), and he ate hummus
topped with chopped meat in a restaurant and bought a glass of
lemonade from a street vendor and smelled the salt water and the car
exhaust and the shoe polish from the bootblacks' ornate metal boxes
and saw the homeless Jordanian day laborers and the wealthy Syrian
merchants and watched mechanics probing underneath trucks and
porters hauling enormous cabinets on their stooped backs and men
selling sticky nut-filled pastries from round platters and heard other
languages—Hebrew, English, German, Armenian, Yiddish, as he later
learned it was called—and the tooting of street musicians and the
revving of engines and the blare of radios . . . and his eyes and ears
and nose were tingling by the end of the day from the strain and emotion and the sheer impossibility of taking it all in.

His head was still buzzing when he reached home—though now
the sensation was not just a matter of physical overstimulation but
also a product of the profit he'd earned, and the fistful of coins that
he was able to present to his beaming father. Abu Taha was, it almost

goes without saying, both grateful and tremendously relieved: at the time, a field-worker's daily wage was about ten piasters, a full-time policeman earned a monthly salary of three or four pounds, and here Abu Taha's skinny young son had gone and made what would amount to an unbelievable five pounds per month—with little evident strain.

What began as necessity evolved into pleasure. Taha had, it was clear, a serious gift for business. And although he continued to enjoy school and loved to read on his own, something had shifted inside him. He had ideas. . . . As he collected eggs and accompanied them on the bumpy ride to Haifa, he began to imagine other ways of earning a living. Now his family had fewer cares and plenty to eat. Meat was no longer a rare treat, and when his mother needed a new dress, it was hers without a crisis. The atmosphere in the house had lightened considerably; his father's laughter washed through all its rooms, and he indulged in telling more elaborate and meandering stories in his madafeh. Abu Taha was, Taha knew, very proud of him—and it pleased him more than anything could to please his father.

Next, as he put it, he opened his window. This was not a metaphor for some new means of perception but the literal unlatching of a small casement that existed in the wall of the middle room in their house, facing the town's main street. Taha had decided that while attending school and dealing in eggs, he also had enough time on his hands to run a small kiosk. Taking some of the earnings from one of his Haifa outings, he bought cigarettes, chocolate, halvah, chewing gum, pens, and—the crowning glory—a block of ice from Nazareth, together with a box of fizzy drinks in different flavors: orange, apple, and lemon. In order to transport this liquid delicacy to Saffuriyya, he borrowed a donkey from Sheikh Saleh and rode into the bigger town, where he paid a call on the Kardosh family ice and lemonade factory near Mary's Well. The man in charge there helped him arrange the frozen cube in an old iron pot and scattered salt on top, and when Taha got the heavy, chilly cauldron home, he stuck the bottled drinks inside and covered the whole with a sack—and he was open for business. He could now charge two piasters for a cold drink and dispense cigarettes individually or in packets. Candy bars were a big seller—especially among the children whom Taha would race back to his own window during the school lunch hour. After class, he opened his window again and sat there from four to ten at night, surrounded by his goods like a king in the midst of his jewels. He would sometimes close early to go collect eggs, or on an afternoon when business was brisk, he might delegate these rounds to his brothers.

Other family members also helped out. His uncle Ahmed the grocer advised him where to buy the best and cheapest wholesale merchandise. English cigarettes, for instance, were readily available in those years through a middleman who bought cartons of Players and Chesterfields from British soldiers at a local camp. At the same time, though, Abu Taha was firm about the ethical paragon he expected his son the budding entrepreneur to be: "Be straight, and when you buy eggs, don't deceive any woman who doesn't know how to add and subtract. . . . He was always telling me, be clean." Taha listened to his father and absorbed what he said—as he drew a few quiet conclusions of his own about how best to do business. He understood such matters instinctively—*honesty is the best policy, the customer is always right*—without ever hearing these snappy truisms. From the stories he'd been told about how, before his own birth, his father had tried and failed at various mercantile ventures, he also realized that you could be friendly with the people who frequented your shop, but you shouldn't let them take over. Influenced, perhaps, by other admirable but decidedly noncommercial codes of conduct, Abu Taha had been far too generous in letting his friends help themselves to what they wanted without paying. So many people owed him money that he eventually closed his store. Taha, however, had other ideas. When a Bedouin once approached his window and asked for an *unqiya* (approximately half a pound) of halvah on credit, Abu Taha ordered his son to wrap it up and hand it over. The boy had then both to deny the nomadic stranger the object of his sweet tooth and to stand his ground before his father. He would, he explained, sell nothing on credit. He was developing a spine.

At the same time, he was cultivating another important trait that would serve him well in the future: learning to ford ahead with what needed to be done, no matter the sometimes dire distractions around him. Responsible for what happened in the house in a way that he hadn't been before, he was different now from children like his neighbor Assad, whose family was so well off that even as a child Assad owned a Parker pen that Taha sorely envied, or his best friend and next-door neighbor, Qasim, who still had the luxury of being wild. A favorite figure in the adult Taha's extemporaneous stories—and the elusive central character in "Fooling the Killers," the title poem of Taha's second book and one of his most powerful poems—Qasim was, according to these tales, an endlessly innovative troublemaker. He was as selfish as he was charming and would, for instance, slip the eggs right out from under his mother's chickens and trade them for cigarettes. Once upon a time, Taha would join Qasim in stealing berries off the basatin trees or hitting birds with a slingshot, and though he himself was by nature much more obedient, he seems to have enjoyed taking part in Qasim's boisterous and sometimes violent games.

Not that Taha had any desire to revert now to these rowdy antics. If anything, he was proud to have assumed his dependable new persona—which also felt like playing a game, though a game of a weightier sort. And he enjoyed being the one to provide for his siblings, who could remain for now more or less carefree. Feisel spent hours fashioning toy cars from wood, while Amin's hobby was—as Taha says and Amin himself confirms with a belly laugh—"fighting." He'd come home with black eyes and scratches, and his father would bellow and hit him for having scuffled, adding to his bruises. Ghazaleh was still young, but she was smart. She liked to take a scarf of her mother's and dance around the courtyard, staging a make-believe wedding, complete with singing and trilled ululation. Yusuf by now was a happy, pudgy two-year-old.

Taha continued to work. He continued to work even as Yusuf developed a precariously high fever and strange creeping rash. After a few nights of the child's sleepless howling and frantic rubbing of his reddened eyes, Abu Taha sent for Sheikh 'Umar, the Egyptian nurse who, together with the Italian nuns, attended to all the villagers' minor medical needs—the dispensing of iodine, bandages, and aspirin—and within just a few seconds of entering the house, the sheikh announced in an odd low tone that the boy must be taken immediately to the Greek doctor in Nazareth. Hearing this, Taha did not need instructions from his father to close and latch the window, wrap the boy in a blanket, and, Abu Taha limping on his cane beside him, carry the crying child to the bus. As the toddler shrieked and the bus wheezed up the hill to the bigger town, the father and his eldest son sat in grim silence.

It was measles. The doctor who examined Yusuf explained exactly what the boy could and could not eat; he wrote out a prescription; he recommended that Yusuf be kept apart from the other children; he wished them a good day.

But it wasn't a good day, and the days that followed were worse. Just as quickly as Abu Taha's laughter had swept in to fill the house when Taha had begun to support them, it drained away now, making room for stifled sobs and distressed whispers. Taha had no choice, meanwhile: he continued to work. There was medicine to buy, along with food for the rest of the family, and if he were to close his window or stop collecting eggs, there would be no money. . . . Perhaps he also continued to work because he found that it helped him to endure the ordeal. Busily arranging packets of chewing gum and chocolate or tallying the columns in his black egg-book gave him the sense that he was *doing* something, and even if nothing could really be done to save his little brother, it was better than sitting and watching illness ravage that tiny body. His parents had both already let their dread take over, and it was consuming them from the inside just as the red spots were devouring Yusuf's soft baby skin from without. Imm Taha wept and prayed and sat up all night with the hot-fleshed child—she had, it seems, let her guard down since all those other Tahas had taken ill, and she had almost forgotten how unspeakably awful this process could be—while Abu Taha waited in bitter, knowing, black wordlessness for the final blow to come.

It came. And when it did, there was nothing else for Taha to do except—after the prescribed period of mourning—travel back to the Kardosh factory in Nazareth for a fresh block of ice and a refill of his soda bottles. Then he reopened his window and continued to work.

HOME FRONT

◆

FAR AWAY ANOTHER DEADLY DISEASE WAS SPREADING and infecting huge swaths of the world's populace: it was war, and although Yusuf's fatal case of measles was infinitely more devastating for Taha's family than the dramas taking place on the distant battlefields of Europe, Japan, or even Egypt, the effects of the fighting did eventually filter into the village around them.

Since Germany had invaded Poland a few years before, the villagers had been following the developments with a wary kind of detachment. They kept abreast of events by means of several-day-old newspapers and staticky radio updates, though it all had a dreamlike, almost make-believe quality. Even word of the Italian bombing of Haifa's oil refinery in the summer and fall of 1940 seemed a bit unreal. So remote did the big city feel from the quiet of rural Saffuriyya, it might as well have been an aerial strike on Tokyo that was being reported.

The men in Abu Taha's madafeh would send Taha to listen to his uncle's radio, and he would then come back and detail for them what he'd heard, like the blow-by-blow proceedings of a soccer game. He gave them a sampling of the various stations: Radio Cairo, Radio Damascus, and the propaganda broadcasts of Radio Berlin, which were delivered by a man named Yunis Bahri, whom Taha remembers as having had a beautiful voice, as well as a tendency (which pleased the people) to focus on the events unfolding in Palestine, with a strong emphasis on the cruel behavior of the British. These broadcasts sometimes also featured Hajj Amin al-Husayni, "der Gross-mufti," whose pro-Nazi sentiments were well known. Taha himself preferred the BBC: "I used to believe exactly what London said. I hated them, but they seemed more objective."

At first the far-off international conflict appeared to have little to do with the people of Saffuriyya, and the men argued for the Allies or the Axis in the same expansive, bantering way they did about so many subjects—neighborhood squabbles, the Bedouin who grazed their flocks on village land, the occasional scandal involving a local girl— over coffee in the madafeh. Taha remembers: "Sheikh Saleh was pro-British. And an old lawyer, educated in Istanbul, he was pro-German. And when Rommel advanced he was delighted, and Saleh was upset. And when the British army was victorious in the desert, in Alamein, I saw Saleh was glad and the Turkish-educated lawyer was in bad shape." A man like Sheikh Saleh might have worried for the future of his own position. Were the Germans to conquer Palestine, he would certainly lose his job as mayor. But for most of the people of Saffuriyya, the war remained an intangible affair.

Anti-Semitism, it ought to be said, appears not to have figured in their thinking at all; the villagers seem to have had no idea what was happening in the death camps. Neither did they harbor a specific hatred of Jews. They simply detested their own political situation and felt the Jews were partly to blame for it. England remained the real focus of their animus.

It is interesting to note that though the village was quite removed from the scene of the ostensible wartime action, these madafeh debates mirrored the larger discussions then taking place throughout Arab Palestine. While the exiled mufti had infamously aligned himself with both Hitler and Mussolini—arguing that he and they shared common enemies in the English, the Jews, and the Communists and soliciting their support for Arab independence throughout the Middle East—the popular Arabic-language Jaffa newspaper *Filastin* urged the people to side with the Allies, and its editorial page patiently explained that "for Palestinians to disagree [with Britain] about local Palestinian politics is one thing, but to consider themselves enemies of Britain is something else. . . . There is not one Arab who understands the best interests of his country who wants to be the enemy of Britain in this war."

A few young Saffuriyya men enlisted in the British army—some for financial reasons, others in search of adventure or a ticket out of town. (One of the characters in an early poem of Taha's is a village

boy named Mahmud Mustafa Abu Eliyyan who joins up and is stationed on Acre's Napoleon Hill, where he "wears pants / and washes
dishes / against the Axis.") Such service was, though, generally frowned
upon. Taha remembers a nineteen-year-old neighbor whose father
cut all ties with him after he went off to fight with the English. Others in the village might have been more subtly skeptical about the ways
the British were using and abusing the local population.

The British army camp near the basatin, meanwhile, filled up
with Indian soldiers, some of them Muslims, whose presence in the
village probably marked the most immediate and obvious change
brought there by the war. The troops sometimes bought cold drinks
from Taha's window, and he often carted eggs to the barbed-wire edge
of the camp—to swap with the soldiers for chocolate, biscuits, or
canned corned beef. He spoke to them in sign language and a broken
hodgepodge of the few English words and phrases he knew: *welcome-
sir, how-much-you-want, is-very-cheap, thank you, yes, no, one, two,
three, bye-bye.* And occasionally he would barter with them for heftier
objects to resell. Dull green wool blankets—stolen from the camp, it
seems, by the soldiers—were a valuable item. Sometimes they would
trade his soda for their specially issued packs of Victory cigarettes,
emblazoned with an English slogan that Taha couldn't yet read: "V Is
for Victory of the Common Man against All Oppression."

The proximity of the soldiers seems also to have induced more
local boys to join His Majesty's armed forces. The archives contain a
plaintive, translated 1941 plea to the authorities from one Saffuriyya
villager who wrote, or more likely dictated, a letter about "my son
Mahmoud [who] escaped from the house and joined the Egyptians
who were working with the military in Saffuriya. . . . As I am altogether lonely and as his mother does not sleep being worried for her
young son, I beg to request your assistance for the return of my son."
The prompt reply was signed by a lieutenant colonel of the Royal Dra-
goons, stationed in Egypt, and its matter-of-fact Englishness must
have broken the father's heart: "As this regiment has now left Palestine I am afraid that I cannot assist you in this matter."

◆

The rains had been scanty during those same years. Sparse crops and
closed wartime ports led the government to impose various forms of

official food control: besides initiating "meatless days"—for three days a week it was illegal to slaughter "cattle, sheep, goats, swine and camels"—the authorities began to distribute flour rations. Because his family's house was relatively large, Abu Taha agreed to let the municipality store the village supply in their middle room, and so Taha's modest window display was crowded for some time by the sacks of Australian flour that would arrive periodically in three or four trucks. Though these heaps filled the room to the ceiling, they weren't nearly enough to feed the village. Taha estimates that the monthly rations were sufficient to sustain a family for a single week. Still, people made do. There were always fruits and vegetables, eggs and yogurt, and the occasional chicken or lamb to eat. And though the supplies of coffee and sugar had also been strictly rationed since the start of the war, Taha now earned enough to pay the extra money necessary to keep his father in madafeh brew. This was not a luxury but an absolute must, and even if it meant buying the beans on the black market, Taha made sure his father always had coffee.

Then one night the war arrived on the family's front step, in the form of the British soldiers who appeared in Saffuriyya in the dark, pounded on the door of Taha's uncle Muhammad Sa'id's house, roused him from sleep, placed him in handcuffs, and—offering his groggy, startled family no explanation—put him in the back of their jeep and drove away.

It was probably the fourth or fifth time Muhammad Sa'id had been taken into police or army custody since the 1932 bombing in Nahalal. And although in principle the family was used to such arrests, in practice each new apprehension and incarceration was a nightmare unto itself. Usually some dramatic event—that moshav bombing or the murder of Lewis Andrews—preceded and accounted for the arrest ("Whenever there was trouble," says Taha now, "they would take him"), but this time the reasons were far less clear. So, too, the soldiers on this occasion had offered no hint as to where they were taking Muhammad Sa'id—and for almost two months, his sons and his brother Ahmed tried desperately to find out where the British were holding him, making frequent, futile trips to the police stations in Nazareth and Haifa. Finally, they were informed that Muhammad Sa'id was being held in the prison fortress at Acre—but it took another two months before they were allowed to see him.

Though Taha remembers the panicked search for his uncle, the precise suspicions that led to this arrest are difficult to ascertain. The only archival record of any of Muhammad Sa'id's legal troubles that I have been able to locate is a single mention in a Hebrew-language Haganah intelligence document from 1942, which describes the "head of the Saffuriyya [Young Men's Muslim] Association [as having] . . . many acquaintances in [the Templar settlement of] Bethlehem." According to this report, "He [Muhammad Sa'id is named in the same document] worked together with one very wealthy [unspecified] German of this settlement who offered money to the association for actions against the Jews and the government and offered them financial assistance. In the end," claims the report, "he informed them that there were in the German Bank 60,000 pounds in his name, all set aside for this purpose." The arrest of "the head of the Saffuriyya Young Man's Muslim Association" for purported "terrorist activities against Jews and the explosion at Nahalal" is then described, along with the bribes that were allegedly paid by the wealthy German to various English and Arab policemen, in order to spring Muhammad Sa'id from jail. No year is mentioned, and various details seem to indicate that the arrest in question happened much earlier, at a time well before Taha might reasonably remember in the sharp-edged way that he does.

Whatever the dubious dealings of which Muhammad Sa'id was accused, it seems likely that his imprisonment did have something to do with the Templars, since he remained on good terms with the Germans—now the official enemies of Britain—who had once been his employers. Since the start of the war, the Templars had been declared prisoners of war by the government of Palestine and been placed in detention camps from which some of them were eventually repatriated to Germany and some deported to Australia on the *Queen Mary.* Muhammad Sa'id, though, maintained a warm connection with his old friends. When one of his sons got married, says Taha, the Templars came to the celebration with the gift of "a car full of sheep." But Taha insists that his uncle spoke no German and that the beefy blond utopians of the Galilean Bethlehem knew only the most basic Arabic. He imitates their way of addressing Muhammad Sa'id: "Inte amin!" You are trustworthy! "Inte mnih!" You are good! The relationship does not, at least in Taha's account, appear to have progressed much beyond the stage of such rudimentary niceties and fleecy wedding gifts.

The possibility that he was involved in terror is harder to evaluate. Although it seems likely that Muhammad Sa'id would have been questioned about his possible involvement in the Nahalal bombing, he was, again, never charged with this crime. Extensive newspaper and archival accounts of the legal proceedings against those involved in that murder do exist, and his name turns up there only in the most neutral terms, as trial witness. Whether Muhammad Sa'id was plotting other such actions in secret we cannot possibly know. Sixty thousand pounds was a huge amount of money, and it seems likely that if so substantial a slush fund did exist—earmarked for pipe bombs and the bloody like, and placed at his disposal by his German friend—the British authorities would have charged and tried Muhammad Sa'id. I have found no records of such a trial or any mention of the affair in the newspapers of the period.

Guilty or innocent, Muhammad Sa'id was placed behind bars in Acre—and, according to Taha, his uncle's wife and children were nearly hysterical with worry. Abu Taha sank further into the gloom that had enveloped him since Yusuf had taken ill. And the arrest must have cast a terrible pall over the village as a whole. Muhammad Sa'id was a respected man and an important figure in the local economy. Many of the villagers relied on his oil press, and with such a prominent member of the community in prison, they must all have felt somehow accused.

Although Taha understood that Muhammad Sa'id's situation was bleak, he was secretly excited to be included in the fuss that followed the discovery of his uncle's whereabouts. Among other things, this incarceration marked the first time Taha ever had his photograph taken: since Muhammad Sa'id's sons were tied up with running their father's various businesses in his absence, the task of traveling to pay calls at the jail fell to Taha and his father. To do so, however, they had to apply for a special permit from the authorities. Acre was a relatively short bus ride from Saffuriyya, but the arrangements for their first visit— the trip to the photographer's shop in Nazareth, the submission of the official request, the waiting period that followed, the tearful assemblage and wrapping of any number of care packages that the family prepared for Muhammad Sa'id—were like those one would make before a lengthy journey abroad. The permit and photo have not survived the years, and Taha's memory of the prison itself is foggy, but he does recall his eagerness to travel to Acre and the *mhammar*—roast chicken with sumac and onions piled on a thin layer of bread—that his aunt and girl cousins had so carefully cooked and bundled for them to take to their sorely missed husband and father.

Perhaps it was after one of these brief, heavy jailhouse visits that Abu Taha realized something drastic must be done to save his older brother from a lifetime in prison, or worse.

So he prepared himself to undertake an even longer and more momentous trip—to Irbid, in Transjordan, where he hoped to ask the help of their relative Sa'id Saleh, chief of the Ligtha clan of the Beni Sakhr Bedouin. Maybe Sa'id Saleh would be able to prevail on his friend the emir 'Abdullah to exert influence on the English authorities in Jerusalem, who might then agree to order the release of Muhammad Sa'id in Acre. Abu Taha was used to smoothing Saffuriyyan feathers, but this plan was a bit grandiose; it had the air of international diplomacy about it, which could hardly be said of the spats over property boundaries and vegetable patch–devouring stray goats in which he usually intervened. Still, he must have felt he had no choice. He ordered Imm Taha to wash his best qumbaz, and when it dried, he donned it, straightened his *kaffiyeh,* tucked under his arm the parcel of food she'd knotted tight, and sat mutely, waiting for the taxi he had ordered to be sent from Nazareth. The presence in this story of the taxi itself seems to indicate the seriousness of Abu Taha's mission. Regular buses ran from Saffuriyya to Nazareth, with connections all the way to Irbid. Yet Abu Taha appears to have sensed that when dealing with tribal chiefs, emirs, and high commissioners, a more upscale form of transport was necessary.

But somehow, without the use of telephones or telegraphs, Sa'id Saleh had already received word of Muhammad Sa'id's predicament and had made his way to Palestine to see what he could do. In Taha's slightly fanciful-sounding version of what happened, Sa'id Saleh arrived in Saffuriyya a mere half hour after Abu Taha's taxi had pulled off in a dramatic swirl of dust. And as soon as Sa'id Saleh appeared— a deus ex machina with a camel and a long, flowing robe—a neighbor was dispatched to halt Abu Taha's trek, and in a brief, miraculous while, all was well.

Just as the charge against him remains obscure, we will probably never know what behind-the-scenes wrangling took place to secure Muhammad Sa'id's release. Taha describes the events that transpired in terms that are short on political particulars but long on theatrical detail. Sa'id Saleh, he says, had gone to Amman and consulted with 'Abdullah, who in turn called someone in Jerusalem, which did the trick. Soon a jeep carrying a British officer and Muhammad Sa'id arrived in Saffuriyya. . . . As Taha relates the story some sixty years later his eyes well up with tears as he laughs—"and my father received him. He told the officer, 'Welcome to my humble home. Would you like me to make you coffee?' He said 'Okay.' My father brought the black coffee and added sugar and took the spoon this way." Taha indicates here how his father stirred a tremendous amount of sweetener into the bitter coffee—understanding, as always, whom he was dealing with and what his preferences would be. "And the Englishman drank it and said, 'Could I receive another cup?' He said, 'Yes.' My father put sugar in the cup, once more. The officer said, 'What is your name?' He said, 'Muhammad Ali.' 'Muhammad Ali! This is the best coffee I've ever had. Thank you very much. And be careful. Now there is a war. Be careful.' And he went home. . . . And the next day my father wrote a letter to Sa'id Saleh, telling him: In the name of Saffuri! In the name of Beni Nijim! Ligtha! A thousand thank-yous to the Emirate. A thousand thank-yous." For all intents and purposes, the war in Saffuriyya was over.

WHAT IF

◆

THE WRITTEN REMAINS OF SAFFURIYYA may be woefully scarce, but to listen and try to account for Taha's own vital yet inevitably fading (and selective) memories is not necessarily to get, or to give, the full picture. What has been blocked out or skipped over, for instance, when he relates in terse terms that he decided to leave school after just four years—two years in the maktab and two in the municipal school—against his father's wishes? "He wanted me to study, and I wanted to work. It was easier to work." Did they argue? I try to get him to be more specific. "No. But it was painful for him that I stopped school." That is all.

Taha tends to accentuate the positive, so it is not surprising that he retreats into a protective turtle shell when discussing the sorrow and anguish that are also a pivotal part of his tale. Describing the short, unhappy life of another sister, Rabba—her appearance in his story is a bit jarring, since he has never, in all the years I have known him, mentioned her before—he is especially taciturn. She was born a year after Yusuf died and was eight months old when she, too, contracted measles. Taha recognized the symptoms and understood. "Sheikh 'Umar came and gave her medicine and we brought her to Nazareth. Useless. She died." He is more expansive when he talks of how his family reacted to this latest death in a seemingly endless chain. His mother would weep, "and then we would weep, then she would say, 'No, no, it's okay, okay, okay. . . . They are all in *al-Janna* [heaven].' My father was about forty-two years old, but after these six deaths he looked like he was seventy. Death changed him. His head

93

went white. And my mother: when you looked into her face, you saw only sadness."

At the same time, Taha's life had shifted into energetic new gear, and he had begun to think seriously of the future. With the end of the war, he invested eight pounds—a small fortune for him—and expanded his business, moving his operations to the little lean-to that his mother had previously used as a kitchen, at the edge of the family's courtyard. He nailed together shelves from planks and wooden crates, drilled a hole in a small table through which coins were to be dropped into a box below. In addition to the sweets, cold drinks, and cigarettes that he had hawked at his original window, he now stocked groceries—canned sardines, dried white beans, sugar, rice, *tehina*, matches, indigo, even gasoline and the occasional freshly slaughtered sheep, as he puts it, "everything." And he worked constantly, even dragging a thin mattress out to the shop and sleeping there, so that he'd be in position to spring into mercantile action when, at five in the morning, laborers would stop on their way to work and wake him to buy a bit of halvah or chocolate, cigarettes to take to the fields. He stayed open until eleven at night and passed his entire day in or in front of the lean-to—selling things, reading, talking with friends, eating the meals his mother would ferry from the house just a few yards away. He arranged several low wooden stools outside the shop, and sometimes his father and his friends would come sit and talk and Taha would listen, hopping up to attend whenever a customer approached.

And then there was Amira. By now she was a tall girl with a quiet intelligence, fair hair, blue eyes, a narrow waist, and a long, lovely neck. And though she had always been there, poised somewhere at the edge of Taha's line of vision, and he had always understood that she would be his wife, this knowledge had been—when he was younger—abstract. Now, though, almost fifteen, he was already a teenager tilting toward manhood, and her presence in his mind—in the life he was planning for them both in Saffuriyya—was growing more and more pronounced. Though the whole village knew that they were to be married, they themselves did not, of course, speak of what lay ahead: they did not, in fact, ever speak more than a few shy words directly to each other. The connection between them was deep but chaste. They were never alone and certainly never interacted the way fiancés would in the West; they never held hands or kissed or wrote letters or even brushed fingertips. "But there was something between us, unexpressed," says Taha now, and offers a dark laugh as he explains that from an early age they'd both been given an "injection," making them immune to the attractions of others.

The sexual conservatism of the village was, says Taha, extreme, and besides a few telegraphically dirty jokes and stories told by the old women, the subject arose only in whispered relation to several honor killings that took place in Saffuriyya: once an unmarried girl got pregnant and was murdered by her father and brothers—an act of which the other villagers strongly disapproved. And though most families slept together in a single room—and the parents continued to produce numerous children—there was, according to Taha, a total embargo on talk of such matters. Did he know what was going on physically between his own parents? "You know, in a primitive way, they were very careful."

But to talk about sex in this context may be misleading—even a violation of the young Taha's virtuous (and virginal) feelings for his cousin. No matter that he was a teenage boy, his attachment to Amira appears to have existed on another, ideal level. It was fueled by the expectations of his family and friends, by her own demure bearing, but also, perhaps unconsciously, by the constant stories he read of another set of cousins, 'Antar and 'Abla, whose exemplary love and eventual marriage were legend. Amira was in all ways a very real girl, someone Taha saw nearly every day and whose trickling laughter and graceful gait had entered his bloodstream so profoundly that she almost seemed to be part of him—but she was, at this point, still also an idea, something to strive for, to imagine.

As he sat in his lean-to and the customers came and the canned sardines went and the coins piled up in the little box, Taha began to hatch a plan that wove both his love of business and his love for Amira. On his trips to buy wholesale merchandise in Nazareth, he had seen the way the shops sat side by side in the suq there, and he envisioned the complex of five or six stalls "each twelve meters deep" that he would like to build and run in Saffuriyya: one for meat, one for groceries, one for clothes, one for gasoline. He would surround the place with fruit trees, and upstairs he would construct a series of apartments—for his parents, his brothers and their eventual wives, for himself and his bride. He planned to build rooms with windows facing west; the air in the afternoons was best in that direction.

And here the older Taha's story breaks off as he pauses—to catch his breath, to linger over some unspoken memory, to grieve? I wait quietly for him to return to his sentence but begin to grasp that there is no way to tell this part of the tale in neat forward progression. He knows—we both know—what will have to come next. And the closer we get to 1948, the rockier the emotional and narrative terrain grows, and the more complicated the process of telling the story becomes.

But what if (I am trying to imagine) 1948 were still a wide-open date in the promising future? What if you were a curly-headed, laughter-prone teenage boy with a small though booming business and a pretty fiancée and History had not yet collided with your life? What if war, inasmuch as you'd ever thought about it, was just something that happened, if it happened, far away? What if?

◆

To tell this story—any story—one must pick and choose what matters, what doesn't. But what matters up close and what matters from a distance are not always one and the same. Of the year 1946, for instance, one could write that on March 6 an Anglo-American Committee of Inquiry arrived in Palestine to investigate and report on the problem of absorbing Jewish concentration camp survivors and war refugees in the country, and that when the committee published its finding some two months later, its members announced their support for a program, backed by American president Harry Truman, for the immediate immigration to Palestine of a hundred thousand Jewish displaced persons; the report stated as well that "because it is a Holy Land, Palestine is not, and can never become, a land which any race or religion can justly claim as its very own."

One could also discuss the fact that the committee was urged to consider the binational option proposed by a group led by philosopher-theologian Martin Buber and Rabbi Judah Magnes, founder of the Hebrew University.

Or one could note that 1946 marked the first summit meeting of the Arab League, whose members declared their support for Palestinian independence and a ban on Zionist immigration; one could refer to the fact that in the United States 1946 was a midterm election year and that—with an eye to the polls just a month away?—President Truman chose the eve of Yom Kippur to make a speech that re-affirmed his backing for mass Jewish immigration to Palestine and bolstered a plan put forth by the quasi-governmental Jewish Agency to partition the country into two states.

One could also type a few thousand words on the subject of why 1946 brought an upsurge in violence by the various Palestinian Jew-ish undergrounds, culminating in the July bombing by Menachem Begin's Irgun of the King David Hotel in Jerusalem.

Or one could say that in 1946 Taha started smoking. In 1946 Taha read his first modern book. This, too, is history—and while it would be a gross distortion to say that Taha's nicotine intake and evolving lit-erary tastes were as important to the rest of the world as the fate of masses of desperate refugees, the policies of an American president, or the deaths of ninety-one people in a Jewish-sponsored blast that ripped an entire side off Palestine's most famous luxury hotel—*these* were the events that most sharply punctuated his own private 1946. And though the actions of the diplomats and terrorists and presidents and kings were present, too, in his consciousness (he'd become a reg-ular reader of the papers *Filastin* and *al-Wahda* [The Union], and with increasing frequency he was called on to read aloud in Abu Taha's madafeh from these newspapers or go listen to his uncle's or Sheikh Saleh's radio and report back on the news to his father and his friends), they existed at a faint remove from his own doings in and around the buzzing grocery he'd established in Saffuriyya. As anyone will understand who lives in a part of the world where "the news" is the chief national export, the "major events" do matter, and some-times desperately so, but—as reported in the bird's-eye terms favored by most history books—such happenings have little to do with what it feels like to wake and work and eat and think and move through the hours of one's day, every day.

Yet background and foreground here are, of course, linked. Taha may have begun smoking simply as a rite of passage. (Men in Saffu-riyya smoked; boys did not.) Or perhaps he turned to tobacco because of current events: the obsessive political talk among his father's friends and the agitated tone of those radio broadcasts might have prompted him to light up. And the first modern book that he bought for himself—*My Brother Ibrahim,* a heartfelt if rather sentimental memoir about the brief, painful life of the poet Ibrahim Tuqan, by his twenty-nine-year-old sister, Fadwa Tuqan, who would go on to become a respected poet in her own right—was, in its wordy way, also connected to the political situation. Known as "The Poet of Palestine," Ibrahim Tuqan was the first important Palestinian poet to take up explicitly nationalistic themes in his work. Though his poems weren't published in book form until after his death in 1941 at age thirty-six, of a chronic stomach ailment, the aristocratic Nablus native was during his short life a genuine culture hero, celebrated throughout Arabic-speaking Palestine for the classically constructed yet groundbreaking (for the time, and for the conservative place) romantic verses that appeared in the newspapers and were read on the Palestine Broadcasting Service, whose Arabic branch he himself directed for several years in the late 1930s. His oeuvre includes erotically charged love and nature poetry and a lyrical hymn, called "Angels of Mercy," about the dovelike nurses who fluttered around his bed and attended him when he was ailing—but he is best known for his scathing political verse. He wrote ironic attacks on "the brokers of the land" (Arabs who were selling their property to Jews), an extended, contrapuntal elegy for three rebels hanged by the British during the revolt, and fervent—some might say florid—odes that glorify the courage and self-sacrifice of various revolutionary stock figures. He rhapsodized, for instance, about "The Martyr" (*al-Shahid*) and "The Freedom Fighter" (*al-Fida'i,* also translated variously as Guerrilla, Commando, or Redeemer): "he has exchanged his pillow for the shroud / . . . His message has been touched with the flames of hell. / He stands at the door, and death fears him." Despite their high fire-and-brimstone content, Tuqan's poems sometimes also worked as quietly eerie warnings to his countrymen. In 1935 he offered up the biting prophecy "People!":

> People, your foe is not of the type
>   to soften or show compassion.
> People, before you lies only flight—
>   you had best start packing.

As the most acclaimed of several Palestinian poets who came of literary age in the years leading up to and during the revolt, Tuqan enjoyed a kind of fame—even lionization—that may be hard for contemporary Western readers (more accustomed perhaps to thinking of poets as asocial aesthetes) to fathom. Despite the loftiness of their diction and themes, his poems played a pivotal role in the broader cultural conversation, and their appeal extended far beyond the reach of the city and its small circles of educated literati. The declamatory passion and patriotism of his work were legendary, and his poems' wide diffusion—on the radio and even through songs like the unofficial national anthem—meant that nearly every Palestinian at the time, literate or no, was likely to know them. He would later inspire several generations of "committed" Palestinian poets. Taha, for his part, would eventually reject the overtly political poetry of the sort that was Ibrahim Tuqan's specialty; nevertheless, Fadwa Tuqan's adoring 1946 portrait of her late brother moved him when he first read it, and the book seems to have whetted his literary appetite for other contemporary works.

But even as Taha was expanding his reading horizons and running his shop, ominous signs of what lay ahead began to loom much closer. Sometime in 1947—as the Irgun organized a campaign of car bombs, road mines, and kidnappings that paralyzed ordinary life in the cities and larger towns—Taha's seventeen-year-old cousin Subhi was shot and killed as he rode on a bus from Haifa. Jewish snipers were apparently stationed on top of the Dagon grain tower and fired on the bus. Taha remembers the funeral: "It was very sad, not like a normal death. People were also afraid and suspected every car that came from outside."

They were right to be jittery when strangers approached. Not only had acts by Jewish terrorists increased drastically of late, but the number of British troops stationed throughout the country had swelled to more than a hundred thousand (at the height of the revolt their ranks were a quarter that size), with many of these uniformed Englishmen approaching their wits' ends; their growing frustrations must not, one imagines, have smoothed their interactions with the locals. According to one historian, "The nerves of ordinary troops and police were frayed, after months of confinement to quarters, of being assailed by shouts of 'English bastard' or 'Nazi' when searching for arms and suspects in Jewish areas, of ceaseless alerts; and above all a pervasive sense of political drift and imperial humiliation." The grim feeling on the ground trickled upward, and back in London opposition leader Winston Churchill "asked rhetorically what all those troops were doing in Palestine, what was the point of their staying on, and at last called on the government to divest Britain 'of a responsibility which we are failing to discharge and which in the process is covering us with blood and shame.'"

The Mandate was obviously on its way out (India, too, would declare independence from Britain that August), and on November 29, some nine months after the English referred the "Palestine problem" to the United Nations, the General Assembly endorsed a resolution that recommended the partition of Palestine into "Independent Arab and Jewish States and [a] Special International Regime for the City of Jerusalem." The vote was thirty-three to thirteen, with the United States and the Soviet Union both strongly advocating partition, all but two of the African and Asian states voting against, and Great Britain, among others, abstaining.

BATTLE DAYS

◆

OIL TANKERS OF INK HAVE BEEN SPILLED on the implications of the UN resolution to divvy the land and on its acceptance by the Jews and rejection by both the Palestinian leadership and the Arab states, who viewed partition as a Zionist plan—a landgrab that would award the Jews a larger, much more agriculturally fertile state than the Palestinians, though at the time Jews owned a mere 10 percent of the country's privately held lands. That many of the Jewish state's new and future immigrants had just suffered the torments of the Holocaust at the hands of European Christians did not, to Palestinian minds, explain why they themselves were being asked to forfeit their hold on vast tracts of citrus groves and fields of grain, to give up direct access to the Red Sea and to the port at Jaffa, or to become—as 40 percent of the Palestinians suddenly would—members of a minority in a Jewish state. "To be the victim of a victim does present quite unusual difficulties," as the Palestinian intellectual and activist Edward Said would later remark about the impossible situation facing his people after World War II. Many ordinary Palestinians seem to have recognized this awful irony in real time, as the drama was unfolding.

In Abu Taha's madafeh, meanwhile, the talk of partition comprised an uneasy mixture of anxiousness and disbelief, threaded through with a surprising strain of cynical amusement. Never mind that the English had immediately begun preparing to dismantle government offices and move troops out and that, the day after the UN vote, anti-American riots flared around the Arab world as violence erupted

throughout Palestine. The men in the madafeh simply did not put
much stock in the UN decision, a fact that is easier to understand
when one stops to consider that the United Nations Special Committee on Palestine—the group that visited the country in the summer
of 1947 and formulated the recommendations that gave way to the
partition plan—was the *eleventh* such international committee sent
to report on the situation in Palestine since 1919. And even though
Abu Taha's friends must surely have understood that the politicians'
rhetoric might be more than hot air this time, they called the partition plan, says Taha, laughing now, "*nonsense*," the work of lunatics.
He imitates the men: "We don't want partition. So when we say
no, that's it. Nobody can divide our country." He stops laughing. "The
people in Saffuri believed that even with partition, Saffuri would
be international, because Nazareth and the villages around Nazareth,
they wouldn't be Arab or Jewish. Jerusalem and Nazareth would be international." (This belief was mistaken and seems to have been based
more on wishful thinking than on any committee's maps.) "But even
if it was international, they still didn't want it." More to the point, the
people had no reason to believe that a new governmental arrangement, should it come to pass, would be any different in its practical
effect from the ones that came before: the Turks, the English—
all these foreign powers came and went but the people of Saffuriyya
remained.

Taha's laughter now is a little opaque, and it is difficult to say if
he is mimicking the edgy snickering that filled the madafeh in the
wake of the UN announcement or if he is chuckling sarcastically in
retrospect at what he calls the villagers' naïveté, their absolute inability to conceive of the nightmare that lay ahead. "I remember . . . a
short, a very short tale. A man from Saffuri, with a rifle, he came to
our place, to our madafeh, then my father asked him, 'What do you
think will happen?' This was a week or two weeks before the with-
drawal of the British army. The man said, 'We are strong, we are okay.
We just want the British to leave, then we will do our business.' My
father asked him, 'How many bullets do you have?' He said, 'Six.'"

To hear Taha, Amin, and many others tell it, the mood in the village and indeed throughout Palestine was in those days nothing short
of schizophrenic: such irrational cockiness appears to have coexisted
with the darkest pessimism and sense of resignation—even fatalism.

"No two people were talking the same," explains Taha. "Everyone had his own thoughts. And the most important thing was that there were no leaders, no intellectual leaders to explain what was happening and what we had to do. Nothing like that. There was only the Communist Party and this was very small. The Communist Party wanted partition, wanted the people to live together with the Jews." And did anyone in Saffuriyya support them? "Noooo. Look, a Communist leader from Nazareth once came to Saffuri and organized a meeting on the roof of the mosque. And people came—about thirty, forty people and they sat down and he started to explain about Communism. He talked about Karl Marx and the struggle between the classes. He talked about the worldwide labor movement. Talked about everything connected with Communist thought. Afterwards he asked for questions, and a man—a handsome man—he said, 'Sir, your talk is nice. Your ideas are beautiful. But 1 don't understand it. Let me ask you a question: what about Hajj Amin [al-Husayni, the mufti]? Are you with the mufti or against him? If you are with him, we are with you. If you are against him, we are against you.'"

Though Taha narrates this encounter now as a mordant joke, the story is, he knows, not funny. The class struggle apart, it is difficult in retrospect to see now how the villagers could have continued to place so much faith in the mufti—an exiled, power-hungry leader whose divisive and often bumbling actions had contributed substantially to the failure of the revolt in the 1930s, who had made a disastrous choice in his wartime support for Hitler, and who now drastically underestimated the political and military challenges that stared his people in the collective face. He claimed it would be easy to defeat the Jews and—by throwing all his weight behind a small, badly equipped volunteer army controlled by his nephew, 'Abd al-Qadir al-Husayni— he did an excellent job of undermining the authority of Fawzi Qawuqji, the same professional Syrian soldier who had come and fought and gone during the revolt and who returned to Palestine at the start of 1948 as the commander of another army of Arab irregulars, this one sponsored by the neighboring Arab states. The Arab states themselves, it should be said, are far from blameless in this story. Just as divisive and bumbling in their actions as the mufti, they failed to provide Qawuqji with the arms and supplies he needed and often put outlandish bureaucratic obstacles in the path of his—also poorly

trained—army. The various Arab leaders were involved in bitter power
struggles with one another, and as one historian has noted, they "remained curiously unwilling to allow the Palestinians to assume control over their own destiny." Meanwhile, the villagers continued to
nurse the fantasy of the mufti as their protector, it seems, for symbolic and emotional reasons—he was a religious authority from a respected family, and he always claimed to be fighting for them—and
because there was simply *no one else*. In the void, they clung to what,
or who, they knew, even if this choice flew tragically in the face of
their best interests.

But this, too, was a part of the schizophrenia. The mufti urged
the locals to rise up and fight the Zionists—which in very large part
they did not do. (The military historian Benny Morris quotes a Jewish intelligence source as writing at the end of 1947 that "the moderate majority . . . are confused, frightened. . . . [A]ll they want is peace,
quiet.") The mufti did not support the invasion of Palestine by the
Arab armies and irregulars since he believed that their presence
would threaten his power, and when Qawuqji's troops arrived in
the country, he issued a warning about cooperating with "strangers."
For Palestinians to do so would be considered treason. At the same
time, many of the villagers who continued to hang the mufti's portrait
on the walls of their homes prayed fervently for the day those very
Arab armies would swoop in to their rescue. The villagers seem to
have understood far better than the mufti himself that the Jews
nearby were much better armed, trained, and organized for fighting
than they. "Look," Taha says, "the people in Saffuri had the impression that the Jewish people, *all* of them were soldiers. Even if he was
not a soldier he was trained in how to use a gun. And they thought
that the Arabs are peasants, and of these peasants, some youngsters
would go to be fighters. That meant from a whole village, maybe five
or ten or six. But of a hundred people from [the moshav] Nahalal,
eighty-five of them could use a gun like a soldier. And they had directions, they had an officer, and the officer was linked to a political leader, and if he was fighting he had rations and equipment and
ammunition."

Denial held sway alongside frantic preparation. During the Mandate, a local man named Nimr had served under the British in the
Arab Legion in Transjordan. Decked out in a regulation red belt and

black fur hat, he had guarded the oil pipeline that ran from Iraq, and as soon as the partition plan was announced, he decided to use what he'd learned from the English to train a band of villagers to shoot and advance and retreat. Another self-appointed officer, Abu Mahmud al-Saffuri, a veteran of the revolt, was now affiliated with the mufti's nephew; he also assembled a group of local men to fight in various battles throughout the Galilee. They donned matching yellow kaffiyehs and set forth. Several other old hands from the revolt tried to organize some of the younger men to defend the village: because a few of the more prominent former rebels had impressively lush mustaches, this small force became known—to the great amusement of the villagers, it seems—as 'Askar Abu Shawarib, the Abu Mustache Army.

Less comical was the appearance that winter of several thousand irregulars from Syria, Iraq, Transjordan, Egypt, and Lebanon who trickled into the country and joined Palestinian fighters, under Qawuqji's command and the turgid title of the Arab Liberation Army (Jaysh al-Inqadh, literally the army of deliverance or salvation), and by late March a whole battalion of ALA soldiers surfaced near the village. They were led by a Syrian Druze named Shakib Wahab, who, says Taha, also had a mustache. He saw Shakib Wahab drinking coffee in Sheikh Saleh's madafeh and heard the people say that he was brave. The presence in nearby Shafa 'Amr of the rifle-bearing Druze irregulars with their khaki uniforms and heavy boots appears to have both calmed the villagers' nerves—well-heeled help had at long last arrived—and created a sense of imminent climax. With the advent of the ALA, most of the villagers entered into a pattern of tense if passive waiting. At one point Qawuqji himself paid a call on Saffuriyya, and everyone turned out to see the man they regarded, says Taha, "as a savior . . . and I saw him in an armored car. He was blond, with green, beautiful eyes, with a good, well-built body." (A more-than-slightly disdainful *Time* magazine story about Qawuqji described him that year as "a red-haired, blue-eyed man, who looked more German than Arab," and noted how "he likes to dress dramatically, to fit his dramatic legend. His favorite garments: a fleece-lined flying jacket, or long sheep-lined cape draped over his shoulders.") Shakib Wahab's headquarters were also in Shafa 'Amr, and on several occasions he, too, turned up in Saffuriyya, his blustery madafeh talk continuing to boost the villagers' sense that the struggle to come would be a cinch.

At first, before Qawuqji and Shakib Wahab arrived in the country,
the radio and newspapers were filled with reports of successful Arab
attacks and strategic advances. There were far more Arabs than Jews
in Palestine, and that sheer numerical fact must have given the villagers a certain sense of invincibility. Armed bands like Abu Mahmud
al-Saffuri's had managed to disrupt road traffic throughout the country and blocked the main Tel Aviv–Jerusalem route for months, holding the hilly, inland city in a serious state of siege. The headlines of
Filastin throughout these months were awash in exclamation points
and grand declarations from foreign Arab leaders pledging to defend
Palestine and "deliver her to her people." As the situation throughout
the country grew bloodier, though, and word of all kinds of defeats
and retreats and threats flooded in, the villagers must have started to
wonder. During the rainy winter months, tens of thousands of well-to-
do Palestinians from Jerusalem, Jaffa, and Haifa were, everyone knew,
packing up and moving—either inland or outside the country.

In Haifa, car bombs and mortars and snipers frightened them,
while soaring prices, closed shops, the suspension of bus service, and
raging unemployment made normal life impossible; by the time the
looting started (often the Arab irregulars were the ones who ransacked
Palestinian homes), food was scarce, and the Arab police themselves
had fled the city. Pandemonium had descended. In Jaffa, the largest
Arab city in the country, the situation was just as bleak, with barbed
wire all over; sniping, explosions, and arson that had become com-
monplace; hospitals filled beyond bursting but few doctors in sight; a
postal service that had ceased functioning; and, in January, a car
bomb set off by the Stern Gang (a radical Jewish group whose leaders included future Israeli prime minister Yitzhak Shamir), which leveled the town hall and killed dozens of people. Though many of those
fleeing Jaffa and Haifa took refuge in Nazareth, safety was a relative
notion: there was also talk of how some of the wealthier citizens of
Nazareth were themselves packing trunks to travel abroad. Rumors
began to circulate about nighttime raids on villages like al-Khisas, on
the northern border, where the Haganah blew up houses and killed
twelve sleeping civilians, including four children, and Balad al-Sheikh,
the village near Haifa where 'Izz al-Din al-Qassam was buried and
where the Haganah retaliated for a riot that had itself broken out

after the Irgun's bombing of an Arab crowd in Haifa—and killed some seventy villagers.

Many of those who survived the slaughter in Balad al-Sheikh fled—and some arrived in Saffuriyya, telling perplexing stories about what had prompted them to run. "They came, fighting. We left." But how—the people asked, incredulous—how could you leave your village, your home? "We didn't want to be killed, that's all." The whole thing sounded, says Taha, vaguely ridiculous—as impossible to imagine as the sky falling. And there was the sky, set as always in its place up above, and there was the radio, set as always on the table in Sheikh Saleh's madafeh, bleating out upbeat news updates at two and six o'clock every afternoon and evening. According to Taha, "They always said the Arabs are victorious in Palestine. And they always said the Jewish newspapers were lying to their people. And when the Arabs suffered a defeat, with ten dead and fifteen wounded they would say two dead and three wounded. They always reduced the casualties." And did the people continue to believe what they heard—even as they saw with their own eyes frightened families fleeing places like Balad al-Sheikh? "They thought the radio was the truth. Propaganda is very strong."

But by April, when 'Abd al-Qadir al-Husayni was killed fighting in the hills near Jerusalem and when the Stern Gang and Irgun, with the help of mortar fire from the Haganah, launched the now-notorious massacre of what the radio said were hundreds of civilians in the nearby village of Dayr Yasin—the villagers of Saffuriyya must have felt themselves torn between fear and assurance.

On the one hand, they were terrified that similar horrors might be lurking and waiting to spring out at them. Besides having to absorb the idea of such a heinous mass murder—committed in a peaceful village that had signed a Haganah-brokered nonaggression pact with their Jewish neighbors—the villagers were forced to take in the accounts of how the surviving Dayr Yasin villagers had been paraded through the streets of Jerusalem before jeering Jewish crowds.

On the other hand, the familiar rhythms of their own planting and milking, tilling and cooking convinced them that things would remain forever unaltered and placid in Saffuriyya. It was one thing to lean forward, puff a cigarette, and listen intently to a transplanted stranger's fantastical-sounding stories of the sudden assault on his city or town—and quite another to picture yourself and your village in a similar situation. Even when, in the middle of that month, a panicked group of Muhammad Sa'id's German friends from Bethlehem turned up in Saffuriyya, offering dazed accounts of the way the British had evacuated the Templar settlement as prelude to their own exodus from the country (the men had, it seems, fled beforehand), many villagers still felt safe—or somehow exempt from the battles and forced departures unfolding so close by. Such doings deeply troubled Abu Taha, who looked toward the future with a new despondency, but sixteen-year-old Taha himself remained hopeful. Outside his window the goats were munching grass, his mother's roses were unfurling sweet blooms, and in the distance he could see the farmers raking the bayader and preparing their scythes as they did every year for the harvest. This season's crops would be, it was said, especially rich because of the abundant rains. "It was a splendid year," says Taha now, speaking in strictly agricultural terms. "Not normal."

Beyond the threshing floors things were also not normal. Just a few weeks after arriving in the area, the Druze officer Shakib Wahab and his men set out for the villages of Hawsha and Kasayir, close to Haifa, from which—at the request of Qawuqji, who was fighting nearby and needed help—they launched sniping attacks on a kibbutz called Ramat Yochanan. Soon the Haganah fought back, the Druze returned fire, and the battle became a hand-to-hand struggle that raged for four full days. "In these battles the soldiers of the enemy displayed great courage," according to the official *History of the Haganah*. Another account, by Moshe Carmel, the commander of the Haganah brigade that faced down Wahab's men, reads, for its hyperbolic part, a bit like *Sirat 'Antar*, "They [the Druze battalion] continued to charge forward furiously, with large knives glittering between their teeth in the sunlight. Despite the casualties they suffered in the field they didn't flag in their attack and they fought face to face, hurling hand grenades and knives at the other side."

Still, the battalion could not hold out. Their ammunition dwindled, they had no reinforcements, no food, little sleep, and though the Haganah fighters were struggling in much the same way—Carmel describes how, when their arsenal was empty, his soldiers resorted to throwing rocks—they did eventually receive additional arms, ammunition, a meal, and even coffee, and so they outlasted the Druze. The Haganah suffered real casualties in this face-off, but these were far less than the substantial losses dealt the five hundred men of the Druze battalion: estimates range from the low-sounding thirty-four dead (this is Wahab's figure, offered right after the battle, along with the grand and apparently baseless declaration that "the enemy suffered far greater losses than we did") to the probably inflated tally of three hundred Druze dead. (This is Moshe Carmel's count. Without citing the number of Jewish casualties, he does go on about the macabre task of having to remove the bodies of his soldiers from the battleground, several days after death: "The cold, bluish-black, and bloodless bare feet looked so strange and aroused tremendous pity.") A contemporary estimate puts the number at 110 Druze and 25 Jewish soldiers killed. Among the dead was then-Lieutenant Colonel Moshe Dayan's younger brother, Zorik, and in the aftermath of this showdown, a group of Wahab's officers met secretly with the grieving Dayan and his men, apparently eager to switch sides and join the Haganah. Though their desertion did not take place immediately—the head of the Haganah was doubtful about their motives and turned down their generous offer—the very contemplation of such double-dealing did not bode well for Wahab or for the people of Saffuriyya. According to one scholar well versed in this particular period and its personalities, "Before leaving [the meeting] . . . the Druze apparently asked for some packets of chocolate with Hebrew handwriting on them, to prove to their friends in the unit that they had actually met with the Jews."

Taha and the other people of Saffuriyya would not learn until later of the dirty doings unfolding behind the scenes in Wahab's battalion, but they did know that the soldiers' supplies had run precariously low. The lines to Damascus had been cut off, and as the men exhausted their bullets and rations, the villagers began to feed them. "Whether they liked them or were afraid of them, I don't know," says Taha. Some fled. "And I myself, in my shop, one of them came and knocked on the door. He said: 'I have a rifle. A Canadian rifle. Do you want it for three pounds?' I wanted very much to buy it. But I didn't have the three pounds and I was afraid. Afraid that my father—he was against dealing in arms. Afraid that Shakib Wahab himself would come and say, 'This is mine!' I told him no."

The commander of the Druze battalion was, as it happens, other-wise occupied. At around the same time that Taha was admiring the deserter's rifle, an apparently desperate Shakib Wahab also met with the Haganah's representatives. In the opinion of one Jewish intelligence officer who participated in the talks, "Our resistance in the face of his troops at Ramat Yochanan had influenced him. We persuaded him that it was possible to trust us." Or perhaps they had persuaded him that fighting back was futile. In either event, Wahab agreed, by refraining from attack, to help the Jews take Acre. The battle known as Hawsha and Kasayir or Ramat Yochanan was the first and last that Wahab's men fought, some of his soldiers did indeed switch sides, and Wahab left Palestine a few weeks after this clandestine meeting.

In Saffuriyya rumors of Wahab's *khiana*—betrayal, treachery, or treason—began to spread. ("Khiana, khiana," Taha repeats the Arabic word several times, in a whisper, as it must have sounded moving from ear to ear and house to house.) No one knew precisely what had transpired; it was rumored that money may have changed hands. "He dealt with the enemy, he talked with them, he received something. . . . But nobody knew what exactly." Besides, his reasons for abandoning them didn't matter anymore. The plain fact was that the people of Saffuriyya were again alone. The village was quiet. It was almost as though all of their troubles had passed.

WHAT HAPPENED

◆

THE HARVEST BEGAN. TAHA PUTTERED IN HIS SHOP. The
bells around the goats' necks clanged, and their bleating mixed with
that flat brass music when the shepherds returned with the flocks
from the fields in the evenings. Abu Taha and his friends sat under
the fig tree in the courtyard and smoked and talked. In the calm that
descended on those warm spring nights it took a concerted effort to
believe the newspapers—which reached the village far less frequently
now—that grave things were happening elsewhere: Tiberias and
Haifa had, they said, fallen. Taha's cousin Sa'id, the late Subhi's older
brother, had been living and working in Haifa, and he'd returned to
Saffuriyya, spilling with surreal-sounding stories about how, for instance, the Jews had fired mortars into a crowd, which caused thousands of Arabs to charge the harbor, desperate to jump onto boats that
were leaving for Acre and Lebanon. Acre itself was said to be filled
with refugees, typhoid was spreading there, and the Haganah had cut
off the city's water and electricity. Safad had been taken, Jaffa was
falling. . . . These seemed like headlines from another planet, though
when Taha traveled to Nazareth to stock up for his store, he could see
the hordes of refugees, feel how sharply the atmosphere in the town
had shifted. One shopkeeper there owned a Philips radio, and the
people always crowded anxiously around it, waiting for news. Meanwhile, the animal market had metamorphosed into a weapons bazaar,
with pistols, revolvers, and machine guns for sale. Taha says that
British soldiers on their way out of town were the main munitions
suppliers.

Such black-market firearms were perhaps the final contribution of the British to Palestine. At midnight on May 14, the Mandate expired, and the last of the English civil servants and soldiers, teachers and policemen were scheduled to have flown or sailed away. On the afternoon of the same day David Ben-Gurion called to order a meeting at the Tel Aviv museum of the (Jewish) National Council and read aloud the Declaration of Independence of the brand-new State of Israel. (The second paragraph of this historic document reads: "Exiled by force, still the Jewish people kept faith with their Land in all the countries of their dispersion, steadfast in their prayer and hope to return and here revive their political freedom.") "Hatikvah," The Hope, the new national anthem, was sung; the Jews—said the radio—danced in the streets. And in Saffuriyya nothing unusual happened at all. Indeed, the hush that had settled over the village must have been loud in the ears of the men who were sitting and waiting under the fig tree . . . waiting for the next day, perhaps, when everyone expected the Arab armies to invade. But when they did, that hush remained and the men kept sitting and waiting under the fig tree. . . .

Time collapses. Time expands. When asked about the period of charged stasis after that famous fifteenth of May, Taha naturally jumps ahead to relate the details of Saffuriyya's final hours—but one imagines that, in the moment, the anticlimax must have grown by the minute, along with a faint but horribly metastasizing sense of communal dread. As fighting raged beyond the village, several young Saffuriyya men died in the battles, Abu Mahmud al-Saffuri and his men fled the fighting in Acre and returned to the village; thousands of refugees spilled onto the roads; a United Nations truce took effect, then expired (after the end of this internationally mediated lull, the Galilee village of al-Birwa fell and then-six-year-old poet-to-be Mahmoud Darwish lost his home); Abu Taha's mood grew even grimmer, and Imm Taha began to putter a bit more desperately around the courtyard and house—sweeping, scrubbing, washing, cooking. She even packed some clothes in sacks. "I asked her what she was doing," says Taha, "and she told me, 'Your father said we don't know what will happen. The situation is so bad. *May*-be we will have to leave the village for a while.'" One of her sisters came to Abu Taha and asked him to take her life savings—thirty-five pounds—and bury it in the garden, alongside the money Taha had tucked away. In the general anxiousness that had descended on the village, she was afraid of thieves.

And though most everyone around him was steeped in this dulled apprehension, Taha carried on, trying to act as though nothing were wrong. This breezy attitude was, it seems safe to say, a calculated decision. He clearly knew as well as anyone else the dangers the future might hold, but he'd decided that there was nothing to do but go on about the business of running his business. Ramadan had arrived, and this was an important time for his shop. Anticipating 'Id al-Fitr, the feast that marks the end of the celebratory Muslim month of daytime fasting and nighttime feasting, he dug up every last coin of his hard-earned money from its own garden spot and made a special trip to Nazareth to buy dates, sugar, rice, coffee, cardamom, cigarettes, chocolate, and—perhaps his biggest gamble to date—sixteen live kids, which he planned to fatten and then sell for holiday slaughter and roasting. "My father told me, 'Taha, don't buy many new things. Don't. Leave some money with us.'. . . I told him, 'There is a holiday. It is Ramadan and we have to prepare ourselves for the *'id.*' But my father, I remember, told me, 'Don't buy things.'" His voice is so low now it is barely audible. "But I insisted. . . ."

On July 13 the radio carried an upsetting story: the poet and self-declared *fida'i* 'Abd al-Rahim Mahmud had been killed while fighting in the nearby town of al-Shajara. A protégé and friend of the poet Ibrahim Tuqan, Mahmud was hailed throughout the country as his mentor had been—though his renown was not solely literary but also relied on his reputation as rifle-bearing hero of the revolt and proud member of Qawuqji's Arab Liberation Army. Long before his final close encounter with the IDF, Mahmud's self-conscious blurring of rabble-rousing poetic themes and his own very martial biography were legend. Like Tuqan, he, too, wrote verses called "The Freedom Fighter" and "The Martyr," but unlike his sickly and citified teacher— for whom such figures were abstract types—Mahmud was a man with a much more literal imagination and what seems in retrospect a howling death wish. 'Izz al-Din al-Qassam's martyrological influence is almost as strong as Tuqan's in 'Abd al-Rahim Mahmud's work, and he appeared in his writing to be predicting, and lauding in advance, his own violent demise. ("And I said to one who fears death: / Are you afraid to face the enemy?") After he was killed, the most famous of his poems—"al-Shahid"—was read over and over on the radio, and the echo of those sonorously rhymed and metered lines must have cast a far darker pall over the village than any droning newscast could:

> I bear my soul in the palm of my hand
> and would cast it into death's abyss—
> for life should gladden the hearts of friends
> or death bring fury to one's foes.

Late that same night—after the Ramadan evening visiting rounds, after the sweets and coffee had been proffered, after the people had gone to sleep—the first arrivals from the nearby village of Shafa 'Amr began to stumble into Saffuriyya. By morning several thousand had poured into the village—limping, weeping, dragging, wilted, each telling a broken piece of the same terrifying story: *The noise . . . the explosions . . . the shelling . . . the shooting . . . .* Taha and his family offered some of the newcomers bread and water, and they listened to their tearful accounts of how the Israelis had arrived, blasting heavy artillery, and how they, the villagers, had panicked and fled. It was much harder now to deny the most ominous forecasts of what lay ahead. "People were afraid," says Taha, "and they believed that their turn was coming, absolutely coming."

Still, they carried on as the eternal good hosts. They helped the Shafa 'Amr refugees arrange mats and blankets in the mosques and the church. The women doubled the amount of food they were preparing for the *iftar,* the Ramadan dusk-time fast-breaking meal, and they welcomed the strangers into their homes. The ragtag Abu Mustache Army and some of the young men trained by Nimr set out to guard the entrance to the village—Taha's cousin Sa'id was among them—and Abu Mahmud al-Saffuri and his men dug in for the battle they had been expecting. They had mined the road from Shafa 'Amr and were now preparing themselves for the worst. They took their positions in the school buildings on the western side of town and hunkered down to wait. Abu Mahmud was said to have promised his friends in the village that his fighters could hold out for at least a week, and since Qawuqji's army would soon be on its way to help, there was no reason to worry. (Unbeknownst to Abu Mahmud and to

Qawuqji, another ALA officer had apparently convinced some of the Saffuriyya villagers to clear the mines on the Shafa 'Amr road by explaining that this would allow a better defense of the village; in fact, he was working for the Israelis and easing the IDF's angle of approach.) At the same time, on hearing word that Shafa 'Amr had surrendered, some of the displaced villagers had begun to make their cautious way home through the orchards and fields, and perhaps the people of Saffuriyya took heart from that fact. Whatever woes might befall one's village, it would always, it seemed, be possible to return.

On the morning of July 15, Imm Taha decided to make mlukhiyyeh for the iftar that night, and she set about the ritualistic work of picking the mallow, then plucking the leaves off the stalks. Ghazaleh, now eleven and a singing, dancing live wire, helped her with that time-consuming task. Next Imm Taha fetched water to rinse the dirt from the vivid green heap, then chopped and chopped until the leaves were nearly a pulp, gathered kindling, lit a fire, peeled garlic, and slowly coaxed the leaves into soup. As the scents from the cauldron rose and tempted, Abu Taha sat indoors in his madafeh. The midday summer sun was unbearable, and fasting made it seem even stronger. Though he also was not eating or drinking, Taha was too busy to notice, so brisk was the business in his shop. Between the extra holiday sales and the cigarettes and canned food he was selling to the Shafa 'Amr villagers who had converged on the town, he hardly had time to be hungry. And his brand-new flock of goats needed to be tended, and arrangements had to be made to send them off with a shepherd in the morning.

At dusk, the end-of-fast call rose up from the mosque, and the whole family drank some water before gathering around the huge platter of shimmery mlukhiyyeh. It was still Taha's favorite food, and its thick, grassy freshness never tasted as sublime as it did in Saffuriyya on an empty Ramadan stomach—as though he were literally ingesting the hillsides around the village. After eating, he washed his hands and face, then set out in the dark with his bleating new investment to wander those same hills. The floppy-eared flock was restless and threatening to eat Imm Taha's garden, so he decided to take the goats to the house of the man who would graze them the next day. Following the dirt path that ran beside the bayader, he walked for about five minutes, and it was then that he heard an odd, low, whirring sound, something circling in the air above. As it lifted to a whistle, then mounted to a roar, he saw a brilliant flash, felt a crash and tremor, and another—then everything was smashing glass and rising smoke, shouts in the distance, wailing nearby, people running, children crying, the sixteen kids yelping in terror as they scattered—

◆

There is—as I've said—no way to tell this part of the tale in neat forward progression. Edward Said has described the characteristic mode of the Palestinian story as "not a narrative . . . but rather broken narratives, fragmentary compositions, and self-consciously staged testimonials, in which the narrative voice keeps stumbling over itself, its obligations, and its limitations." To add further to the built-in complex of restraints that attend the telling of any such tale, this one that I am writing is not, would never pretend to be, a Palestinian story alone. For better or worse, there are others in this picture, and I am one of them.

It is late May 2005, and I am sitting in a plain Israeli living room by the sea, drinking homemade seltzer and having a Hebrew conversation that seems at once completely natural and utterly bizarre, the product of a series of historical ironies too great for me to absorb at once. I have traveled by bus and train today from Jerusalem to Nahariya, a sleepy Jewish—and/or largely Russian-speaking, to judge from the Cyrillic signs all around the train station—town near the Lebanese border, to talk to a man named Dov Yermiya. At age "ninety and a half," as he counts it, he is an incredible figure. Terrifically energetic and lucid, sharp in his opinions, dry in his quips, he is best known in today's Israel as an outspoken advocate for peace and coexistence. Several recent television news programs have featured stories about his twenty years of devoted volunteer work teaching music to Bedouin children in Galilee villages that remain unrecognized by the government (they receive no water, electricity, or other services), and it is clear that the idea of an elderly Jewish man playing the accordion and singing nursery rhymes with a roomful of cute Arab kids is easier for the general public to stomach than more direct protests against the warped status quo. But Dov has hardly held back from expressing himself in straightforward ways as well. He has been an activist for

Arab-Jewish political, social, and cultural cooperation for decades now, and unlike many who bat around such fine-sounding words as "humanity" and "justice" without stopping to consider what they mean, he has, more than once, put his money where his morals are and suffered the consequences.

After service of more than fifty years in the Haganah and IDF—complete with a wartime injury so serious that death notices were mistakenly printed in the newspaper—he performed perhaps the bravest act of his military career and published an account of what he had seen in the 1982 Lebanon War. He was, at the time, a sixty-eight-year-old senior officer in charge of a unit that administered aid, distributing water, medicine, and powdered milk to the civilian population of the Palestinian refugee camps that bore the most brutal brunt of the IDF's initial onslaught. As soon as excerpts from the book appeared in the Hebrew press, he was expelled from the army without explanation. That he did not submit the diary to the military censor was, it seems, the technical reason for his dismissal, though more likely his clear-eyed honesty and refusal to hide behind the usual slogans was what really got him in trouble: "The Jewish, Israeli soldier, whose hypocritical commanders and politicians call him the most humane soldier in the world," he wrote, "the IDF, which claims to preserve the 'purity of arms' (a sick and deceitful term), is changing its image. For this is what I ran into every step of the way: despicable actions of humiliation, of striking at women and children who wander, confused and miserable, along the sidelines of the war and its aftermath, not knowing their own souls in their fright, hunger, and thirst."

By now, these words may not sound terribly shocking to Western ears—the Israeli army has, alas, been charged with far worse crimes—but to understand the stir they caused when they were first published and to grasp why it upsets people when Dov in particular continues to talk unflinchingly about what he calls "the apartheid state" and "fascism" that, as he sees it, now exist in Israel, it is also necessary to realize who Dov Yermiya is and where he comes from. A member of the state's most mythic generation, he is one of Israel's founding fathers, and in so many senses he stood—and continues to stand—for all that is good and admirable about this troubled country. When a patriot like Dov declares that he has no patience with the Israeli flag because "under that flag horrible things have been done," he speaks without malice and only with a sadness that sounds like it physically hurts him.

He was born in 1914 in one of the first Jewish settlements in the Galilee to an idealistic socialist-revolutionary Russian father and a mother who came to the country as a pioneer with the legendary Joseph Trumpledor, whose apocryphal last words—"It is good to die for our country"—are engraved more sharply in the secular Israeli consciousness than the prayers of the Jewish liturgy. Dov's family soon moved, and he grew up on Nahalal, where he went to school with Moshe Dayan, two years his junior. According to Dayan's biographer, Moshe deeply resented Dov, whom he saw as the teacher's pet and main rival for attention, especially among the girls. "A gentle, good-looking, gifted, and musical boy who played the violin at school parties," Dov was carried to school on his father's shoulders, "so that his clothes would not become soiled. Dov wore outfits made of soft corduroy, and everyone admired his cleanliness, good looks, curls, and rosy cheeks. But as soon as his father had deposited him on the relative safety of the mat and gone on his way, Moshe—in clothes made from his father's discarded outfits—would jump on him and beat him." (In a very painful—and public—act of retribution for perceived childhood wrongs, the notoriously womanizing Dayan would, in the late 1950s, have an affair with Dov's much younger second wife, who then wrote a book called *Passionate Paths* about her romance with the mastermind of the Sinai Campaign. David Ben-Gurion himself was forced to deal with the aftermath of that scandal.)

Meeting and being welcomed with unstinting warmth and generosity by Dov—a slight man with perfect posture, a trim gray mustache, and almost feminine, dark-framed glasses—and hearing him talk in his elegant but unadorned old-world Hebrew about his profound disappointment with what Israel and Zionism have become ("I've been pessimistic for fifty years now"), it is difficult not to wonder what would have happened if he, and not the bully of his pastoral youth, had wound up with so much power. And yet, the two former classmates' very different professional trajectories were not a mere matter of chance: Dov was offered—and rejected—a high-profile career early on when, right after the war in 1948, he turned down the job of military governor of Nazareth as a matter of principle. He saw immediately that this sort of regime would become, in his words, "a political tool in the hands of the government." And the rest is—literally—history.

As he was growing up, Dov worked in the fields and studied what he describes as "classical and Jewish literature, painting, and humanistic thought and ethics." But music was his true love, and besides playing the violin he sang in a choir. He also learned to speak fluent Arabic. He had friends in the local villages and Bedouin encampments; often the fallahin would come to sell vegetables on the moshav, and the settlers would take their wheat to be ground in one of the nearby Arab villages. He calls his relations with the Palestinian peasants at that time "alternately friendly and hostile, depending on the situation in the fields." After he joined the Haganah as a fifteen-year-old in 1929, Dov was, together with Dayan, part of a band of Jewish horsemen who guarded the fields around Nahalal. The teenagers who were part of this privileged group were taught by a veteran of the Cossack regiment in the czarist army to ride bareback and perform fancy equestrian tricks.

When Dov was twenty, he joined Hashomer Hatza'ir, the pioneering socialist youth movement that sought both to promote Jewish culture and settlement in Palestine and to encourage among its members more general humanistic values. (The movement was inspired by the mystical-romantic Zionism of the Russian-born Jewish Tolstoyan A. D. Gordon, among others, who wrote in 1920 that "we must create a new people, a human people whose attitude toward other peoples is informed with the sense of human brotherhood and whose attitude toward nature and all within it is inspired by noble urges of life-loving creativity.") Soon he left Nahalal for ideological reasons. He was more of a socialist than the other people on the moshav, where he says it was forbidden to celebrate the first of May. He helped to found a more leftist kibbutz, Eilon, and became what was known as the kibbutz mukhtar, performing many of the same tasks as a mukhtar in a Palestinian village—entertaining guests (Jewish, Arab, English), meeting with the authorities, acting as all-purpose communal mediator, serving coffee in a special room, designated by the kibbutz. Eventually, Dov set out for Tel Aviv, where he planned to study music—piano, composition, and conducting—but, as he explains, "at exactly that time, the disturbances of '36–'39 broke out. That was one thing that caused me to give up on that dream." Putting aside his musical plans, and with them the hopes for a very different life, Dov soon became a full-time soldier. He volunteered for the Jewish Brigade of the British army during World War II, serving in North Africa and Syria and eventually participating in the Allied invasion of Italy. After the war, he helped the Haganah to organize the illegal immigration of Holocaust survivors to Israel. In 1947, with partition looming, he and his comrades in Hashomer Hatza'ir advocated the establishment of a binational state.

"As soon as a binational state wasn't established," he explains, in the most clipped and matter-of-fact fashion, "the UN decided on the state of Israel, and the Arabs descended on us, and we fought." During February 1948, he had enrolled in a one-month officer's training course at a British army base in Netanya, still filled with British soldiers. Because of his experience in the Jewish Brigade—and, though he doesn't say it, because of his obvious ability to lead, whether an orchestra or a battalion—he jumped ranks quickly, and by April, when he was posted near Jerusalem, he was in charge of guiding army transports in that region. He later returned to the Western Galilee, where he was shot in battle and almost died (a British officer saved his life by bringing him penicillin), then returned to fight and remained there for the rest of the war.

And so it was that on the night of July 15, 1948, as Taha was making his way across the threshing floors in the dark with his raggedy herd of kids, Dov Yarmonovitch, a company commander in the Twenty-first Battalion of the IDF's Carmeli Brigade, was preparing to ride southeast from Shafa 'Amr with his soldiers in a convoy of three buses, several jeeps, and a mortar-bearing armored car. They had been sent to travel the nine miles "through enemy territory" to Saffuriyya with their headlights off—to meet up with another battalion and attack and conquer the village. The real goal of this operation, known to the Israelis as Dekel, or Palm Tree, was to take Nazareth, but Saffuriyya and the nearby village of 'Illut stood in the way, and so Dov—who had not yet changed his name to the more Israeli, less diasporic-sounding Yermiya—was charged with leading this stage of the assault.

Growing up in Nahalal as he had, Dov held the same dim view of Saffuriyya and its people that many of the nearby Jewish settlers did. "I personally had a score to settle with them," he admits. He had been at Nahalal when the bombing took place in 1932. "And in the morning when I heard that during the night someone had thrown a bomb into a hut and Ya'akobi and his son were killed . . . I went to see and I saw what I saw, and my first reaction was to compose an elegy for violin—no more and no less! 'In Memory of the Father and His Son,' it was called." As he approached Saffuriyya in the July dark, Dov may or may not have been thinking of Ya'akobi. When he details the blow-by-blow of what happened that 1948 night—and writes about it in an unfinished six-hundred-page memoir that he doesn't plan to publish but from which he hands me a thick Xeroxed chunk almost as soon as I walk through the door—he leaves out such personal feelings and confines himself to logistical accounts and the drier description of the various-sized mortars, cannons, and half-tracks that he had at his disposal during the campaign. He was a soldier doing his job, and that job was, to his mind, a matter of life and death. "I said then clearly . . . either we fight and win, or they'll throw us in the sea and slaughter us. There was always here . . . somewhere . . . the Holocaust. We saw the Holocaust with our own eyes. The first ones who saw the Holocaust were the soldiers who met the . . . ." He trails off without describing what he saw. "We fought with a clear understanding that we had no choice but to win, at least in this war."

Dov says he "did what he had to do" during the war and stood on principle throughout—at one point, against serious resistance and even physical threats from the other soldiers in his battalion, bringing charges against a company commander who had murdered three dozen Lebanese prisoners. But he did not, by his own admission, grasp the implications of what these actions would mean for the expelled Palestinians until much later, well after the war. "We, the kibbutzim . . . in this area, they [the government] gave us land from the [northern border] village of [al-]Bassa. A lot of good land—and they divided it between us. And I myself went, I was a fallah"—he uses the Arabic word without irony—"I went on a tractor to dig up the olive trees so that there would be land there for us to plant. And I didn't think of it then. It took me a few years until I understood . . . especially when I met the refugees from Bassa . . . and I understood what we'd done." Still, when he talks about the war he insists: "It was a historical necessity, which it was impossible to prevent, especially because it involved the Holocaust. The question about the Holo-

caust . . . is if we would come out of that more human or less human.
And we didn't come out of it more human. That's the problem."

Putting aside such philosophically charged questions for now,
I ask Dov to tell me about what happened, from his point of view,
on the night of the attack on Saffuriyya. He explains: "We knew
that there was a gang there that was still there from the time of the
disturbances . . . and there was a commander, [Abu] Mahmud al-
Saffuri, and they had a lot of weapons, more modern weapons and
they were really a military unit. So we expected a battle." The civilians, it is clear, were not part of Dov's and his immediate commanders' strategic thinking, though he was grateful that the villagers fled
as they did "when we came." "It was," he says, "good for the soul that
the village was empty and there was no killing." (The village was not,
in fact, entirely empty, as Dov would discover the next day.)

According to Dov, there was a great deal of confusion at the entrance to the village, near the Qastal spring. He and his company of
some fifty men arrived well after midnight, and the other battalion—
led by Ben Dunkelman, a Canadian volunteer—was late and lost, and
when Dunkelman and his soldiers finally arrived, he began firing his
Bren gun on Dov, mistaking him for "the enemy." (In his own memoir, Dunkelman tells a similar story, though he depicts himself as the
one making decisions and doesn't mention getting lost or unleashing
his friendly fire on Dov, whom he describes as a "wiry kibbutznik . . .
a born soldier and a man of enormous courage.") An Arab sniper
killed one of Dov's men, and Dov realized he would have to act soon
if he wanted to invade before daylight. He recounts the conversation
that ensued with Dunkelman, who did not speak Hebrew. "'He
[Dunkelman] said to me, 'But do you think you can do it?' Like that,
in English. And I, you know, without even thinking. . . .'" Dov now
breaks into slightly British English: "What do you mean? Can I do it?
I *must* do it." And back to Hebrew: "After me!'" And so he charged up
the hill. . . .

By now my own narrative compass has gone completely haywire:
my perspective is scrambled. This is not a matter of taking sides, of
Arab or Jew, right or wrong, but simply of trying to piece together the
story in a plausible fashion. . . . I have heard the Palestinian version
of this assault dozens of times and it is always the same—and very
much at odds with Dov's account. Just after dark, the villagers say,

several airplanes came and dropped a series of primitive bombs on Saffuriyya; this caused a tremendous amount of noise—the crashing that Taha heard as he walked with his goats—and some serious damage. People and animals were killed (the names of the dead are often offered up), and the villagers—expecting a ground attack—were taken by surprise, so they fled to safety, first to the orchards nearby, and then, when the Israelis had entered and occupied the town, northward—many of them heading for Lebanon.

"What planes?" asks Dov, genuinely baffled, when I explain to him what I've heard.

I repeat for him the story of the planes, the bombs, the dead civilians, sheep, and donkeys, and he shakes his head emphatically, though he is, it is plain, troubled by what I am saying, and begins to ruminate aloud: "No. It couldn't be. It's not possible that I could be that involved in things and not know. I would have known about it." As adamant as he sounds, however, Dov is thinking hard, trying to make some sense of all I've said. "There was one Iraqi plane that appeared in the morning. Maybe they thought . . . I'll tell you. . . . When we'd already conquered the village, in the morning, an Iraqi plane, a heavy one, was circling around, and it dropped bombs—either on us or on Nazareth. Maybe they were confused. . . ."

But the people fled in the night, I say gently. Besides, it doesn't make sense that *everyone* in the village could be mistaken. Not only had I heard about the planes from Taha, Amin, Imm Nizar, and every other Saffuriyya native I had met in Nazareth, I'd read and heard accounts by refugees elsewhere that matched their version exactly. In 1978, the Palestinian historian Nafez Nazzal published an English-language book called *The Palestinian Exodus from Galilee, 1948,* and in it he interviewed Saffuriyya villagers then living in Lebanon who related the very same tale. A former farmer told Nazzal: "Three Jewish planes flew over the village and dropped barrels filled with explosives, metal fragments, nails and glass. They were very loud and disrupting. . . . They shook the whole village, broke windows, doors, killed or wounded some of the villagers and many of the village livestock. We expected a war but not an air and tank war." Searching for other testimony, I'd stumbled onto a Web site called www.palestine remembered.com that featured similar written (Arabic) chronicles of the events of July 15, 1948, and, under the rubric of something called al-Nakba Oral History Project (*al-nakba*—the catastrophe—is the standard Palestinian term for the events of '48), also offered for sale lengthy camcorder interviews with refugees from different villages and towns, now living in Jordan. After sending in my twenty-dollar check, I received a package postmarked Illinois and decorated with magic-marker smiley faces, slipped the enclosed disk into my computer, and—pausing to consider the weird, out-of-body bridge-crossings made possible by modern technology—found myself face to face with one 'Ali Muhammad al-Hassan (Abu Amin) Nijim, an eighty-eight-year-old Saffuriyya *fallah* in a white kaffiyeh and thick plastic glasses. From his living room couch in a refugee camp in Irbid, some fifty miles from Amman, Abu Amin describes Saffuriyya and its people and crops and customs at length, then goes on to narrate in singsongy dialect ("Shayf kif?" You see? he adds, as punctuation, to almost every sentence) the exact same story of the planes and the bombs. . . . And in Elias Khoury's *Gate of the Sun,* his polyphonous novel about the nakba and its legacy in the wretched camps of Lebanon and the Arab villages that now lie within Israel's borders—based on years of the Lebanese author's research and interviews with refugees—the same story is *again* recounted by a Saffuriyyan character whose wife and three children were killed when their house was demolished by a bomb from one of those infamous planes. Could it possibly be that all of these scattered people had managed to misremember, concoct, or conspire to relate the same details?

"Bubbe meises!" Dov proclaims now, using the Yiddish for "old wives' tales" and obviously unconvinced by my stack of multimedia, second-, and thirdhand evidence. "Everything they write. . . . There is," he offers, "something called the Oriental imagination."

"There's also the Jewish imagination," I suggest, laughing a bit uneasily.

"Of course!" agrees Dov—but now I'm the one who's baffled. What would a man like Dov stand to gain by suppressing what really happened that night? If anything, he has made a career of demanding accuracy and fairness in all things. And he is hardly, at this late date, an enemy or denier of the history of the Palestinian people: he is even friendly with Amin and has met Taha and eaten a dinner and appeared in a documentary film with him; they have various friends, both Arab and Jewish, in common. Perhaps—I do not like to admit this, but my day with Dov makes me suspect myself—my empathy for the people of Saffuriyya and their undeniably bitter fate has clouded my ability to distinguish between fact and fantasy? Although I trust Taha's honesty absolutely, I cannot dismiss the possibility that his memories have evolved over time in complex, not always conscious or reliable, ways. Every Palestinian account of Saffuriyya's fall that I've heard or read has been recalled aloud across the decades—decades of suffering and hardship whose painful unfurling would understandably have colored the recollection of what took place back then. It's true that Dov himself is also an old man whose memories may be faulty as well, but a measure of doubt has already crept into and begun to spread through my thinking. . . .

If one peers closely at footnotes, for instance, one realizes that numerous history books—including Walid Khalidi's *All That Remains* and Benny Morris's *Birth of the Palestinian Refugee Problem*—rely on the account provided by the villagers in Nazzal's book for their information about the events of that night. The realization that three out of five of Nazzal's interviewees belong to the same family, Mau'ad, might cause one to take their version with a grain of salt. Skewed or collectively exaggerated details could, after all, begin to metamorphose into "certainty" were they repeated often enough. And Web sites like the one that brought me the amiable Abu Amin and his Jordanian living room couch are hardly dispassionate bastions of critical historiographic thought. Advertised as "The Home of All Ethnically Cleansed Palestinians," the site makes for often depressing reading, featuring as it does a Saffuriyya guest book that spews forth raw, ungrammatical diatribes, Islamist doggerel, and the inadvertent comedy and poetry of semiliteracy. Interestingly, the vast majority of the messages that appear in this guest book were written in places like Melbourne, Dallas, and Riyadh by descendants of villagers who have themselves never set foot in the village. "The day I logged on to this web site is when patriotism in me again reached a higher level. First I want to thank ALLAH for making this possible. Second, I want to thank the inventor of this amazing web site" and "SAFFORYI AS I LIKE TO SAY IT LIKE TO WRITE IT. IT IS THE ENDLESS DREAM THAT WE HAVE ALL TO FIGHT FOR IN ORDER TO BE ABLE TO MAKE IT A TRUTH IN SPITE OF WHATEVER HAPPENS AND WHOSOEVER IS. OUR VILLAGE WHICH WE HAVE NOT SEEN WAS BORN TOGETHER WITH US FROM THE FIRST DAY WE CAME

TO THIS WORLD. WE ALL DID FORGET MANY THINGS, BUT THE UNFORGET-
TABLE THING WAS OUR MOTHER PALESTINE AND HER DEAR DAUGHTER
SAFFOORYI. SOONER OR LATER WE WILL RETURN AND REBUILD IT WITH
LIFE AGAIN." And the pithy: "siphoriss; my sweety town is a part of my
holly home land PALESTINE. We shall return, END OF ARGUMENTS."

After some five hours spent in animated talk with Dov, who has
already come to seem like my long-lost great-uncle, he walks me
briskly to the train station, and by early evening, I am sitting with
Taha (more grandfather than uncle) at the plastic table under the nut
tree in his Bir el-Amir back courtyard—which often seems to me the
calmest swatch of concrete and shade in the whole Middle East—and
telling him about my conversation with Dov. He laughs wearily, insisting with the same unflinching certainty that I'd just heard in Nahariya, "There was an airplane. I remember like I remember yesterday. Of course." He sounds exhausted by the subject. "Otherwise why
would the people leave?" But could it possibly have been an Iraqi
plane? Could it have been the next day? I ask him gingerly, feeling a
bit guilty that I'm calling into question any of the particulars of the
story he has told me so many times and with such emotion. Israelis
are chronic doubters—especially in relation to all matters Palestinian—and the last thing I want is to assume that standard cynical pose
or revert to those predictable, defensive gestures. "No. . . . It was
night, and there was an airplane, a very simple one. Like an agricultural airplane—you can ask anybody. And I remember when the
rocket came—zzzzzzhhhhooooomm!!!—I remember it exactly."

My vertigo is now extreme. Whose memory should be believed?
And on what grounds? The term *narrative* is a catch-all called upon
too often to explain the warring versions of Arab and Jewish history
that steer hearts and minds in Israel/Palestine. The struggle for this
small piece of land, we are told and told again, is in fact a struggle between conflicting narratives. Did 1948 mark the War of Independence
or the nakba? It depends on the narrative to which one subscribes.
And within each of these broad designations there are, of course,
hundreds if not thousands of ideological and hermeneutical grada-
tions of belief. While the question of what precisely took place in this
country in 1948 is nothing new to me in the abstract, I've never been
faced with such baldly irreconcilable, *Rashomon*-like versions of the
same discrete event, and from two such credible and sympathetic wit-

nesses as Taha and Dov. Meanwhile, the contradictory stories they tell are not a simple case of diaphanously relativistic impressions or of variable perceptions molded by clashing worldviews: either there was a plane or there wasn't a plane in the skies of Saffuriyya that night. Either some of Taha's former neighbors were killed by falling bombs or they weren't. Both accounts cannot possibly be correct.

When I return home to Jerusalem, I begin to comb through other Israeli military accounts of what transpired—and, to my increasing confusion, find Dov's version repeated. And repeated. There are no planes in the Jewish accounts.

Battalion commander Ben Dunkelman was heir to the Tip Top Tailor clothing-store fortune of Toronto and, in his own words, a formerly "flabby, pampered boy" who found excitement and romance, muscles and meaning in Palestine, where he first came in the early 1930s to pick oranges. ("All my life I had been accustomed to living well, with plenty of comfort and all the luxuries I could ask for. . . . But then I had never experienced the kind of deep satisfaction which comes from tilling virgin soil.") He went back to Canada but returned to Palestine later—having since been decorated as an armored corps commander during World War II—now a high-ranking officer in Machal, or the IDF's Mitnadvei Chutz L'Aretz, Volunteers from Abroad, of which at least 2,400 served during the 1948 war, many in positions of authority. In his often lively memoir, Dunkelman—or his gifted ghostwriter, Peretz Kidron—describes in swashbuckling and slightly self-aggrandizing terms the plan to sneak up on Nazareth: in the dead of night two teams would take on separate targets, one heading for 'Illut and the other for Saffuriyya. As soon as 'Illut was captured, the attack on Saffuriyya would begin. This late-night, two-tiered assault was, he says, "extremely unorthodox . . . a calculated risk, which would prove costly if something went wrong, but would pay big dividends if it came off." The advance troops bound for Saffuriyya left Shafa 'Amr at 11 pm, according to his watch, and a few hours later Dunkelman and his own men set out:

> Driving conditions were impossible, and normally the . . . reluctance [of the drivers of the armored cars] to move on into the pitch darkness would have been sensible and prudent. But this was not a time for prudence, and I ordered them forward,

while I followed closely behind in a jeep. It was a ride to remember, probing slowly in the pitch darkness, between black
hillsides, expecting at any moment to run into a ravine or a
shoulder of rock, or an enemy ambush.

But, he writes, "We were lucky. . . . [T]he enemy was obviously taken
by surprise," and, after a brief survey of the situation and a consulta-
tion with Dov, who "pressed for permission to go ahead," Dunkelman
gave the command. "Almost as soon as I told him to go ahead, his two
three-inch mortars opened up, and the infantrymen stormed forward,
up the hill. In an amazingly short time, Dov reported back: 'Saffuriya
is in our hands!' The company had one man killed, the villagers had
fled. The capture of Saffuriya was the turning point. Our force was
now secure, and we had overcome the biggest obstacle on the way to
Nazareth."

Moshe Carmel, the same brigade commander whose soldiers had
struggled with Shakib Wahab's Druze battalion at Hawsha and
Kasayir/Ramat Yochanan, also writes about that night and outlines
the same creeping approach through the dark and the surprising
angle of ground approach, chalking up Saffuriyya's fall and the villagers' flight as Dunkelman does to the superior cleverness of the
IDF: "The attack on Saffuriyya came at the Arab fighters from an unexpected direction, and startled them completely, confusing their
strategy for defense, so that they abandoned it, without any serious
attempt to defend and to fight." Lieutenant Colonel Natanel Lorch,
one-time chief historian of the IDF, writes of the assault in his chronicle of the war, *The Edge of the Sword:* "Mass and surprise attack
combined to break the villagers and the Liberation Army garrison [sic:
these were local fighters] after feeble and sporadic resistance. At
dawn they deserted the village." According to *The History of the War
of Independence,* compiled and published by the IDF, "With rapid
movement [the force] arrived at Saffuriyya—that is, Tzippori. . . .
They immediately organized to attack, and did so that same night.
The people of Saffuriyya were always known throughout the Galilee
as brave fighters, but because of the magnitude of the surprise, the
village fell almost without a fight." And so on and on. The soldiers'
memoirs and official Israeli histories are multiple and slightly monot-
onous. And reading them in rapid succession one begins to sense that

the villagers of Saffuriyya—and the Palestinian peasants in general—
were not just unlucky to be the victims of the victims in this grand
historical drama; they were also cursed to have found themselves, a
basically oral people, wrestling rhetorically with perhaps the most
print-obsessed people on the planet.

Although many of the Jewish accounts of this time were recorded
years after the events, they have achieved the status of "fact" in the
minds of many simply because they were written down. It seems reasonable to think that one of the reasons the official Israeli version of
the 1948 war has managed to dominate in the West for so many
years—this is the David-and-Goliath myth of the scrappy little army
of Holocaust survivors and strapping yet ethical Paul Newman–esque
Sabras that had to defend itself against all odds and the huge might
of the united, bloodthirsty Arab world—is in large part a function of
such a textual proliferation. (The reductio ad absurdum of all this
frantic memoir-and-history-book-writing by various IDF officers and
Zionist functionaries is perhaps *The Book of the History of the Haganah*: a three-volume Hebrew opus that describes only the events
leading up to May 31, when the Haganah formally metamorphosed
into the IDF—and weighs in at sixteen hundred pages.)

The Palestinians may have told their stories often to one another
and to other Arabs, and they may have longed to convey those stories
to the wider world, but until recently, when various memoirs and oral
histories of 1948 began to emerge, there were just a handful of accounts of the nakba from the Palestinian perspective—the most important of which remain untranslated into English and out of print in
Arabic. The presence on the scene of a fiercely articulate, American-
sounding advocate like the late Edward Said may have advanced
awareness in the wider world of the Palestinians as a people with a
past and present of their own, but as Said himself would surely have
agreed, the West remains, in large part, oblivious to the particulars of
the Palestinian saga. For this skewed state of affairs, one might blame
an ignorance and suspicion of all things Arabic, the Jewish Lobby, or
any number of shady propagandizing forces, though as Said himself
once noted, the Palestinians haven't helped matters on this front.
"I recall during the siege of Beirut," he wrote in 1984, "obsessively
telling friends and family there, over the phone, that they ought to
record, write down their experiences; it seemed crucial as a start-

ing point to furnish the world some narrative evidence, over and above atomized and reified TV clips, of what it was like to be at the receiving end of Israeli 'antiterrorism.' . . . Naturally, they were all far too busy surviving to take seriously the unclear theoretical imperatives being urged on them intermittently by a distant son, brother, or friend."

Said sympathized with his loved ones' wartime distraction, but he also realized the scale of the mistrust the Palestinians were up against—both in short-term political and in long-range historical terms. I am not a professional historian, yet I, too, understand why most scholars prefer weathered paper proof to retrospective oral accounts. Benny Morris explains his own near-fetish for documents and wariness of interviews by describing the "enormous gaps of memory and terrible distortion and selectivity born of 'adopted' and 'rediscovered' memories, ideological certainties and commitments and political agendas." His traditional approach has been rightly criticized for underestimating the political agendas that also hold sway in real time, as documents are written. It does, though, complement the tack taken up by academics of a more fashionably postmodern stripe who choose to study oral accounts not for anything so old-fashioned as "the truth" but as a means to unpack—in the words of one young American anthropologist who writes about Palestine—the "constructed nature of . . . experiences and recollections."

My mind now whirling with a storm of contradictory certainties and hesitations—I've begun to doubt no one so much as myself—I set out in search of ink.

◆

The Tel Hashomer army base is one of the largest military compounds in modern-day Israel, and for one like me who has never set foot on such a base anywhere, being there is slightly frightening. Almost a small city unto itself, it occupies a substantial area of land in suburban Tel Aviv, and special bus lines circle its interior. But Tel Hashomer is a most peculiar city, populated, as it appears to be, almost entirely by eighteen-to-twenty-two-year-old men and women in uniform, with rifles slung over their shoulders. The only other older people and/or civilians I see as I wait for my bus are the few who work at the forlorn sandwich and falafel stands near the entrance to the base, which has, to judge from the flaking paint and dirty concrete all around, seen better days. Most of the teenagers waiting with me look exceptionally bored. Like most Israeli soldiers, they do not carry themselves in the alert, spit-and-polish way that is expected of recruits in other armies but slouch and let their hems hang out or roll up their sleeves or unbutton their shirts as they suck on popsicles, chomp gum, or chat into cell phones. There are fat girls and pimply boys, and pretty girls and square-jawed boys, and some of the young women try hard to look sexy, wearing their standard-issue khakis low on their hips and piling on the mascara while, with their paler uniforms and the pistols they tend to lodge in the back of their pants, the male air force cadets—traditionally the elite of the elite—pose and strut as if on some imaginary catwalk.

Even after a few minutes at the bus stop with this crew—whose motley young members could easily be the sons and daughters of my neighbors and friends—I am no longer afraid, though I am still uncomfortable, conscious not just of how, as a grown woman with a flowery blouse and American gait, I stick out like a throbbing thumb here, but also aware, in the most tactile terms, of just how deeply, and probably irreversibly, the military runs through this culture. This is hardly news, of course, but with its belligerent and bedraggled air, Tel Hashomer strikes me now as an awful microcosm of the battered armed camp the whole country has become in the past few years. I've lived in Jerusalem long enough so that I'm no longer fazed by the constant sight of guns—but the sheer number of M16s that surround me at the bus stop today seems by any standard grotesque, as do the passive expressions on the faces of these armed-to-the-teeth children.

The bus arrives at last, and after asking the driver to let me off near the recruitment bureau, I soon find myself alone in front of the formidable hedge of dusty oleander and the high fence that surround my true destination—the IDF Archive. Several locked gates, intercoms, metal detectors, and security searches later, I make my way into an overly air-conditioned and sterile library, where a number of gray-haired, athletic-looking men in blue jeans and Birkenstocks are working in stony silence.

One does not arrive unannounced at this archive but must call to schedule an appointment in advance and submit oneself to a tele-

phone interview of matter-of-fact but vaguely nerve-wracking sorts. I
had been coached for this gauntlet by a historian friend who re-
searches "sensitive" material, so when asked, I knew to outline my
project and particular archival quest in the vaguest terms, not men-
tioning Dov or Taha by name but using the army's jargon, referring in
Hebrew to Operation Dekel and the conquest of Nazareth. The
archivist was curt but polite, and as I explained myself further, I wondered what unspoken questions I had actually just been asked. If I'd
called and made the same request with an Arabic accent, for instance,
or in English—what would the response have been?

Defying my skepticism and even prejudice, the archivist—a roly-
poly middle-aged man with wire-framed glasses, a beard, and a scruffy
cotton shirt—turns out to be, in person, by far the most helpful,
knowledgeable, and businesslike of all the Israeli archivists I have
dealt with in my work. Ironically enough, it is the army's unflappable
efficiency that makes its archive run smoothly. (The comparison to
the chaotic state archive is both sad and telling.) A strict system of
cataloguing is in place, as are large amounts of money and man-
power—or, really, girl-power, since besides the archivist and security
guards, the whole photocopying and library staff appear to be young
women in uniform. Strict attention has been paid to which documents
the public is and is not allowed to see; the most incriminating and
incendiary records are not—it is clear from several journalistic inves-
tigations and drawn-out, highly publicized court cases—available.
But the formidable repository of declassified documents from Israel's
many wars and from the years of the military government has been
scanned and placed on the library's computers, and within a short
while I am sitting in front of a screen, scrolling through pages whose
coordinates are provided by the archivist on a neatly ordered printout.

First I make a foray into once top-secret operational plans. The
guidelines for Operation Dekel, issued a week before the attack on
Saffuriyya, do not mention airplanes or civilians and relate only to
Qawuqji's forces, describing as the ultimate goal of the Nazareth-
bound mission "to surround the enemy and in the final stage completely destroy him." A surreal list of the operation's Hebrew code
words follows: girls' names (Ditza, Gila, Rina) stood for certain roads,
while Syria, Yemen, Iraq, Egypt, India, and Lebanon indicated particular villages and towns slated for conquest during Dekel. (Saffu-

riyya = Yemen.) All of this is interesting, though not precisely what I am looking for, and just as I begin to wonder if this wild-goose chase will yield anything besides a few stray feathers, my search comes to an end.

At the sight of the first flight report, I gasp audibly and puncture the hush of the chilly room. Here is all the ink I could possibly ask for: the name of the pilot (Moshe), the type of plane (Auster), the hour of airfield take-off (21:25) and the precise time that four bombs were dropped on Saffuriyya (22:00). The size of the bombs is also scrawled there (three A20s and one A8), as are the terse declarations "fires sighted" and "the strikes were on target." The second flight report accounts for the five incendiary devices and three twenty-kilogram bombs ejected over the village ten minutes later from another Auster, flown by a pilot named Dubi or David: the handwritten name is not clear. Dated the next morning at 8 am, a further communication—whose order to "destroy after reading" was obviously ignored by its recipient or a filing clerk—states in flat but final terms: "Saffuriyya . . . [was] bombed by our planes a number of times in the course of the night."

So it was. And so the villagers of Saffuriyya did not flee because the army outwitted their defenders on the ground or because they were cowardly or weak or told by their leaders to do so. They fled because a pair of Israel Air Force planes pummeled them with bombs from on high, sending up flames and sending down mayhem. (Saffuriyya was not alone in this respect. The army files contain flight reports that chart how the same was done to many villages in the vicinity that same week, and one chronicle of the Israel Air Force's actions during the 1948 war calculates that "in early July [the Galilee Squadron] had registered 91 bombing sorties and dropped a total in excess of one ton of bombs. All of this had been achieved with four Austers"—which are crop duster–like propeller planes, just as Taha described.) They fled because they were driven out by someone or ones who *wanted* them to flee.

Why commanders like Dov Yarmonovitch and Ben Dunkelman did not know about the plans for the air strikes—which I believe they truly did not—remains a mystery. (When I eventually show copies of the flight reports to Dov, he is amazed—but now says he believes the Saffuriyyans' story.) Perhaps the person who gave the order to bomb

the village several hours before the ground forces were scheduled to
arrive understood that such a violent assault on unarmed civilians did
not quite meet the standards of "the purity of arms" and preferred to
let the officers think they had taken the village in a more "honorable"
or "fair" way. Maybe the failure to alert them was simply a matter of
poor coordination. I do not know. And neither, suddenly, do I care to
spend much more time in the company of this relentlessly military
mind-set. It is Taha and his terrified goats who concern me now. It is
Imm Taha abandoning the unwashed iftar platter with a shriek, and
the lame Abu Taha, desperate somehow to grasp his cane and run for
cover as the first bomb hits; it is the frightened fifteen- and thirteen-
year-old Feisel and Amin, and it is Ghazaleh—who is sobbing because
of the noise and her mother's stunned expression. It is Sheikh Saleh
Salim and his three wives, grabbing their children and scrambling to
flee, and it is il-Hajj Taher, so panicked that he leaves behind his precious shelf of books. It is Qasim and it is Amira. It is Saffuriyya. It is
the people escaping into the darkness as the sky above them falls.

LEBANON

◆

Before me my longing,
And behind me fate.

'Umar ibn al-Farid
(1181–1245)

GOING

◆

THEY WALKED FOR TWO DAYS AND MUCH OF TWO NIGHTS, and under the fig trees of Bint Jbeyl, the people at last came to rest. The harsh July sun had followed them across the border, and thousands of children and women and babies and men sat in exhausted groups, the "lucky" ones finding space beneath the only semblance of a roof in sight—the wide pointed leaves of the trees. Infants bawled, old women whimpered, mules brayed, truck brakes screeched, and those who found refuge in these foreign orchards and fields were surrounded on all sides by a constant, anguished din.

Noise or no, it was perhaps the first time in the course of those long hallucinatory hours since they'd left the village that Taha and his family and the people huddled with them had a chance to pause and try to reconstruct what had just happened.

This is what Taha remembered: when the bombs crashed down and his kids fled, he had run alone back to the house—but found that his mother, father, brothers, and sister had already gone, taking nothing. Someone, a neighbor, told him: Your father is looking for you. Your family is waiting at Benat Ya'qub—an ancient tomb at the edge of Saffuriyya—so Taha sprinted in that direction (the family had in fact arranged a full month in advance to meet there "in case of trouble"), and as soon as he was reunited with them, they made their way, as almost all the villagers had, first into the orchards and then north across several miles toward what seemed the safer remove of the Battuf Valley, beyond the village lands on the way to Kafr Manda, where they hoped to sit out the night and then return to their homes.

Thinking ahead, Muhammad Sa'id had ordered one of his sons back to his stables to get a horse—a strong white one—for Abu Taha, and so he was able to traverse the hilly territory with the rest. Muhammad Sa'id also commanded his son to bring a cow, which then waddled along beside them.

After walking a short distance, Taha and his mother, seeing that many of their neighbors and friends were carrying satchels on their heads and under their arms, decided to risk sneaking back to their house to retrieve the sacks she had packed full of clothes and Abu Taha's coffee-making equipment, as well as her sister's thirty-five pounds, which they hadn't yet managed to bury. They moved quickly and got out before the Israeli ground forces arrived. Later, though, just before morning, they heard the rounds of artillery fire that echoed from the village; they heard shooting from the Qal'a. And as the next day dawned they saw, according to Taha, clouds of dust rising in the distance. The Israelis had destroyed the girls' and boys' schools. They were also razing houses.

By now Abu Mahmud al-Saffuri and the fighters who had survived the Israeli onslaught had fled and joined the other villagers, scrambling northward, or east. At first, it seemed, they simply *moved,* as fast as they could and without a clear sense of where they were going but feeling, as Amin later described it, the "war at our backs." Hearing the explosions and seeing the smoke from the village, they understood the impossibility—indeed, the mortal danger—of immediate return, and though it seems unlikely that anyone had yet formulated a distinct plan, they gradually peeled off in different directions, drawn by the various magnets of family and friends or by proximity or chance. Some were bound for Lebanon, others for Syria, and still others for the towns and villages nearer by—Nazareth, Reina, Kafr Manda, 'Arraba. For reasons that Taha cannot now reconstruct, his childhood companion Assad headed with his family toward Jordan, while his best friend, Qasim, and his clan decamped for Syria. Taha would never see either again. Nor would he see his nineteen-year-old cousin Sa'id, who had stayed behind to defend Saffuriyya and been discovered asleep by some Israeli soldiers. Finding him armed, they put him in a jeep, took him to a field, and shot him dead.

Assuming that the Israelis would soon advance in their direction, Taha and his extended family were themselves moving toward

Lebanon—where his uncles had friends and acquaintances who
they thought might be able to help them. They traveled as a group of
some thirty people, which included Muhammad Saʻid and Ahmed
and their wives and children, Amira among them. There are, of course,
no photographs of their specific departure, but the painful scene is
not hard to picture, so archetypical does this long cavalcade of tired,
hungry, frightened exiles seem. After the wakeful night spent in the
Battuf, they must have looked like sleepwalkers. Feisel and Amin
went barefoot the whole way, and as Taha tells it, his family was quiet.
The sobbing started only the next day. In a poem written forty years
later, he describes a night when "we had / neither night nor light,"
when "no moon rose":

> We did not weep
> when we were leaving—
> for we had neither
> time nor tears,
> and there was no farewell.
> We did not know
> at the moment of parting
> that it was a parting,
> so where would our weeping
> have come from?

They may not have known that it was a parting—but Taha, Feisel,
Amin, Ghazaleh, and their various young cousins understood that
something grave was happening and realized they should speak in no
more than a hush. Sterner than ever, Abu Taha sat perched with their
satchels behind him on the white horse; his brothers and their wives
walked, clutching bundles and baskets. Imm Taha may have been the
first in their group to cry, bursting into tears when she realized that
her mother had remained in the village, together with one of Imm
Taha's sisters. There was, though, no possibility of turning back. No
choice but to keep going. And going, stopping once or twice to rest
fitfully in a field or a grove, then going, even after they realized that
all but one of the sacks with their belongings had somehow fallen off
the horse and disappeared into the night. Now even Abu Taha's precious coffeepots were lost, and they had not a single object from Saf-

furiyya left to cling to. (The remaining bag contained underwear.) But they kept going and passed through Kafr Manda and Sakhnin and close to Dayr Hanna.

Near the village of Rama, says Taha, a Syrian officer stopped them at a roadblock and demanded to know their destination. When they told him "Lebanon," he ordered them back to their village. Taha laughs. "We went about one kilometer and then went around him. We took another route." And the laughter stops. "We thought that we were deceiving him, but later we realized that we deceived ourselves." This story, incidentally, corresponds with the findings of contemporary scholars concerning the popular misconception that the Palestinians were ordered by their leaders to leave. No documentary proof has ever been found to support these claims, which appear to have been the extremely successful creation of several pamphleteers in the Israeli foreign ministry, circa 1949. Taha, for his part, is adamant when asked if he ever heard such evacuation calls from on high: "Believe me, *no!*" In all of the months leading up to that night in July— as he listened hard to the radio and read the newspaper aloud in his father's madafeh—he says he never once heard such an appeal. If anything, he remembers exhortations from the leadership, urging the people to hold fast, be firm.

They had no food and nothing to drink. Eventually, they found water in village wells along the way and would cup their hands, gulp, then carry on. In this small sense, they were better off than others. Oral historian Rosemary Sayigh has interviewed refugees who remember "drinking from cattle pools" as well as "eating grass and drinking their own urine" on this terrible trek.

Taha claims now, a bit implausibly, that he was thrilled to be going to Lebanon—that at the time this journey seemed to him a marvelous adventure, an opportunity to see Beirut. He says that he and those around him were sure that the United Nations would insist that partition be implemented and that such a decision would allow them to return to Saffuriyya. The idea of staying in Lebanon did not even flit through their minds. When asked if he fathomed what was happening as they walked, Amin, however, gives a grimmer assessment of their mood at the time: "We were conscious. And we understood everything. We understood that Saffuri was gone. Palestine was gone. We'd become refugees. We lost everything we owned." Perhaps their true awareness lay somewhere in between these bright and dark versions, between complete denial and full comprehension. It seems likely that they knew something awful was unfolding—but didn't yet grasp the scale of that thing.

It may not have taken them long. Less than a month after Taha and his family, together with tens of thousands of refugees from all over the Galilee, crowded into Lebanese border towns like Bint Jbeyl, 'Adayssa, and 'Abbasiyya, the Syrian intellectual Constantine Zurayk coined the term *al-nakba* when he published in Beirut his book *Ma'na al-nakba* (The Meaning of the Catastrophe)—a scathing indictment of both Zionism and what he called the "impotence" of the Arab states and the Palestinian leadership—which opened with these words: "The defeat of the Arabs in Palestine is no simple setback or light, passing evil. It is a disaster in every sense of the word and one of the harshest of the trials and tribulations with which the Arabs have been afflicted throughout their long history."

Taha did not know of the book at the time, and the word "nakba" may not have been used immediately by the refugees themselves to describe what had happened to them, but there is no doubt that they soon sensed in their bones—and in their sinking hearts and empty stomachs—the Meaning of the Catastrophe. By July 18, the day after Taha and his family staggered across the Lebanese border, when a second truce was declared in the fighting, the number of Palestinian Arabs who had taken refuge in neighboring countries is estimated to have been about half a million—of a population of 1.3 million Palestinian Arabs. By the formal end of the fighting in January 1949, thousands of others had been driven out or had fled. (The total number of refugees is, like much else about the war, a matter of debate: figures vary widely and range from Israel's official count of 520,000 to the United Nations' 726,000 to an Arab estimate of 1 million.) Few disagree, meanwhile, that a mere 160,000 Arabs remained in the new state of Israel.

Such abstract figures are perhaps difficult to absorb, though Taha's description of the desperate throngs of thirsty, bleary-eyed people who had massed in the border town of Bint Jbeyl and who now sat, stunned, as Lebanese workers from the Red Cross slowly circulated, transcribing names and handing out canned sardines and bread—is not. Neither is Amin's account of how, in the days that followed, "the people went around, begging from the people of Bint Jbeyl a loaf of bread, something, anything to eat. The children were crying. There was no milk. The mothers—they were all crying, all weeping." And no statistic is as powerful as the image of the dark little room Taha describes as "really a wide corridor" which their immediate family rented that same week and where the six of them lived in cramped and squalid conditions for the next thirty days.

◆

In *The Meaning of the Catastrophe,* Zurayk writes, "Difficulties and hardships—even disasters—are an incentive to individuals and groups and are one of the causes of their awakening and their renaissance. But they do no not have this effect in all situations, for in some cases they will cause destruction and collapse, even extinction." Although Taha was surely not thinking in such terms, he appears to have grasped instinctively these very opportunities and dangers. He would turn seventeen late that month, but he was already an older hand at survival than many men twice his age, and he knew what he had to do. "I went to work," he says, without fanfare. He looped a belt through two holes in the sides of a wooden box and fixed this contraption, a makeshift vendor's rig, around his neck. Then he set out to try and find a grocer who would agree to advance him a sampling of simple wares—combs, lighters, matches, razor blades, tobacco, soap—which Taha could then sell to the Palestinians who, as he calmly puts it now, "had nothing."

Taha's knack for business was nothing new, and in such a sink-or-swim situation his mercantile sense must have kicked in almost automatically. But he was, too, helped on this score by the particulars of the place into which his family had stumbled. Just two miles from the border of Palestine and very close to Syria's edge, Bint Jbeyl had long been a bustling market town, a bit smaller than Saffuriyya, populated almost entirely by Shiite Muslims. It was locally famous as "Lebanon's gate to Palestine" and a town from which traders driving caravans of goods had for years set out, heading south—sometimes bound for the markets of Haifa, Tiberias, or Nazareth and other times using Palestine as a land bridge all the way to Egypt. Taha remembers men from Bint Jbeyl arriving in Saffuriyya with animals to sell at the weekly livestock market. Before World War I, at the close of which the French and English sliced into separate countries the territory that had for centuries been an undivided, Ottoman-ruled entity, no strict borders had existed in the area, and the people of the region had crossed back and forth casually, without passports and without, it seems, thinking twice. And even after the nations known as Palestine, Syria, Iraq, and Transjordan had come to be, movement—and trade and even marriage—across the borders was basically free.

Although the events of 1948 would mean the slamming shut of all those open doors—and although the relationship of most Lebanese to the masses of newly arrived and newly impoverished Palestinian peasants would soon grow much darker and more complicated—for now the bonds between a Palestinian like Taha and the Lebanese traders of a town like Bint Jbeyl were trusting enough so that a young man with Taha's particular gifts could arrive empty-handed one day and set up shop the next. He said nothing to his family but ventured out to survey the market stalls and observe which businesses were thriving; he asked the advice of some of the locals; then he fixed his sights on a prosperous wholesaler named 'Ali al-Bazzi, from "a famous Shiite family in Bint Jbeyl." When Taha approached al-Bazzi, he introduced himself: "Sir, my name is Taha Muhammad Ali. I am from Palestine, from Saffuri. Could you give me things to sell and I'll return your money to you at the end of the day? Be*lieve* me I will not run away." Al-Bazzi fixed Taha with a somber, probing look and asked him to repeat himself, then—somehow convinced by Taha's open face and respectful manner—agreed to the arrangement: Taha would wander the streets selling al-Bazzi's merchandise at whatever price he saw fit. Then he would reimburse al-Bazzi its cost at the end of the day and retain the profits. "He gave me a little of this, a little of that. In the evening I counted how much profit I had made: *six Palestinian pounds!*" Taha says this was enough to buy "two goats or one and a half sheep." (The currency circulating through Bint Jbeyl and other border towns like it was, according to Taha, a scramble of Palestinian and Lebanese coins and paper, with a Palestinian pound then worth approximately nine Lebanese pounds.) In one remarkable instance—"the climax," he calls it—Taha earned an unbelievable twenty-eight Palestinian pounds in a day. Given that Taha's family was renting their small room for ten Lebanese pounds a month, this was indeed a fortune.

Somehow, they got by. Though the family's collective mood had reached an all-time low—Abu Taha did nothing but sit glumly all day in that small room; Imm Taha cried endlessly, worried about her mother and sister, of whom she'd had no word; Feisel, Amin, and Ghazaleh were restless and had nothing to do, while Taha was single-minded and obsessive in his work—they at least had food to eat. With the money Taha earned, he bought meat and coffee, a Primus for his father, a frying pan for his mother.

And one flicker of light came when a man from Saffuriyya found them and brought them Taha's missing kids. He had collected all sixteen the night the bombs fell and had shepherded them, together with his own flocks, north and across the border. Abu Taha offered the man a goat in exchange for this unexpected and extremely generous act. The man refused. According to Taha, he said, "I did not feed them from my own pocket. They ate from the land and drank from the water of God. I don't want anything." Taha did as his father told him and sold fifteen kids; then, on the end-of-Ramadan 'id, he slaughtered the lone remaining member of the flock and invited the whole family—uncles and aunts and cousins—to come and eat the bittersweet feast.

◆

Documentation of pre-'48 Saffuriyya from the villagers' point of view may be scanty, but the written, first-person Palestinian record that remains from this early Lebanese period is even worse: it simply does not exist. Chaos created by the rapidly mutating political situation explains this lacuna in part, as even the most literate of the refugees would have been too busy trying to survive to think to take notes or save papers. If by some miracle they had somehow scribbled a few words, those scraps themselves would have been unlikely to have withstood the physical uncertainty and repeated uprootings to which their authors were subject during those difficult months.

Mention of this void may sound ironic, since, at precisely this time, the United Nations and other international observers, aid organizations, and missionary societies had begun to produce a veritable Matterhorn of memos and cablegrams, registration cards, letters, draft resolutions, resolutions, reports, decisions, press releases, ration slips, powdered-milk distribution plans, and calorie-intake charts. One recent study estimates that since 1948 the various archives that hold documents about the Palestinian refugees have accumulated some eighty million sheets of paper. This is a figure that doesn't even take into account the "many documents . . . scattered in file cabinets, boxes, and storage rooms across the Arab world" or the nine tons of documents that the International Committee of the Red Cross reportedly destroyed in Beirut in 1950. However massive the quantity of documents such groups produced, it is clear that the Palestinians had now become, in the eyes of the outside world, primarily a Problem: a humanitarian disaster or statistical nightmare ("a public health menace of the first magnitude" according to one official) to be at best *managed*.

A United Nations Disaster Relief Project was instituted in mid-August, as though the refugees' sorry plight were the chance result of an earthquake or hurricane, and the rhetoric that surrounded such efforts was by necessity dry and practical. That month the UN Department of Public Information issued, for instance, a typically brass-tacks statement about how "64 per cent of the Arabs are bedded . . . in private houses, hutments and derelict and deserted shelters; 15 per cent are under tents—either used military tents or camel's hair Bedouin tents; the remaining 21 per cent live in the open, mainly under trees." More subjective or reflective descriptions of those early months are scarce: the Quakers wrote eloquent accounts of their relief work with refugees in the Gaza Strip, and one dedicated Anglican missionary, a former Jerusalem girls' school headmistress stationed in Transjordan, somehow found time amid the pandemonium to compose letters about how, for instance, "few Arabs used banks; they mostly had their wealth in their houses and many had large stocks of food, wheat, rice, olive oil, etc. Now many have had their houses destroyed, or at any rate all food, furniture, etc. looted and if they lose their houses and land they have literally nothing." In Transjordan, "The Palestinians are crying out for work, but there is not work for these strangers and they are depressed and resentful at their condition."

Visiting the West Bank town of Ramallah in early August, UN Mediator Count Folke Bernadotte was faced with a scene so horrendous that it shook even this most sanguine and usually serene of diplomats:

I have made the acquaintance of a great many refugee camps; but never have I seen a more ghastly sight than that which met my eyes here at Ramallah. The car was literally stormed by excited masses shouting with Oriental fervour that they wanted food and wanted to return to their homes. There were plenty of frightening faces in that sea of suffering humanity. I remember not least a group of scabby and helpless old men with tangled beards who thrust their emaciated faces into the car and held out scraps of bread that would certainly have been considered quite uneatable by ordinary people, but was their only food.

Similar verbal renderings of the conditions in Lebanon are limited to a few sketches of what one Red Cross official called vaguely "the appalling state of affairs." An Anglican priest living in what was then known as "the Lebanon" noted that some of the refugees there had "fled [Palestine] in their nightclothes."

It almost goes without saying that such outsiders rarely if ever attempted to set down more precisely the refugees' own point of view, a fact for which they can hardly be blamed, given the Sisyphean nature of the job that had been hastily thrust on them. They had not only to help the forlorn people on the ground but also to try and rouse foreign support among those who had, it is clear, absolutely no idea who the Palestinians were or what their real needs might be. "While I was in Beirut I managed to get possession of a number of odds and ends of relief goods," wrote one church official:

I brought back with me as far as Amman a case . . . labeled "Vitamins." Vitamins are desperately needed at the moment in the refugee camps in Transjordan, and I was very happy to be able to take so large a stock with me. . . . When I reached Amman I opened the case and, to my amazement, discovered an indescribable assortment of odds and ends that reminded me very forcibly of a clearance sale in a Wehlan drug store. Fifteen minutes' search revealed no vitamins, but we found practically everything else, including, I think, a small table lamp.

He also cites "swiss cheese and fish powder" as being both strange and useless to the refugees, as were some of the items of donated clothing that they had received, among them "bathing suits."

The Lebanese government first oversaw aid to the newcomers in that country, handing out a monthly "ten kilos flour or bread and 3 Lebanese pounds [to] . . . each refugee," but it later wilted and gave up under the burden, which was swallowing 20 percent of the national budget, and passed the difficult work on to the League of the Societies of the Red Cross, under the supervision of the United Nations; the Red Cross in turn eventually handed the responsibility over entirely to the United Nations and its newly formed subsidiary, the United Nations Relief for Palestine Refugees, UNRPR, which evolved into the United Nations Relief and Work Agency, UNRWA. UNICEF and the WHO (World Health Organization) were also involved—which is to say that the alphabet soup of nongovernmental organizations and UN subdivisions that governs so much of Palestinian life to this day had already become central to the refugee diet—both figurative and literal.

What is striking, however, is the heaviness of the hush that descends when I ask Taha and Amin, Imm Nizar and the others—even now—to tell me what they remember of that time.

This silence is no surprise. One need not be a psychologist to recognize the reasons for the descriptive holes that riddle their accounts of the sudden rending from home, neighbors, village, country. And that is to say nothing of the obvious humiliation that attended then, as it attends now, the awareness of this unexpected loss and its anatomy, let alone the assumption of that stinging title, *refugee*. When Taha tells this part of his tale, he offers no particulars—just a barebones summary of the family's scraping by, then cuts to another, more upbeat chapter of his story—and he must be coaxed to slog back to that time and to recount what he saw: "people living in a miserable situation." It is as if some sensory part of himself shut down when he left Saffuriyya, as a sanity-preserving reaction both to the sorrow of that departure and to the suffering that surrounded him on all sides in Lebanon.

Taha has, of course, agreed to let me write this book and to let me probe his past. Indeed, he has labored with me in getting it right by sitting with me over the course of uncountable hours, weeks, months, years, and telling his story in the most exacting detail possible, clarifying and elaborating as I cross-check what he says, or try to, with written accounts and the versions of others who were present. (He has even taken to referring to these marathon interview sessions as "our work.") And since he prides himself on holding up his end of any bargain, he feels, it seems, that he has to answer me straight. But I can see that the process costs him. And his responses are less concrete, less vivid than are his answers to questions about things that he loves. To truly conjure those days would mean to experience them again. And why should he want to do that?

However understandable, though, this reticence makes it hard to know just what happened to his family during those months. And as with so many of the pieces of this puzzlelike story, the accounts range widely—even between brothers.

After a month in Bint Jbeyl, says Taha, his father and uncles decided to try the family's luck elsewhere, and the large group set out— still hoping for the best—bound for the Beqaa Valley and the town of al-Qara'un, some thirty-five miles north as the Palestine sunbird flies, where Muhammad Sa'id had a business associate who they thought might be able to help them.

After a month in Bint Jbeyl, says Amin, buses arrived and the Palestinians were ordered to get on. (Who ordered them? The government? The Red Cross? Neither Amin nor the historical sources, which do suggest that such transports may well have taken place, are clear on this point. At one stage—probably a bit later—the Lebanese army seems to have gathered refugees onto tractors and taken them to camps, at a remove from the Israeli border.) The family was deposited without ceremony in the coastal city of Sidon and from there resolved to make their way inland again, to al-Qara'un.

Whoever initiated the journey, the brothers agree that they traveled first to Sidon and then to Beirut, where they stayed for just a few hours, enough time for Taha to become entranced. It was, as he puts it, like "a big Haifa." There were "private cars and beautiful buildings and women with pants. For the first time I saw women with pants." He longed to stay, but his father and uncles were eager to move on— and so the whole family boarded yet another bus for yet another village, this one near al-Qara'un, to which they then had to walk a dirt path. (How Abu Taha managed this hike is not clear.) The man whom Muhammad Sa'id knew in al-Qara'un was a well-respected trader and would, they imagined, have the means to intervene politically on their behalf. Perhaps, they reasoned, this business associate of Muhammad Sa'id's could arrange for them to return to their village. . . .

Muhammad Sa'id was a man who was used to wielding his influence—and there is something poignant in the notion that he and his family still believed that the power and connections of one small-town Palestinian businessman might be enough to sway the international diplomatic community, to say nothing of the half-dozen regional armies now locked in a bloody, multifront struggle. (The dedicated Anglican school headmistress who wrote about her work with the refugees in Transjordan described a similarly painful loss of political perspective: "It was difficult not to raise false hopes. In one case . . . I heard one of the hangers on of our little party explaining me to one lot of refugees thus: 'She is from the Mission and she is going to write to King George and of course when he hears all about it he will send help.'") In the end, the man in al-Qara'un gave Muhammad Sa'id and the others a warm welcome and a hot meal, but he had little to offer them in the longer term. He couldn't, in fact, even help them find jobs since, as it turned out, he himself worked in Beirut, not in al-Qara'un, as Muhammad Sa'id had understood. The sight of thirty needy refugees on his doorstep was probably a bit overwhelming, but he did what he could and offered to at least try to arrange their local lodging.

An old French army camp existed near al-Qara'un, and the barracks had been hastily converted to housing for the Palestinian refugees who had flooded into the place. Taha's family, though, chose to use the money Taha had earned to rent a small room in the village itself, half an hour by foot from the camp, and as soon as they were installed, Taha again went to work. He quickly found several local grocers with whom he evolved business relationships like the one he'd established with 'Ali al-Bazzi in Bint Jbeyl, and in the morning he would rise and walk to the camp and spend the day wandering with his wooden box between the barracks, selling, as he calls them, "humble things." His profits here were much less than they'd been in crowded, mercantile Bint Jbeyl. In al-Qara'un his customers were all refugees—the poorest of the poor.

When pressed, he digs back—slowly, carefully—for more details and admits that spending his days in the camp was extremely difficult. He remembers the tin-roofed barracks, crammed with families who hung blankets in a futile attempt to separate themselves from the others. The United Nations provided the camp dwellers hot food once a

day: rice with chickpeas and often, he recalls, stones. They also regularly received small quantities of basic foodstuffs, and in these rations
Taha discovered a new way to support his family. He would buy the
UN-issued allotments of white beans from the refugees, sell them at
a profit to a local merchant from whom he would then buy more desirable goods like lentils, which he would then sell back to the people
in the camp. The white beans, he says, required hours of cooking, and
the refugees were so impoverished they could not afford to keep a fire
burning long enough to soften those tough skins. Seizing on this fact
and on the relatively short cooking time of the local lentils, he made
a regular business of this bean-trading and even invested in two small
aluminum plates, which he attached to strings and a stick, creating a
simple greengrocer's scale.

Families with children under age fifteen were also granted cans of
corned beef as a nutritional supplement, but this soft processed flesh
seemed strange to the peasants, who were used to fresh chicken and
lamb. So they were happy to sell the cans to Taha, who would take
them to town and resell them at a profit—until, that is, he was ordered to report to the Canadian official responsible for rations in the
camp. The man warned Taha to stop this practice, since it was, he said,
depriving the children the protein they needed to grow. "But the
people want *real* meat," Taha explained. "With the money I pay them,
they can afford to buy a little." The man was not interested in his cultural savvy or culinary logic—and the second time he caught Taha
carting a quantity of canned meat he both threatened him with arrest
and poked holes in the bottom of all of his cans. Even after this close
brush, though, Taha continued his illicit corned beef trafficking—
though he took care to vary the route that he walked into town.

With the modest sums that Taha earned, meanwhile, his family
could cook their own basic food, and sometimes they augmented their
meager supplies with wild greens they picked nearby—mallow and
chicory. After a short time, the villagers who were renting them a
room told them to stop paying rent: you are our guests, they told
Taha's family. Still, in exchange for their hospitality, Abu Taha insisted
that Taha bring them lentils and beans and even some of those black-
market cans of corned beef.

But despite the welcome his family received, the situation was
bleak. Taha describes the scenes that he saw in the camp, people

waiting in line for food and shouting with impatience. "The men there said, 'We want a line. Be calm.' And the people were shouting, 'We have been waiting one hour for your terrible food.' And the police usually came and tried to calm the people. Forced the people to be calm. And forced them to stand in a line." Amin for his part remembers the "very hard conditions" and the paucity of the rations: a bag of beans, a bag of rice, a can of meat, a bit of flour. "And people began to think—what are we going to do?? They started to look for work. They went to the villages around the camp. . . . People started to leave, to work the land, in the villages near al-Qara'un. This one earns half a pound. That one a pound. In order to buy bread, to feed his children."

Although their days were occupied with the all-consuming, near-at-hand challenges of getting by, it is likely that word of far-off woes reached Taha and his family and the other refugees. That September, for instance, they must have heard the news about Count Bernadotte. A day after the UN mediator—who had been assigned in May to broker a settlement to what he called "the ugly-looking conflict between Arabs and Jews which had broken out in Palestine"—put the finishing touches on a 120-page report about "his mediation efforts, truce supervision, refugee aid," the personal representative of the UN secretary-general Ralph Bunche sent a frantic cablegram from Jerusalem to the international organization's temporary headquarters in Lake Success, New York: "COUNT FOLKE BERNADOTTE, UNITED NATIONS MEDIATOR ON PALESTINE, BRUTALLY ASSASSINATED BY JEWISH ASSAILANTS OF UNKNOWN IDENTITY, IN PLANNED COLD-BLOODED ATTACK IN THE NEW CITY OF JERUSALEM AT 1405 GMT TODAY FRIDAY SEVENTEENTH SEPTEMBER."

Even before the people of Saffuriyya had left their homes, Bernadotte—a debonair career humanitarian best known before he came to the Middle East for securing the release of some thirty thousand people, many of them Jews, from Nazi concentration camps toward the end of World War II—had been desperately trying to cobble together a solution to the conflict raging in Palestine/Israel. He had been one of the most prominent and outspoken advocates for the repatriation of the Palestinian refugees, "these innocent victims of a needless conflict," in his words, who "should be assured the right to return to their homes, if they desire to do so."

"A simple man despite his high birth," this nephew of the Swedish king was widely criticized in his lifetime for being naive or worse. At the time, Arabs and Jews could agree about little besides their disdain for Bernadotte's various proposals, which included giving Jerusalem to Transjordan, establishing an Arab-Jewish union of two independent but economically and politically linked states, and letting almost all the refugees return home. He has been described variously since his death as having been a pawn, a fool, "a crusading Don Quixote who liked to see the world as an arena where evil fought goodness and himself as an unbiased roving knight," or just a good ("rather ignorant") man cruelly out of his element in the Middle East, someone who "lacked the suppleness of mind for the task assigned him." Perhaps he really was oblivious to the disparate forces working against him; maybe he lacked the cynical knowingness that was shared by the other political players in this terrible game. His successor, Bunche, reportedly told Ben-Gurion that Bernadotte was "not a brilliant man, but he was decent." Whatever his limitations, however, Bernadotte's vision seems in retrospect remarkably prescient. A lone voice in praising the mediator, American-born Hebrew University founder Rabbi Judah Magnes wrote that Bernadotte had "done more to advance the cause of peace and conciliation in Palestine than all other persons put together."

The report Bernadotte completed the day before his death states that "the Jewish State is an established fact," proposes substantial revisions to his earlier plans (jettisoning his idea of a Transjordanian Jerusalem, he now put forth the suggestion that the city be placed under international control), and includes an assessment of how the refugees might be helped by warning gravely about "the desperate urgency of this problem." In this final accounting, he declared, "I believe that for the international community to accept its share of responsibility for the refugees of Palestine is one of the minimum conditions for the success of its efforts to bring peace to that land."

But as the fighting continued, Israel's reluctance to allow the refugees back had grown fierce: one American diplomat described the new Jewish state's stance on this subject as "rigid and uncompromising." Not long before his death, Count Bernadotte wrote that the Israelis' military successes during July had "gone to their heads." And the destruction of villages had already begun in a quiet but systematic way. By August the government had established an official "transfer committee" to institute a "plan for the transfer of the Arabs and their resettlement." Liberal foreign minister Moshe Shertok, later Sharett, gushed in a letter that "the most spectacular event in the contemporary history of Palestine—more spectacular in a sense than the creation of the Jewish State—is the wholesale evacuation of the Arab population. . . . The opportunities which the present position open up for a lasting and radical solution of the most vexing problem of the Jewish State are so far-reaching as to take one's breath away." Land expropriation and the demolition of villages had by now swung into high gear, and according to historian Benny Morris, "orders went out to all IDF units to prevent 'with all means' the return of refugees."

In this context, it is obvious that Bernadotte's efforts on behalf of the displaced Palestinian civilians would not have made him many friends in Jewish Jerusalem; neither would have his attempts to draw a parallel between recent Jewish and Arab suffering. It was, he wrote, "an anomaly that the Israeli Government should advance as an argument for the establishment of their state the plight of Jewish refugees and . . . demand the immediate immigration [to Israel] of [Jewish] displaced persons at the same time that they refused to recognize the existence of the Arab refugees which they had created." His murder at the hands of Jewish assassins may indeed have been an "UNSPEAKABLE VIOLATION OF ELEMENTARY MORALITY," in the anguished words that Bunche blasted at Shertok right after the murder, but it was also a highly calculated act—designed to foil any Arab homecoming plans, as well as all attempts to separate the Jews from Jerusalem. And though Shertok quickly shifted tonal gears and cabled the UN secretary-general a condemnation that referred to the killers as "DESPERADOES AND OUTLAWS WHO ARE EXECRATED BY ENTIRE PEOPLE OF ISRAEL AND JEWISH COMMUNITY OF JERUSALEM," no one was ever charged with the murders, and those responsible, members of the Stern Gang, were not punished. One of the group's leaders, Natan Yellin-Mor, was arrested for belonging to a terrorist organization and found guilty, but he was instantly released and pardoned, and was soon elected to the first Knesset. Another mastermind of the murder,

Yitzhak Shamir, later became Israel's prime minister, and the gunman himself found lifelong employment as one of David Ben-Gurion's security guards.

In a sharp letter to the editor of the *New York Times* written right after the assassination, Judah Magnes did term the murder of Bernadotte "a historic tragedy" and strongly condemned the general resort to crocodile tears. "It is very easy to join in the cry that the Jewish terrorists are responsible for this atrocious crime," he wrote. "But who has been responsible for the terrorists? We all bear some responsibility. Certainly the large number of American supporters in Palestine do—the Senators and Congressmen, the newspaper publishers and writers and the large number of Jews and others who have supported terrorists morally and financially."

Magnes died of a heart condition within a month, and by October, the Arab states and Israel had united, after a fashion, to reject Bernadotte's plan formally. Though parts of his proposals were integrated several months later into the notorious UN General Assembly Resolution 194, which declares that "the refugees wishing to return to their homes and live with their neighbors should be permitted to do so at the earliest practicable date," the resolution has—as of this writing some six decades later—never been implemented. A year after the murder, meanwhile, the Israeli cabinet made its single collective gesture of apology to the Swedes and to Bernadotte's widow by grudgingly discussing a proposal to plant a Jewish National Fund forest in memory of the count—on "abandoned," that is, formerly Palestinian-owned, land.

To Taha and his family, of course, such arboreal diplomacy must have seemed distant indeed. Winter was approaching, and their situation would, they knew, soon grow still more dismal, since Lebanon was cold and wet, and often even snowy. "Everywhere you see fallen tents . . . a sea of mud, and children shivering in the cold," as one UN pamphlet written around that time described the refugees' rainy season. Living in their small, unheated room, with few prospects, the family relied on Taha to eke out a living by selling his lentils and combs, and he, understanding this, equipped himself for the task: somehow he got hold of an extra blanket and paid a tailor to sew him heavy snow pants from the cloth. He invested in a wool hat with ear flaps, and he continued to make his way daily to the camp, where he says a thick haze of smoke hung everywhere, as the families tried to warm themselves beside fires built of damp kindling. (The fires seem to have helped little in those bitter temperatures. One historian quotes a description of a child in al-Qara'un "who went out to the toilet in the night and was found frozen stiff the next morning.")

Soon the snow began to fall, until it was, says Taha, "half a meter high, covering everything." But he pushed on, working all day, returning after dark, and in the evenings smoking cigarettes and—to stave off the cold—drinking tea with his uncles and cousins or a new Lebanese friend his own age, Jamal, who lived and grew grapes in al-Qara'un. Despite the family's grave circumstances, they seem to have found during this period a kind of weary equilibrium, as life, anyway, went on. They were obviously waiting for some seismic shift to take hold, but in the meantime, they had simply to ford through each day. Amin remembers the goodness of the people of al-Qara'un as having given comfort. They "were ready to help, but they were poor. They didn't have anything. But they would sit together with us, spend time, laugh." Abu Taha had what Taha calls a "tiny madafeh," two or three local men whom he had befriended. He talked with them and brewed them coffee on the new Primus that Taha had bought.

What did they talk about? What was their mood? It is hard to say, from these thumbnail descriptions, though Taha says his father was "without joy," and around this time one observer of the more general scene wrote that "the most tragic impression to my mind was the hopelessness of the men; children, if healthy enough, will always make their own amusements, and the women at least had some 'household' chores and the children to look after. But the men just loll about and brood, and there lies the danger."

Remarkably, Taha kept reading throughout it all. He would buy cheap editions—either secondhand or from a grocery in town—and, after a long workday, would absorb the same sorts of stories he had read so avidly as a child in Saffuriyya, *Sirat 'Antar, A Thousand and One Nights,* and the legends of *Zir Salim,* a folk epic that recounts what are known as the Battle Days, or wars of the pre-Islamic Arabian tribes. To vary things, he sometimes also read Egyptian dime-store translations of novels about the French "gentleman burglar" Arsène Lupin. Ghazaleh, meanwhile, was popular with the girls her age in al-Qara'un, with whom she often played, and she and Amin and Feisel also concocted various games together. Imm Taha, though still upset about her mother and sister, had by necessity sunken into a routine: she cooked on a fire in the cold outdoors and worked hard to keep the small room clean.

Sometime that winter, word reached them that their Bedouin relatives in Jordan were offering Abu Taha and his brothers and their families refuge: *Come!* their cousin Sa'id Saleh of the Beni Sakhr tribe sent a message, promising them tracts of land for free. A man from Saffuriyya who was also living in al-Qara'un had traveled to Jordan and returned to Lebanon with the news. "This is *yours*," Sa'id Saleh told his emissary to tell the family. "But my father and my uncles of course refused," says Taha, because their minds and hearts were still set on returning to Palestine and in fact to Saffuriyya. That said, both of Abu Taha's brothers were struggling at the same time to establish businesses in Lebanon. Muhammad Sa'id and a Palestinian partner invested in a soap factory, which failed after several months; Ahmed and one of his sons tried their hand at a butcher shop, but this, too, bottomed out.

Meanwhile, the scraps of information that reached them from Palestine—now Israel—were confusing. "We heard two kinds of stories," says Taha. "One was a smiling story, which said you can come and receive an identity card. The other story was very gloomy: the people here are looking for work. You are not allowed to return to Saffuri but must stay in Reina, Nazareth, Kafr Kanna. And if you have no identity card then the army will capture you and send you to Jordan and refuse to deal with you at all." The gloomy story was, in fact, much closer to the truth, and though the legal particulars of the situation could not possibly have been clear to them at the time, they did hear rumors about, for instance, Abu Taha's Saffuriyya friend Hassan—who had been living in al-Qara'un and made the journey back home on foot, returning to the village and sneaking into his own house at night to try and retrieve some of his belongings. He was caught—people said—and shot dead on the spot.

The unfortunate Hassan could not have known that in December the Israeli government passed its Emergency Regulations Regarding Absentee Property, which would eventually evolve into the infamous Absentee Property Law of 1950. This stated in the plainest language that anyone who "was a Palestinian citizen and left his ordinary place of residence in Palestine for a place outside Palestine" after November 29, 1947, when the partition plan was announced, and before September 1, 1948, had forfeited the rights to his or her land and belongings, which were now placed under the care of a custodian. In other words, the fledgling Israeli government confiscated them. The same was true for those who had left their homes for "a place in Palestine held at the time by forces which sought to prevent the establishment of the state of Israel or which fought against it after its establishment." Israel profited hugely from this clever, retroactive law: it is estimated that 350 of the 370 Jewish settlements established between 1948 and 1953 were built on "absentee" land.

To add insult to injury, a census had been conducted by the Israeli authorities that autumn, and anyone who had not been counted and granted an identity card was also considered an absentee, no matter how present they might have been. (And indeed the Orwellian official term "Present Absentee" would soon become their official designation.) Without such cards, those returning to their own country and homes would be considered illegal aliens—trespassers or, in the army's punishing terminology, "infiltrators."

By means of a tortuous legal obstacle course, the government meant to limit severely the number of Arab residents—and, in the end, citizens—in the Jewish state, which was rapidly filling with new Jewish immigrants who were granted ID cards almost as soon as they stepped off the boat or the plane. Some 350,000 arrived between May 1948 and the end of 1949, and the Jewish population increased by half; in July 1950 the Knesset passed, by unanimous vote, the Law of Return, which allowed any Jew anywhere to immigrate to Israel. By the close of 1951, the number of Israeli Jews would be more than double what it had been at the state's founding. Meanwhile, the idea behind the strict limits imposed on Arab would-be citizens was, in euphemistic official terms, "to liberate [Israel] from the presence of people with suspicious pasts or whose present behavior does not ensure that they will be quiet and desirable residents." However quiet, Taha and his family and friends were no longer desirable and were subject to no law of return.

LEAVINGS

◆

ON THE HOT MAY DAY in 1941 when the Bratislava-born Jewish poet Tuvia Ruebner arrived at Kibbutz Merchavia, near Nazareth, he saw a monkey tied to a pine tree and went to pet it on the head. The monkey bit Ruebner in the leg. The greeting was, it seems, fairly typical of the welcome the young immigrant received in Palestine, a place that flooded him with ambivalent emotions from the first day he set foot there.

He was seventeen and had just bid good-bye to his family in a Slovakian train station ("I had a vivid feeling that I would not see them again," he said later, and he was right), and traveled to his new home through Hungary, Romania, Turkey, Syria, and Lebanon. He belonged to a Zionist youth group—Hashomer Hatza'ir, the same left-wing movement in which Dov Yermiya had been active—but Ruebner was not enthralled. "I have no talent for ideology," he explained many years later to a journalist. "Because it demands loyalty from its followers and I am capable of being loyal only to people. Not to ideas." He was also deeply disappointed with the kibbutz, where all his private property had been confiscated and handed out to veteran members on his arrival; he now had to endure the sight of a stranger wearing his favorite hunting cap and, more seriously, to continue to live among these tough, hardworking people who were not especially interested in or sympathetic to the needs and desires of a sensitive young European intellectual. Perhaps it was the collective cold shoulder he received that caused him to continue writing in German for another twelve years—a private act of linguistic rebellion that would have been audacious at that time and in that society, when speaking and writing in Hebrew was a profound ideological statement. *Not* to do so was almost a rejection of Zionism itself. Although he would later ease his way into Hebrew and become quite passionate about the language, emerging as a respected figure on the local literary scene, he told the same reporter in 2005 that "the first sounds a person hears in his life, and the sights and landscapes—that is the foundation of his psyche. I love the landscape of Israel, but inside I am connected more to the landscape of the Carpathians."

What an odd experience it must have been, then, for Ruebner to find himself, in late July 1948, clutching a rifle as he faced someone else's childhood landscape: the hills and houses of the conquered village of Saffuriyya. Or—as he and the other soldiers who had been mobilized to guard the place had already taken to calling it—Tzippori, "restoring" the town's Mishnah-era Hebrew name.

Ruebner was a reluctant soldier. Not only did he have ideological doubts and lack military experience, he had suffered a serious case of hepatitis several years before, and as a result was called up during the war for just a month. He spent the whole time stationed in Saffuriyya/Tzippori, and his memory of this period is very partial. When my husband, Peter, and I sit with Ruebner and his wife in the living room of the small house in Merchavia where he still lives at age eighty-one, he at first insists he remembers "nothing." Eventually, however, he dredges up a few fragments, which he delivers in the flattest terms: it was summer. The village was empty. There was a strange smell in the air. Several bodies were decomposing in the street; they were black and swollen. Together with the other soldiers, he slept in the citadel. He estimates that there were thirty or forty men altogether but can't remember the name or number of the battalion or unit and says he would be surprised if he had known it even then. He had been issued a rifle, though he doesn't recall if he was taught how to use it. He felt, he says, disconnected from everything taking place around him. His mood was dark. The soldiers would go out occasionally on patrols around the village—and once his platoon commander stopped an old Arab man and asked what he was doing. Looking for my camel, the old man said. The commander didn't believe him and thought he was a spy. Though they had explicit orders to deliver any prisoners back to the citadel, the commander told the man to walk ahead. The old man

fell to his knees and pleaded for his life. The commander told the man
to get up and walk—and then shot him dead. The rest of the soldiers
were silent and didn't react. Neither did Ruebner. As he would write
in his autobiography, "I did not protest on his behalf. No one saw anything wrong with the act. I accepted it as a depressing fact like the entire experience in which I was caught up."

He spent his time, he tells us, "reading and rotting."

Once he found an old oil jug in the courtyard of one of the
houses; later, when he got it home to the kibbutz, he discovered that
it dated from the Middle Bronze Age. Aside from the old man whom

his commander killed, he doesn't remember
the presence of any Arabs in the village—
though he realizes that some of them must
have remained, since he himself snapped photographs of a few. (He can't, he says, summon
any specific memories of taking these pictures
or of wandering alone through the village with
his camera.) A serious amateur photographer,
he seems happier talking about photography
than Tzippori and offers to go have a look for
the prints. He disappears into the house's crammed upstairs loft, descending a short while later with three black-and-white photographs.
Two are studied, studio-style portraits of Saffuriyya peasants—a blind

man with a delicate mouth and an older man
with a white kaffiyeh and silvery beard. Both
of these anonymous fallahin are framed in
tight close-up, and they appear to be posing
for the photographer. The old man tilts his
head toward the light, in a nearly ecstatic expression. The blind man turns his eyes toward
the lens or just off to the side—and the shad-
owy composition of Ruebner's photo makes
them look hollow. The photos are peculiarly

"artistic," dating as they do from this period and place. Given the fractured nature of Ruebner's memories and the necessary silence of the
two men themselves, however, one can only stare hard at the pictures
and try to imagine the scene that surrounded the photographer and
his subjects as he leaned in to get the right angle.

The third photograph is perhaps the most unsettling. Labeled in Hebrew "Tzippori, 1948, landscape," it was shot from so great a remove that—were it not for Ruebner's scribbled inscription—one would have no way of distinguishing it from any other rural Palestinian setting of the last century. In the shady foreground, a tall knot of sabra cactuses twists in that oddly emotive—almost imploring, human—way that they will; beyond and below, in the distance, sit what must be (it is hard to say from their indistinct shape) a cluster of pale houses, drenched in the summertime sun. The photograph is at once weirdly idyllic and somehow abstract. No people or animals are anywhere in view. Everything is still. It is a lovely, spooky picture—very possibly the last photograph ever taken of Saffuriyya. It is also a record of the emptiness that one depressed émigré poet, a young Jewish soldier in the victorious new Israeli army, saw as he pointed his lens down at Taha Muhammad Ali's village and carefully closed the shutter.

Saffuriyya was, in fact, hardly empty. Even as most of the villagers had run for their lives on that black July night, several hundred people—mostly, but not entirely, the sick and the elderly, including Taha's grandmother, and his aunt, who did not want to leave the old woman alone—had stayed behind in their homes and waved white flags when they saw the soldiers coming.

Dov Yermiya remembers giving orders the day after the village was conquered to round up the men "in order to register them and explain to them the restrictions that applied to them while the fighting continued, and in order"—it would sound grotesque from anyone else, but this is Dov talking, and he means it—"to hear any special requests they might have had." Some fifty men were herded into one of the larger houses at the center of the village, and according to the story that Dov writes in his memoir: "When I entered the house and approached them, one of them suddenly stood up, came toward me, and—before the startled gaze of all present—fell on my neck, crying and kissing me with great excitement. *Ya mukhtar! Ya mukhtar!* What a surprise. It's so good that you're here! Save us, *ya mukhtar!*'" The man was 'Isa, a Saffuriyya villager who had once guarded the forests near Dov's kibbutz, and the two had been good friends. When Dov tells me the story in person, he elaborates in slightly more ominous terms. "'Isa said, 'Dov, save us. We're afraid of the soldiers, they . . . don't behave well with us.' So I calmed him down. And everyone was shocked, all the soldiers, and the Arabs too, and I said, 'Everyone go back to their houses!' And I gave an order to my soldiers to protect them—there'll be *hell* to pay if someone does something! And they went back to their houses. Before evening I made the rounds again. And I came to 'Isa, and he said, 'The soldiers are bothering my daughters.' They were flirting with them. So I went out, and I said, 'Guys, if anyone does anything to a single Arab, I'll shoot him.' At 'Amqa [a village the battalion had previously conquered] I had already said that. And really, I was very sharp on that score."

But Dov left the very same day. That night, just after dark, a jeep arrived in the village and whisked him off to Nazareth, which—he learned only then—had surrendered to the Israelis. Dov says that when he arrived in the larger town, Ben Dunkelman "hugged me and said, in English, 'You have taken Nazareth for us'—that's what he said. The fact that I conquered Saffuriyya meant I opened the way."

In the *New York Times* photograph of the capitulation signing ceremony, Dov stands with a group of blank-faced officers who crowd
around the one man looking a bit warily into the camera: the fez-
wearing mayor, pen in hand.

Meanwhile, the remaining Saffuriyya villagers were left to fend
for and defend themselves. They lived off the supplies they had stored
in their homes—most of which were still intact—and scavenged some
from their neighbors who'd left. To judge from Dov's description of
'Isa's tears, and from Tuvia Ruebner's account of the corpses in the
street and the old man's pleas and murder, it seems clear that the villagers were petrified—too frightened even to bury their dead. It is
likely that they would have tried to remain as inconspicuous as possible while the soldiers were camped in the Qal'a. During this time, it
appears that Taha's grandmother crept back into the remains of her
house—which was one of those the army had destroyed—and tried
to collect some of her belongings. "Among the stones and dust," says
Taha, she found her wooden bridal chest, shattered, and managed to
take from it a few things, including the white dress in which she
wanted one day to be buried.

Yet even as the villagers tiptoed and whispered and watched, life
must have started to assume a kind of rhythm. The people would certainly have tried, for instance, to harvest what they could of their
crops that summer and autumn. In October and November the national census was conducted, and those still resident in the town were
granted identity cards, which listed their address, in Arabic, as Saffuriyya. Along with all the other Palestinian Arabs who had remained in
Israel, they were now bound by a battery of rules that, among other
things, severely restricted their freedom of movement. Based on British
emergency regulations issued in 1945, these martial laws derived from
the code the English had concocted to quell the 1936–39 revolt.
Maybe—remembering the revolt and how it was crushed—they believed that these restrictions were temporary and would be lifted once
the war was over. Perhaps they trusted that soon their relatives and
neighbors would return and that life would revert to something like
normal. (In fact, in 1950 the same rigid laws created the foundation
for the military government, and the draconian statutes this regime
imposed on the Arabs of Israel would remain firmly in place until 1966.)

With time, indeed, their numbers grew. As the fighting wound down in late autumn, many of those who had decamped for nearby villages had begun to come back, and by winter government officials had noticed and were worried. One formerly secret document from the files of the so-called Committee for the Transfer of the Arabs bluntly states, "The people of Saffuriyya must be moved immediately, since the number of residents in this village is growing from day to day and one assumes that if the village isn't evacuated in its entirety, the population will increase considerably in the future, and we will be facing the reality of a large settlement in the village." At the same time, the authorities had already set their eyes on the rich soil of Saffuriyya: "Next to Nazareth is a village . . . whose distant lands are needed for our settlements," wrote one official. "Perhaps they can be given another place."

And so the new year began for the people of Saffuriyya. On the morning of January 7, 1949, trucks arrived, and soldiers ordered all the remaining villagers to get on. That day, 550 people—many of them legal residents, with ID cards marked "Saffuriyya"—were expelled to nearby villages and towns. A week later the minister of minority affairs received a neatly typed note, whose telling parenthetical aside appears in the original:

> RE: Saffuriyya
>
> Monday, 1.10.49 was the last date that was given to the residents of the aforementioned village to vacate their village. A large number of them "moved" (were moved) to the village of 'Illut and a small number infiltrated into and set themselves up in Nazareth and the villages in the area, such as Kafr Kanna and Reina.
>
> The Military Governor of Nazareth put at the disposal of the aforementioned residents a number of military vehicles, to help them in moving their belongings.
>
> The evacuation was carried out without any incidents with the army.

One Palestinian account—by the son of Saffuriyya's leading religious authority, a sheikh trained at al-Azhar in Cairo—describes "the mighty explosions" heard by the villagers who had been forced out of their homes in January and who then watched and listened from the neighboring towns as Saffuriyya's buildings were reduced to rubble: "Columns of smoke and dust rose to the heavens above Saffuriyyeh. . . . The Jews had blown up the houses with dynamite. In many houses only the ceiling fell in, while the walls remained standing." As far as the government was concerned, though, everything had gone "smoothly," and by February, Kibbutz Sde Nachum had received 1,500 dunams (375 acres) of Saffuriyya land; Kibbutz Cheftziba took 1,000 (250 acres). Nearby Kibbutz Hasolelim would later receive another chunk, three times that size, and late that spring a new moshav, Tzippori, would be founded on much of what remained of the village land, and the Arabic name "Saffuriyya" would be replaced once and for all with the Hebrew "Tzippori" in all official documents. (On June 13, 1949, to be precise, a tiny story ran on the front page of the Hebrew tabloid *Yediot Achronot* announcing, "This week Bulgarian immigrants will arrive in Tzippori, near Kfar Choresh. The village of Tzippori was known from the start of the war as one of the dens of the gangs, and its residents were among the first to flee.") A Zionist historian of this period describes the reluctance of many of the new immigrants—some eighty-five families, who also came from Turkey and Romania—to settle in this strange and, in their eyes, harsh place. Most of them, he says, would have preferred city life and felt themselves "cheated." There were, however, also those who in his words, "truly and genuinely wanted to participate in the project of Judaizing the Galilee." He writes of the "small, shapeless concrete structures" that were built among the ruins of the village houses and how,  despite the difficulties they faced, the newcomers eventually made Tzippori flourish—so much so that it "became an object of envy among its former residents."

Another Hebrew account of the conditions on the moshav in its trying first days was written by Shmuel Dayan, Moshe's hard-nosed father, who describes how "the Arab town has been demolished and the stones from the walls have been thrown in heaps. Walls are on the verge of collapse and the dust of generations and dung rises in the air. . . . In every ruin thieves and murderers are hiding."

Dayan also describes in strangely lyrical and, it seems, not fully conscious terms the confrontational relationship of the moshav dwellers to the spectral remains—one might even use the government's phrase, "present absence"—of the former villagers:

> On a summer day, at dusk, a man and his wife were resting on the small porch of an ancient stone house in Tzippori. . . . Dense, twisted sabra cactuses surrounded the house, which had come into their hands, and they had to prepare and uproot the sabra. . . . It was hard, says the man—every day I opened my eyes and I saw the loathsome sabra. I continued to uproot it, because I could not stand to see it, and even at night in my bed, when I closed my eyes, I saw the sabra falling under my saw and hoe. Each bit of additional land that I cleared of it gave me great satisfaction—until I saw before my eyes, in my dream, clean land, and I fell into a deep sleep.

At the same time, Saffuriyya had been declared by the authorities off-limits to the villagers themselves, and their presence there could result in death. This designation also meant that in 1952, when those residents who had received identity cards marked "Saffuriyya" appealed to the Supreme Court to be allowed to go home, their case was rejected out of hand, without so much as a hearing. Saffuriyya was, in the eyes of the court, a "closed military area," which meant the expelled citizens had no legal recourse.

But we are getting ahead of ourselves. At the start of 1949, Taha's grandmother and aunt settled anxiously into a small rented room in the old Nazareth suq and awaited news of their family. At the same time, Taha and his parents and siblings also huddled and waited in their cold, cramped room in al-Qara'un. Everyone, says Taha, dreamed of Saffuriyya.

◆

Throughout that hard winter, Taha continued to rise early and walk to the camp to sell his modest odds and ends. One late February morning, he remembers, Ghazaleh showed him the hole in her stocking and asked him to bring her a new pair.

He was the oldest, she the youngest, and as big brother and little sister they had a playful connection: he would tease her, she would snap back, and their catlike game—a protracted mock feud, almost (it sounds) a kind of flirtation—would begin. As the baby and only girl, she was certainly the most protected of the children, but as she approached adolescence she had also metamorphosed into a tough, poised, and extremely outgoing young woman. Having grown up with all these boys, she could hold her own. She was close to her mother and spent most days helping with the housework, and though Imm Taha had been tearful and clutched since they'd left Saffuriyya and her own mother behind, Ghazaleh still managed to make her laugh with her stories, quips, and songs. Ghazaleh and Amira, a year her senior, had also forged a close bond; they would giggle and argue like sisters, and in Lebanon, especially, they spent hours and hours together, holding hands and whispering. Taha remembers that once they fought, and Amira hit Ghazaleh. Ghazaleh cried but a few minutes later improvised a song for Amira, a kind of musical peace offering, which she accompanied on the small drum that Taha had once bought her as a gift.

The family had little, so Taha couldn't afford to spoil Ghazaleh, but he enjoyed giving her things, and that morning, as he collected his wares from the grocery, he bought not one but *three* new pairs of stockings for his sister, as a special treat.

When he returned that evening, Ghazaleh was napping, alone in the room. Taha went to her and tapped her on the shoulder, said, "Look Ghazaleh, I brought you what you wanted."

"No," she said, turning away. "No."

"What do you mean no? Look!"

"No," she muttered, drifting back toward sleep. "I'm dying."

Taha says now that he thought she was joking. What else could he possibly think? She had been perfectly fine when he left the house that morning. As she did every day, she stayed home and worked alongside her mother, sweeping, cleaning, cooking—and though at some stage she had complained that she had a headache, whatever ailed her hadn't seemed to Imm Taha anything serious. And even by the time Taha returned from work, it appears that no one had yet registered the gravity of her situation. Ghazaleh's cheeks were burning and she was lying limply on a straw mat, but Imm Taha and the others thought she had a slight flu and had left her to rest—and then Taha came home, and it all happened so quickly, they hardly had time to grasp what it seems Ghazaleh herself already knew. Well before a doctor arrived and diagnosed a "very dangerous" case of meningitis, she stopped speaking; her breathing grew labored; she slipped out of consciousness. The doctor hurried off to make arrangements for an ambulance to be sent immediately to take this extremely ill patient to quarantine in Beirut. But it was too late. "All of her suffering," says Taha, "lasted less than a day." Within hours of mumbling that her head hurt, the twelve-year-old Ghazaleh was dead.

And with this, Imm Taha snapped.

She had already buried six children—three infant Tahas, one baby Milad, and the toddlers Yusuf and Rabba. She had no idea if her own mother and sister were alive. She had just lost her house, her belongings, her neighbors, her fruit trees, her village, her country, the only life she had ever known, and she was now exiled to a single freezing-cold room in a strange land, with absolutely no sense of what the future might hold. So when her only daughter, her constant companion and comfort died—when Ghazaleh died—she snapped.

The doctor, meanwhile, had returned and ordered them not to bury Ghazaleh. An ambulance sent by the Ministry of Health would soon arrive to take her body to Beirut for autopsy. But Abu Taha had no plans to wait or to hand his daughter over to these strange officials in lab coats, and as soon as the doctor left, he ordered his sons to wash Ghazaleh and dig her grave. Within the hour, they finished the wrenching task.

For better or worse, the graveyard lay right beside the house where they were renting a room: from the front door, one could look across the field of tombs or set out to wander between them. And that is precisely what Imm Taha did, for days. Clutching Ghazaleh's little *mandil*, her headscarf, she would stumble through the cemetery then take up her post beside the grave and wail and wail, until Abu Taha would send one of the boys to lead her gently home. Then she would sit at the entrance to their house and face the graveyard and wail again. For days on end. Then, as Amin puts it, they began to worry that perhaps "she *had something*." Because of the way she was acting, in fact, they decided to leave al-Qara'un. "My father thought that we must go far away from this place. If we stay in this place, Imm Taha will go mad."

At first, Abu Taha announced that they would go to Beirut, where work might be easier to find. But something in this plan seemed to trouble him, and for several days—as Imm Taha sobbed and the boys tried to calm her and Amira began to arrive in the mornings to help Imm Taha cook and clean, assuming without comment the role of the future daughter-in-law, that is, a necessary set of extra female hands—he stewed in one of his dark, silent moods and then declared, suddenly, "We are returning to Palestine." Abu Taha believed that Imm Taha's agony would be tempered once she was reunited with her mother and sister; according to Taha, this decision also constituted an admission of "the mistake we made by leaving." Abu Taha wanted to right this wrong, "to compensate, to come back."

It took them several months to arrange their affairs and gather enough money to make the trip, but once Abu Taha had made up his mind, that was that. Taha says, "He was the one who decided. We obeyed him." The five of them would travel together with Muhammad Sa'id's and Ahmed's oldest sons, who would scout for their families and see if return was possible. The others—Amira among them—would stay behind in Lebanon. It was springtime. They had been living in Lebanon for the better part of a year.

"And before we left al-Qara'un" says Taha, "my mother told the woman who rented us a room there, near the graveyard, 'Imm Muhammad, keep an eye on Ghazaleh, please.'"

The whole family accompanied them to the bus—bound first for Beirut, then south to Ermesh, on the border—and they said more farewells. Taha did not wish Amira, his bride-to-be, a special good-bye. "I said good-bye to them all. Not especially to her. But of course she received her share." He hoped to see her soon.

REINA

◆

PRESENT, ABSENT

◆

IN ERMESH THEY BOUGHT A DONKEY and *dibbis*, the thick fruit molasses that is eaten with bread. (Saffuriyya dibbis was made of grapes or dates, but this foreign-tasting Lebanese batch came from the pulp of carob.) Imm Taha baked a pile of flat loaves over the fire, then they filled bottles with water and quietly prepared themselves to cross over to Palestine—or, as they would need to get used to calling it, Israel. From the way the brothers describe that day now, it seems no one talked about what lay ahead. The donkey was meant to carry Abu Taha, and the dibbis would fortify them for the long trip. They waited until dark, when a large group of them would begin to make their cautious way across the fields. Palestinian refugees had been dashing anxiously over the border for months now, and on this particular night, the ranks of the returnees had swollen to almost a hundred. They believed, it appears, that the passage was best attempted en masse. "Il-mawt bayn in-nas na'as," Abu Taha liked to say: To die among others is like drifting off to sleep.

Still they were, says Amin, terrified. The soldiers who were guarding the border would shoot at anything that moved, and they had all heard stories of people killed just trying to go home. True, they didn't *see* any soldiers—but they couldn't be sure what or who was lying in wait. It was so dark they could barely make out the shapes of their own feet, and every few minutes someone would start at a sound, and the whole group would, he says, "jump with fright." A few people turned back, they were so scared—but one man traveling with them, from the village of al-Farradiyya, acted as a kind of guide, or goad, urging them on, trying to calm them, assuring them that everything would be all right.

By morning, they were deep inside, and when they sat to rest and eat the dibbis, they offered it all around, and among the people who joined in this spontaneous repast were some they knew from Saffuriyya: Abu Taha's cousin, the well-to-do widow Radia Abu Najj, took part, as did her children, including her youngest, a bashful eight-year-old girl named Yusra Qablawi. (They had not planned to meet Taha's family and had arrived on a series of trains and buses all the way from Damascus.) Later, as the group moved south and they reached a stream, Radia Abu Najj asked the teenaged Taha to please lift the little girl over the water. He did so, and they continued to walk together.

Radia Abu Najj's husband had been murdered in mysterious circumstances near the British army camp in Saffuriyya in 1943. Some

Egyptian soldiers who'd been billeted there by the English were suspected, but the police found no tracks and no arrests were ever made. With his death, she had inherited the handsome stone house that she herself had helped to build, as well as a large team of workers, many goats, sheep, and cows, and a wide swatch of rich land on the boundary dividing Saffuriyya from Reina. In the years before 1948, she had become a serious farmer and businesswoman. Those in the area regarded her, according to one who knew her well, as "mannish and smart." With the help of her formidable entrepreneurial skills, her three boys, five girls, and widowed mother—who was herself "a very proud person" and who was one of the only Arab peasants in those days and that vicinity to wear eyeglasses, which were considered "strange"— Radia managed her nearly one thousand dunams of land and her accounts, overseeing the harvest and sale of corn, wheat, watermelon, tomatoes, and especially luscious pomegranates. When the fig-picking season arrived, extra workers and their families would

come live in tents scattered among the groves or camp out in a cave on her property. During the autumn and winter rains, she let others take refuge in its dry darkness, and she was generally known for her hospitality. On Ramadan evenings she hosted huge, song-filled parties at her house, and she enjoyed sending care packages of her choicest produce to neighbors, relatives, and friends.

It was a small agricultural empire that she commanded—and though she and her family considered themselves Saffuriyyans and had fled with the others when the planes attacked, leaving behind everything, including the livestock, a full year's worth of supplies, the crops in the fields, and all her gold jewelry, she was now also hoping that luck, or the unspoken but obvious Israeli policy of sparing "friendly" villages, had saved her home. While by the time she returned to what was now Israel, she and the others knew that Saffuriyya was gone—and with it, she understood, the extensive olive orchards that were part of her husband's legacy but that lay within the limits of the conquered village—nearby (really next-door) Reina had been left untouched. Its people, a good number of them Christians, were still living in their homes; they had flown white flags and relinquished their arms immediately after Nazareth surrendered to the Israelis. So after nine months spent living in the most squalid conditions in Lebanon and Syria, where she and her family had gone in search of shelter and where she had been forced to swallow her aristocratic sense of herself and worked cleaning houses in order to make ends barely meet, Radia Abu Najj had decided that the time had come to reclaim her land in Reina.

It seems that she, too, was moved to return by the death of a daughter. Her eldest child, a twenty-one-year-old mother of four, was pregnant when they left Saffuriyya, but living in a room with broken windows and no roof in a village near Damascus she had taken ill and, giving birth, died, as had her newborn daughter. Now Radia was responsible for supporting her late daughter's other children as well as her own, along with her bespectacled mother. In Reina, Radia hoped, she would be able to provide for this large, hungry brood.

◆

Taha and his family had also fixed on Reina as the most logical place to live for now. It was not Saffuriyya, of course, but it was at least

close to the remains of their village, and they knew its hills and paths.
They had received word that many people from Saffuriyya had taken
refuge there, among them the former mayor of Saffuriyya, Sheikh
Saleh Salim, and his family. And they had heard that their old friend
had retained his pre-'48 influence with the authorities, a fact that
might help them to obtain the documents they needed to reside in the
country legally. Sheikh Saleh had, it seems, a knack for endearing
himself to the powers that be, whichever powers they were.

According to the story that one of Sheikh Saleh's sons would later
tell, his family had first fled Saffuriyya for Kafr Manda, sending the
younger children ahead to Lebanon and safety with their grandparents. But as Sheikh Saleh's entourage moved northward, the
mukhtars of the various villages had pleaded with him to stay put—
and eventually a priest was dispatched by the wealthy families and the
religious authorities of Nazareth, asking that Sheikh Saleh return to
the area and take up once again the mantle (or the qumbaz) of respected communal leader. He was well known before 1948 for having
negotiated a series of sulhas, reconciliation ceremonies, between two
important and constantly feuding Nazareth families, the Fahums and
the Zu'bis. Taha remembers, in fact, the dazzling feast that was prepared and eaten in Saffuriyya on one of these occasions. Sheikh Saleh
not only hosted this grand banquet but paid for it himself, arranging
for Saleh al-'Afifi to use his entire fleet of buses to transport the rival
Nazareth families and their many friends and associates to the village,
where—after performing the necessary ritual gestures—they feasted
on fifteen roast sheep and twenty trays of sweet cheese pastry, *knafeh*,
prepared by a special chef.

The local Palestinians themselves were the ones now begging
Sheikh Saleh to return and shepherd them; perhaps this was a last-
ditch effort to grasp the frayed end of the rope that linked them to the
life they had known before 1948. But it is clear that the Israelis, too,
had a vested interest in maintaining his authority and the authority of
other regionally respected old-school "notables" like him. Although
almost all the educated—and urban, politically savvy, nationally
known—Palestinian leaders had left the country before or during the
war (one government official described post-'48 Israeli Arab society as
being "like a headless body"), a more traditional and acquiescent stra-
tum of tribal chiefs and peasant potentates had remained. By doling

out small perks and the trappings of power to these men—and such representatives of the old patriarchal clan system were, it hardly bears stating, all men—the government was able to win their support and the support of the people who looked up to them, even under the punishing conditions imposed by the emergency regulations and eventual military government.

This was no small achievement, since these laws were so harsh—and so crushing in their political, psychological, and intellectual effects—that when they were used by the British before 1948 to crack down on Jewish undergrounds like the Stern Gang, future Israeli attorney general Ya'akov Shimshon Shapira, among others, had strongly condemned them, saying, "Even in Nazi Germany there were no such laws. . . . It is our duty to tell the whole world that the defense regulations . . . destroy the very foundation of justice in this land. . . . No government has the right to draw up such laws."

Yet after 1948 the laws remained in place, and the critique among the members of the ruling parties evaporated. By 1950, the regulations had given way to a system of military government which made it a criminal offense for the Arab citizens of Israel to leave their own villages or cities without special permits. The military governor could, if he liked, issue a permit that designated the precise time and route of the trip or decline a permit without explanation on the grounds of "security." Freedom of speech and the press were severely limited. All books, articles, stories, and poems slated for publication had to be submitted to the military censor, and any foreign publication could be banned as the censor saw fit. Land could be summarily confiscated or declared off-limits, even to its owners—again, on the enigmatic yet all-encompassing grounds of "security"—and the military governor had "the power to proclaim any area or place a closed area . . . which no one can enter or leave without . . . a written permit from the military commander or his deputy." At the same time, information about which areas were considered closed was the well-guarded secret of the military governor and his men, a situation that often led to a terrible Catch-22 in which someone was charged with violating a closure order that he could not possibly have known to exist. The military governor could also impose curfews at will. An individual whom the governor suspected or simply wanted to punish could—without ever being charged with a crime—be placed under police supervision and

ordered to live in a city or village of the governor's choosing, "report-
ing his movements to the authorities or to appointed persons . . . at
set times according to instructions." And so on and on—through a
tortuous litany of restrictions, degradations, and legalistic booby-
traps. "Kafkaesque" is a worn-out term—but it really does apply to
this dark, absurd, and often destiny-determining code.

If anything, then, the regime needed the help of men like Sheikh
Saleh to exert its force and keep tabs on the villagers. And the selective easing of these tough laws was often used as a way to shore up
support for such obeisant figureheads: a special travel permit might
be rewarded here, an incidence of "infiltration" overlooked there—all
as a way to win the frightened people's silence and submission.
Threats to anyone who spoke up or lashed out against the repressive
web of controls might also be easily made through the same channels.
And so a system of quiet collusion was instituted almost immediately
with the founding of the state, and several Zionist political parties, including Ben-Gurion's ruling Mapai, the forerunner of the Labor Party,
created special "Arab lists," which put some of these men in the
Knesset, Sheikh Saleh among them.

In his white kaffiyeh and black 'igal, or rope headband, Sheikh
Saleh was an unlikely Mapainik. (Most of the party's other representatives were Eastern European socialists with wide-open collars and
manners.) But he would serve the party in the Knesset from 1955 to
1959. The power that Saleh and the others commanded, however, was
largely an illusion. According to one account: "The moral support
given the Arab members by the party was as meager as the material
benefits. Mapai regarded its Arab Knesset members as mere hangers-
on, whose duty it was to vote the party line and support it during the
formation of a government. They were never consulted about the
composition of the government nor given ministerial or high offices."
Amin relates with a rueful guffaw that even his constituents made
jokes about Sheikh Saleh, "a fallah," serving in the Knesset, since he
spoke no Hebrew and often fell asleep during parliamentary debates.
Someone would have to knock him in the ribs to wake him whenever
there was a vote.

Whatever his limitations as leader at the national level, though,
and however piddling the spoils he controlled, Sheikh Saleh held the
reigns locally. One Hebrew document from the files of the Ministry

of Minority Affairs, dated August 26, 1948, records the protocol of a meeting "initiated by Sheikh Saleh Salim of Tzippori, a man of great influence in all the towns of the [Nazareth] area." Sheikh Saleh had summoned the mukhtars, priests, and dignitaries of twenty-eight villages nearby to meet with the military governor and various Israeli army commanders. In respectful—some might say fawning—terms, Sheikh Saleh and the others offered their allegiance to the new Jewish state and asked in exchange that the government treat their people decently, help with the steady distribution of commodities, protect them from falsely inflated prices, and allow the harvest to take place as usual. The military governor responded by expressing his happiness at the chance to meet and promised that "at the end of the war we can all live together freely, regardless of religious or racial differences."

In exchange for his help, the authorities were quick to extend certain benefits to Sheikh Saleh. By the time the remaining Saffuriyya villagers were ordered onto trucks and out of town in January, Saleh had already settled into a spacious "abandoned" house in the center of Reina. He had also taken hold of another fine stone structure on the outskirts of the village—none other than the house built and owned by the widow Radia Abu Najj. Sheikh Saleh's wives and children lived with him in town, though he had dispatched several families of "his" workers, former Saffuriyyans, to occupy Radia's property, so that he could lay claim to her lands and the fruits of those lands. On discovering that her house, her crops, and all her belongings (even her children's clothes) had been requisitioned, Radia crumpled into a faint—when she came to, declaring her faith in the goodness of the respected Sheikh Saleh, who would surely make things right. But when she realized he had no plans whatsoever to return her land or her house, she promptly launched a legal battle to wrest back what was hers. Sheikh Saleh seemed to have been banking on her "inferior" status as both a single woman and an "absentee," while the patriarch of one of the families now living in her house dismissed her claims by saying that she had gone crazy in Syria from "the apples they eat there." Radia, her children, grandchildren, and mother were forced to live in a single room of their own house—sharing a roof with these other refugees who had become their avowed enemies and who often beat them, stole their things, and hurled verbal abuse at them, "like in an Egyptian movie," according to the memory of one eyewitness.

It took three lawyers five years, but Radia eventually won citizenship and her court case and so took control, wearily, of the whole of her home and all her property in Reina. As it happens, this battle was not her last, and she would be forced over the course of the next decade to fight, often physically, to hold on to the land that remained—at one point throwing herself down in front of a bulldozer, which proceeded to break her leg. The Israeli government was also eager to expropriate her fields, and it proved a much more formidable force to be reckoned with than Sheikh Saleh. However greedy and self-interested his actions might have been, he was an aging Arab peasant, himself a second-class citizen and refugee whose clumsy attempts to grab land from a homeless widow seem in retrospect more pathetic than evil.

Although Radia cut off all contact with the Sheikh—refusing even to speak to him—her youngest daughter, Yusra, remembers that several years after the court's verdict was handed down, she and her mother passed the former Saffuriyya mayor one Friday as he was walking alone toward Nazareth, bound for noontime prayers at the White Mosque. According to Yusra, he was shuffling, his hands folded behind his back, pitched forward as if deep in thought. He stopped when he saw Radia. He wanted to tell her, he said, that he realized now that she had always been right. He was sorry. Whether his apology was genuine or a manifestation of his well-known penchant for staging dramatic reconciliation ceremonies is impossible to tell. Neither can we say how Radia understood his pronouncement. In any event, Yusra insists her mother was never afraid of Sheikh Saleh: "He was powerful, but she was stronger."

When Taha and his family finally arrived in Reina, meanwhile, they had nowhere to live. They knew they needed to be extremely careful since they were considered infiltrators and could be arrested and expelled from the country at any moment. The irony of their status as trespassers in their homeland was not lost on them; neither was it discussed. But they were hoping that Sheikh Saleh could help them, and so they made their way straight to his house at the center of town, where he welcomed them grandly. His wives cooked them a special meal and arranged bedding for them on the madafeh floor. The next day Sheikh Saleh promised that he would, in due course, try and arrange for them to receive ID cards. Abu Taha was not just any old friend, after all, but an honored and trusted companion. For now he used the power vested in him as local boss and bestowed on them a home of their own on the far edge of town: a low, two-room stone hut, alone in a field, shielded by trees of olive, fig, and almond.

◆

It was quiet in the field. It was quiet in the hut. All the crowding and strife that had surrounded them in Lebanon felt light-years away from this strangely pastoral hideaway, and though as legal residents of no country on earth they remained caught in nerve-wracking limbo, the family was enormously relieved to be restored to the familiar Galilean landscape. Imm Taha still wept often at the memory of Ghazaleh, but she no longer seemed to be teetering on the edge of madness. After nine anguishing months, she had been tearfully reunited with her mother and sister, which soothed her. Abu Taha was grateful for that fact, and he appeared calmed—cheered would be too upbeat a word to describe his brooding mood—to be near some of his old friends. Muhammad Sa'id and Ahmed's sons had ventured off to search for work, while Amin and Feisel enjoyed running in the open meadows around the house: for fun they hunted birds with slingshots. As minors who were not likely to be asked to show their (nonexistent) ID cards, they were also charged with the task of walking regularly to the mukhtar's house in the center of town, where they would collect the Red Cross rations on which the family relied.

For the first time since he was a boy, Taha did not work. He *could* not work, since if he wandered too far from the hut, he might be arrested. Instead, he displayed his usual knack for making the best of a bad situation and began to read with a new hunger, venturing into the unfamiliar realm of Western novels and plays. In Arabic pocketbook translations that he borrowed from friends in Reina, he eagerly took in *The Three Musketeers, Romeo and Juliet,* and Tolstoy's *Resurrection* and *Anna Karenina.* And it was then—left to loll with the masters under those trees—that he began to think seriously about becoming a writer. The way he tells it, this growing awareness of his literary calling came to him not as a dramatic epiphany but as a gradual realization of something that he had always known deep down.

It was also, at this preliminary point, a highly theoretical, fairly romantic notion. He had never written much and was probably capable of composing just the simplest sentences. Though he loved to relate tales aloud, the careful arrangement of words on the page was an alien practice he would need to learn. But with Amira waiting for him in the Lebanese distance, he was, he says, inspired by the "love stories" he encountered in these books. (It is perhaps worth noting that many of these "love stories" end in pain, separation, and death.) And as he tells it now, his despair at the loss of Saffuriyya had also begun to push through to the surface. The break from the village made him conscious of the place in a way that he hadn't been before: it would in fact be decades before Taha even attempted to conjure the village in his writing, yet the germ of the idea that would give way much later to his best poems and stories seems to have been present then, when he was just eighteen years old. At this stage, he says, his feelings toward the place remained inexpressible, and he had no desire to render the village literally in his writing; in those early years, he considered his experience of Saffuriyya an invisible emotional girder or a source of silent inspiration rather than his subject matter. Novels and stories, he believed then, should take on grand themes and not "small, simple things." For now he was like an oyster nursing a grain of sand.

Fiction was Taha's first literary love and what he set out then to try and write. And though he knew no writers personally and had no teacher to guide him, he seems to have understood—in the same instinctive way that he set up his egg business and grocery in Saffuriyya—that he needed to devise a concrete plan of action. He would, he decided, return to the basics of Arabic grammar. His few years of schooling in Saffuriyya had provided him the simplest tools, which allowed him to understand what he read, but the architectonic intricacies of classical fusha were something else altogether. One could spend a lifetime studying its contours and still not master it. He would refer to the language later as "a sea," and though he understood it might take years before he even stuck in a toe, he wanted to read the great works of morphology (*sarf*) and syntax (*nahw*, a term that was also defined by one important eighth-century grammarian as a "way" of behaving ethically). He was determined, once he had improved his Arabic, to begin a systematic study of the pre-Islamic poets, the Qur'an, the *hadith* (the sayings or deeds of the Prophet Muhammad), and *tafsir* (qur'anic exegisis). This, too, might take years, if not decades or a century, but Taha's intellectual goals at this early stage seem to have been characterized both by a young man's soaring, almost limitless ambition and by a much mellower sort of modesty in the face of this vast, difficult, and infinitely rich tradition. Little by little, he hoped to absorb the best of Umayyad verse and the work of the great Abbasid poets—Abu Nuwas, al-Mutanabbi, Abu Tammam, al-Ma'arri. . . . And he wanted, too, to read modern Arabic stories and novels and criticism and maybe even to teach himself English: that would allow him to drink up what he could of world literature in translation. To read it all would take several lifetimes, but there were names he had heard—Anton Chekhov, Guy de Maupassant, Edgar Allan Poe, Percy Bysshe Shelley, Christopher Marlowe—and though he had no idea who these men were or what they had written, he was ravenous to find out. This desire had surely been building within him for years, but it exploded now—whether as refuge from thoughts of the world he had lost in 1948 or as a natural station on an intellectual pilgrim's progress that he would also have reached were he still selling halvah, dates, and indigo from his small shop in Saffuriyya, we will, of course, never know. In any event, Taha was seized by the need to read and to learn, and he found himself in the peculiar position of at once dreading profoundly what the future might hold (discovery, arrest, expulsion, even death) and looking forward with thrilled anticipation to all he hoped lay ahead (knowledge, expression, publication, marriage to Amira). It would be another twenty-five years before Taha's friend-to-be, the novelist Emile Habiby, would dream up his most famous character, the ur-Israeli Arab, Saeed the Pessoptimist, but Taha already found himself living poised between the realms of gloom and light.

◆

The gloom, alas, was everywhere around him, and it often threatened to prevail. First he was hired to carry out the most dismal work—and spent several weeks picking olives from the commandeered trees of Saffuriyya. Together with dozens of other refugees, he was employed at a measly daily rate to harvest his village's olives on behalf of Moshav Tzippori. It seems the authorities knew that some of the laborers were "infiltrators" but had chosen to turn a blind eye, wanting to help the new immigrant Jewish settlers to market the crops as quickly and cheaply as possible. Taha is, again, unusually taciturn when asked to describe the thoughts and feelings that swept him as he shook the green fruit from his former neighbors' trees. "It was hard," is all he'll say.

Then one night, shortly after the family arrived in Reina, Ahmed and Muhammad Sa'id's sons appeared at the hut and announced that they had decided to return to Lebanon. The situation was just too risky for male "infiltrators" their age, whom the Israelis considered armed and dangerous, and so they had, they felt, no choice but to bid their cousins and aunt and uncle good-bye—and to go. This development was, as Taha puts it, "very terrible," since it meant not just the immediate loss of these two young men toward whom he felt tremendous affection and who were as close to him as his brothers but also that their extended family would, it was clear now, be separated for a long time to come—and that Amira would not be arriving in Israel anytime soon. Bidding farewell to his cousins felt, Taha says, "as though we were leaving Saffuri for the second time."

One morning, other visitors arrived unannounced at the hut: it was early and there was a pounding on the door. Taha had been asleep, and his father—fearing the worst—whispered, *"Cover your head with the blanket!"* He did so, but when three Israeli soldiers with rifles entered, Taha drew a corner of the blanket back to peek; he was spotted and, after being asked for an ID card and admitting he had none, he was immediately ordered from the house and onto a waiting truck. (His brothers were too young to interest the authorities, and it seems that Abu Taha's lame leg saved him. As a woman, Imm Taha appears not to have been perceived as a threat.)

What followed sounds like a bad waking dream, but Taha relates the particulars of his arrest now matter-of-factly, almost without emotion: he and the other men on the truck were driven first to the Austrian hospice in Nazareth, where they were corralled into a single large room, together with many others. They were ordered to remain standing. An officer who spoke a bit of Arabic interrogated them in turns. "You!" the man said to Taha, "What is your name?"

"Taha."

"Taha what?"

"Taha Muhammad Ali."

"Taha Muhammad Ali what?"

"Taha Muhammad Ali 'Abd el-Mo'ti."

There was a pause.

"And Muhammad Sa'id 'Abd el-Mo'ti—what is he to you?"

"My uncle."

"And where is your uncle now?"

"In Lebanon."

The officer may or may not have believed this claim—but the mere fact that Taha shared both blood and a name with a notorious "troublemaker" like Muhammad Sa'id seems to have been enough to have sealed his fate. Within minutes, he found himself being blindfolded and pushed roughly onto another truck, together with some seventeen or eighteen others—all local men in their late teens and twenties. They were utterly silent as the wheels began to turn and the truck to lurch: perhaps each was trying to figure out from the pitches and turns in the road where they were being taken; maybe some were praying and others plotting how to escape. Taha says he believed that he might soon be shot dead.

In fact, when the truck arrived at its destination—which they later discovered was right on the armistice line (that is, the border) with Jordan—the soldiers removed their blindfolds and ordered them at gunpoint to "*Go!*" and the prisoners began to scatter eastward. Then the truck pulled away and, after a brief, tense while, a group of them came together and decided to wait until dark to try and sneak back toward Nazareth. One of the men had already been put through this hellish ordeal several times before. The soldiers would arrest him, blindfold him, expel him, and he would return, then other soldiers would arrest him, blindfold him, expel him, and he would return. . . . It was by now a kind of routine, and—despite the guards and mines and army patrols that stood between this man and his home—he had only grown more determined. He promised them he could guide them back: he knew the way all too well.

◆

If the start of this story rings of a nightmare, the end—in Taha's rather sardonic telling—sounds more like a joke. Nightmares and jokes, though, often seem bound in this pessoptimistic context.

After walking for some twelve hours in the dark, an exhausted Taha stumbled across the meadow in Reina and saw the door of the hut propped open. His parents had been waiting up all night, and though others had assured Abu Taha that his son would return ("they always come back"), they had both been racked with worry. Now, at the sight of her eldest, safe and sound, Imm Taha threw her arms around him and wept—this time for joy. His father, meanwhile, chastised him harshly for having pulled back the blanket and shown his face when the soldiers had entered the hut. "Why did you do this? Why?" he demanded to know.

Taha could only grin sheepishly in response: "I had never seen a Jewish soldier before. I wanted to have a look."

NAZARETH I

◆

AFTER THE FLOOD

◆

PASTORAL, UNSULLIED NAZARETH—the glowing little village of pilgrims' picture postcards—may always have been something of a fantasy. So, too, the immaculately peaceful place conjured by certain biblically minded nineteenth-century Western chroniclers: "untainted harmony" ruled there according to one European traveler who paid Jesus' hometown an extended visit in 1846. Yet however sanitized such depictions-for-export may have been, up to the end of the British Mandate, the smallish city, or overgrown hamlet, had somehow managed to maintain its rural aspect and essentially tranquil mien.

Even as, throughout the Mandate, building had spread well beyond the warren of low stone structures that made up its traditional core, the town had somehow always melded with the countryside—both physically and psychologically. Cultivated fields and threshing floors, olive, fig, and Lebanese pine groves spilled over its steep slopes, all the way down to the curving main street. Because their clay-roofed, one-room homes lacked indoor plumbing, the poorer women and girls made regular trips to draw water from the famous fountain known as Mary's Well. (The better-off sent their servants.) But modernization was slowly creeping in: by the 1940s, the town boasted a tennis court, printing press, cigarette factory, movie theater, electric streetlamps, and swank British Council reading room. There was a literate, white-collar middle class, and an aristocracy that lived in large houses appointed with stained glass, red Marseille roof tiles, modish yellow-brown plaster, and even intricate ceiling frescoes. Nonetheless, many of the townspeople continued to live off their land and flocks. The old village clan structure was, too, still very much in place. Extended families lived close together in distinct neighborhoods, and for better or worse, people kept an eye on one another around the clock. Christians made up more than 60 percent of the population during these years—the Greek Orthodox community was roughly equivalent in size to that of the various Catholic, Protestant, Maronite, and Coptic sects combined—and everyone, Muslims included, got along more or less.

If gradual change and the dynamic give-and-take between very different social forces had marked the previous century of life in Nazareth, all of that ended—or came crashing down—in a matter of months. In fact, had a Nazarene Rip van Winkle dozed off in early November 1947 and then roused himself awake just a year later, he would have rubbed his eyes in disbelief. The quiet old town, by turns bucolic and genteel, was gone: it had been swept away by a flash flood of desperate, coursing humanity.

Tiberias, Haifa, Beisan, Safad, Acre—as each of these cities was besieged and eventually fell to the IDF throughout the winter and spring of 1948, refugees had scrambled for safety toward Nazareth. At the same time, many of Nazareth's richer residents had decamped to safety in Lebanon or points farther off. There were ominous signs of what might lie ahead, including what one memoirist describes as "a large number of men in striped uniforms roaming around the meat-broiling kiosks that had begun to fill the area in front of the Casa Nova building in the main street. These men, I was told, were Arab prisoners released from the famous Akko [Acre] Prison by the [British] authorities ahead of the deadline for the departure of the government." And sure enough, after mid-May, a low-grade sort of anarchy did kick in. Municipal salaries went unpaid, the public school was shut down, and the district court ceased to function since, according to the presiding judge, Nazareth was now subject to no country's laws. Soon after, when Palestinian irregulars and several platoons of Fawzi Qawuqji's Iraqi soldiers requisitioned different buildings in town and reportedly stole from and otherwise abused some of the residents, there was no authority in place to stop them.

This fact did not prevent literal torrents of Palestinians from pouring into Nazareth as the July battles raged in the nearby villages and towns. Meanwhile, other citizens left in fear as the Israelis drew closer. The chaos and crowding were intense, and by 6:15 on the evening of July 16, when the town's mayor, Yusuf al-Fahum, and several religious authorities approached IDF headquarters—bearing a white flag and announcing their desire to surrender the city without a fight, since they apparently believed that "resistance would end in defeat and the city's destruction"—it is estimated that Nazareth was home to sixteen thousand permanent residents and twenty thousand refugees.

Over the next several months, as the fighting pounded on in other parts of the country, a highly unstable situation reigned. Of the refugees who came from cities and villages where an Arab population held on, many managed to return to their homes. The vast majority, though, hailed from towns that had been emptied and so continued to camp out in Nazareth. Subject to extremely rough conditions, they slept in churches, convents, mosques, schools, in makeshift tents or shacks—even on the floor of the movie theater. Some bedded

down with family or friends; one businessman recalls how thirty-five people packed themselves into his small home during the week of the conquest. While military law and a strict curfew were immediately imposed on the town—at first from 2 pm to 10 am, later from 7 pm to 6 am—along with an order preventing entrance to or exit from the city limits, refugees appear to have been coming and going often over those months, searching desperately for housing, food, and work, to say nothing of peace of mind.

Israeli documentation from this period is extensive and detailed. The military governor, the minister of minority affairs, the press, and various welfare, health, and religious authorities reported constantly on the situation in Nazareth as it evolved, a fact that stemmed both from the humanitarian challenges posed by the newly bloated size of the town (which would soon become—and remain—the largest all-Arab city in the country) and from the authorities' keen awareness of

Nazareth's delicate international political status or, in the plainer words of one historian, "the public relations problem." Conscious that the eyes of the world—or at least the eyes of the Vatican—were watching, David Ben-Gurion himself had made special provisions before the conquest to safeguard the holy sites in the town, and he had ordered that any soldiers caught looting should be shot "with machine-guns, mercilessly." As one army officer put it: "Because of its importance to the Christian world—the behavior of the occupation forces in the town could serve as a factor in determining the prestige of the young state abroad." The orders handed down to the troops that day warned gravely against harming "a single object or thing in this city," and protested a bit too much perhaps that "our soldiers are enlightened, cultured, and will behave with respect and courtesy toward the religious feelings of the other."

Bizarrely enough, given this official compunction about protecting on pain of death every last Nazarene altar, steeple, and chalice, a day after the town's surrender, a high-ranking commander issued an order to expel all the civilians from Nazareth. Newly appointed military governor Ben Dunkelman said he was "shocked and horrified. I told him I would do nothing of the sort." And although Ben-Gurion eventually stepped in and cabled that the residents should be allowed to remain in their homes, the principled, scandalized Canadian was relieved of his duties as governor. Several weeks later, when Ben-Gurion first toured the conquered city, he is said to have been startled by what he saw: "Why so many Arabs?" he reportedly asked. "Why didn't you expel them?"

Various reports and protocols preserved in the files make reference to the "satisfaction" of the residents and describe how they "look well," are "well-behaved and cordial," and "don't want to leave Nazareth." In the opinion of the minister of minority affairs, offered the week of the surrender, "The people of Nazareth are ready to recognize Israel." He and the other officials emphasized the urgent need to re-. turn the town as quickly as possible to "normalcy" and as such asked the mayor and members of the city council, along with the ranking district court judge, to stay on in their positions. They agreed, as did the 88 members of the Mandatory police force (of an original 170) who remained in town and continued to wear their old British uniforms. One contemporary Jewish newspaper reporter chirped excitedly about what seemed to her the big block party that was "the first 'Israel' Monday in Nazareth," July 19, 1948. According to this slaphappy version of the events, "hundreds of Nazareth residents had abandoned their homes," but many "were joyfully returning." And "how," wonders the reporter, "does the Nazareth population feel about the occupation?" She answers her own question: "The picture is varied and it would be a mistake to imagine that all the population has burst into a united 'Hatikvah.' Much of the present 'hawaja'-ing [ma'am-ing, in Arabic] and 'shalom'ing is merely business with those who are naturally resentful. Some with a backbone even throw you a dirty look that is quite refreshing."

Other newspaper stories from around that time take up the same glib tone or vary it with something a touch more defensive. Toward the end of 1948, for instance, the Mapai-boosting *Palestine Post* made it its business to publish details of the visit to Israel of "Mrs. Zelda Popkin, noted American novelist":

> An assimilationist Jewess until a visit to European D.P. camps "shocked her into Zionism." . . . Mrs. Popkin had gone to Nazareth to see what the town looked like under Israeli occupation. Before going, in her mind's eye she had the picture of Frankfurt under American military occupation in 1945, and of Athens. But in Israel-held Nazareth, she said, she was amazed to find that the Army of Occupation stayed in the background, laying down policy, but tactful, discreet and careful.

At the same time, this rosy view of life in the occupied city is sharply contradicted by the words preserved in many documents lodged in the Israel State Archive files. If the people who'd found refuge in Nazareth weren't eager to leave the town, it may simply have been that the situation beyond its borders was more menacing for being unknown. And the dirty looks that the Jewish journalist found so refreshing were, it seems safe to say, the product of profound shame and confusion brought about by the people's newfound status as second-class citizens, confined by law to their homes for long hours each day and forbidden from leaving town without permission. Many of their great-great-grandfathers were born in Nazareth, and now they were subject to a rigid set of laws imposed on them by a government made up largely of recent immigrants. (The peripatetic Mrs. Popkin, of course, was constrained by no such rules.) Meanwhile, we read of how "there are a large number of residents and refugees without the ability to pay for the most basic goods, and they live off the help they receive from different institutions." Even before the occupation, more than six thousand people had registered to re-

ceive hot meals from a charity established by a Belgian church mission. "But due to lack of funds, they are able to distribute just one
portion of bread and soup every two days." The Baptists, the Red
Cross, UNICEF, the English and French hospitals, the Anglican orphanage, and various convents were scrambling to help feed and
clothe the refugees, but the demand was far greater than the supply.

Throughout the autumn and winter, the people of Nazareth continued to suffer from a severe water shortage, widespread hunger, and
"deplorable" sanitary conditions, especially among the refugees. In
December, at the behest of the Israeli welfare authorities, the Christian Arab social worker Sami Jeraysi wrote a report in which he estimated that five thousand refugees were still housed in the town and
warned that "the vast majority . . . are facing the danger of hunger and
cold because of the lack of food and clothing, most of them having
been forced to sell all their belongings to feed their large families." He
also predicted that the size of this uprooted population, along with
the widespread unemployment and lack of supplies and "the tremendous differences in the outlooks between the different classes," was
bound to "sow discord among them, and lead them down crooked
paths." With no room for them in the Nazareth schools, the refugee
children, Jeraysi wrote, "run shouting through the alleys at all hours
of the day." The number of shoeshine boys and "loiterers" in Nazareth
had, he noted, increased drastically of late.

Another Palestinian employee of the new Israeli government was
Dr. M. A. Shammas, the Nazareth District's chief medical officer. A
Jerusalemite and veteran of the British army during World War II, he
patiently wrote a monthly English-language report on the health of
the troubled town. Reading his regular, dry, though evocative summaries now, one can almost smell the sorrow in the streets—not to
mention the sewage.

> Although [the refugees'] places were sprayed with D.D.T. so-
> lution and they were all inoculated against typhoid, yet we
> find that no improvement could be achieved in the sanitary
> conditions of their dwellings and, therefore, the health stan-
> dard between them is very low. Add to this the shortage of
> water supply, and the poverty prevailing, will make it difficult
> to improve their condition. It is requested that this problem

will be attended to from the Medical and Human sides, and
that all the refugees in Nazareth may be returned to their former places. If this is done, diseases will drop down, sanitary
conditions will greatly improve, and the water supply might
suffice the needs of Nazareth['s] original population.

The Jewish military governor of Nazareth, for his part, tended
to condescend where matters of sanitation and health were concerned. "Here," one document quotes this lifelong liberal as explaining to the members of a visiting UN delegation, "we have run into objective difficulties: it is difficult to supervise the Arabs where hygiene
is concerned."

Not all the Israelis were as patronizing as the military governor.
One of the most powerful descriptions of the squalor in which the
refugees languished was written by a Jewish official from the Ministry
of Religions, whose acute concern was twofold—for the Palestinians,
forced to suffer, and for the Israelis, who bore the primary responsibility for their plight: "I have worked in this city for a month now . . . ," he
writes in a letter addressed to the minister of religions, but obviously
aimed at those still higher up, "and I have come to the conclusion that
there will be little value in all of our efforts, and our achievements will
not last long if no solution is found to the central problems that come
from the miserable conditions—both in the material and spiritual
spheres—in which the Arab residents and refugees here live." He
continues: "With my own eyes I saw 500–600 refugees crowded into
one building, sick children ailing on a dirty floor, elderly men crying
like boys because of the lack of work and bread." He warns that if help
isn't given—"for both humanitarian and Jewish reasons"—there will
be chaos, and "there will be no value to what we've done. . . . The
honor of Israel requires that the few Arabs remaining in the land of
Israel find in it conditions befitting every human being above whose
head the heavens stretch."

Identifying the problem, though, was one thing; fixing it was another. By now, the powers that be clearly recognized the gravity of the
situation and understood that it had somehow to be improved, whether
out of moral, political, or "security" considerations. Early in 1949, the
military governor himself wrote that "these people [the refugees] live in
Nazareth in the very worst conditions, without anything," and consti-

tute "a heavy burden." Various high-ranking government committees were soon formed and proposals put forth, suggesting a range of complicated schemes for handling the matter. The most popular idea was to return the Haifa refugees to that city and concentrate all the rural refugees in a single village, far from the border and from their old homes. Although the Haifa dwellers were eventually allowed to go back and some of the peasants were sent to live in Shafa 'Amr, nothing ever came of the more grandiose relocation plan. A list of possible jobs for the remaining Nazareth refugees was brainstormed—at a workshop for the manufacture of curbstones, fifty jobs; at a garage for car repairs, twenty jobs; and so on—and as part of its official recommendations, the Interministerial Committee for Nazareth Matters asserted that "refugee-ism should be stamped out" once and for all.

Alas, the thousands of refugees who had no choice but to stay on in Nazareth—in 1951, they constituted a quarter of the town's population—seem not to have heard the news.

◆

In the autumn of 1949, when Taha and his family finally arrived in the crowded town, they had somehow to try and make of the battered city a home.

The brand-new Israeli identity cards they had just received in the most dramatic circumstances allowed them to stay in the country as legal residents. And though that may sound an unspectacular thing— every one of them, after all, was born in Palestine and, with the exception of the brief, spontaneous sojourn to Lebanon, had spent his or her entire law-abiding life within a single Saffuriyyan square mile, which is to say, three miles from Nazareth—receiving these little blue booklets was hardly a given. But after Taha's arrest, expulsion, and safe return on foot from Jordan to Reina, Sheikh Saleh Salim had decided at long last to intervene with the authorities on behalf of his old friend Abu Taha. In his typical, rather pomp-heavy fashion, Sheikh Saleh had arranged for a banquet to be served to the Nazareth military governor and the chief of police, as well as a contingent of other Jews in uniform. Various former Saffuriyya villagers were also invited, as was Sheikh Saleh's retinue from Reina, and the large group of men assembled in the area of the old Saffuriyya basatin—the orchards—

to eat the lavish spread Sheikh Saleh had provided, as it seems that he did regularly for the governor. He was, it is worth noting, far from alone in practicing what one historian of the period dubs "mealtime bribery." In this charged context, food became a political tool, as Jewish officials exploited the Arabs' famous hospitality, frequently partaking of extravagant repasts in the homes of the most impoverished and terrified Palestinians, who had little choice but to play gracious host to any member of the military government who happened to pay a call. So, too, Palestinians desperate to secure their legal status in the country would host "weekly parties" for Israeli officers who they believed, often wrongly, could help them. Like these others, it appears Sheikh Saleh understood that in order to have the governor's ear, he needed first to get to his stomach.

Abu Taha, meanwhile, had not wanted to attend the lunch at all and had to be coaxed by the sheikh into coming. It is clear from the way that Amin and Taha both relate the story that their father had no interest whatsoever in playing groveling games to curry favor. He had eaten little and talked less during the meal, and now—after the roast lamb and spiced rice were served, after the fruit and sweets and black coffee proffered, at the first significant pause, that is, in the highly choreographed proceedings—Abu Taha stood to speak. He was a man with little left to lose, and so he did not mince words and addressed the governor directly. Amin relates what he said now, playing the role of his father and fixing me straight in the eye, as if I were the military governor. He neither pleads nor accuses, but states: "I left my village. I lost everything. I have nothing. I cannot live this way. My children cannot work. And now I want to ask something simple of you: either put my family in a car and drive us back to the Lebanese border, or give us ID cards and let us stay here."

The gamble paid off. After Sheikh Saleh vouched for the family's uprightness, one of the governor's men was ordered to transcribe Abu Taha's particulars, and a week later Taha and his father received a summons to appear downtown at the headquarters of the Nazareth military governor. There an Arab clerk pummeled them with questions: Where have you been? What work did you do there? Who told you to come back? Which route did you take? What did you bring with you? "It was nonsense," according to Taha. "These are questions that need no answers." But they responded honestly, he says, and that very day they each received a temporary ID, followed several weeks later by the true blue thing. They did not know it then, but the numbers they were issued were coded to indicate that they had left the country and returned. Even now, almost sixty years later, Taha says, Nazareth bank, health clinic, and post office clerks will look at his card, see his number, and ask him about his time in Lebanon. It follows him like a shadow. The Israelis had also seen fit to assign Taha a new name. Never mind that Palestinians are traditionally known by their name and their father's—that is, Taha Muhammad Ali; the authorities decided unilaterally that Muhammad Ali was Taha's middle name and "gave" him a last name, 'Abd el-Mo'ti, after his grandfather. And though this remains what he is called on all official documents, Taha has always written and published on his own terms, as Taha Muhammad Ali.

When asked what it felt like to first carry an Israeli identity card, Taha looks at me a bit blankly and makes it clear that steep philosophical thoughts about national belonging and the meaning of citizenship could not, at that point, have been further from his mind. The family was relieved, he says, to be allowed to stay, and the period following their arrival in town was marked for him by a resolute sense of what must be done to survive, both physically and intellectually. He meant not only to provide for his parents and brothers but to proceed along the writerly road that he had mapped for himself while reading and thinking in Reina. Physical survival took priority, of course, though perhaps the promise of those other, internal pursuits added incentive to establish a steady income as quickly as possible.

The most pressing order of Nazareth business was to find a place to live, which they did right away, renting a dark vaulted room deep in the old suq. This was once a grand house that had been the home of a single wealthy family, but now the owner, one Abu George, lived upstairs and rented the downstairs rooms individually, each to a family of refugees. Taha estimates that six or seven families, each of six to ten people, lived without electricity around the small courtyard that year, sharing a "primitive bathroom." To reach this community outhouse in the dark, Taha says, one would have to take a kerosene lantern and make the perilous trip out across the slippery stones. "More than once someone would—" he indicates with great hilarity a slapstick fall on the backside. Every month Abu George would appear at their door, "with the fez on his head and the cane in his hand," saying, "Give me the money, the rent money."

Taha's second act on coming to Nazareth was to buy himself his first-ever pair of long khaki pants and a cotton shirt and to discard his qumbaz and skullcap for good. He was eighteen years old, and with his trim little mustache and a fair, sometimes unruly pompadour that he tried to train with a bit of pomade, he now looked like a dashing young man of the city. This appears to have been a conscious choice. His father, for his part, wore his long qumbaz, white kaffiyeh, and black 'igal until his dying day.

Appropriately outfitted for his new urban clime, Taha then did what he'd learned in Lebanon and collected some wood scraps, fashioned a portable display box, and set out again to sell lighters, needles, and the like, this time picking a spot near Nazareth's central bus station. He also added a twist to his usual merchandise and began hawking black-market chocolate bars and cans of jam, which later gave way to more serious contraband, like black-market sugar, coffee, and even ration book "points" for buying shoes and clothing.

Since May 1949, when the Israeli government had passed its controversial Austerity Plan, the black market had been thriving throughout the country. The plan, based on British World War II–time rationing and price controls, was designed to help—in the words of its mastermind, Canadian-born minister of supplies and rationing Dov Yosef—"a small nation in a poor country, a nation that must absorb masses of immigrants, build them houses, settle and bring back to life the desolate areas of the country." As Yosef's rhetoric should make clear, the plan was presented to the Jewish public in patriotic terms. "Pioneer Poverty" it was dubbed by the fiercely nationalistic poet Uri Tzvi Greenberg, while future prime minister Golda Meir offered an ultimatum: "either ration immigration or ration food and clothing."

And while furious Knesset debates raged around the amount of albumen found in milk powder and whether or not "sweet potatoes were just as nourishing but one-third cheaper than ordinary potatoes" or how many "points" equaled the value of diapers, dishcloths, and cotton pajamas—almost no public mention was made of the 160,000 Palestinian residents of the state, who were also subject to the austerity menu and forced to line up with their ration booklets in hand, just like their Jewish counterparts, but who were given little of the same high-minded communal inspiration to limit their caloric intake or go without new shoes. The rations themselves, which included distinctly northern items like margarine, herring, frozen cod, and egg powder, must have seemed very strange indeed to the Palestinian palate, as must the officially regulated loaves that were the only sort that were produced legally in the country's bakeries during those years. This so-called black bread was really soft, white, and sliceable, a distant cousin to the round—flat or pocketed—sorts of wood-oven breads that Palestinians usually ate.

As the government budgeted rations for dried onions, halvah, and macaroni, the black market boomed among Jews and Arabs alike, with individuals selling off coupons their families didn't want and shopping illegally for the items they preferred or needed. At the same time, kibbutzim, wholesalers, stores, and factories floated far more serious scams, and a complex subterranean economy developed. These under-the-table transactions became so ubiquitous, in fact, that one contemporary Hebrew account called the black market "an illness that's gnawing at the gut of the Yishuv." Though here and there a Jewish citizen might have felt a modicum of guilt at cheating the national coffers this way, a Palestinian in Taha's position would have had little reason to think twice before buying up goods that certain people did not want and selling them off to others who did.

Most of his customers were Jews—many of them soldiers—who traveled to Nazareth for the express purpose of doing business on the black market, and Taha had two friends with whom he worked, Muhammad Tawfiq, from a distinguished Nazareth family, and Hussein "the Red-Head," a refugee from Tiberias. The three were organized and would divide, for instance, a large bag of sugar into ten smaller parcels, each labeled according to its amount, then they'd deposit the sacks in a hiding place—a stairwell or the foyer of a house. The transaction would unfold with one of the trio first offering a passerby something legal like matches or shoelaces, then asking—under his breath and in the few words of basic Hebrew that he had just started to learn—"You want to buy sugar? You want coffee?" If the answer was yes and a price agreed upon, Taha or one of his colleagues would dash off to retrieve the goods, and many times, he says, they returned to the site where they'd concealed their cache to find it missing or its quantity drastically reduced. Knowing the young men had no legal recourse against the theft of black-market goods, people simply helped themselves to whatever they found.

Though extremely common, such wheeling and dealing was risky. There were inspectors all around, and every now and then Taha and the others would be caught and arrested—as, it seems, would many of those whom David Ben-Gurion himself called "small fry." The big industrialists ran off with huge profits, the prime minister complained, while the prisons spilled with petty offenders. Indeed, the Israel Police files labeled "War on the Black Market" are crammed with documents like the one that describes the criminal investigation opened in 1950 against the owners of Jerusalem's (now-illustrious) Alba Pharmacy, where "a search was conducted and certain [illegal] quantities of cotton balls were discovered." Taha, meanwhile, spent the night in jail on several occasions, locked in a cell with thugs and crooks of all sorts. Was he scared? "The first time, sure. You see the whole world as this small room. Then you get used to it, and it starts to seem normal."

But what choice did he really have? In the morning, he says, he would pay his ten-lira fine—two full days' earnings—retrieve his box of odds and ends, then make his way back to the street.

LIKE WATER AND AIR

◆

WHEN LITERARY HISTORIANS—and Palestinian writers them-selves—describe the Arabic cultural landscape that existed in Israel immediately following 1948, they tend to resort to the starkest, most el-emental vocabulary: "Culturally speaking," writes a Galilee-born jour-nalist and novelist, "the Arab reader [in Israel] lived in a desert." In the words of one of the more charismatic local poets who came of age dur-ing that time, "For ten years Israeli Arab intellectuals were starved of any nourishment from the sources of current Arabic literary creativity." Another novelist ups the ante and writes that "for twenty years the Arabs of Israel breathed with one lung." And in the apocalyptic terms favored by perhaps the greatest Palestinian prose writer to have lived through that time in Israel, "Nothing was left here but a dying ember and a few mouths breathing in cinders, and a raging wind blowing across the desolate wasteland, scattering ghosts of ash."

In objective terms, all of this was true: the vast majority of Pal-estine's intellectuals had fled the country during the fighting and opted for exile after it ended, leaving those who stayed behind or snuck back—a battered-down and largely illiterate peasant population—to fend for themselves both politically and culturally. It was, as one out-side observer put it, "a demoralized, disillusioned, disorganized, het-erogeneous remnant. Its leaders had gone; it had no spokesmen." Of those who clung on in Nazareth, "not a single inhabitant had published a book. The 'capital' of Galilee," according to another eye-witness, "boasted neither publishing house nor printing press [at first], and when I came to live there in 1958, there was but one poor bookshop." For a full decade, almost no Arabic books were available for sale in Israel, a situation brought about by the Arab states' blockade of Israel and Israel's strict censorship policies. Arabic books were neither imported nor printed within the country for several years, and even after initial attempts were made to publish locally, the number of volumes that emerged was minuscule. One scholar who has surveyed the situation that prevailed during the first ten years of Israel's existence counted just eight books of Arabic poetry, written by five poets—this, though poetry had been for centuries that language's most privileged and popular form of literary expression.

Even the local Arabic press was severely circumscribed. While the Israeli Communist Party offered a small flicker of intellectual light in the otherwise smothering darkness and did continue to publish and distribute by hand its important Arabic weekly, *al-Ittihad* (The Union), which had been founded in 1944, the only Arabic daily in Israel during those years was the government-sponsored *al-Yawm* (Today), described variously as "a small paper, poor in both shape and content," "a mouthpiece for official propaganda," and—by the Baghdadi Jewish immigrant who once served as its editor-in-chief!—the "laughingstock of [those] it was supposed to serve and give expression to." Reading old copies of that amateurish, clumsily whitewashing newspaper now, all these characterizations seem like generous understatements. What was a Palestinian reader living under the watchful rule of an Israeli military governor to do with a news item about the ceremonial opening of a Jewish Agency office in West Berlin or with the Arabic translation of a speech by Prime Minister David Ben-Gurion titled "The State of Israel Belongs to All the Jewish People"? How should she regard the festive blue ink in which the paper was printed in honor of Israel's Independence Day? All Arab teachers and government employees, meanwhile, had the cost of a subscription to *al-Yawm* deducted automatically from their salaries. The overall situation was perhaps summed up best in a single line (novelist Anton Shammas calls it the "best known [line] in local Arabic literature") written in 1956 by the Nazareth poet Michel Haddad, who had then recently come to be one of Taha's best friends: "Farewell to thee, ability to breathe!"

But one does not choose the era into which one is born, and for those aspiring young writers like Taha and the smattering of his Palestinian contemporaries who were beginning to make their literary way in Israel during these years, there was little choice but to make do with what was at hand—often literally. Stories abound about the feverish transcription into school notebooks of the few Arabic books that did exist and were passed from desperate reader to reader. Na'ila Zayyad, the widow of the poet and legendary future mayor of Nazareth Taw-fiq Zayyad, described to me how, sometime in the early 1950s, her husband-to-be—then an impoverished construction worker—had bor-rowed the tenth-century poet Abu al-'Ala' al-Ma'arri's darkly satirical prose work, *The Epis-*

tle of Forgiveness, from Nazareth's one tiny lending library, the only "bookstore" in town, and spent several frenzied nights writing it out, word by word, so that he would have his own copy to keep. Not only was al-Ma'arri himself medieval, so was this scribelike method of tex-tual reproduction.

The Nazareth human rights lawyer and story writer Walid al-Fahum remembers how, when he was in high school, one of his Christian friends traveled to Jordan. At that time, certain Israeli Christians—those who were politically "kosher" in the eyes of the government—enjoyed privileges that Muslims and Communists did not and were allowed to make Christmas pilgrimages to the holy sites across the border in then-Jordanian East Jerusalem. When his friend returned from abroad, he came bearing an unbelievably precious gift for Walid—a book of poems by Fadwa Tuqan, which Walid then cir-culated throughout his high school class according to the labor-intensive method these poetry-hungry teenagers had already per-fected: one student would copy the poems by hand, then pass this notebook version along to the next student on the chain, who would recopy them into his own notebook, then pass on *his* notebook to an-other friend . . . and so on until, as Walid estimates, some twenty stu-dents would possess (literal) copies of the book.

The poet Hanna Abu Hanna, who was already working as a teacher at the municipal high school in Nazareth in 1948 and who had managed as a student in pre-nakba Jerusalem to accumulate a small but serious library for himself, found that he could not, during those difficult later years, refuse needy friends who came asking to borrow particular titles. "On the contrary," he laughs ruefully. "I used to say, take this book." Most of the volumes were never returned, and in this way, his collection slowly dwindled. Abu Hanna also recalls the "funny, tragic" instance in the autumn of 1948 when Palestinian workers from Nazareth were recruited—as Taha had been, in what had become Moshav Tzippori—to harvest the olives of Lydda and Ramla. Almost all of the some sixty thousand Palestinian residents of these neighboring towns had been driven out by the Israeli army during the same week that Saffuriyya and Nazareth were conquered, and besides forsaking the bounty of their groves, many of them were forced—by troops operating under the command of, among others, Moshe Dayan and Yitzhak Rabin—to leave their doors unlocked and their well-appointed houses wide open: some of the Nazarene olive-pickers ventured into these empty homes and took the books they found there.

Abu Hanna remembers in particular an edition of *Kitab al-aghani*, Abu al-Faraj al-Isfahani's magisterial "Book of Songs," the multivolume, tenth-century anthology of poems, biographical sketches, and historical miscellanea that many consider the greatest compilation of classical Arabic literature in existence. (Taha himself has said that if he were sent to live on a desert island and could take only a single book, he would choose *Kitab al-aghani*—a choice that echoes the words of the medieval philologist, belletrist, vizier, and renowned bibliophile al-Sahib ibn 'Abbad, who, according to one chronicle, "when travelling, used to take thirty camel-loads of books about with him, but on receiving the *Aghani* . . . contented himself with this one book and dispensed with all the rest.") Its arrival in Nazareth was, Abu Hanna says, "something great!" and whatever uneasiness the workers may have felt at looting the libraries of the Lydda and Ramla refugees, their act seems to have been viewed by others as understandable, even admirable. Besides, the Israelis had already sent trucks to start carting off furniture from the homes and goods from the shops. In this harsh, finders-keepers context, the olive-pickers could view their own theft of this literary jewel as a kind of rescue mission—for the sake both of the abandoned volumes, which would now find an appreciative new audience, and of themselves, so thirsty for reading material. The ironies, of course, were multiple—not least the fact that

Kitab al-aghani owed its composition to historical circumstances so painfully distant from those that now faced Taha and Hanna Abu Hanna, Tawfiq Zayyad, Michel Haddad, and the others. According to a later commentator on Abu al-Faraj's masterpiece, which had been composed at the height of Baghdad's Abbasid glory: "[Abu al-Faraj] used to go into the bazaar of the booksellers when it was flourishing and the shops were filled with books, and he would buy numbers of volumes which he would carry home. And all his narratives were derived from them."

◆

Here and there, other cracks opened up, and a bit of air from the outside world slipped through. Some of the Iraqi Jewish immigrants, for instance, brought Arabic books with them when they arrived in the country: Sasson Somekh, the distinguished, Baghdad-born scholar of modern Arabic literature, was himself an ambitious seventeen-year-old Arabic poet when he left his family and the mounting anti-Jewish hostility behind in Iraq and came to Israel, "not from Zionist motives, but rather out of an urge for adventure and rebellion." Along with this appetite for the unknown, when he stepped off the airplane in Lod in 1951, Somekh carried the precious cargo of three modern Arabic books, one of them inscribed to him by Badr Shakir al-Sayyab, the groundbreaking Iraqi poet.

For nearly a millennium and a half, Arabic poetry had, with rare exceptions, been written in either a regular, two-hemistich line, using a fixed meter and single end rhyme, or according to a prescribed set of rhymed strophic modes; it tended to rely as well on an extremely fixed stock of images. Then in the late 1940s, together with the Baghdadi woman poet Nazik al-Mala'ika, al-Sayyab had introduced enjambment, uneven line lengths, and irregular rhymes, along with a whole battery of mythic and symbolist tropes taken over in large part from Baudelaire, T. S. Eliot, and other European moderns. In doing so, he had broken free of the classical—by-then highly mannered and calcified—*qasida* (ode) form and, in the course of just a few years, made Arabic poetry newer than it had been for centuries. The formal and conceptual changes wrought by these two poets and their successors launched modern Arabic poetry as it is now known. And although

the technical ins and outs of their then highly controversial innovations may sound almost comically arcane (instead of following one of
the standard quantitative meters from end-stopped line to end-stopped
line, the new poetry—known in Arabic as *shi'r hurr,* free verse—was
based on the repetition as the poet saw fit of a single kind of "foot"
throughout a poem), it is important to note, as many have, that this
revolution in form corresponded directly to the political and social
upheavals then rocking the Middle East. New circumstances demanded new poetry. And though the complex processes of cultural
modernization and literary regeneration at work had their origins
in the *nahda,* the "revival" or "renaissance" that had been gaining
ground and bringing Western forms and ideas to bear on Arabic literature and life throughout the Middle East since the end of the nine-
teenth century, the fall of Palestine in 1948 marked more decisively
than any other event had the cataclysmic end of one era and the start
of another.

Yet—odd as it sounds—while such poetic earthquakes were leveling literary landforms from Cairo to Beirut, the Palestinian epicen-
ter remained mostly still. Raised in cosmopolitan Baghdad, with its
literati-filled cafés and cutting-edge bookstores, Somekh for one found
in Israel of 1951 something of an Arabic intellectual void. He was
quick to befriend the small group of devoted Communist writers and
activists who were publishing *al-Ittihad* in Haifa—and who had, that
same year, founded the party's seminal literary magazine, *al-Jadid*
(The New), then the sole local outlet for Arabic letters. (The Communist Party, it is important to note, was in those years the single political party in Israel to admit Arabs as full members.) But he says quietly
now that "they were totally isolated, totally. And that was the saddest
thing." Though the work of al-Sayyab and others was taking the rest
of the Arab world by storm, "they'd never heard [of him] before. . . .
And I couldn't let them borrow my book. That was too dear to me, because I got it from Sayyab himself. But I had a few things that I'd cut
from newspapers before I left." He passed these clippings on, to be
read, hand-copied, and circulated, and gradually the new forms began
to seep into the local literary imagination, soon coming to dominate.
Indeed, much of the most famous Palestinian "poetry of resistance"
that would be written in later years would take its cues from the so-
called Iraqi style of free verse, though Mahmoud Darwish, Samih al-

Qasim, and the other poets who would become celebrities throughout the Arab world for writing this fiery sort of political verse were, for the most part, still children when Somekh arrived with the word from Baghdad. And although his behind-the-scenes role in the development of contemporary Palestinian literature in Israel was clearly important, he speaks with real modesty about it now and laughs, saying he feels like the first man to import a tomato from the New World.

The intense isolation Somekh describes is confirmed by the local poets themselves—including the Reina-born Hanna Abu Hanna, who had at around the same time also begun, on his own, to experiment with jagged lines and uneven rhyme schemes. Then a young Communist who had been writing and publishing his poems before 1948, he was, he says, inspired both by the revolutionary spirit of the British Romantics and by the Soviet rebel Vladimir Mayakovsky's charge to, in Abu Hanna's words, "match the rhythm of a poem with its meaning and atmosphere," and he felt that he must push past the constrictions of classical Arabic verse: the historical moment demanded an engaged poetic and political response. He had, he says, never heard of Badr Shakir al-Sayyab and Nazik al-Mala'ika (neither did he yet know Somekh), and only several years after he attempted his own first poems in a freer mode did he encounter their verse and come to understand that this wasn't his own private paradigm shift but that, as he put it, "the time had been ripe" for shattering the old forms.

Taha, meanwhile, was at a very different stage in his literary and political development. With just four years of dubious Saffuriyya schooling behind him and a reading life that had been rich, though— Fadwa Tuqan's *My Brother Ibrahim,* a few Arabic translations of Tolstoy novels, some detective stories, and one Shakespeare play aside— largely confined to pre-Islamic poems, the Qur'an, and popular Arabic epics, he had probably never heard of Mayakovsky, let alone Badr Shakir al-Sayyab. But he was also wise enough to know how much he didn't know, and, determined to carry out the plan he'd devised in Reina, he began at the absolute beginning: he somehow got hold of a series of Arabic textbooks and started his work on the first page. What is a noun? What is a verb? He worked intently, methodically, pushing forward from book 1 to book 2 to book 3. At the same time, he began to study English on his own, and—using a similar set

of elementary primers—he progressed from the alphabet to simple
vocabulary and grammar to the most basic texts. When he finished
the five levels of that introductory series, he graduated to abridged
versions of English books published by Palestine's Mandate-era Ministry of Education. These included *Treasure Island, Robin Hood,* and
The Loves of Carmen. He estimates that he borrowed and devoured
some fifteen volumes this way before he proceeded with great excitement to his first "real" English book, *The Prisoner of Zenda.* And from
there, he made his way to a secondhand copy of Cleanth Brooks and
Robert Penn Warren's 1936 *An Approach to Literature,* which offered
a selection of European and American stories, essays, and poems, together with such no-nonsense New Critical questions as "This story,
like most stories by Guy de Maupassant, has an ironical effect. From
what does this irony spring?"

At the same time, he had happened unexpectedly on a treasure
trove that he would later refer to as "my first serious school." A neigh-

bor who knew that Taha liked to read offered him hundreds of back issues of the
widely read and respected Cairo literary
weekly, *al-Risala* (The Message, Letter,
or Treatise), among the most popular of
the many Egyptian periodicals that had
flooded the middle-class Palestinian market in the years before 1948. The neighbor was the father of a Communist activist who had left the country during the
war and who had been a faithful sub-
scriber since the magazine's inception in
1933. Taha was thrilled to receive the
stash, for which, he says, he insisted on paying, despite the man's
protestations that he had no room and no need for the heaps of old
journals.

So it was that Taha came to immerse himself over a short period
in several heady decades' worth of literary essays and cultural commentary by, among many others, the trailblazing critics 'Abbas Mahmud al-'Aqqad and Muhammad Mandur, and by the greatest of all
Egyptian men of letters, Taha Hussein. Each of the three played a
central role in defining modern Egyptian culture—which is to say, *the*

modern Arab culture of its time. Each was also, in his distinct way, strongly influenced by European thought and letters and, at the same time, devoted heart and soul to the study, analysis, and even lionization of the classical Arabic literary tradition. Known as a poet and novelist as well as a critic, al-'Aqqad drew his methodological and stylistic inspiration in large part from Shelley, Coleridge, and William Hazlitt, as he wrote articles and books about al-Ma'arri, al-Mutanabbi, Abu Nuwas, Ibn al-Rumi, and other major ancient Arabic and Islamic poets. Advocating what he called the "poetry of personality," he wrote of the need for the poet to express his own quirks and "inner life," instead of simply speaking on behalf of the tribe: "the poet who cannot be recognized from his poetry does not deserve recognition." Mandur also drew from both Occident and Orient and, in his theorizing about medieval Arabic literary criticism and contemporary Egyptian theater, wrote under the influence of such nineteenth-century French critics as Charles-Augustin Sainte-Beuve, Georges Duhamel, and Jules Lemaître.

The blind, village-born al-Azhar–trained Taha Hussein was, meanwhile, by far the most important Arab intellectual of his time: the first graduate of a modern Egyptian university and later its first native dean of the arts, he earned a doctorate from the Sorbonne—by writing about the great fourteenth-century historian Ibn Khaldun under the supervision of Émile Durkheim, the French father of modern sociology. Hussein then returned to Egypt and went on to become a prolific and accomplished essayist, critic, polemicist, short story writer, memoirist, novelist, and translator, president of the Academy of Arabic Language, and eventually Egypt's minister of education, in which capacity he brought to the most remote rural reaches of that country the newfangled notion of free schooling. "Knowledge," he declared, "is like water and air" and should be available to all.

Writing in an elegant yet unfussy style, the very lucidity of which was part and parcel of his democratic vision, Hussein was the foremost proponent of an Egyptian nationalism that advocated outright the "adoption of Western techniques and ideas." He even put forth the concept that Egyptian culture was essentially Hellenistic and belonged to a hybrid, Westward-looking "Mediterranean Culture," as opposed to a pan-Arab one. "We must follow the path of the Europeans," he wrote in 1938, "so as to be their equals and partners in civ-

ilization, in its good and evil, its sweetness and bitterness, what can
be loved or hated, what can be praised or blamed." At the same time,
he wrote with passion about the entire corpus of Arabic literature,
most famously and scandalously, in his critical studies of pre-Islamic
poetry—which he claimed was in large part a much later creation. By
implication, he suggested that the Qur'an, too, was a fiction and not
the word of God.

The influence that these critics would one day exert on Taha
Muhammad Ali's writing life cannot be underestimated: his freedom
of thought, his lack of pretension, his devout secularism, his tolerance, his clarity, his willingness to learn lessons from East and West,
universal and local, old and new alike—these are perhaps the most
notable traces of their ideas on his work. Although there are certainly
sharp differences between these critics and Taha as well—most notably in their stern defense of a "pure" (noncolloquial) Arabic and in
al-'Aqqad and Hussein's rigid insistence on the need for poetry to possess both meter and rhyme—the criticism he absorbed then, whether
consciously or not, appears to have affected him in other ways. Both
al-'Aqqad and Mandur wrote quite explicitly about the role of art in
society and politics, demanding, for instance, as al-'Aqqad did: "Give
us a poet who composes a poem in which he makes the Egyptians love
the flower, and I guarantee [that it will give us] the greatest national
benefit and the truest renaissance." For much of his life, Mandur advocated the detachment of art from ideological concerns; Taha shares
with him the refusal to see literature as beholden to any straightforward political program or party. (All three Egyptian critics were, it is
worth noting, attacked by left-leaning writers who saw their Romantic ideas as being antisocial, hermetic, and reactionary.) Mandur's
idea of al-adab al-mahmus, "whispered literature," also seems to have
left its mark on Taha, whose work is free of "the declamatory tone
which has dominated and corrupted Arabic poetry since the days of
[the great tenth-century panegyrist] al-Mutanabbi," in the words of
one scholar, describing Mandur's term.

And perhaps most important of all, al-'Aqqad wrote of how the
figure he calls the wayfarer "sees poetry, if he wishes, everywhere . . .
he sees it in the house he lives in, and in the street he walks every day,
in the shop windows, in the car . . . because all these are linked with

daily life and everything which is linked with human life is entangled in our feelings and is therefore fit to be expressed."

It would, again, be years before Taha would begin to express such feelings on paper or try to conjure the lost daily world of Saffuriyya in his poems. But the lessons he was learning on the pages of *al-Risala* were crucial—and his apprenticeship as a writer in training had at long last begun.

◆

Many of the ideas put forth on the yellowing newsprint of these old copies of *al-Risala* were, by the time Taha encountered them, "out of date." The world, and especially the Arab world, had changed dramatically since 1933, and even the blocky art deco outline of the Cairo skyline that often graced the journal's brightly colored cover must—with its few spare minarets, domes, and leaning palms—no longer (if ever) have borne much relation to the actual, crowded thing. But this didn't matter to Taha, who felt he had a lot of catching up to do and who seems also to have subscribed instinctively to E. M. Forster's notion of the contemporaneous quality of all good writing. ("Time . . . is to be our enemy. We are to visualize the English novelists . . . as seated together in a room, a circular room, a sort of British Museum reading room, all writing their novels simultaneously.") What difference did it make to him whether an essay was fifteen years old or a poem dated from 1253? If it had something to teach him, it was utterly fresh.

Oddly enough, Taha's belated introduction to twentieth-century letters, along with his readiness to take on the humbling, exhilarating role of the autodidact, appears to have made it easier for him to endure the cultural depredations of that post-'48 period. That is, while his more formally educated and worldly contemporaries were achingly aware of all the books, journals, and bold new ideas from which they'd been cut off because of the political situation, Taha was starting from the ground up and so was thankful for every text that came his way. His intellectual glass was more than half full, and he read with the most catholic curiosity and sense of gratitude. He did not, meanwhile, take the job of autodidact lightly but invested both effort and money in the project of educating himself and began, at this time, to commit to memory large chunks of Arabic poetry, especially by al-Mutanabbi, a practice he says was like the process of building up muscles. And he relates now how he saved to buy the very best ten-volume Arabic dictionary, *Taj al-'arus* (The Crown of the Bride—a medieval Arabic forebear of the *Oxford English Dictionary*), which a Jewish peddler from Jaffa sold him for thirty liras, or some eighty-five dollars. "In the fifties, with thirty liras you could buy a dunam of land. I decided to buy the dictionary."

Taha had also begun to look for a steadier way to make a living, and after several months of exhausting black-market hustling, he had a promising new thought. Surveying the traffic flow in downtown Nazareth and noting in particular the popularity of the Empire Cinema, which sat smack-dab at the corner of Nazareth's busiest intersection, he rented a tiny, nearly closet-sized kiosk right across from the theater, then arranged to buy black-market cooking oil and chickpeas—and set up shop as Nazareth's newest and perhaps most erudite falafel vendor.

It was a family affair. Every night he would soak the beans and early each morning his mother would rise and cook them for several  hours, then his father would sit in their dark room in the suq and, using a simple hand grinder, mash the chickpeas to a pulp. Since they'd arrived in Nazareth, Amin and Feisel had been hawking baklava to bus passengers from wooden boards balanced on their heads, but now Amin took a break from selling sweets and came to help Taha for a few hours a day at the kiosk, shaping the bean mixture into balls. Taha himself was responsible for buying and chopping vegetables, mixing tehina, frying the falafel, then composing the sandwiches—sold as whole and half portions in fresh pita bread—and interacting with the customers. He sold, he estimates, about a hundred portions every day, which required several hours of preparation, then a full day of sales and another hour of sweeping, scrubbing, and tidying up: he worked from eight in the morning until eight at night. On Saturdays—which Israeli soldiers and male Nazarenes or married couples would make their big night on the town—he readied an extra-large batch and worked late. Half of what he took in for each falafel was profit. And although he did make some money and estimates that his pay each month was twice that of a manual laborer, it was, he soon saw, a great deal of work for not enough profit. There must be a better method of making money, he reasoned—and a method that might also allow him more time each day to devote to his Arabic and English grammar books and his immersion in *al-Risala*.

Help came from an old Saffuriyya friend, Anis al-'Afifi, who was Taha's cousin a few times removed and his senior by several years and who had opened a small grocery store in his family's bus company building downtown. This single room was the only part of the building that the government had not confiscated in 1948—together with most of the 'Afifis' buses—after some family members left for Lebanon during the fighting.

Anis had now been running his shop alone there for nearly a year, but "he saw," says Taha, "that I could easily persuade the customer to buy this or that." Hearing that Taha's biographer would like to talk to him, Anis has put in a rare 2005 appearance at Taha's souvenir shop. As he explains, "I asked Taha to be my partner because he is a relative, because he was here, and because he is a *gentleman*." He declares this in Arabic, but lands with a flourish on the English word, which he punctuates with a guffaw. Taha joins in with a most ungentlemanly cackle. But it is, insists Taha, *Anis* who is the gentleman, descending as he does from such a noble Saffuriyya family. "They were the cream!" announces Taha grandly, and in bizarrely high literary Arabic, meant to honor Anis—by the time I interview him, a dapper and slightly deaf eighty-something widower with thick glasses, a kaffiyeh, a neat suit and tie, and an infectious sense of humor. Taha continues: "He and his friends were the elite of Saffuriyya! They went together to weddings. They dressed very nicely, with money in their pockets! Nobody in Saffuriyya had money in their pockets! But Anis did, all the time. True? Isn't it true?"

The two of them are chuckling throughout this exchange, which Taha has turned into a genuine theatrical performance and a good-

natured parody of one of our own question-and-answer sessions: he
alternates playing the roles of narrator and interviewer, and whenever
I ask Anis a question in colloquial Arabic ("What did you and Taha
sell in your shop?"), Taha then "translates" for his old friend into a
much more formal Arabic register and at extremely high volume, referring to himself in the third person. "WHAT WERE THE ITEMS THAT
YOU AND TAHA OFFERED FOR SALE IN YOUR ESTABLISHMENT?" Under normal circumstances, no childhood friends would actually speak to
each other in the elevated literary tones that Taha has trotted out like
his best china for the occasion, and even Anis seems a bit confused
by the rhetorical game Taha is playing. Yet for all the silliness of the
back and forth, it is startling to see the elder Taha transformed before
my eyes into the role of the younger, poorer man, working hard to
make his distinguished guest feel honored—or more likely, knowing
Taha, to keep him entertained.

However large the gap in their social standing, it was a fortuitous
match: Taha's charisma and his extensive shopkeeping experience,
combined with Anis's stability (he was already married and a father),
his capital, and his family connections, made their business a success.
They worked together for several years without fuss or strain; perhaps
their common Saffuriyya legacy made a certain shorthand possible.
They sold cigarettes, canned food, and cold soda, which they cooled
on a block of ice delivered daily by the Kardosh family. They also kept
dealing in black-market goods—chocolate, sugar, and ration "points"
for clothing, and they stocked, too, a substance called *kaham,* a coffee substitute that they bought once from a Jewish middleman. The
kaham was not subject to rationing, but it got them into trouble with
an inspector who was sure that the two sacks of ground brown stuff
behind the counter were actually black-market coffee. Taha and Anis
were both taken into police custody and eventually tried—though
they were acquitted after presenting the judge with a declaration from
the man in Haifa that "this is not coffee." In fact, says Taha, it wasn't
even close and tasted terrible.

With the money he was now bringing in, Taha was able to save
enough in a short time to move his family to a much more spacious
apartment in the suq, near the White Mosque. Their new home was
perched on the second story of an elegant old house that, according
to local lore, had once been the home of the poet, intellectual, and

literary socialite Mayy Ziyada, who was born in Nazareth in 1886 and spent most of her life in Cairo. The apartment consisted of six rooms that looked down on an open courtyard; it had electricity. And "drip by drip," as Taha says, they were able to buy things to make it more comfortable: armchairs, a radio, a small cooking stove. Taha's mother began to fill tin cans with roses that she crowded along the windowsills and outdoor, stone staircase, and Taha now claimed a shelf of his own, where he lined up his magazines and small set of books, the seeds of a library.

When the government finally—after a drawn-out court case—returned the 'Afifis' confiscated property, Anis sold Taha his share of their shop and went to work as one of the managers of the bus company. By 1953, Taha was running the grocery by himself, and as he set down new roots, he established new rhythms: the White Mosque's muezzin would wake him early each morning, and then, in the half-light, he would rise to read and study grammar for a few precious hours before setting out for work.

That same year, Taha also heard his first Beethoven symphony, and it moved him deeply. The concert was the first of its kind performed in Nazareth since the Israeli conquest, and the event was momentous enough to warrant an article in the *New York Times*, which described how the military governor had set up a stage and seating for five hundred "in the courtyard of his residence at the top of a hill overlooking the church spires of the city . . . [and] the citizens of Nazareth streamed up through the cobblestoned streets and filled every seat and crowded the surroundings to hear the unfamiliar Western music." Works by Palestrina, Haydn, Darius Milhaud, and Arcady Dubensky, along with a gavotte composed by a local Anglican priest, were all on the program, as was Jean Sibelius's *Valse Triste* and the overture to Beethoven's *Egmont*.

Taha, for one, was carried away by the music and the outdoor spectacle—and fascinated by the American conductor's presence, "his face, his hands, his body." He decided on the spot to expand the scope of his autodidactic curriculum. "To be a writer," he explains now, "you have to know about painting, about music." He decided to study the violin, and though he had no illusions of becoming a serious musician, he wanted to learn the rudiments and so arranged to buy an instrument at a reduced rate from a local teacher and to take weekly lessons at the Casa Nova. Now his studies lasted from those early morning reading hours until late at night, when—after returning from a full day's worth of soda and cigarette sales—he would stay up to practice his scales.

◆

At long last Taha and his family again had a home, and it is clear from the generous proportions of the apartment they'd chosen that they meant to stay put for a good long while. There were rooms and room enough for the family to grow, for the sons to marry and bring their wives to come live together with the aging parents. And then the babies would start to arrive, and there would somehow be space for everyone, just as there was seemingly always place on the stairs for another can of roses.

Something, however, was missing—or, more accurately, someone. In the years since Taha had said good-bye to Amira as his family boarded the bus in al-Qara'un, he had never doubted that they would soon be reunited and that their marriage would shortly follow. But the longer they had been apart, the darker his feelings had become on this score. And here it is important to remember that the same barriers that kept Arabic books from entering Israel also completely blocked contact between Palestinians on what had come to be known as the "inside" (that is, within Israel's borders) and those on the "outside" (everywhere beyond). Taha's extended family had, in other words, been utterly torn asunder by the events of 1948. Without access to an American or European intermediary—in the case of a peasant clan such as Taha's, a serious improbability—there was no way to write a letter or even telephone those living in an Arab state like Lebanon, and the single opportunity to communicate with relatives or loved ones across the borders was by means of the now-infamous transmissions of the Arabic service of the government radio station called (it seems cruelly ironic in this context) the Voice of Israel.

At 2:35 pm, several days a week, "Messages of Listeners to their Relations" would play for ten minutes—between love songs sung by Farid al-Atrash, Umm Kulthum, and Muhammad 'Abd al-Wahab—and telegraphic tidings would be broadcast over the airwaves. (After a few years, the program's title was changed to the more explicit "Messages of Israeli Arabs to Their Relations on the Outside," and a decade later Mahmoud Darwish would write of these plaintive dispatches in his poem "Letter from Exile": "On the radio I heard / the greetings of the homeless . . . to the homeless. / They all said: We're fine. / No one is sad.") Although Taha had neither sent word nor received any news of Amira for four years now, he says he never even considered contacting her this way. "I was ashamed," he says. "People were listening so this was no good."

But Taha was, understandably, becoming impatient. He was twenty-two years old and ready, in all ways, to marry the girl who'd been promised to him since her birth. He felt this deep down in himself, and those around him—his parents especially—had also made it clear that the time had come for him to wed. After waiting patiently, and futilely, for the political situation to change in a way that would make a legal reunion possible, his faith in such general solutions had clouded, and he had begun to consider taking more drastic, private steps. Without telling a soul, save his black-marketeering friend Muhammad Tawfiq, he decided to leave his family and travel to Amira in Lebanon. Taha says that Muhammad offered to go along, but Taha refused him, "because it was a very dangerous trip," and indeed as he describes his plans now, he uses terms that make the journey sound like an especially precarious knightly quest to rescue a fair damsel: he arranged for a man to transport him to the border for, as he puts it, "three English golden coins." Defying the military government and its strict permit system, the man agreed to deliver Taha at dusk to the mined and army-patrolled border, where he'd leave him to continue on foot, in the darkness—bound for Amira and the unknown.

Taha's will was (and remains) formidable, and once he had resolved to do something, there was usually nothing that could stop him—save, it seems, his *father's* will and his rather uncanny ability to sense a thought or scheme brewing in the mind of his oldest son. Without Taha saying a word, Abu Taha understood what he was planning and confronted him. According to Taha, "My father said to me: Your brothers are young. What will happen to us if you go? What should we do? Beg for money in front of the mosque? Then I said I would not go, and I stayed. I promised." And that—abruptly—was that. Taha says he never again considered escaping to Lebanon.

But neither did he give up on Amira. In fact, the family now began to organize and look even harder for some means to bring her to Israel: father and son arranged to speak to representatives of the Red Cross, and they met with church officials who had contacts in Lebanon and who they hoped might somehow be able to help. Everyone said they would do what they could. And Taha began a painful period of waiting. And waiting.

SPARKS

◆

TAHA'S LONG VIGIL FOR AMIRA WAS NO DOUBT DIFFICULT, but he was hardly mooning in silence alone in his room. On the contrary, his keen social instincts kicked in with full force during these years, as he came to know some of the men who would become his closest companions for life.

He met them all at his store. During the same period—apparently without conscious design—he had begun to host an impromptu salon in his shop, a sort of modern, mercantile madafeh, and he spent long hours every day plunged in conversation with the various visitors who would drop in and perch for an hour or two on one of the low, straw-bottomed wooden stools that were crowded into the small room. Before the shelves of sardines and chocolate bars, a seemingly constant conversation would unfold among a few people at a time, and though the cast of characters would evolve over the course of a day—with one man getting up to leave as another made his entrance, and then another joined in—the back and forth would continue, the talk changing tack and tone slightly with the addition or subtraction of a particular guest. As a chain-smoker lights the next cigarette from the last, so the

spark was passed on. And given the era and the social milieu, nearly everyone who gathered to sit there was also an inveterate *literal* chainsmoker, Taha included.

One exception to the nicotine-dependent rule was the journalist, teacher, publisher, and later poet Michel Haddad, who was among these close new friends of Taha's and someone who logged endless hours at the smoky shop. Though Haddad was himself an avid tennis player and sometimes soccer coach and eschewed tobacco for health reasons, his notorious—even chronic—amiability and generosity were epitomized by the fact that he often carried cigarettes with him, so he could offer them to others.

Haddad was a tall, slender man with a penetrating gaze, eyebrows so dark and thick they look charcoaled on, and a matching black mustache. A Greek Orthodox Christian born in Nazareth in 1919 to a distinguished middle-class family (his maternal grandfather was the town's first mayor), he was educated in Christian elementary schools

and was a graduate of the municipal high school. As a young man, Haddad appears to have fancied himself a sort of professional amateur, someone with many minor talents and no strong single passion. He took pride in his waggish sense of humor, his good sportsmanship, and the active role he played in the extracurricular lives of the various schools where he taught, supervising student clubs—drawing, drama, literature, singing, soccer, basketball, volleyball, even the harmonica—with a vengeance. In the mid-1940s he received a correspondence course diploma from a journalism school in Cairo and went on to write children's programs for the Arabic Service of the Palestine Broadcasting Corporation and to publish articles in various locally produced Arabic journals.

Haddad's personal and professional interests darted this way and that, and might ultimately have led him in any number of directions had the events of 1948 not played out as they did. But with the sudden departure of so much of the Palestinian intelligentsia that year, the already small pond grew even smaller. In an instant, Haddad and a tiny group of writers, editors, and publishers who had already been working before the nakba—including Hanna Abu Hanna, the young Communist Emile Habiby, nationalist lawyer Hanna Naqara, Cambridge-educated Marxist historian Emile Touma, Trotskyite critic Jabra Nicola, and a few others—faced the daunting task of salvaging what they could of the local Arabic intellectual culture and attempting to build a new foundation.

Different approaches to the same challenges emerged almost immediately, and in the absence of contemporary Arabic books, the press—newspapers and magazines alike—played a uniquely charged role, serving as the single source of freshly printed sustenance for the Palestinian citizens of Israel. In those early years, admittedly, only the smallest readership existed: many Palestinians who remained after 1948 were not literate and relied on the radio for their news and high-cultural nourishment. With the years, though, and with Israel's enforcement of laws both enlightened and repressive, demand for the written word increased exponentially. On the one hand, school was now mandatory for all citizens; by the next generation, most Arab teenagers would be able to read. On the other hand, dissatisfaction brought about by the severe restrictions of the military government and the racism Palestinian citizens faced daily was mounting—and with it the desire for ideas (in the form of poems, stories, essays, critical articles) that might offer hope for change. By the late 1960s, the various Arabic magazines published in Israel would become a major force in the local political and literary culture—the two were, in this context, twined at the root—and each new issue was awaited eagerly by workers, students, and shopkeepers alike.

At this nascent stage, all those responsible for bringing forth the local Arabic publications seem to have seen their mission as broadly educational. Regardless of the distinct approaches taken up by each set of writers and editors, literature was considered primarily a tool, a way of swaying the masses—however reduced their numbers. When the Communists turned their newspaper supplement *al-Jadid* into a freestanding literary journal in 1953, its editors declared it "a platform open to all [ideologically] clean writing, not just to Communist writers." Despite this official nonpartisan policy and the attention paid in the magazine to both the classical Arabic tradition and to older and emerging Palestinian literature, however, many of *al-Jadid*'s pages were dedicated to articles on Marxist thought, Soviet writing, and Arabic translations of work by foreign "progressive" or "committed" poets and fiction writers: Nazim Hikmet, Federico García Lorca, Pablo

Neruda, Paul Éluard, Bertolt Brecht, Louis Aragon, and others. Maxim
Gorky was a perennial favorite. This emphasis on translated literature
was as much a matter of necessity as it was a choice. As Hanna Abu
Hanna explained to me, "We were accustomed to reading Egyptian
literature, Lebanese literature—and all of a sudden, everything was
cut off. . . . So we came to rely on European literature. It was a kind
of substitute—though you cannot really make a substitution here.
This is needed and *that* is needed."

Ironically—though perhaps not coincidentally—1953 also
marked the founding of the Beirut literary magazine *al-Adab,* the
most important journal devoted to the literature of "commitment" in
the Arab world. The editor of *al-Adab,* the critic and novelist Suhayl
Idris, had recently returned from studying in Paris, where he had
seized on Sartre's idea of "engagement," which translated easily into
the Arab context, as so much tumultuous Middle Eastern history was
then unfolding and writers felt themselves charged with the duty to
respond. Although the concerns of the editors of *al-Jadid* were very
similar to those of Idris—who declared in the first issue of *al-Adab*
that "literature . . . influences society just as much as it is influenced
by it"—it is not at all clear that they had, in those early years, ever
seen a copy of his magazine.

There was, as it happens, a similar time lag when it came to absorbing the word from the Soviet bloc. *Al-Jadid* ran ads for pamphlet
collections of articles and speeches by Stalin—several decades after
the Moscow trials, his name seems not to have carried any taint in
local terms—and its editors were plainly most interested in the literature of "the struggle," a term they were already using in that inaugu-
ral 1953 issue, whose cover featured a cheerful Maoist woodcut, titled
"We Are the Owners of the Factory." At the same time, they were prepared to take real rhetorical risks to defend the rights of "the people,"
Arab and Jewish alike. They were outspoken from the outset in their
calls for all the workers to band together, regardless of religion, race,
or nation, and alongside essays about Arabic literature and culture,
the magazine published frequent surveys of modern and medieval
Hebrew literature and philosophy, as well as a regular "Letter from
Tel Aviv," which offered reviews of the latest plays running at the
major theaters in that city—*The Crucible, The Caine Mutiny Court
Martial,* and *The Wild Duck* received special mention—and new
books of Hebrew poetry and fiction were also discussed. Lenin and

Maimonides sat side by side on the magazine's pages, and together with native-born Palestinian Communists, leftist Iraqi Jewish immigrants like Sasson Somekh and the Hebrew novelist-to-be Sami Michael, then an Arabic essayist known as Samir Marid, were regular contributors. A spirit of upbeat defiance fueled the journal from that first issue, in which the editors proclaimed that the "literature of the people . . . can't be hidden behind barbed wire or prevented by law from moving around, and it is the only 'infiltrator' whose breath can't be extinguished by a shot from a gun!" They went on: "We . . . believe that the people in its struggle must find the necessary weapons, and [our] weapon is literature."

Michel Haddad, for his part, took what seems on the face of it a much more cautious route. He was, in the words of one who knew him during those years, "not a daring person" and is also remembered as having been a churchgoing Christian whose house was filled with crucifixes and pictures of the Virgin Mary, a fact that would have put him at serious odds with the local Arabic-speaking Communists—most of whom were also Christians but loudly lapsed ones, men whose prophet of preference was Karl Marx.

But to call Haddad's actions cautious is not to underestimate the profound way that 1948 appears to have changed him or worked to crystallize his sense of communal and literary purpose. In a few short years, he had founded his own magazine, *al-Mujtama'* (Society), which also waved the banner of social progress, opening its first issue in 1954 with an address to its "respected readers," to whom Haddad apologized for not making promises he couldn't keep. In the past, he noted, these promises led to "catastrophe . . . and an entire society was destroyed, its fragments scattered." The magazine's goals were, he explained, to promote local writing, to "discuss problems in society and seek their cure, to examine the situation of women [and consider how this is] an inseparable part of the situation of society at large," as well as "to bring closer the perspectives . . . of Arab and Jewish citizens [and encourage] the exchange of opinions."

Unlike the editors of *al-Jadid*, whose salaries were paid by the Communist Party and who didn't hesitate to speak in plainly ideological terms, Haddad was eager to maintain political independence—or, some might say, to sidestep conflict—and *al-Mujtama'* never officially aligned itself with any political party or perspective. The magazine was initially welcomed by one of the most outspoken and visible of

the Communists, Knesset member Emile Habiby. Habiby's blessings,
however, bore a pointed warning: "We know how much such independence costs." And as might have been predicted, the magazine
would eventually come under scathing attack from the Communist
competition, who saw it as an Arabic mouthpiece for the Jewish authorities. By 1956, Emile Touma, for one, was denouncing Haddad's
magazine with the ferocity typical of the intellectual debates of that
time and place, accusing it and its editor of cowardice and accommo-
dation: "[It] trembles with fear [at the thought of] publishing a poem
that contains [so much as] a flame from the fire of the struggle or a
breeze of revolutionary inspiration."

Touma's hot-and-heavy rhetoric may leave much to be desired,
but he had a point. The list of social priorities set forth in the initial
issue of *al-Mujtama'* is perhaps most striking for what it leaves out:
liberal causes such as promotion of the rights of women and friendly
intellectual relations between Arabs and Jews were not especially audacious, and floating mild ideas like these hardly brought with it the
threat of censorship or arrest—both of which, it should be said, the
editors of *al-Jadid* regularly faced. Meanwhile, Haddad makes no mention of the military government or the severe restrictions under which
the magazine's writers and editors were living and working. This may
have been the cost of accepting modest government financing to pay
his printing bills (the magazine was partly funded by the Ministry of
Education), or it might simply have derived from his own naturally
tiptoeing nature.

The poet Samih al-Qasim—who was an ambitious young high
school student, newly arrived in Nazareth from his own Galilee village when he met Haddad in 1955 or 1956—has written and spoken of
the "air of joy" that Haddad kindled. But al-Qasim sees a darker aspect to all that insistent cheerfulness. Looking back, in 1981, al-Qasim
understood what he had missed before: "For twenty years I didn't realize that behind the abundant mirth that Michel Haddad would spread
all around him, behind that cheer lay in his heart a profoundly deep
sadness, bordering on depression in the clinical psychological sense."

Taha, for his part, describes Haddad with affection as having been
highly distractible, flitting from conversational subject to subject, always amusing with his banter but rarely settling down into a single serious thought. Still, he and Taha logged hours and hours together,

"laughing so hard we almost cried," as Taha would later put it, with a complicated sigh.

◆

As Haddad—it should come as little surprise—so his magazine. When applying to the government for a license to publish *al-Mujtama'*, he described the proposed journal as an Arabic *Reader's Digest*, and its contents generally hewed to this innocuous middle-brow model, comprising an odd mixture of highfalutin and flyweight. Essays introducing readers to the work of Mahatma Gandhi, Taha Hussein, Tchaikovsky, and Benjamin Franklin sat beside breezy articles called, for instance, "Are You Tired All the Time?" "Is There Life on Other Planets?" and "How to Help Your Husband Get Ahead," and the occasional color story: "Danny Kaye in Nazareth." Classically rhymed and metered poems with generic titles like "Autumn" and "Springtime of Love" shared pages with earnest disquisitions on "Women's Freedom," "Marriage," and "Social Striving and the Development of Society," while translated stories by Edgar Allan Poe, O. Henry, Chekhov, and "the Swedish writer John Steinbeck" were followed by local sports scores, club news, and a special joke page, complete with a monthly contest: "The winning joke wins a kilo of baklava!" The magazine's contributors often included Jews—some of them recent immigrants from Iraq, "establishment" poets like Salim Sha'shua', who was known for writing florid Arabic panegyrics to the wonders of the new Jewish state and his vague longing for what he called "Arab-Jewish brotherhood," which he described in poems such as "Spring in Israel" and "Cooperation." ("Through cooperation, we shall yet build a world / Whose purpose is peace.") Others were official "Arabists" of the Histadrut, the powerful labor union that represented the interests of Ben-Gurion's ruling Mapai party. Their occasional lectures and articles on cultural topics were translated from Hebrew and reprinted in the magazine. "Is there any hope for distinctive literary production among the Arabs of Israel?" one of these Jewish "experts" condescended to ask, on the pages of one of Israel's first Arabic literary magazines.

Ideology aside, there is no question that *al-Mujtama'* does not begin to approach *al-Jadid* in the intensity or quality of the work it published. And it may in fact be tempting just to dismiss Haddad and his magazine as second-rate and wonder why so many pages of a life and times of Taha Muhammad Ali are being cluttered with a discussion of this mediocre publication and its timid editor. But it is, it seems to me, much too easy simply to label Michel Haddad a "good Arab"—the local equivalent of an Uncle Tom—and to brush off his magazine as "saltless," as one veteran of the period and its literary battles did when talking to me, adding that in the 1950s he and his left-wing friends had considered Haddad "a lackey." Although he was in his time shunned by the Communist literary establishment and has since been overlooked or condemned by those scholars and critics who view Palestinian literature solely through the lens of "the struggle" (the politician and English professor Hanan Ashrawi, for instance, uses bald, show-trial language to denounce Haddad as one of a group of "individualistic, personal poets who are totally detached from their people and setting"), the role that Michel Haddad played in those gestational years—both in Arabic culture in Israel at large and in Taha's development as a writer—was essential.

Not only did Haddad open the door to the possibility of a Palestinian literary life in Israel that was not bound by the dictates of a political agenda, but he was the first local poet to write totally free verse. This work is known in Arabic as *shi'r manthur* or *qasidat al-nathr*, literally, a poem of prose, that is, verse with neither meter nor rhyme. (This is the form in which Taha himself would one day write—consciously or unconsciously, it seems, influenced by his good friend.)* Haddad did not publish his first collection of poems until 1969, but in the early 1950s he was already attempting unmetered and

---

* The terminology here can be extremely confusing for Western readers—and indeed even in the Arab world a state of what one critic has called "unprecedented terminological chaos" often seems to prevail. To put it as plainly as possible: "Shi'r manthur" is not the same as "prose poetry" in the American and European sense of heightened or somehow metaphorical language offered in the approximate shape of a paragraph; in the Arabic context it simply means verse without rhyme or meter and so is in fact the equivalent of English or French free verse. To further complicate matters, the term "free verse" in Arabic (*shi'r hurr*) is, as previously explained, usually confined to poems written in the metrically fixed "Iraqi style," which contain a single repeated foot—though Arabic-language poets themselves have been arguing about the best way to describe these myriad forms for as long as modern Arabic poetry has existed.

unrhymed poems in a loosely Romantic vein, inspired, it seems, by the work of Mahjar (Diaspora) poets and critics like Kahlil Gibran and the Nazareth-educated Mikhail Naimy. These Lebanese and Syrian Christians had emigrated to the West at the end of the nineteenth and start of the twentieth centuries and continued to write in Arabic, though theirs was a freer and much more idiosyncratic Arabic than what was then being written in the countries of their birth. Naimy for one sought to unleash Arabic prosody from, among other things, "the Arabic type of rhyme, which . . . ," he wrote in 1923, "is nothing but an iron chain by which we tie down the minds of our poets." And despite the flower-power reputation in the West of *The Prophet*, Gibran was and remains a respected figure in the Arab world; his work is considered to have, in the words of one veteran scholar, "revolutionized literary art in every sphere of its activity."

What was welcomed as novel and refreshing in Prohibition-era Arab-American émigré circles was, however, still strange, even scandalous, in 1950s Nazareth. And when Haddad printed his preliminary free-verse attempts—"Feelings," he dubbed them, a bit mistily—in his magazine, they were usually met with a scornful chorus of snickers from his neighbors and even his good friends, who considered these displays self-indulgent and decidedly unpoetic: "a joke" in the blunt estimation of one who was there. But by the time he published his first collection of poems at age fifty, he had jettisoned the sometimes mawkish spiritualist approach of Gibran and evolved a much sharper poetics, closer in spirit and tack to the avant-garde shi'r manthur that was being written and published in Beirut and Damascus in the late 1950s and early 1960s by the major poets of the day—Adonis, Mahmud al-Maghut, Yusuf al-Khal, Unsi al-Hajj, and others. It isn't, however, at all clear that his readers in Nazareth had stopped giggling at what they perceived as a plain *inability* to employ the standard meters. It was a charge that Taha himself would face in later years—and continues sometimes to reckon with now. (Although Taha just laughs at such accusations, Haddad felt it necessary to write one book in traditional meters—apparently just to prove that he could.) In the decades since, shi'r manthur has flourished elsewhere and has come to be accepted by intellectuals in many parts of the Arab world, yet it remains to this day unusual and even controversial in the conservative context of Palestinian letters.

For all of his social prudery, then, Haddad was—and even after his death remains—a genuine radical in formal terms. And though one may wonder at the pain his friends' derision caused him deep down, he insists in his memoir that he "didn't pay any attention" to the laughter that surrounded his early poems. Ironically enough, he was more of a radical in an artistic sense than many of his politically radical detractors, who tended to confine their poems of protest to much more traditional metrical modes. At the same time, a tiny cadre of Haddad's friends did support him from the outset. Among them was Taha, who had not yet published any of his own poems when he wrote the introduction to Haddad's first book but who used the occasion to explain and defend the basics of shi'r manthur to a local audience, tracing a lineage for Haddad's work—and, by unspoken extension, his own—that included the Lebanese school surrounding *Shi'r* magazine and European modernism. Haddad's book, wrote Taha, was "a courageous step on a path to adventure."

Haddad was also one of the first publishers of Arabic books in Israel. In 1955, he edited and brought out an anthology, featuring the work of seventeen local poets, called *Alwan min al-shi'r al-'arabi fi Isra'il* (The Varieties of Arabic Poetry in Israel). This collection was extremely primitive in its way: it was filled mostly with poems in that wan, dreamy "Springtime of Love" mode, and many of its contributors were high school students, members of an organization Haddad had recently formed, Rabita Shu'ara' al-'Arabiyya fi Isra'il, the Association of Arabic Poets in Israel. By founding this group and giving it this name, Haddad was invoking and hoping, it seems, to emulate the work of al-Rabita al-Qalamiyya, the Pen Association, a pioneering literary society founded in 1920 in New York by those same émigré Romantic poets, Gibran and Naimy. Haddad's older brother had left Palestine for the United States before Michel's birth and was friendly with the poets in this circle. Because of this connection and Haddad's literary bent and journalistic experience, he had been invited in the early 1950s to move to America to edit the group's newspaper, as Gibran himself had once done. According to Haddad's own account, he was poised to emigrate and had begun to prepare his young family to go and even shipped off several crates of his books when word arrived of his brother's death. In an instant, his dreams—of escape, of freedom, of literary immortality—fizzled, leaving him to oversee this motley group of eager Nazareth teenagers instead. But I am putting words in his mouth. "The wind," he writes in his memoir, "doesn't always take the boat where it wants to go."

It may sound a bit preposterous to compare Haddad's ragtag Rabita to its illustrious American antecedent: in the end, his group more closely resembled one of the after-school harmonica clubs that he so loved to supervise. The miniature, passport-style pictures that accompany each selection and show the poets with their neatly knotted ties, smoothed pompadours, and wide-open baby faces give the collection the poignant air of a yellowing high school yearbook. But the intellectually and emotionally cramped circumstances with which Haddad had to reckon in post-1948 Israel were, it hardly bears stating, a far cry from those that greeted Gibran and Naimy on the wide avenues of 1920s New York, and he was making the best of a bad situation. Meanwhile, the very presence of such a volume in the world marked an important first—a gently ironic retort, perhaps, to that same article published by the Histadrut expert on the pages of Haddad's own magazine. Is there any hope for distinctive literary production among the Arabs of Israel? Among the contributors to that slender 1955 volume was the young poet and embattled local legend-to-be Rashid (pronounced RA-shid) Hussein. "Born in [the village of] Musmus in 1936," Haddad's introduction to Rashid's selection explained, "he is now in his final year of high school in Nazareth. . . . Influenced by the poetry of [the great medieval fatalist] Abu al-'Ala' al-Ma'arri . . . his poetry is marked by the imprint of identification with others and feeling for the hardships of the people."

Rashid (as he was known to one and all) wasn't alone. Haddad served as encouraging avuncular figure and welcoming publisher to many members of the next generation—no matter their differences of formal approach. His younger cousin, Taha's contemporary, the poet Jamal Qa'war, was the poetry editor of *al-Mujtama'* and a regular contributor from the magazine's founding, though his own monorhymed and classically metered odes could not possibly have been further from Haddad's free-form poetic meanderings. (The two argued constantly about what counts as a poem, as Jamal and Taha still do.) In 1955, Taha's own fledgling short stories and critical essays—his first published work—would begin to appear in the magazine.

On the pages of *al-Mujtama'* Haddad would, too, eventually pub-

lish some of the earliest work ever written by Samih al-Qasim and
another poet who would go on to become a household name throughout the Arab world, Mahmoud Darwish. Several years younger than

Rashid, al-Qasim and
Darwish were, re-
spectively, nineteen
and seventeen years
old when they began
to publish there in
1958. As a bright-
eyed high school stu-
dent, al-Qasim even
wrote a regular col-
umn, "The Magic
Carpet," in which he
surveyed with a little boy's glee the various books and journals being
published locally. "And now whoever is reading these lines . . . ," his
first column bubbled, "I call to you to set out with me on a journey
on this wondrous enchanted carpet. Let's set out together into the
skies, where we'll peer down at everything and afterwards we'll talk
about it all!!"

And talk and talk they did. By the time al-Qasim and Darwish arrived on the scene, Taha, Michel, Jamal, Rashid, and the others had
been talking nearly nonstop for several heady years. Taha was first introduced to Michel and Jamal in 1954, and the three became close
quite quickly, forming the core group that was always enveloped by a
billow of smoke at the center of Taha's store—which he had changed
over to a souvenir shop at about this time. (His rationale, he said, was
simple: even thrifty people splurge when on vacation.) Almost immediately after they met, Michel invited Taha to be the fiction editor of
the magazine, and he was given the task of choosing the stories that
would appear there each month. Taha was, perhaps, an odd addition
to this well-bred, educated, Christian clique. He was much more of a
peasant and much less concerned with middle-class propriety than
they. However secular, he was a Muslim. His way of speaking was
more forthright and exuberant; his table manners were cataclysmic;
he had no interest whatsoever in acting proper or in joining civic
clubs or genteel associations. (Michel was a proud member of both

the local YMCA board and the Rotary.) But their differences hardly seem to have stopped them from talking endlessly—about poetry, grammar, novels, history, and . . . the world. So addictive did this talk prove that, after store hours, they would often simply pick up and move the conversation along to Haddad's small house in the Ortho-dox quarter behind Mary's Well.

Thinking back, Taha and Haddad's widow, Imm Adib—still strik-ing in her eighties, with clear blue eyes and a softly regal demeanor—each relate the same story of how Taha and Michel would finish these garrulous evenings with Michel walking Taha home through the empty Nazareth streets, the two immersed in banter. When they reached Taha's front door they would turn around—and then Taha would walk Michel back home, and when they reached Michel's front door they'd turn around and Michel would walk Taha back home, and . . . on and on they would walk and talk, late into the night.

COMPENSATION, CONTAGION, CONSUMPTION

◆

IN OBJECTIVE TERMS, TAHA'S LOT WAS BETTER NOW than that of many around him: he had lucrative work at the souvenir shop, lively friends, a full head of hair, citizenship, a steady diet of his mother's cooking, a superior ten-volume Arabic dictionary, violin lessons, and an unflagging sense of humor; his family was clothed, housed, and healthy; his English was improving; he had undertaken a course of serious Arabic study that would keep him engaged for decades to come.

Nonetheless, he says, his mood, was "black." Amira's continued absence—and the ebbing prospect of being reunited with her—had begun to eat at him in the most immediate way. At the same time, Saffuriyya had evolved from being a tangible place to which he and his family believed they might return to a cruel and abstract symbol of all that had befallen them. Nazareth was so close to the village that the smell of the seasons there was the same as the smell of the seasons in Saffuriyya, but now the winter rains and the hot spring winds and the harvests each year brought nothing but a mocking reminder of how far away his hometown really was. Distance, after all, wasn't measured just in miles.

And then—it happened suddenly—Taha took ill. Although it may be tempting to ascribe his sickness to a psychosomatic paroxysm brought on by his private disquiet or a more general, societal Hans Castorpian malaise, what ailed him physically was actual and serious: he grew pale and weak and began to lose weight, and when he started coughing blood, he conceded to his parents' worried urgings and finally agreed to go see the "Austrian doctor," one Dr. Konitzer, who was in fact German but whom everyone knew by this name because he'd worked at Nazareth's Austrian hospice for years. Dr. Konitzer checked Taha, sent him to have an X-ray, and diagnosed him on the spot with tuberculosis, ordering him hospitalized right away, confined for months if need be to the compound of buildings and barns known almost mythically to the people of Nazareth simply as "Schneller."

Once a Lutheran agricultural school, Schneller was perched on an airy hill southwest of town, and because of this slight remove from the city center, it had been pressed into spontaneous service as a smallpox hospital when, in the autumn of 1948, several cases of the dread disease were diagnosed among the villagers of nearby Kafr Kanna and a more severe outbreak threatened.

By 1954, when Taha was ordered to don a pair of standard-issue white pajamas and take up residence at Schneller, the smallpox threat had passed and the place had been functioning for several years as a hospital for the treatment of TB. It was Israel's single institution intended for the treatment of Arab consumptives, and because of its relative isolation from town, it had been selected by the Ministry of Health to serve as a sanatorium. The need for such distance was essentially medical: contagious patients housed there would, it was reasoned, be kept out of contact with the general populace. But the far-off calm of the compound and its pastoral mien seem to have served Taha, for one, in more psychological ways as well. Relieved by doctor's orders of the burdens of running his business (his brothers managed to keep the shop open while he was gone, with Anis al-'Afifi occasionally helping out), he spent the next nine long months sleeping, eating, resting, befriending his German-Jewish doctors and an Iraqi Jewish orderly named Yosef Averra, or Abu Amir, with whom he became especially close. More important, he was sitting and reading and musing. For the first time since he'd been hiding from the army in Reina, he lived more or less in his head.

This opportunity to lounge and brood was, as he tells it, both a curse and a blessing. On the one hand, he describes how his mind was divided in half, "but the mind has about eight halves. One half was in Lebanon [with Amira], one was in the shop, one was studying Arabic and English, one was on my disease." On the other hand, the forced rest cure—days empty of any obligations, free copies of the *Je-*

rusalem Post, which a friendly Dr. Lichtenstein passed on when he'd finished reading them and with which Taha practiced his English, lights out at seven o'clock—allowed him the luxury of time and calm in which to think and study and prepare himself to write. During this period he read, he says, as though he were "on fire," and immersed himself in Arabic translations of short stories by Poe, Maupassant, and Chekhov. Taha's particular strain of TB was not contagious, and after the first month of treatment, the doctors allowed him to wander the grounds and receive visitors. So Michel and Jamal would visit him often and the three of them would sit together under the tall pines that hemmed the compound's stone buildings and talk for hours, as they would in his shop. "I began to recover. I gained about four kilos, and my face wasn't pale. . . . And Michel and Jamal they used to come and talk and they would say to me, 'You are okay, why you are here?' But I would tell them: the face is okay, but inside there is something wrong."

Although Taha is speaking in medical terms—he goes on to recount the course of his illness, the doctor's plans to operate on his lungs, and the brand-new, imported drug that Dr. Lichtenstein eventually tried out on him instead of surgery, permanently curing his

TB—he seems also to be describing a more elusive inner state, one that wouldn't show up on any ordinary chest X-ray. Neither would it surface in the few snapshots that exist from that time: in those pictures, Taha looks surprisingly relaxed and happy, surrounded by smiling young men in white hospital pajamas, their arms thrown around each other as though convalescence from serious pulmonary disease were the most fun-filled sort of vacation. But Taha makes it clear that his smile was in fact barely masking a profound sense of grief.

He was not alone in this distress. As Taha recuperated at Schneller, letters from former residents of Saffuriyya and addressed to everyone from the Nazareth military governor to the attorney general to the prime minister himself accumulated in the government files, their tone mounting from fawning respect in the early years (1949: "We desire wholeheartedly to live together with our brothers the Jews, who live in our village, who we know will protect our rights better than the Arabs") to more insistent and desperate as the clock ticked on and the unwillingness of the politicians and bureaucrats to help became plain. (1952: "I ask that you [the prime minister] answer me promptly, completely, and in a positive fashion, since I can no longer bear the disgrace and uprooting, and [ask] that you permit me . . . [and my family] to return to our village, Saffuriyya.")

Meanwhile, it is obvious from documents that remain in the archives that the authorities had no intention of ever allowing the villagers to return to their homes—even those who had stayed on in Saffuriyya during its conquest, been issued ID cards, and whom the army drove away on trucks in early January 1949. The official memos and letters preserved in those files take shape as a long, mazelike series of blunt refusals, cagier attempts to stall, and the occasional grudging agreement that compensation might indeed be due that small group of refugees who had been counted in the census. Although the case of Taha and his family and the thousands of other Saffuriyyans who had been forced out by the army and its airplanes on that terrible July night was never even mentioned, the several hundred ID-card holders persisted, realizing that legally—not just morally—the state was in the wrong. By 1954, their letters were short and plain:

> We are former residents of Saffuriyya, and it is six years now
> that we have suffered great material deprivation . . . as a re-
> sult of the government's confiscation of our lands and our
> groves, the source of our livelihood. We are farmers and we
> have no other profession or trade besides farming. We ask that
> you judge us fairly . . . and that you treat us in accordance
> with the laws of the government.

From the paper trail that has survived, it seems the authorities themselves understood the state's legal obligation to the ID holders— and by the time this last letter was written there were already various plans afoot for "the rehabilitation of the Tzippori refugees," that is, suggestions of other swatches of land that might be offered in exchange for all claims to Saffuriyya soil. But for now this theoretical admission of responsibility brought little practical relief to the people themselves. And as always, the army could be counted on to erect the brick wall of Security:

> Regarding the problem of the rehabilitation of the Tzippori refugees, the Chief of Staff has decided that their return to the area of Tzippori-Nazareth is not in the security interests of the area and should be prevented. Therefore I ask that you inform the [relevant committee] of the cessation of all contact with the refugees of Tzippori regarding their return to the aforementioned area.

Although the military man who composed this memo felt no need to prove his concerns with the help of evidence, the date of his declaration—September 1954—makes it clear that it was written in the shadow of a startling act of violence that had taken place just the year before on Moshav Tzippori. That act was, in many ways, exceptional for its time and place, yet the punishment it visited on the displaced people of Saffuriyya was in that same time and place completely to be expected.

The crime in question was the grisly double murder of Marcel Feder, the Romanian-born moshav grocer, and his wife, Helena, on Passover Eve, 1953. According to a police telegram sent the night of the murder, the couple had been dressing to go celebrate the Seder meal with their neighbors when, through an open door, an unknown assailant shot Marcel fourteen times and Helena six with an automatic weapon. Their "mean and aggressive" dog had been drugged. No jewelry or money was stolen, and the grocery next door was completely untouched. The police dispensed trackers and acted quickly to find the killers. As the headline of the Hebrew tabloid *Yediot Achronot* screamed as soon as arrests were made: ARAB REVENGE GANG CARRIED OUT THE DOUBLE MURDER IN TZIPPORI. According to the article that followed, the police theorized that former residents of the village had retaliated against "the settlers of Tzippori [who they believed] took their houses and land."

By the next day, though, the shrill tone had been tamped, as it became clear that the chief suspects, two young Arab shepherds, originally from Saffuriyya, had bought cigarettes from Feder's grocery earlier in the day, which accounted for the presence of their footprints nearby. "The police," the newspaper noted, "are also investigating other leads"—some of which pointed in the direction of a politically over-heated bodice ripper. Helena Feder had, it turned out, been a Christian, and according to one newspaper story, a priest at the Tzippori/Saffuriyya convent had fallen in love with her when she came to pray on Sunday mornings. She did not return his affections, and he decided to take his revenge by "inciting the two young Arab extremists to murder by telling them that Marcel Feder . . . had turned the abandoned mosque [of Saffuriyya] into a movie theatre." This seems to have been sheer fantasy, as was the notion that one of the shepherds was a relative of the late 'Izz al-Din al-Qassam, "whose gang . . . was well-known for their extremism and hatred of the Jews." The scenario was, not surprisingly, adamantly denied by various high-ranking church officials, one of whom wrote a letter to the newspaper—and many others, more adamant still, to the superintendent of police—in which he pointed out that the priest was seventy-seven years old and spoke only Italian. His relations with the Jews of the moshav were excellent, and he had never met either Helena or Marcel Feder. The police themselves, meanwhile, seem not to have put much stock in the journalist's highly imaginative account of what had transpired.

But even as the detectives were inspecting dusty footprints and sending their dogs to sniff for other clues, damning judgment had already been brought in the court of public opinion—against *all* the refugees of Saffuriyya. One Hebrew newspaper article explained that "everyone in the know understands that this group of refugees constitutes the greatest danger to the state, of all the members of the Arab minority," and went on to relate that the Saffuriyya refugees had "demonstrated rejectionism and stubbornness and asked to have, of all things, those lands and houses that had been theirs in the past. . . . Until the murder, the authorities made various attempts to find a solution for the refugees. . . . But the murder of the Feder couple in Tzippori was a turning point in the relationship [between the government and refugees]. Land was no longer granted to them and various restrictions were placed upon them." Another article recounted in more detail the government's attempts to "rehabilitate" the refugees from Saffuriyya. In this version of events, several families had been given land elsewhere, "taken from Hebrew settlements" and all had been well:

> But "the golden age" quickly came to an end. . . . The Arabs, with their artificial attitude to democratic rule, saw in the . . .

attempts of the government to help them signs of weakness
and impotence. Their confidence and daring grew until it bor-
dered on insolence. Incidents of infiltration increased, with
many of the refugees almost outwardly providing assistance.
Armed gangs began to wander the hills of the Galilee, several
confrontations with the security forces took place, and the
lawlessness reached its height with the murder of the settler
couple on Moshav Tzippori.

After the murder, the article goes on to explain, the government hard-
ened its position toward the Saffuriyya villagers and stopped even
talking about compensation.

Meanwhile, as the refugees saw their prospects of return fading
fast in the wake of the murder, the two Saffuriyya shepherds had been
quietly released by the police. No evidence against them existed, and
the authorities could not build a case. And as it happens, the inves-
tigative files and the stories told in hushed voices by some of the
twenty-first-century members of Moshav Tzippori point to another
scenario entirely. This plot had nothing whatsoever to do with the
refugees, though it also welled up from the desire for revenge:

> PLEASE [goes the scrawled draft of one internal police
> telegram] TELL ME   IF EVER   A COMPLAINT   WAS MADE AGAINST
> MARCEL FEDER,   A NEW IMMIGRANT   FROM ROMANIA-BUCHAREST,
> 45 YEARS OLD,   ABOUT THE   ABUSE OF JEWS   WHEN HE WAS
> IN CHARGE   AT A FORCED   WORKCAMP   DURING THE WAR

Marcel Feder had, it appears, been a Kapo, a fact that would have led
police detectives—had they pushed—in another, uncomfortably Jewish, direction. It seems they preferred to avoid such a mess, and to
this day the couple's killers have never been apprehended.

◆

Although he and his former Saffuriyya neighbors were those placed
behind figurative bars because of the crime, Taha says that he knew
of the Feder murder only "as in a dream." Like most doings in nearby
Jewish society, it was for him something far-off and hazy. (The same

was true, it should clearly be said, of Israeli Jews and their sense of the Arab society that existed so close by, yet in another galaxy. As the headline of one 1955 *Jerusalem Post* story about Nazareth put it, "Town Is Terra Incognita to Most Israelis." The same could still be written today, as could the reporter's words: "One might truthfully state that our newspaper reading public is better informed about Rangoon or Saigon than about Nazareth, one of our largest urban centers. Some people have forgotten or have never known that Nazareth is in Israel. Some ask what money is used there.") Taha's confinement to Schneller placed him at an even greater remove from the outside world, though there was one other violent event that same year, 1954, of which he was well aware. And in this case, the people of Saffuriyya, and Taha's family in particular, were brought more closely than any of them would probably have liked to the Jews of Moshav Tzippori.

It happened in early April that year—and it happened to Ahmed Qablawi, the eldest son of the widow Radia Abu Najj, Abu Taha's cousin who lived on the Reina-Saffuriyya border and who had struggled against Sheikh Saleh to take back her house and fertile land on the return of her family, with Taha's, from Lebanon. Recently married and in his midtwenties, with soft lips and a firm stare, Ahmed was the father of two infant girls, whom he adored. Ever since his own father

was killed mysteriously when he was a child, he had been the man of the house but had also grown used to a home dominated by women— his mother, grandmother, multiple younger sisters and little nieces—and when his wife gave birth first to a girl he announced that she was "as good as ten sons," a fairly unusual declaration to make in that conservative, male-centered village milieu. He was considered progressive in other ways as well and would sometimes accompany his grandmother (she with the eyeglasses) to the movies in Nazareth—disapproving neighbors be damned. As his mother, Radia, regained control of her groves and fields, he had been her greatest help. She relied on him to oversee the plowing, planting, harvesting. Like her, he was known for having a spine.

The border between Radia's land and the edge of the moshav was vague, and one day Ahmed and his younger brothers wandered across the invisible line that separated their present-day property from the property that had until recently also belonged to them. Perhaps it was an innocent mistake; maybe they knew they were trespassing and didn't care. It is altogether possible that Ahmed still considered it his right to pluck wild greens from those particular meadows. Whatever the case, as they were picking mallow, several settlers from the moshav approached and ordered them to leave. It is not clear what language the watchmen spoke when they called out to Ahmed and his brothers. Neither is it known how the young men responded, if at all, or at what point precisely one of the guards, a fifty-year-old new immigrant from Iran named Chanuka Ben Shalom Arbili, pulled his gun from its holster and shot Ahmed twice in the head.

After that, things happened quickly: other settlers rushed to find a car and drove Ahmed to the English hospital in Nazareth, where he continued to bleed profusely; the police arrived at the scene of the shooting and arrested three men, including Arbili; he confessed, claiming that he had meant just to fire a warning shot. Radia and her entire brood took up a vigil at Ahmed's bedside. Yusra, Radia's youngest child—then a wise, quiet thirteen-year-old, slightly in awe of her outspoken older brother—remembers that Ahmed was not conscious and that her mother the widow wept the whole time, moaning to herself that "this land is covered with the blood of men." And after a day and a night, Ahmed Qablawi died.

When they tell this story, the members of Ahmed's family understandably focus on the man himself and on the terrible loss his death meant for them. His baby girls were now considered orphans; his young wife was a widow. Radia—known as Imm Ahmed—was forced to carry his name everywhere with her, as if she were trailing a shroud. Yusra and her other siblings had lost their beloved big brother, the only father figure they had known.

The written record, meanwhile, relates another tale altogether, and one whose outlines are worth recounting not just for the light they shed on this particular event but for what they say more generally about the world in which the twenty-three-year-old Taha Muhammad Ali lived—and the complicated ways that guilt, forgiveness, and revenge, compensation, compulsion, and absolution were being used and sometimes abused all around him. Decades later, Taha's poetry would take up many of these very themes, and although it is impossible to know how much effect these precise proceedings had on Taha and his writing, what happened in the wake of Ahmed Qablawi's murder clearly lingers on, if only in Taha's unconscious.

According to the Hebrew-language files of the Israel Police, the family of Chanuka Ben Shalom Arbili "put pressure on the Jewish Agency" to arrange a sulha, a traditional Arab reconciliation ceremony enacted between the perpetrator of a crime and representatives of the victim, designed both to make symbolic financial amends and to halt the cycle of bloody score-settling. (By accepting the *diya*—or blood money—the family of the victim agrees not to avenge his murder.) This would be the first such ceremony ever performed between Arabs and Jews in the new state of Israel. While Arbili was described in one Hebrew newspaper just after the murder as being "a grown man, known as responsible and serious" and may well have felt real remorse and been genuinely interested in repenting, a more cynical reading of the situation also strongly suggests itself, since his family was urging that a sulha take place "before he was brought to trial." Presumably they assumed that if the Qablawi family had already formally forgiven Arbili for the murder, a judge would be more lenient in his sentencing. The Jewish Agency's representative, a former military governor of Nazareth, turned for help to Sheikh Saleh Salim, and he agreed to act as intermediary.

Somehow—despite the fact that Radia had refused to speak to him since their battle over her house—Sheikh Saleh prevailed on the Qablawi family to participate in the sulha. Neither the official documentation nor the spoken accounts of those who were present specify how he managed to persuade them—though plain old-fashioned intimidation seems highly likely. The Nazareth chief of police and a representative of the military governor were among the affair's distinguished invitees, and given the tenuous nature of Radia's status in the country and her desperate need to hang on to her land near the moshav, she would have had little choice but to agree: this was forgiveness offered under extreme duress. As it happens, her name is not mentioned in the neatly typed and dryly remarkable summary of the proceedings that lies buried in the police files. This begins with a curt description of the arrival one day in September of "the intermediaries and the representatives of the Chanuka family from Moshav Tzippori" at a leafy area on the edge of the settlement, known as the Persian Grove—once the basatin of Saffuriyya. Soon "the Arab dignitaries from Nazareth and the area who were invited by the intermediaries also gathered in the same grove and awaited the arrival of the representatives of the authorities," each of whom is listed in the document with his full name and rank. Then, in a passage startling for all it does—and does not—say:

> At 12:30 the intermediaries and dignitaries went up to the house of the Qablawi family, which is located one kilometer from the site of the ceremony. As they approached the house, a member of the Qablawi family came out and received the group and the chief intermediary told him of the reason for the arrival of the dignitaries. The family member allowed the group to enter the house, where the brother of Ahmed Qablawi, the deceased, and his cousin were sitting. After the group was asked to sit, the chief intermediary, Sheikh Saleh Salim, asked the members of the family of the deceased to sit in the middle of the room, and when they sat he recited before them passages of the Qur'an which remind the believer of the Muslim faith to forgive all those who seek peace. He reminded them that because the group included government officials, it was incumbent upon them to accept the request for a peace pact. The representatives of the family accepted the offer [the diya] of the intermediaries.

From here, the whole party proceeded outdoors, where Sheikh Saleh kicked off the more theatrical side of the ancient ritual and "three knots of a kerchief were bound on a stick." The first he tied "in the name of the murdered man, and the second in the name of the Chanuka family. The third knot was tied by the representative of the military governor . . . in the name of the authorities, as a witness to the enactment of the peace pact."

Of course, no one's emotions are recorded in this most matter-of-fact account—though one can only imagine how Radia must have felt as she stayed at home with her mother, daughters, and now-fatherless granddaughters while her adolescent sons and their male cousins were then ordered to walk all the way to the Persian Grove alongside Sheikh Saleh, who held the kerchief-bound stick high over their heads. When they reached the grove the boys were placed at the head of a line of people, and another group was dispatched to go bring "the suspect in the killing, Chanuka Ben Shalom of Moshav Tzippori, to the ceremony. When Chanuka and his relatives arrived . . . they were placed beside the Qablawi family under the kerchief tied to the stick, and here Sheikh Saleh Salim lectured about the ceremony itself and its traditions and the responsibilities of the Qablawi family after the enactment of the peace pact."

When Sheikh Saleh finished thanking the authorities for their presence, other Arab dignitaries rose to speak in turn: one school-teacher from Sakhnin waxed poetic about how "under the shade of the mulberries and the pomegranates, for the first time a 'sulha' between the two sides of the people was held, the first side Jewish and the second side Arab. . . . Now we feel that there is no racial discrimination between Arab and Jew in this country, according to the law or in cultural life." He then offered profuse thanks to the military governor, the former military governor, the police chief, and Sheikh Saleh. The Qablawi family was praised for their "appropriate behavior" and warned again that it was incumbent on them to respect the sulha. Then, as "lunch was served according to the custom of the tribes," another sheikh spoke and "said that he hoped that this small sulha would be the beginning of a sulha between Israel and the Arab states."

"With the end of the meal, and the drinking of bitter coffee," the report concludes, "the counselor of Moshav Tzippori paid the sum of 2,000 IL [worth about $1,100 at the time] to the Qablawi family as a 'diya' . . . and all those assembled returned to their homes."

But that is not quite right: the military governor, the former military governor, the police chief, Sheikh Saleh, the thankful school-teacher, and the hopeful sheikh all returned to their homes, as did the people of Moshav Tzippori, among them Chanuka Ben Shalom Arbili. (He never served time for the murder.) Radia's sons and nephews also made their way back over the fields and into her house. Although when they presented her with the diya, Radia refused it in disgust— saying she didn't want to touch that tainted money—another relative stepped in, collected it, and eventually purchased land in the name of

Ahmed's small, orphaned daughters, Hadra and Amina. If they could not have a father, at least they would be promised some security in the future.

The Saffuriyya refugees who were present that day, meanwhile, did not return to their homes but retreated to their rented rooms and to the fading hope that they might once again be allowed to work the earth of a place like the Persian Grove with its mulberries, its pomegranates, its forgiving shade.

TWO FRIENDS

◆

IN JUNE 1955, TAHA'S FIRST SHORT STORY APPEARED in *al-Mujtama'* alongside a photograph of the mustachioed twenty-four-year-old author, looking serious, smooth-browed, and a touch cross-eyed. "The Two Friends," as his four-page debut was titled, is an unrelentingly bleak bit of melodrama—the tale of a young man named Amin whose father's two wives spend all their time battering each other with abuse and obscenities. "As a child . . . ," he writes, "I would memorize these curses and insults. And often I would go out into the street and hurl all that I'd learned at the passing children, women, and men." Soon Amin's mother dies, his father's second wife runs away, and "my father came out of this painful battle with mind and nerves shattered. And they say he was walking aimlessly when a large car hit him and killed the last living creature I knew."

The story hurtles along its gloomy course, sending Amin into a life of "evil, ignorance, and corruption." He drinks, he smokes, he "craves debauchery" (the prose turns fairly florid and euphemistic here, though the word in Arabic, *fujur,* also means "fornication" or "whoredom"), he takes to stealing to pay for "these vices." And then—just as he has declared his "spirit darkened . . . and youth withered"—a "miracle" takes place, and he is befriended by a stranger named Salim. "He

was in his thirties, tall, with white skin, blue eyes, fine clothes, and a
gentle manner that made itself known with each word that he uttered,
and calm flowed from every one of his movements." With time, Amin
begins to believe that Salim is "a generous messenger sent from the
heavens to [help] my miserable spirit," and soon the two friends have
decided to open a small shop together in the suq. At first, their sales—
of "basic provisions, cigarettes, a few games for children"—are modest, but because of Salim's "radiant face and the charming smile he
would offer everyone who entered the store," their business is shortly
booming.

   "And it was the night of the 'id and the people rejoiced in the holiday, and on this happy occasion there was a great deal of selling and
buying." The friends take in a large quantity of "liras and pieces of sil-
ver, large and small," and when the time comes to close for the
evening, they leave the money inside a jar in the store, each placing a
key in his pocket and bidding the other good-bye.

   Such camaraderie, prosperity, and cheer are all well and good, but
any story that starts with angry wives spitting curses at each other is
not likely to end happily, and from here on in, the grim climax looms:
on his way home, Amin is accosted by an old friend from his days of
depravity, and the man invites him for a cup of coffee. Amin resists,
but is coaxed into a café, "in honor of the 'id," and soon finds himself
drinking heavily, playing cards with a roomful of leering men, and
even wielding a switchblade. In a moment of desperation (he needs
cash to stay in the game), he lurches, drunk, toward his own shop, to
steal from the holiday stash—only to discover that a light has been
turned on inside. "Who is the thief who dares steal from us?" He
clutches his knife, sneaks into the shop, and, finding the thief emp-
tying the jar of coins, crouches and prepares himself to stab the in-
truder in the chest, "but I stopped suddenly because the thief who
was standing before me was none other than my friend Salim."

   "The Two Friends" is without question an awkward, derivative
work, and one that Taha himself now dismisses completely, as he does
almost all his early stories. Poe is here (Amin's descent into debauchery strongly recalls the "miserable profligacy . . . rooted habits of vice
and . . . soulless dissipation" of, for instance, the American writer's
"William Wilson"), as is Maupassant (in the story's all-pervasive irony
and final, devastating revelation), along with any number of Egyptian

B movies. The story is not in any meaningful way representative of the fiction and poems that Taha would later write: its texture, tone, register, and basic themes are not yet recognizably his own.

And yet, as a snapshot of Taha's frame of mind, circa 1955, the story is fascinating. The bitterness, fatalism, and even misanthropy that ooze from almost every word are palpable, and the last, damning flourish—in which Amin discovers that Salim is not just a crook but in effect *no better than he himself*—offers a startling glimpse at Taha's grievous sense of the world and of himself at that time. All the characters (save, perhaps, Amin's broken father) are corrupt to the core and are depicted in the most unforgiving terms—the narrator included.

"The Two Friends" is, to be fair, the work of an absolute beginner, and though it is not a tale that demands—or would withstand—probing textual analysis, it does seem reasonable to read it against the historical scrim before which it was composed, understanding that Taha himself was probably not conscious of the effect of this backdrop when he sat down to write. To hear him tell it, he was simply interested in crafting a story after the fashion of the foreign models he'd been gobbling up while hospitalized at Schneller. There is, if anything, a temporally vague and physically unanchored quality to the story's action. With the exception of a few "local" details—those two wives, the shop in the suq, the liras—the story might be set anywhere on earth and in any era. But the fact that "The Two Friends" is permeated with cynicism, suspicion of self, and almost universal mistrust cannot be a coincidence. Nothing in the story is uniquely "Palestinian," yet the whole of it seems to be Taha's sublimated attempt to express his own lancing sense of having been betrayed (and perhaps betraying), both personally and as a member of his people.

That said, one must be careful not to read all of Taha's work in this way. Connect-the-historical-dots interpretations of his far richer and more complex later stories and poems give out quickly, as pat glosses on the author's nationality or class don't begin to account for what would in time become his writing's power. And here it is instructive—and even a bit spooky—to flip fur-

ther through the yellowing pages of *al-Mujtama'*, pulled up like a time
capsule, on a dumbwaiter, from the closed stacks of the National Library in Jerusalem. There one encounters the voice of Taha as a
young critic, holding forth on the very question of the writer's relationship to his social setting. Since he is a true son of oral, archive-
less Saffuriyya and has never kept a notebook or diary, preserved a
draft, or saved a letter in his life, such criticism constitutes the only
extant written record of his thoughts as a young writer.

Already in 1955, the same year he published three earnest but
slightly ham-handed stories in Haddad's magazine, Taha had begun

to formulate the ideas about literature that he would evolve
and apply much later on. His
critical mind was, in a sense,
more developed at that stage
than his fiction (the influence
of the Egyptian essayists he'd
been reading in *al-Risala* is

clear), and in one particularly telling 1955 exchange—a conversation
that took place at Haddad's house and was later published in his magazine under the title "Whither Literature?"—Taha and several other
writers were asked to address a series of massive, basic questions:

* Does the writer write for himself and for his own pleasure or
  does he write in order to improve [others] and enlighten?
* Must literature be committed [the Arabic word also means
  "obliged" or "compelled"] or free?
* Should the writer draw his material from society and the environment or write about his own feelings and experiences?
* Should literature be for literature's sake, or for life's sake?

Taha plunges right in and declares that committed writers view
the primary function of literature as being "advancement and better-
ment [of the reader]," and although books like those by Tolstoy do call
for such things and will indeed last, there are many great works of
world literature that don't and will also endure. He then rattles off a
list of masterpieces—*Romeo and Juliet, The Sorrows of Young Werther,*

Alexandre Dumas fils's *Lady of the Camillias,* Poe's "Black Cat," Wilde's "The Nightingale and the Rose"—which will, he says, "remain, as long as there are human beings who perceive beauty." The basic condition, then, for a work to be preserved over time is not the "improvement" it encourages but its "artistic quality and its distinctive beauty."

He goes on: partisans of "commitment" demand that writers draw their inspiration from "the outside" and leave no room for personal inspiration. But "we know of no literary work of Arabic or world literature worth preserving which is not a true mirror that reflects the feelings and personality of its author—not the feelings and personality of the society with which he is contemporaneous." And while Taha emphasizes the need to read literature with history and economics in mind, he gives several examples of great works whose force is drastically reduced by limiting them to sociological interpretation. It is not necessarily the sort of disquisition one expects from a young grocer with four years of formal schooling:

> If we studied the political, social, and economic concerns that occupied the people of Florence in particular and Italian society in general at the end of the thirteenth century, we could not truly understand *The Divine Comedy* since we would have learned about Italian society in a given day and period but not about the immortal Dante, which is to say that we would have learned all about the White Guelphs and the Black Ghibellines and their struggles but we would not have come to know the beautiful Beatrice, who loosened the knot of poetry

on Dante's tongue and who was the greatest influence on the creation of the eternal *Comedy*. In short, one could say that we had learned about collective consciousness and not about individual consciousness—the consciousness which is the basis of all art.

After offering up a similar critique of certain readings of al-Ma'arri and making it clear that he realizes all writers are influenced by the lives of the societies in which they live, he declares that "the true writer is the writer who writes his own feelings and ideas. In other words, he writes for himself."

To twenty-first-century Western ears, Taha's aesthetic pronouncements may sound so obvious as to be almost banal. But in the context of 1955 Palestinian letters, they put him squarely on the fringe. The year before, for instance, one of Taha's Nazareth friends and occasional visitors to the shop, Communist Knesset member Emile Habiby, had held forth on the pages of *al-Jadid*, saying, in essence, the opposite. "The literature we are calling for," wrote Habiby, "is the literature of the people. Literature that serves the people in its struggle toward a brighter future, literature that awakens consciousness of itself in the souls of the people and grants the people an understanding of its role and an understanding of the world that surrounds it and an understanding of the basic conflict that exists between those who seize hold of a morsel by the sweat of their brow and those who steal that morsel."

If these words ring more of a stump speech than a writerly meditation on the function of art, that may be because during these years Habiby—an educated, Haifa-born Protestant with a dashing manner and bold, unflappably energetic public persona and a man who would go on to pen some of the most singular, lasting, and truly inspired works of Palestinian fiction ever composed—was consumed by politics in the most day-to-day way, and for him at that stage the line between art and protest did not really exist. Which is not to say that he wrote mere agitprop. His own first story, "Mandelbaum Gate," published in 1954 in *al-Jadid*, under the pen name Abu Salam, "father of peace," blends in a remarkably sophisticated and even tender way his personal experience with a plain political message. (Habiby had in fact named his first son Salam, so that he himself would bear that pacific agnomen.)

The story is based on an episode in Habiby's life and recounts the day when he and his family accompanied his elderly mother to Jerusalem—in order to see her off through that titular gate, which separated the Arabs of Israel from the rest of the universe. After 1948, their family, like so many other Palestinian families, had been torn in two, and in order for her to travel to her other children who resided in that netherworld beyond, she would have to pass through the army checkpoint, out of Israel and into Jordan. Located amid "the rubble and green" of the border neighborhood al-Musrara, Mandelbaum Gate is the dividing line between "here" and "there," and Habiby's story becomes a riff on the illogic of these very notions. When, after bidding the old woman good-bye and seeing her pass over into the other, foreign zone, suddenly "a small body pulsing with life, like a ball kicked by the foot of a skillful player toward the goal of the other team"— Habiby's own small daughter—goes shooting out from their small group, across No Man's Land, and into her grandmother's arms. The story ends with the narrator marveling at "the ignorant girl . . . the naive child" who cannot tell the difference between the soldiers on one side and the soldiers on the other, her grandmother on one side and her father on the other, Hebrew on one side and Arabic on the other. In Habiby's sentimental but potent scheme, the child is the wisest of them all.

This pair of stories—Taha's "The Two Friends" and Habiby's "Mandelbaum Gate"—were written within a year of each other and within just a few Nazareth blocks by men who knew and liked one another. Yet everything about them is different, from subject to style to timbre to worldview. As Taha himself would probably now agree, Habiby's is by far the more mature and convincing of the two: in it are the seeds of much that he would eventually write. Taha, meanwhile, was a much later bloomer in literary terms, and ultimately fiction was not his primary form; neither was his engagement with politics ever as direct or practical as Habiby's. And here it is perhaps worth stepping back to recognize that Taha's life and work are not just the sum total of what he did and wrote. They also emerge in large part from what he did *not* do and did *not* write—for whether he himself chose to participate actively in the struggles waged by a writer like Habiby, they filled the very air that he and his contemporaries took in with each breath. Until the past few decades, Taha's stories and poetry, along with his much less deliberate approach to politics, were marginal in the Palestinian context. And in order to understand what takes place in the margins, one must know something of the page itself.

LIVES OF THE POETS

♦

YEARS LATER, EMILE HABIBY would describe himself as having spent his life carrying "two watermelons under one arm"—the watermelon of politics and that of literature. (He would also, in his final days, admit that this was a physical impossibility.) In the immediate wake of '48, however, and despite his eagerness to write fiction, he gave himself over in the most tireless fashion to hauling that first heavy fruit.

For Habiby, politics, too, was a verbal challenge. Hanna Abu Hanna writes in his memoir of first meeting "comrade Habiby" in 1948, post-conquest Nazareth and discussing with him the educational challenges he and his colleagues in the schools were facing "in this new period." Abu Hanna showed Habiby a notebook thick with pedagogic instruction, left behind by the British Mandatory Department of Education. "You'll need this now," Habiby told him, "with no house or furniture. . . . All that's left to us are words."

And words, it seems, flooded from Emile Habiby's pen. As editor of *al-Ittihad* for some thirty-five years, he wrote—in his own name, unsigned, or under a pseudonym—thousands of editorials and articles. The words also poured from his mouth, whether at his own naturally high volume or amplified by a megaphone. At gatherings held regularly throughout the 1950s by Maki—the Communist Party of Israel—at Nazareth's Empire or Rex cinemas, at al-Jabali's banquet hall or al-Sabagh's coffeehouse, Habiby would speak at length and with passion before crowds ranging from thirty to four hundred. On these occasions, he did not harangue so much as strive to inspire his listeners—a tack that appears to have worked. One British journalist who met him at that time described how Habiby was "full of the joy of life [and] not a bit like the surly misanthropes that Europeans are accustomed to associate with the name of communist. . . . For all his brilliance, he is respected and liked as the local family man—

with a gift for putting everybody's feelings into words." He had, it seems, ample occasion to do so. According to the records of the Israel Police—not surprisingly, given the repressive controls that the state used to monitor and intimidate its Arab citizens at that time, an all-too rich archival resource—Habiby held forth on everything from Ben-Gurion's refusal to allow the refugees to return, to the cruelty of the military government, the need to hold free and fair municipal elections in Nazareth, the persecution of Communist Party members, the government's moves to prevent "closeness between Arabs and Jews," the confiscation of Arab-owned land, and the firing of teachers on political grounds. (Teaching, it should be noted, was one of the few jobs open to Arab high school graduates in Israel.)

But these local battles were just part of a larger struggle. Habiby's disquisitions would veer sharply from the near at hand to the very far off—all, to his internationalist mind, part of the same grand design. At gatherings held throughout 1954, for instance, he vowed that "Maki will continue to fight against the government and against unemployment, in favor of Jewish-Arab brotherhood and in favor of establishing a mixed Jewish-Arab state in all of Israel," as he also offered fervent calls to "fight against the construction of . . . [American] military bases in Turkey . . . and the Turkish-Pakistani-American military pact, which constitutes a war against peace." In one instance he decried "the conspiracy to keep your rights from you and to intensify the military closure." (The police informant noted that Habiby had delivered this speech "with great excitement and had often spoken in simple folk language, in order to get his message across to the illiterate.") And on the next occasion he "surveyed the victories of the Communist Party throughout the world and the escalation of the people's struggle against imperialism and in favor of freedom and independence." Another time he spoke for a full hour and a half and compared the battles that the local people were fighting "to the righteous struggles being waged throughout the world, in Vietnam, Guatemala, and elsewhere." By 1955 the scope of his talk had widened further, and he expounded on current events that were then stormily unfolding in Egypt, Korea, Cyprus, Jordan, Algeria, and India.

From the very outset, poetry, too, played an important role in these combative yet festive conclaves—just as the nature of such assemblies would soon change the sort of verse local poets were writing. As early as November 1948, on the occasion of a Maki gathering at the Empire Cinema in honor of the thirty-first an-niversary of the Russian Revolution, Hanna Abu Hanna read a poem in the traditional Arabic "heroic" (*hamasa*) style. He himself describes how his words were greeted warmly by the listeners, though he was left feeling that in reciting such a poem in a classical vein, he "didn't blaze like a live coal but rather looked at it through a window pane." This is when his thoughts first turned to Mayakovsky and the idea of a new, "realistic" verse, appropriate to the political and social context: he was keenly aware of the need to write poetry that would be, in his words, "a platform," "transparent," and "easily grasped by the listeners." Over the next few years most Maki rallies featured a special "artistic program" in which poetry was a crucial ingredient— and served as a rhythmic verse extension of all the speechifying that had come before. After an address by Habiby, Tawfiq Zayyad, or one of their comrades from the Communist Party secretariat, Abu Hanna would read one of his rousing, topical poems about the imprisonment in Jordan of the former leader of the Communist Party of Palestine or, quite simply, "The Land." The al-Tali'a Choir also sometimes performed anthems for which Abu Hanna wrote lyrics, with titles like "The Return."

He was hardly the only one writing and reciting his pointed political poems during these years, and by the mid-1950s an extraordinary new phenomenon had begun to take shape throughout the Galilee: the now-fabled poetry festivals, held sometimes in cities but most often in villages without electricity or paved roads and attended by hundreds, even thousands, of people, old, young, male, female, all of whom were living under the smothering restrictions of the military government and many of whom could not read. Even those who were literate had, in those years, scant access to the unfiltered printed word; the recitations that took place at the festivals were one way around the censor. Which is not to say that the military government and the Shin Bet (General Security Service) did not do everything in their power to keep certain poets from reaching the festivals. And those who did manage to avoid roadblocks and police threats and reach the villages were also often punished later for having traveled without a permit or for defying an army closure. Many were imprisoned or placed under strict curfews and surveillance because of their participation in the festivals; teachers and other government employees who took part seriously risked losing their jobs—and often did. Still, many dared, and so their poetry managed to reach its needy audience.

In many ways the poets' defiance seems to have infused the eager crowds with a sense of possibility and strength. By all accounts, the festivals also instilled a crucial brand of cultural, linguistic, and communal pride that had been sorely lacking since 1948. The mass nature of the festivals made it possible for the people to stand up—or, more literally, talk back—to the authorities and to do so on their own terms. It hardly seems a coincidence that those terms involved poetry. The medieval historian Ibn Khaldun famously wrote that poetry is the "archive of the Arabs," and the notion seems even truer in the Palestinian context, where almost all other archives are lacking and where poetry has long been a basic fact of life. It is no exaggeration to say that, in their time—which lasted, with the military government, through the late 1960s—the festivals made poetry the most important means of political expression for the hemmed-in, cut-off Palestinians citizens of Israel.

The festivals were usually organized by local clubs or individuals associated with the Communist Party, and they took place most often in the main square of the village, which was lit with kerosene lanterns and which the people filled to bursting, some sitting on small straw stools but most standing or squatting for hours on end, so hungry were they to listen. Others—those who were especially afraid of the miseries that the military governor and his men might visit upon them for attending such a provocative political event—would listen from inside their houses or sit on their rooftops and take in the poems' echoes from afar.

And what echoes they were: sounds bouncing back across more than a millennium. Despite early attempts by Hanna Abu Hanna, Sasson Somekh, and a few others to introduce enjambment, irregular meters, and other new techniques to local verse, in the early years, most of the poets—including Tawfiq Zayyad, Hanna Ibrahim, 'Isam 'Abbasi, 'Isa Lubani, the Iraqi Jewish émigré David Semah, and others—preferred to retain the constraints of the classical, two-hemistich ode or to employ standard strophic modes. Both these forms pulsed in the "festival poetry" with what one observer called "oratory stress." He also describes the way these familiar sound patterns brought the poetry "close to the feelings of the people," who were, whether literate or not, steeped in the rhythms of the traditional Arabic meters almost from birth. Most of them had also absorbed a tremendous amount of oral folk poetry—*zajal*—to say nothing of whole lifetimes of Qur'anic recitation, and they knew that book's rhymed prose cadences like their own heartbeats. The classical forms were obviously musical and easily committed to memory, both excellent qualifications for the soapbox poetry the situation demanded.

At first the poets adhered to a few basic, local themes: the cruelty of the military government, the misery of the refugees, the preciousness of the land, the courage of villagers who had defied government plans to confiscate property or expel "infiltrators." Later—as word of revolutionary events from the world at large trickled in—the poets expanded their rhetoric slightly to include other stirring themes, and odes were composed to those waging civil wars, revolts, and insurrections in Algeria, Lebanon, Yemen, Vietnam, Sudan, and Syria. And behind or before all these other coups and armed collisions, the most important revolution of all was Gamal Abdel Nasser's. A few years after the Free Officers' revolt of 1952—when a band of young Egyptian veterans of the 1948 war in Palestine overthrew the corrupt, English-sponsored King Faruq—the charismatic conspirator turned president of the Egyptian Republic seized the imaginations of Arabs everywhere, and the Palestinian poets began to write paeans to the man they considered a present-day Saladin. Nasser's daring 1956 move to defy the Western powers and nationalize the Suez Canal in particular became the source of tremendous inspiration to the local poets. "Port Said" was the title of innumerable encomia. Later that year, during the Suez Crisis—when Egypt took on Israeli, English, and French forces to protect Egypt's control over the canal—the poems in his praise continued to abound at festivals, where listeners greeted them with wild enthusiasm.

Meanwhile, a bold new form of politically charged elegy had emerged in response to the massacre of forty-eight Palestinian citizens of Israel by the border police in the village of Kafr Qasim. At 4:30 in the afternoon of October 29, 1956—the same day that Israel and its French and English allies invaded Egypt—the authorities announced a 5 pm curfew in this village and others in the area, near the Jordanian border, along with a shoot-to-kill order for all violators. It was, however, too late to warn those villagers who were working in their fields and groves on the outskirts of town, and that evening, when they returned home on foot, truck, bike, and donkey, the soldiers began to fire. The murdered included six women, six girls, and seven boys, one just eight years old. News of the massacre was initially suppressed. Nearly two weeks afterward, Ben-Gurion's office would merely admit that some people in the region had been "injured," and only after serious pressure was applied by the Communists and a few maverick journalists did word of the mass, cold-blooded killing leak out and the prime minister acknowledge the "shocking incident."

Many Israeli Jews did express distress at what had happened ("One must write of no other subject," declared Hebrew poet Natan Alterman), but they generally perceived the massacre to have been, in the words of one contemporary commentator, a "misfortune," "mistake," or "regrettable incident." A trial was held and several officers were convicted, though they were all eventually pardoned or had their sentences commuted. Some were promoted to higher ranks, and while the commander of the unit responsible was later brought to trial and found guilty on a technicality, so that the true source of the order, his own higher-ups, would not be subject to legal scrutiny, he served no jail time and was punished with a fine of one piaster. A year after the massacre, a sulha—a much grander and more highly publicized version of the reconciliation ceremony to which the family of the murdered Ahmed Qablawi had been subjected—was also imposed on the surviving villagers of Kafr Qasim, who were all but ordered to break bread with (and so "forgive," as the cameras rolled) a smiling crowd of cabinet ministers, Knesset members, and union functionaries. The government must have thought that this "peaceful" rite meant the end of the troublesome matter.

For the Palestinians of Israel, however, the massacre, its whitewashed aftermath, and the humiliating sulha quickly emerged as the ultimate symbols of the state's punishing treatment of them—and a popular theme among the local Arabic-language poets. They rallied to commemorate the dead of Kafr Qasim in their verse, often defying military closures to sneak into the village and read their poems on the anniversary of the bloodbath. They were frequently arrested for doing so. Literary memorials were held every year on that date throughout the country, and the poetry of Kafr Qasim became, in a sense, a genre unto itself—and a particularly dramatic one at that. When a poet read his verse about the massacre aloud before a crowd it took on extra meaning, as though he were speaking not just for himself but for the group as a whole and as if the grisly event were not unique but the sum of so many others. It was in a sense a return to the pre-Islamic notion of the poet as voice of his tribe and as lucid guard of collective memory. A great number of the poems were quashed by the censor, so that their recitation grew doubly important: they were memorized and passed along orally, though this hardly seems to have lessened their force.

And even when a poem on the subject was printed, it was often subject to the censor's all-powerful eraser. "There is no monument, no rose, no memorial—" wrote the young Samih al-Qasim:

> neither a line of poetry to delight the murdered
> nor any curtain for the unveiling.
> There is no blood-stained shred
> of a shirt our upright brothers wore.
> No stone to bear their names.
> Nothing. Only the shame.
>
> Their spirits are hovering still,
> digging graves in the rubble of Kafr Qasim.

Though the second half of the poem (which followed) was excised by
the censor from al-Qasim's book, the poet insisted on indicating the
deletion and left eight lines of mute Xs where the words used to be.
These function almost like rows of tombs in the village cemetery, silent
but somehow expressive.

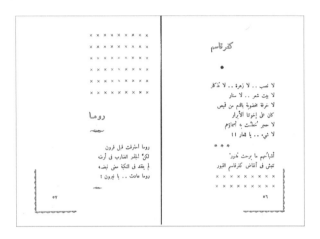

Beyond the obviously political function of such mass gatherings,
the festivals served a critical educational purpose, in the sense formulated by those pre-'48 cultural nationalists like Khalil al-Sakakini and
Is'af al-Nashashibi, whose ideas had influenced Taha's brief Saffuriyya schooling. This was patriotism that took hold through language
and literature. Then a fledgling Arab nationalist, later expelled by Israel
for his political activities, the high school teacher and poet Habib
Qahwaji sometimes participated in the festivals, and he has described
the "tremendous influence" these assemblies had, "by planting in the
hearts of the new generation the love of poetry, and by driving them
to read from the Arabic literary heritage and that of all mankind."
    Among the members of that new generation was Mahmoud Dar-
wish. At first a young boy in the audience, soon one of the festivals'
brightest stars—he participated in his first festival in Acre, in 1958—
he would later remember these gatherings with what he called "true
happiness" as having been "folk celebrations to which the people would
look forward." Still later, though, he would admit to far more mixed
feelings about the festivals. On the one hand, they offered the people
a terrific feeling of hope and provided them with a crucial means of ex-

pressing themselves politically; on the other, more sinister hand, they limited the poets drastically in terms of possible themes and tone. It would, he later said, have been impossible to have stood up at a festival and recited a love poem.

Darwish's high school classmate and friend Salem Jubran was another writer who started out listening to the festival poetry and wound up composing and intoning it, becoming one of the crowd's darlings in the process. (As teenagers, the two would share the poetry books they'd copied out by hand—by the Iraqi neoclassicist Muhammad Mahdi al-Jawahari and the Syrian love poet Nizar Qabbani—and would spar poetically according to the medieval Arabic tradition of literary dueling, a practice that entailed elaborate rhyming games and metrical challenges.) He also comments on the thematic limitations imposed by the festival setting but remembers in glowing terms the thrill the poetry would bring to people like his mother, who had never gone to school and could not read, "But when she sat in the main square, under the mulberry tree, and the poets were reciting"—he imitates how she would clap her hands—"she'd get more excited than me!"

The poetry festivals were, says Samih al-Qasim—who was a few years older than his friends Darwish and Jubran and would also rise to widespread fame by way of the festival stage—a form of "popular passive resistance," and he, too, remembers these gatherings as having been enormously important in context. His budding sense of himself not just as a Palestinian and as a poet but as a member of the wider Arab nation was also strengthened by his participation—or forced nonparticipation, as the case sometimes happened to be. He was first arrested as a nineteen-year-old in 1958 simply for planning to appear at a festival in the village of Kafr Yasif. The man who arrested him was, he recalls, an Ashkenazi police captain who spoke Arabic and called himself Abu Nimr. He was "blond, tall, handsome," and it enraged him that al-Qasim, a Druze, would "betray" the state with such actions. "Shame on you," the captain told al-Qasim, "You're a Druze. How can you participate with Muslims and Christians in something like that?" According to Samih, "I laughed, and said, 'I participate because I'm a poet. What does that mean, I'm a Druze. They're my brothers. Arabs like me.' And he got angrier, 'You will not participate!' and he arrested me."

Under Nasser's influence, Arab nationalism had, by 1958, become *the* rallying cry and cause célèbre throughout the Middle East. And although in the Israeli context the local Communists and nationalists would soon officially be at each other's throats because of the Qasim revolt, which took place in Iraq in July of that year, and the subsequent decision of the Soviet Union to throw its support behind the new Iraqi prime minister—instead of Nasser—in the intricate and often arcane isometrics of Cold War politics, allegiances were much blurrier up close and at ground level. The Communists were steadily gaining electoral popularity among the Palestinians of Israel. (Between the vote for the fourth Knesset in 1959 and the seventh in 1969, the Communists went from winning about a quarter of the Arab vote to taking almost half.) But Nasser and his pan-Arab vision were also beloved to an almost unprecedented degree. As one writer neatly put it: "Communism was a label and nationalism was what you felt in the pit of your stomach." When Nasser addressed a crowd and his words were broadcast on Radio Cairo, the streets and cafés of Arab Israel went utterly silent. Hanna Abu Hanna describes the way this voice "nailed" everyone in place and how, as he himself—then a devout Communist—listened, he "imagined that those present were all huge ears, sitting on the edges of their chairs."

Before the break between the camps in 1959, the Communists and nationalists drew closer, while the poets of the various streams also put their differences aside and appeared together at the festivals, making them even more popular with the ordinary people. With the exception of those in the cities and a few "red" villages, like Kafr Yasif, Bi'na, and Tayba, which had proud and active traditions of local involvement with Maki, these people may not have espoused one ideology or the other outwardly, but they identified almost instinctively with the goals of both.

One gathering in particular drew together a wide array of writers and thinkers and attracted a good deal of attention as a result. This was a Conference of Arab Poets and Intellectuals, held in the late afternoon and into the evening of January 2, 1958, at Nazareth's Empire Cinema. To judge from the fairly hysterical accounts of the event that remain in the police files, the powers that be were quite concerned by the convergence of talents that such an assembly represented. While it seems they could not stop the group from meeting—since the organizers had obtained legal permission to assemble and by this time permits were not required to travel to Nazareth from within the Galilee— they could, and did, monitor the proceedings and punish many of the participants afterward.

The police report states that some four hundred people filled the hall, half of them high school students. (Educated teenagers were rapidly becoming some of the most politically active Arabs in the country.) Poets, teachers, the entire Maki secretariat, priests, the son of the local *qadi,* or Islamic judge, and several politicians were also in attendance. Communist Knesset members Habiby and Tawfiq Toubi are mentioned by name, as are Tawfiq Zayyad and Mansour Kardosh, who now ran a small café next to his family's Nazareth ice and soft drink workshop while also emerging as one of the most articulate spokesmen for Arab nationalism in the country.

The proceedings included a speech by the poet 'Isam 'Abbasi, whom the report describes as "a known extreme nationalist and supporter of Maki." He "appealed to the Arabs of Israel to support Arab nationalism and the liberation movements that had recently awakened among the peoples of Asia and Africa," and the crowd responded with cries. The Communist poet and teacher 'Isa Lubani "discussed the value of the Arabic language and the early writers; he emphasized in his speech . . . cultural matters and the promotion of the Arabic language," and several other poets and teachers spoke and read, demanding "the release of the Arabs of Israel in the same way that the people of Asia have been freed from the yoke of imperialism." And "when Hanna Abu Hanna got up, all of those present greeted him with applause and cries." His poem was "dedicated to [the idea that] our world lives with a question mark and we must fight for freedom. And here the students were unable to control themselves and continued calling out in appreciation for the words of Hanna Abu Hanna."

Of all those who spoke on that wintry late afternoon, though, no one was greeted with more furious clapping and jubilant cries than yet another poet who was also a teacher, the twenty-two-year-old Rashid Hussein. This was the same Rashid who had made his debut in Michel Haddad's magazine and poetry anthology as an al-Ma'arri– loving high school student. When his first book of poems, *With the Dawn,* was published in 1957, it had immediately established him as one of the most popular Arabic-language poets writing in Israel. He was now preparing to bring out a second book, *Rockets,* and by the time he rose to recite a poem on the stage of the Empire Cinema, the audience already knew and loved Rashid for his simple style and rhetorical passion. There was also something a touch glamorous about him: he was handsomely tousle-headed, young, dark, and animated, with a constant half-smile and steady bass voice, and his demeanor was different from that of the older, stiffer, and more proper Communist poets, who were—according to one who remembers the period and its poetry well—viewed as "preachers" with a specific, Muscovite message to spread. He seemed at once fiercer and freer; he was an Arab to the core, but he also spoke Hebrew and he had Jewish friends. He thought of himself as both Palestinian *and* Israeli. He was a peasant who loved the city. The first of the prominent Palestinian poets to go without a mustache, he was also the first to have graduated from an Israeli high school, and this gave him a window onto both Hebrew literature and world literature in Hebrew translation. This window worked in complex ways, making him more sympathetic perhaps to the feelings of his Jewish countrymen—while it also granted him the insight to write, as he would that same year, that "whoever denies us [Arabs] the right to express our suffering and our hopes must also deny Bialik and [Hebrew-language Russian-Jewish poet Shaul] Tchernikovsky most of their nationalistic poems." Rashid would go on to translate a book of Bialik's poems into Arabic; he was hired to do so by the editors of a series sponsored by the Hebrew University, but it was an assignment of which he was proud.

Although Rashid had been writing in *al-Ittihad* under the pseudonym "Abu Iyyas," he was not a Communist. Like dozens of other politically engaged teachers, he had taken refuge behind a pen name in an attempt to both speak his mind and keep his job. He was identified with Mapam, a socialist Zionist party that had hitched its own Jewish nationalist wagon to the growing feeling for Arab nationalism all around, and he would later write incognito for the bulletin of the soon-to-be-banned nationalist movement al-Ard (The Land). But for all of these disparate affiliations, he seems not to have thought of himself in strictly partisan terms and rather to have acted and written from the gut. And it was this immediacy, this knack for expressing intimate feelings in a grand public way or of making the national personal, that so endeared him to "the people." The descriptions of his appearance at that 1958 Nazareth gathering certainly sound different from accounts of other poetry festivals, in which the physical presence of the poets almost never figures. Dressed in shirtsleeves and a traditional kaffiyeh, it is said, the striking young villager from Musmus stood on the stage and recited his classically metered, monorhymed poem "I Am from Asia"—a declaration of deep identification with Nehru and his people's struggle—and "set all hearts afire."

Rashid Hussein was the first celebrity poet to emerge on the Arab-Israeli stage—Mahmoud Darwish would, decades later, call him "the star"—but his appeal was not all about good looks and scene-stealing poise: his poems themselves marked a watershed in the development

of the local Arabic poetry, and when the other poets speak of him now, they do so in almost unanimously elegiac terms. Samih al-Qasim describes "the new atmosphere" Rashid created by lacing nationalism into his verse, and he has written of being dazzled by Rashid's recitations. Rashid was, as Samih puts it, the oldest brother in this "family of many poet-brothers" that was then taking shape. Samih was several grades behind Rashid at the municipal high school in Nazareth but had become part of his poetry-obsessed circle, while Darwish and Salem Jubran were students in Kafr Yasif and had written a letter introducing themselves to Samih, who had in turn introduced them to Rashid.

According to Darwish, Rashid showed them that it was possible to write about "human things"—refugee camp tents, bread, and hunger. Salem Jubran recalls in particular the way that Rashid declaimed his poems: "It was more beautiful than singing," he says, and people would come to festivals especially to hear him reciting his work. And Taha himself once wrote about Rashid, praising him—in terms unusual for Taha—as "the model of the patriotic, committed poet, the cultured youth, the sincere human being, . . . the prince of Palestinian poetry."

◆

Rashid was also—by all accounts—a singularly restless and even tortured soul, someone who was, no matter what the setting in which he found himself, unflaggingly generous, vulnerable to the point of recklessness, gentle, frank, affectionate, caustic, kind, at home both everywhere and nowhere. Indeed, of all the poets who emerged during this period, he was the one who appears to have suffered most for the contradictions he struggled to embrace. He is also the poet whom all the others mention the most frequently and with the most tremulous quiver in their voices. And this is not just because he died young and tragically—in self-imposed exile, lonely and alcoholic—of smoke inhalation in a New York apartment that caught fire when it seems he fell asleep clutching an ever-present cigarette. (The year was 1977 and Rashid was forty-one.) No, something else about Rashid causes his name to buoy up into the middle of nearly every conversation about that time and place and its poetry.

In the course of writing this book, I met no fewer than seven individuals who announced that Rashid had been their "best friend" and, to judge from the abundant written testimonials that also exist, Rashid had best friends everywhere. He seems to have possessed an uncanny gift for making each of those around him feel his confidant in an instant, as many of his friends were also driven by the need to try and protect him—most pressingly, from himself.

Taha, for one, recounts his first meeting with the teenage Rashid, five years his junior. Taha was at his shop when a fistfight broke out near the front door. Rashid and another, larger boy were pummeling each other, so Taha separated them, sent the other boy off, took Rashid inside, cleaned the blood off his lip, and plied him with a glass of water. "Why are you fighting?" he demanded to know, and Rashid burst into tears. He would soon become a regular at the store. He'd bring poems for critique and ideas for swapping, and he would tell Taha how much livelier he found this makeshift academy than the municipal high school where he was officially enrolled: "If only our teacher talked about al-Mutanabbi the way you do!" he said, and made a point of coming by almost every afternoon for a conversation about classical Arabic literature.

But Rashid's hunger didn't stop with Arabic and Arab society. As he grew older, he was also fascinated—and almost desperate to be accepted—by Israeli Jewish society. He craved Jewish friends and seems to have had a particular penchant for Jewish women; he loved Hebrew talk, smoky cafés, flowing booze, late-night parties. He was drawn, moth-to-flame-like, by the flash of this other world, which could not possibly have been further from his humble and teetotaling roots in Muslim Musmus. After graduating from high school and teaching for several years, he was fired for his political activities—his friend I. F. Stone was correct to write in relation to Rashid that "it seems as if there are forces in Israel which fear the Arab friend more than the Arab terrorist"—and late in 1958 he moved to Tel Aviv to edit and write political articles for Mapam's Arabic-language magazine, *al-Fajr* (The Dawn—named, it appears, after Rashid's first book). He also worked for the party's Arabic Book Company, the first local press since 1948 to publish books from around the Arab world. He threw himself headlong into the Jewish city's bohemian life, befriending Hebrew-speaking writers, artists, journalists, actors, musicians— though even as he mixed it up, he worked hard to promote the cause of his own people.

That October he helped to organize the country's first formal meeting between Arab and Jewish writers: this was held at the Tel Aviv studio of the Hebrew writer Binyamin Tammuz and was designed to foster understanding between the two utterly separate literary communities. In a sense, this was Rashid's personal mission, though he found willing partners in several Jewish editors and writers affiliated with the newspaper *Haaretz*. Many leading Hebrew and Arabic writers were invited, and the event began with cardamom-scented coffee that Rashid had prepared for the guests in a traditional gesture of welcome—but little that followed flowed as smoothly as that hot drink. By all accounts, the rest of the evening was difficult, and part of the controversy about it that later burst forth on the pages of the local press derived from a Hebrew translation (by Sasson Somekh) of Rashid's Arabic poem "The Locked Door," read aloud at the gathering. The poem was dedicated, "To my Jewish friend who asked me: why don't you describe the Negev and kibbutz and moshav in your poetry?"

> You tell me to describe the beauty of the kibbutz and moshav
> And the Negev and the Yarkon that drapes its sands as a gown.
> But you have forgotten, my brother, that you've locked me out.
> Do you want me to be a lying clown?
> You've locked me out.

Two other, more aggressively aggrieved poems—"The Land" by Hanna Abu Hanna and 'Isa Lubani's "Tale of a Struggle"—were also presented, and the reaction of the Hebrew writers was "total silence. [Poet] Avraham Shlonksy glanced at [novelist] Moshe Shamir. [Poet] Haim Gouri stared at the floor . . . everyone waited for his colleague to speak first." Shlonsky, according to one account, "recovered first. . . . He begged that the discussion remain focused on the poems' literary aspects." But soon after, the conversation descended into a murky pool of blunt political declarations, angry challenges, and sharp accusations—with Haim Gouri putting forth the standard Israeli Jewish plaint that "we came here to talk peace; but is there anyone in Damascus willing to print an article in the newspaper about peace with Israel?" Jabra Nicola, meanwhile, "hit the nail on the head by posing the disturbing question: how many of you know how to speak Arabic? Nearly all of us [Arabs] present . . . speak Hebrew. How do you intend, therefore, to communicate with us?" Gouri did at least have the decency to be startled later when, by his own account, "One [of the Arab writers] rises tottering, leaning on his cane, announcing he must take his leave. His colleagues explain that he has to go now because of the curfew. We are dumbfounded. It is far easier to deal with abstract matters."

Instead of new friendships, the event led mostly to acrimony, the reasons for which ranged from petty to pressing. Controversy arose about the exclusion of Communist Jewish writers from the guest list, and though 'Isa Lubani was fired from his teaching job after his poem was reprinted in *Haaretz*, none of the Jewish writers came to his defense. But the problem, more essentially, was that these two isolated islands—of Arabic and Hebrew writing—seemed for the time being unbridgeable, and the Arab writers clearly felt that their Jewish colleagues were not making much of an effort to understand their perspective. Hanna Abu Hanna put it plainly, "The greatest obstacle was the Jewish writers' ignorance about the problems of our people." Taha was also present at the gathering and dismisses it with a dark laugh now as "nonsense." He says one of the Hebrew writers asked where he was from, and Taha answered, in English, "Nazareth," but the man corrected him, saying "Natzrat" (Nazareth in Hebrew). "To sum up tonight's meeting," Taha clears his throat in a mock-official manner, "We have traveled from Nazareth, and now we'll return to Natzrat."

To judge from the imperious response to the event by the influential Hebrew literary critic Gabriel Moked, Abu Hanna was right: the Jewish writers did indeed lack a basic empathy for their Arab counterparts. Moked wrote and published a lengthy dismissal of the poems that were read at the gathering, claiming they bore "no relation to literature." They were "placards, primitive in their simplicity," whose place was not in the literary supplement of a distinguished paper like *Haaretz,* since "one must not conduct a political debate using the guise of literature." He went on: "One cannot ascribe to the poetry of Hanna Abu Hanna, for instance, any qualities that might distinguish it from a fervid patriotic essay by an elementary or high school student from Musmus or [the Arab town of] Umm al-Faham." (The nasty allusion to Musmus seems to have been aimed like a dart in Rashid's direction.) "We must be prepared," he condescended to elaborate, "to talk with Abu Hanna, Hussein, Lubani, etc., as citizens, as Arabs. But we are not obliged to see poetry in their poetry or intellectual thinking in their intellectual thinking, because this poetry, this art, this thinking seems, to me at least, as lagging more than a hundred years behind." His sense of poetry's purity had been offended, and he would not let go, insisting that "a primitive graphomaniac is a primitive graphomaniac, whether he is a fascist, a communist, a democrat, or Arab nationalist."

Rashid was not one to let a gauntlet, once thrown down, lie in the dust. He seized it up and wrote a passionate response that was published in Hebrew and shows him at his excitable, eager-to-communicate best, as he wondered:

> What is the literature that Mr. Moked longs for? Of course we could compare the moon this time to a bald head and that

time to a plate full of honey, this time to a little pat of margarine and that time to a golden boat, this time to a princess
swimming with her daughters the stars and that time to an
American cowboy. . . . But that wasn't what we wrote or read
at the gathering. It seems to me that if we'd read poems of this
sort . . . Mr. Moked would have clapped his hands and wept
with feeling.

Rashid wasn't just being a wise guy. For the benefit of Moked or
whoever was reading, he patiently explained the essence of his own
literary project and of the other writers whose work was read aloud
that night. These poems, he wrote, "come from the pain and bitterness that well up from a certain situation in which certain people live.
Never will a Tel Aviv dweller understand, sitting in his comfortable
room and listening to records as he tries to forget the past or flee from
it. Certainly, a reader will be moved by them who grew up in Germany
and hasn't forgotten that yesterday he was expelled or fled from his
home!"

Though the newspaper debate dwindled after a few months, and
though it took many years for another official attempt at literary rapprochement between Israel's Arab and Jewish writers, Rashid continued to battle to bring about some kind of exchange—with friends,
with enemies, with anyone who would agree to wrestle.

◆

But life in Tel Aviv wasn't all argument. If anything, Rashid was determined to enjoy himself there. As al-Qasim recounts it, Rashid rel-
ished his new role as peasant-turned-playboy: "Sometimes he'd invite
me, if a singer came from Spain, a guitarist from Argentina. . . . He
was too generous, and whatever he earned, he wasted."

Wasted. The term comes up often in relation to Rashid and refers
both to his tendency to squander cash and to his frittered talents:
after those first two books, Rashid continued to write constantly—
scribbling on cigarette boxes and stray scraps of paper—but he didn't
always finish what he started and published sporadically, bringing out
his third and final volume of poems only two decades later, a year

before his death. Although he dashed off a great deal of playful yet biting journalistic prose while he worked at *al-Fajr*—articles on everything from the sorry state of Arab education in Israel to Otto Preminger's *Exodus* ("If I were a Jewish youth and I saw this movie, I would come out hating Arabs, all the Arabs!")—many say he sacrificed his poetry on the altar of hackwork, of politics, of the good life. Some simply point to the bottle.

It seems telling that almost everyone who writes or talks about Rashid mentions food and drink, and in particular his almost desperate need to shower with edibles all those he loved. He appears to have had an acute, nearly physical compulsion to make his affection tangible and would, for instance, treat his friends to extravagant lunches he could not afford. Al-Qasim recalls how Rashid once insisted on wining and dining him at a Tel Aviv restaurant. "Did Rashid win the lottery?" Samih asked Rashid's then-girlfriend (later wife) Ann, a freshly pretty American Jew, who later explained that Rashid had been paying for a manual typewriter in monthly installments—and that, on a whim, he'd hawked it for half the price a few hours before, to pay for the lavish meal. Ann herself remembers Rashid's extreme generosity as having  been a matter of stubborn insistence, Arab hospitality taken to an almost perverse extreme. But she also recalls the gifts he'd lavish on his family back in Musmus. They had very little, and when Rashid visited from Tel Aviv (where he was living with Ann in a box-sized studio apartment with a breezy balcony, where they'd often entertain), he'd come bearing multiple chickens.

In 1966 Rashid followed Ann to Ohio, where she studied for a graduate degree in psychology and he floundered and drank and continued to scribble, teaching himself English by watching old Westerns on TV and reading any text he could find. Before Christmas, the great hope of Palestinian poetry found work in the perfume section of a downtown Columbus department store. It was, says Ann, a job for

which he was oddly suited, since he could charm any male shopper into buying scent for his wife and coax any woman to splurge on her man's aftershave. He would, she remembers, come home reeking of eau de cologne. The job did not last long, however, and after the couple's impromptu 1967 road trip to Montreal, to see Expo and old friends, Rashid was stopped at the U.S. border and almost not allowed back into the country. Threatened with his deportation, he and Ann decided to marry—soon moving to Manhattan, where he enrolled as a student at New York University ("not because I love to study but because people here are judged by their degrees," he wrote in a letter). He also did odd translation and copywriting jobs for the newly formed Palestine Liberation Organization delegation at the United Nations and continued to drink, scribble, and drink more.

All the while he bombarded his friends back in Haifa with sometimes nagging aerograms—listing all the other friends who hadn't answered his letters and then turning to the correspondent at hand to plead for attention and ask, "Why don't you find a few minutes to respond to my letter?" But sometimes these missives were more quietly eloquent and ominous: "As regards my writing, I write. . . . But what I write is different from what some people want to hear, so I read to myself what I've written, in a resounding voice. . . . Then I throw it in the drawer and forget about it. And then the day comes when I remember where I put what I wrote." He was surrounded by friends, but he was homesick, and he'd cook *mjaddara* for anyone who would let him, as if presenting a steaming bowl of this ur-Palestinian peasant rice-and-lentil dish might somehow induce Musmus right on the spot—even if that spot were in Manhattan. The poet and activist Fouzi El-Asmar describes visiting Rashid in New York and walking with him through a street festival in Little Italy. "He bought all kinds of foods, drinks, candies and desserts. When I insisted I didn't need them he said simply: 'It doesn't matter. Just take it and throw it away.'"

Such painful anecdotes have a way of accumulating around the memory of Rashid Hussein. And it is, of course, tricky to untangle the postmortem legend from who he really was—the Arabic-language memorial book describes him repeatedly as a "hero" and "martyr," as if he had fallen in battle, and one posthumous Lebanese source claims, absurdly, that he was "expelled by the occupation forces and

banished from his homeland"—but from all the tales about him, it is clear that Rashid was in his friends' minds both a singularly gifted, anguished individual and the symbol of something much larger than himself. The Israeli peace activist and journalist Uri Avnery recounts a story that Rashid himself related, "a tall, thin youth standing before me and in a soft voice, telling me what happened" the day, sometime in the mid-1950s, the military commander summoned the high-school-aged Rashid to his office and informed him he would be hosting an Independence Day reception for Arab notables. "I want you to write a nice poem honoring the State of Israel," the commander told Rashid, "and I want you to read it at the gathering."

According to Avnery:

Rashid Hussein was a sensitive man—perhaps the most sensitive man I ever met. He was insulted to the depths of his soul.

"I don't write poems upon demand," he answered, with resolute pride.

The commander didn't waiver. "Look, you're a young boy from a good family. Help us and don't worry. It will be worth your while and your family will come out ahead."

In a somewhat more threatening manner he added: "After all, we all love the State, don't we? Certainly you want to express your love."

"I oppose the regime and everything it does," said the trembling Rashid. "The government stole our land. The government prevents me from moving around the country without a travel permit. The very existence of the military regime

symbolizes the oppression of the Arab minority in Israel. And
you want me to write a poem praising the military regime? Do
you think I'm a whore?"

At this stage, writes Avnery, the commander changed tacks and warned
Rashid that if he did not obey, "his whole family would suffer." But
Rashid continued to refuse—and when he returned to his village, he
found the women of the family "falling on the ground, tearing their
clothes, letting out bloodcurdling cries. The men sat to the side, silent
and mournful. 'Who died?' Rashid cried. 'You have killed us! You have
murdered the family,' replied one of the women." The authorities had
already sent word that the entire family would be made to pay dearly
for Rashid's intransigence.

Rashid was "torn between his loyalty to his family and to himself—
both to his ideals and to his conscience." Faced with that terrible
equation, he buckled and immediately wrote the governor a short
poem in praise of the state. In Avnery's view, "That was the day Rashid
Hussein died. The twenty years that followed were a dark depression,
a depression that choked him like a hangman's noose tightening ever
so slowly."

Avnery's account of Rashid's struggle is perhaps a bit melodramatic and reductive: surely the pain of no man's life can be explained
in its entirety by recounting the events of a single dreadful day, and
Ann Hussein for one reads the story differently, saying that the incident actually *focused* Rashid by first alerting him to the power that his
poetry could command. But there is clearly something to Avnery's version. Rashid was in many ways the victim of his circumstances, and
those circumstances were, of course, not just his own but his entire
people's. Although he found himself trapped between all these warring forces—political, familial, poetic, economic—he was not alone.
His vexed life simply raised to the level of symbol what so many others
also faced. I. F. Stone would later write that Rashid had "died of homelessness, a homelessness for which we [Jews] are responsible," something that could be said—whether literally or figuratively—of tens of
thousands of other Palestinians. Rashid himself, meanwhile, seems
never to have blamed the Jews alone for his plight.

In 1961, after traveling to Belgrade as a journalist to cover a
conference of nonaligned nations, Rashid wrote in despair of "the

tragedy of the Israeli Arabs," scorned by both the Israeli government and the Arab world: "Of course," he wrote, "I did not expect the Arab reporters to embrace me, but I was not prepared to read in their eyes, and certainly not to hear them express in words, the very same charges that are leveled against me in Israel. . . . I no longer knew who I was, a nationalist Arab loyal to his people, or a suspect Israeli citizen." And even after his political rhetoric had been radicalized by his work with the PLO and by brief stints in Beirut, Cairo, and Damascus, he spread his critique around democratically, going so far as to hang in his New York bedroom a map of the Arab states, affixed with his own handwritten warning: "Thought forbidden here."

However keen his critical faculties, though, the loosely stitched fabric of his life was quickly unraveling. After much misery, Ann had left. Rashid's constant drinking, his Old World male possessiveness, and his maddening habit of spending on trifles whatever money she earned had made life with him next to impossible. Looking back over the decades, she muses that Rashid drank to numb himself. Other poets may have found solace in writing, but for Rashid, poetry itself had turned into a thorn in his side—and the very act of verbalizing his own and his people's sorrows had become almost unbearable. After they divorced he began to drink still more heavily, was evicted from several New York apartments, and became a certifiable, if still somehow endearing, wreck. At around this time he appeared at the Village Gate with Pete Seeger and folksinger Theodore Bikel in an evening of "Israeli and Arabic music and poetry," and wrote one of his most famous poems, "Without a Passport," which would become a kind of anthem among displaced Palestinians: "I was born / without a passport, / raised without a passport / and saw my country turned into jails." Eventually he found steadier work as a correspondent for the bulletin of the Palestine News Agency, and though Rashid was hardly one for strict deadlines and regular hours, he was soon promoted to bureau chief and granted the unofficial title of PLO spokesman. The Libyan mission named him a special adviser—yet these various honors seem to have washed over him in a flood tide of vodka and grief.

Edward Said was yet another friend, and he describes the Rashid he knew during this period as having existed in a "state of living anarchy." But, he says, there was still some method to Rashid's sadness.

Said writes of how the "sense of a squandered, wasted life he communicated—too much drink, too much tobacco, too little self-discipline and care and intellectual attention—never really burst through, did not really destroy, the basic order of his being." For Said, Rashid's weaknesses were redeemed by his embodiment of a grander design: "It seemed enough for him, as for anyone who came to know him, to be a Palestinian, as if, in its existential and complicated state, our unfortunate lot as a people *was* a political statement, which, in his now totally authentic way, Rashid lived. Therefore, he talked, walked, breathed, dreamt and acted the Palestinian agony with pride, a complete lack of self-conscious posing, and a simplicity, more dignified and coherent, than anyone I knew."

If Avnery's account is reductive, Said's version may be overly romantic—an elegant attempt to make sense of a most inelegant life. And yet, taken side by side, as dots in a pointillist painting, the testimonials begin to fuse into a convincing portrait, and one that explains the uncanny hold that Rashid had—and continues to have—on the imaginations of all those who knew him and his poems.

Ten days before Rashid's death, some three weeks before his body was flown back to Musmus, where it was greeted by what news reports described as more than ten thousand mourners and a large sign declaring, "Rashid welcomes his honored guests!" he sent a note to his estranged wife. It was adorned with a colorful 3-D figure in traditional Palestinian dress and handwritten crookedly, in clear if sometimes-misspelled English:

Dear Ann,
Thanks for the card, in fact thanks for remembering that I still exist. And happy New Year to you and all those you love. . . .

I feel very sad while writing to you. My post is like the post of ambassador. I have fifteen employees. But feel misrable. To be the director of a News Agency and adviser to the Lybian mission, at the U.N. and the U.S. is not my cup of tea. Last month the Lybian embassy at the U.N. gave a party in the U.N. in the "honor of R. Hussein." Believe me, I don't remember even one name of the 300 guests except those I knew before.

I had a new book published. Its third edition is coming out next week in W-D.C. (Arabic).

But all the prestige and big sallaries are nothing. What is lost cant be compensated. I ~~hope~~ wish you the best. Call if you come to N.Y.

Rashid

"The question wasn't how to live," Said writes in his essay about Rashid. "But how, in the close to desperate morass of the Palestinian situation, one could *be* at all." Perhaps the greatest riddle that attends the troubled memory of the troubled Rashid Hussein—as it also hovers over the lives of all the Palestinian poets, Taha included—is why some sink, some swim, some flail, some float. What force of history or character or sheer bad luck was it that drove Rashid to his smoky death in that cramped apartment on East Forty-sixth Street, while thirty years later Mahmoud Darwish received interviewers from all over the world in a grand office in battered, army-checkpoint-encircled Ramallah and Taha Muhammad Ali sat poring intently over a dog-eared dictionary in his Nazareth souvenir shop?

A LEAP OUTSIDE

◆

THE EVENTS OF MAY 1, 1958, should not have surprised the Jewish authorities. On that day, at a rally in Nazareth, the frustrations felt by the Palestinian minority burst forth in a geyser of hurled stones and angry cries for justice.

The ongoing and stifling presence of the military government, the overwhelming lack of political power held by Arabs in Israel, discrimination both social and economic, the confiscation of huge tracts of Palestinian land (including the large hill that looked down, so to speak, on Arab Nazareth and that would eventually become the Jewish town of "Upper Nazareth")—all combined to create these frustrations, which were exacerbated by Israel's plans to celebrate its tenth birthday that month. Grandiose military parades and folk dancing in the streets were scheduled, and the powers that be were eager to show off the progress the state believed it had brought to its Arab citizens. Toward this end, the Ministry of the Interior had selected a Turkish bathhouse in the old city of Acre to play host to an "Exhibition of the Folklore of the Minorities," complete with mannequins dressed in traditional garb and "authentic" Arab coffee and sweets for all comers.

Far less desirable for PR purposes was that Nazareth May Day demonstration, conceived weeks in advance by the Communist Party. Anticipating trouble, the authorities had given preference to the Histadrut and Mapam rallies, meanwhile denying the Communist organizers a permit for the hour they'd requested, raiding their headquarters, arresting many of them days before in a "preventative" sweep (the "administrative detainees" included Emile Habiby, Hanna Abu Hanna, and Tawfiq Zayyad), and eventually banning the rally outright. Yet the party decided to press on, and by the scheduled 10 am start time, vast numbers of baton- and shield-wielding police had massed near Mary's Well, all but inviting the demonstrators to join them in a violent showdown. Clashes inevitably followed, as did widespread beatings and arrests. Harsh punishments were meted out to many who took part (up to two years of jail time), and both Hebrew and foreign newspapers characterized the day's events as a "riot," laying the sole blame with the Communist Party for having "used the excuse of the day of the workers to demonstrate its hostility to the state of Israel." At a cabinet meeting a few days later, one indignant Ukrainian-born Jewish minister went so far as to call what had happened in Nazareth a "pogrom."

Arab descriptions of that May Day stand in stark contrast to this official version. Many speak proudly—almost mythologically—of the collective strength the people showed that day, in the face of the "truncheons and vicious abuse" the police wielded against those they'd arrested. Heroic accounts are offered by everyone from the novelist Ghassan Kanafani—who was not himself present but who recounts the way the violent events inspired the composition of hope-giving popular songs, since "the word does more than gunfire and can burst through the blockade around it"—to one Abu Ghanem, the burly, balding owner of a modest Nazareth hummus restaurant with whom I once drank coffee. A native of Saffuriyya with a contagious laugh, Abu Ghanem recounts the role played in the demonstration by Arna Khamis, the Jewish wife of Communist organizer Saliba Khamis. She was very pregnant at the time and, he tells me, fearless: bellyfirst, she lead the crowds into battle while the Jewish cops taunted her mercilessly: "You whore of the Arabs!" Meanwhile—Abu Ghanem wants me badly to know and leans in across the Formica table for emphasis—"it was important to us that she was a Jew," standing up for the rights of others.

And where, while all of this stormy history transpired, was Taha?

"In the shop," he tells me matter-of-factly, when I ask him about his whereabouts on that notorious day. "I heard about it from people."

His answer is both slightly incredible and somehow plausible. On the one hand, the shouting, chanting throng had swarmed the center of town, which must have brought it well within earshot of Taha's souvenir shop, located near a main intersection. How could he not have ventured outside, at least for a quick look? On the other hand, Taha had made his choices early on about where he wanted to stick out his neck and where he didn't or felt he couldn't, and the fact that

he neither took part nor seemed to have paid much attention to the furious roar mounting just down the street is in keeping with much else about his story. Taha was not an activist in the usual sense, yet he, too, had chosen to act—to support his family, to educate himself, to preserve the memory of his village, to welcome all kinds of people to speak their minds openly in his shop. Although by then he had begun to vote for the Communist Party, he never became a member, and he would not join the protest that day.

As it happened, 1958 also marked a turning point for Taha, though of a very different sort. This was the year when word reached him— by letter, via a cousin working in Saudi Arabia—that Amira, who was still in Lebanon and had waited for Taha for ten long years, had married someone else.

Taha was, naturally, devastated. He says he barely ate for weeks on end, and he grew so thin, pale, and agitated that his parents—to whom he could not bear to relay the news at first—believed that his TB had returned.

Realizing that reunion with Amira had become a next-to-impossible prospect, they had gently been trying for years now to steer him toward another wife. Taha himself had, though, rejected out of hand each match they proposed, and while he was at twenty-seven considered old to be single, he did not care a bit. He'd had no word from Amira since they parted, but he would have waited for her for another decade if need be. In the meantime—and quite unusually for this social setting, in which the eldest son almost always married first— Amin had agreed to a match with a woman from Saffuriyya (Taha had first been offered her hand and refused) and had wed before both of his older brothers. He already had two small children.

Taha finally told his parents the truth and almost immediately thereafter let them arrange a marriage for him with someone else. Given the prolonged wait for Amira—which had begun, in essence, when he peered through the iron cradle bars at the day-old baby she'd been when they were betrothed—the preparations for this other wedding went by in a flash. It was decided: Taha would marry Yusra Qablawi, daughter of the widow Radia Abu Najj, sister to the murdered young Ahmed Qablawi, and the little girl whom Taha had lifted over a stream when their families returned together from Lebanon and shared a meal of dibbis and bread.

In 1959, the year they were married, Yusra was eighteen years old. Bright, pretty, and exceptionally good-natured, she had grown up surrounded by women and girls in Radia's house, and this experience had rendered her equal parts tough and sheltered. She had inherited or absorbed much of her mother's and grandmother's fortitude, intelligence, and industry. From an early age she'd helped her mother to cook, sew, clean, plant, and harvest, and she says now that already as a child she understood how to stand up for what was hers. She had then, as she still has, Radia's down-to-earth dignity and total lack of guile. She knew how to speak her mind. But she was, too, the baby of the family, and her loving female minders had been desperate to protect her from even the perception of harm to her person or reputation. So it was that after just a few weeks of attending the first grade, her mother had pulled her out. Some boys had called to Yusra as she walked alone to school, and Radia had decided that her daughter's honor was in danger. That was the end of her schooling.

Aside from their one (fateful?) encounter over the spring near the Lebanese border nearly ten years before, Yusra and Taha had never had any direct contact: they had certainly never spoken. Their grandmothers were sisters, and in many ways, the match was conceived as a marriage between the branches of an extended family rather than the joining for life of two distinct individuals. That would have to come with time. After a Sunday afternoon meeting of the entire crew at Radia's house, Taha gave his taciturn consent, though the shadow cast by Amira's Lebanese wedding hovered heavily over the proceedings. It was not mentioned, of course, but Taha's lengthy engagement to his first cousin was well known to everyone present that day, as sweets were nibbled and coffee was sipped. Although for years to come Taha would remain wrapped in a kind of mourning for Amira and all that her loss represented, he had resigned himself to this new arrangement and went along with the plans.

Yusra herself had heard about Amira, but she was so excited at the idea of her own marriage to Taha that she says she "was flying." He was considered, she says, "educated and good-hearted, from a good family. And he worked at a newspaper [al-Mujtama'] and he had a shop." Taha was by now earning real money, and he had the means to pay the traditional bride price and buy her the gold jewelry that was expected by young women at the time of their engagement. (In Muslim culture, the groom's family pays the dowry.) It was important to him that Yusra start her married life with the appropriate number of bangles, necklaces, and rings, as well as four complete new sets of clothing, sewn of the best imported fabrics by an expert dressmaker in Haifa. With one of her aunts as chaperone, the couple took a taxi all the way to the shop, Yusra tells me, and when they returned, Taha's mother served them a celebratory meal of *mansaf,* lamb with rice and a rich yogurt sauce. Then in the months after the engagement—when the wedding contract was signed and the opening lines of the Qur'an were recited—Yusra was sent to the convent school that was the only pre-'48 Saffuriyya institution still operating in what was now Tzippori: there she learned to embroider, crochet, make lace, and needlepoint. Her mind awhirl with thoughts of all that lay ahead, she slowly prepared a bridal chest, sewing coverlets, sheets, and pillowcases. On the fanciest of these she fixed a small tin hoop and through it stitched rosebuds and twining vines with delicate silk thread.

◆

The wedding was a low-key affair. Taha's family, says Yusra, "didn't like a lot of noise" and preferred to keep things subdued. But her mother did throw a party for the women at her own house the night before. Radia played the oud, and the usual ululations and songs were accompanied by homemade stuffed cookies and "bought" baklava. The next day, according to tradition, Taha's family came to Reina to fetch Yusra—who wore a simple, almost girlish white dress with long sleeves and a modest lace-trimmed bodice—and they brought her back in a car to Nazareth, where a lunch for some forty people was held at the family's apartment near the White Mosque. And with that Yusra became Taha's wife and a member of the household at large, so coming to share her life—as well as a kitchen, a bathroom, and many long hours of every day—not just with her new husband but with his entire family.

What was it like to be married suddenly to someone you barely knew? How did it feel to leave the people, rooms, trees, and objects that had almost always surrounded you and wake up the next morning in an unfamiliar city house full of near-strangers? How did the others relate to the presence of this eager teenager in their midst? What about sex? About the early months of this marriage, the biographer must make do with vague speculation and terse answers to a few gingerly phrased questions. "That is how it was done," it is said. "It was normal." (Few subjects are off-limits in my interviews with Taha and Yusra, but I myself prefer to pull the shades down when it comes to asking about the more intimate connubial particulars.) Both of them make a point of telling me that Taha tried early on to teach Yusra to read. They had gotten hold of an old copy of the elementary level of Khalil al-Sakakini's Mandate-era primer, which they still refer to with the nickname *Ras Rus*—"Head, Heads," for the first words in the book—and the two began to work their way through it together. She did learn to sign her name, but at a certain point the grand project of making her literate was abandoned, and Taha instead took to reading aloud to Yusra. She had, and still has, an incredible sensitivity to words, says Taha, and with time, she would become his first—and most important—"reader." Every story and poem that he has written since they married he has read aloud to her before all others. And she is an appreciative but critical listener, offering pointed suggestions along with her praise.

And here, with the start of this new phase of Taha's life, a calmer, less dramatic pace took hold. In Taha's telling, these years are collapsed, and the events that bear mention fall under the rubric of happy but expected occasions, like the birth of their first child, a son, the year after the marriage: Taha named him Nizar, after the poet Nizar Qabbani, and so became Abu Nizar, as Yusra was now Imm Nizar. This was followed several years later by the birth of a daughter, Layla.

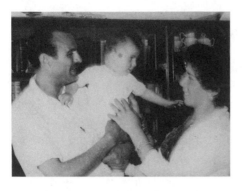

Amin's wife, Sabha, had also borne several more babies. As Taha continued to serve as the main breadwinner for the rapidly expanding crew—whose number, within a few years, would swell to thirteen—Amin took responsibility for the day-to-day management of the household, the women cooked for everyone, and the cousins played together in the courtyard. It was, in a sense, like a small commune, with everyone doing their part.

In 1960, Taha was offered a chance to buy a shop on Casa Nova Street, the road that leads up to the Church of the Annunciation and into Nazareth's main suq. It was a prime location for a souvenir shop. This was the year that construction had begun on the imposing basilica whose conical stone and blackened copper cupola now loom over the center of Nazareth. Designed by the Vatican to be the largest church in the Middle East, it replaced the much more modest stone structure—built in 1730 over the ruins of Byzantine and Crusader chapels—that had formerly occupied the same space. So pilgrim traffic there was almost sure to increase. The only problem with Taha's proposed move, how-ever, was the money it required: he had managed to save some 1,500 liras, but the purchase of the new shop demanded three times that much.

By now Yusra was deeply involved in the workings of the shop and of her husband's heart and head; they had become quite close, and his priorities had evolved into her own. Without thinking twice, she says, she offered to sell off most of her be-trothal gold to help Taha make the purchase. Keeping for herself just one ring and one bracelet, she cashed in the rest, and Taha soon moved to his new shop, a tiny box of a place that he packed full of olive wood rosaries, camels, and crucifixes, bottled "holy water," postcards, old coins, worry beads, and a ragtag menagerie of candlesticks, trays,

beakers, mortars and pestles, broken watches and stopped clocks, decorative plates, engraved cups, and dented coffeepots, all of it heaped in tag-sale fashion on shelves of his own construction. Over the whole he then hung a hand-painted English and Hebrew sign, announcing to one and all that the NIZAR SOUVENIR SHOP was open for business.

◆

Taha had, for the time being, given up writing fiction. Due to lack of funds, *al-Mujtama'* had folded in 1959. (By then he'd published five stories there, along with various book reviews and translations.) But he says the real reason he stopped was because he understood that what he had written to date just wasn't good enough. He knew he must prepare himself further and "Read, learn, read." He studied "Maupassant with his 272 stories" and "always dreamed about the masterpiece I would like to write."

As part of his preparations, he agreed to take on a new critical project, and late in 1960, he and Michel Haddad began to publish a regular literary roundup, called "A Window," in *al-Yawm*. Although the newspaper's government-boosting politics were, he says, "far from me," he and Michel were given free rein to write about whatever books or writers they wanted. Published most Fridays, this half page or so of tightly packed newsprint was described on its debut as "a narrow window that attempts to look out on a wide area that knows no boundaries."

That initial installment was typical of what would follow—a generous hodgepodge of thoughts and quotations and critical ideas, not unlike the jumble of objects that filled the shelves of Taha's shop: a brief article about Taha Hussein and innovation in poetry was followed by a poem by the Lebanese symbolist Sa'id 'Aql and an excerpt from an article about "'Antar . . . the Knight and the Poet," reprinted from an Arabic magazine published in Buenos Aires. A translation of a story by the fin-de-siècle French writer Jules Renard appeared, together with a brief introduction. Finally, this "Window" contains an article—the most explicitly critical of the lot—about the disproportionate influence of Nizar Qabbani on the younger local poets, who are mentioned by name and include Mahmoud Darwish, whose first book had just been published that year, and Samih al-Qasim, who had brought out his maiden volume in 1958. "Nizar Qabbani is an original poet," wrote Taha or Michel (the piece is not signed, though to judge from the prose style and unflinching tone, these are likely Taha's words). "And we see nothing wrong with a young poet reading and being influenced by great poets in various ways. But . . . he must search for originality within himself and his environment and develop a style and a path to express himself uniquely, as Nizar himself did."

And they were off and running. Over the next few years they would publish some thirty installments of this "Window," filled with short articles that ranged from appreciations of writers as various as Fadwa Tuqan, Henri Bergson, Tawfiq al-Hakim, and Françoise Sagan (also André Gide, Rabindranath Tagore, al-Ma'arri, Goethe, Salah 'Abd al-Sabur, and Frédéric Mistral, to name just a few) to surveys of "Berber Verse," "Artistic Form and Literary Responsibility," and "A New Direction in Sudanese Poetry." While none of the articles was profound—they were clearly written in haste and were for the most part summaries of other people's ideas, designed to provide information rather than analysis—they do offer a running log of what Taha was reading at this stage of his literary apprenticeship, as well as a chronicle of his aesthetics-in-formation.

In the context of this "Window," Taha also reckoned for the first time with the radical modernist poetics then being put forth in Beirut by the Syrian-born Adonis and Yusuf al-Khal on the pages of their groundbreaking journal, Shi'r. Founded in 1957, Shi'r—which means simply "Poetry"—stood at the forefront of the Arabic literary avant-garde, as its poet-editors advocated a drastic rethinking of the entire Arabic tradition: this was not an abandonment of the canon, they insisted, but a fundamental reimagining of its various parts. They also called for immersion in other languages' literatures (French poetry, and surrealism in particular, would exert a tremendous influence on Shi'r, and translation was central to the project of the magazine), an Eliotic turn to the realm of myth (born 'Ali Ahmad Sa'id, Adonis had renamed himself after the resurrected Tammuz of the story's Greek version), and a nearly total break from the classical Arabic forms. Shi'r manthur, prose poetry, would become the signature mode of many of the poets of this group, and some of them experimented with writing in colloquial Lebanese Arabic, so taking up Eliot's notion that "the music of poetry . . . must be a music latent in the common speech of its time. And that means also that it must be latent in the common speech of the poet's *place*."

Adopting a grandly mythopoetic view of Near Eastern history and drawing deeply from the well of Sufi mysticism, Adonis for one viewed poetry as "a vision. And a vision, by nature, is a leap outside of existing understanding and a change in the order of things . . . a revolt against the old poetic forms and methods and a refusal of the style and positions that they represent. . . . By leaving behind the classical forms, modern poetry helps us to see in existence what familiarity and habit have hidden. It exposes the face of the veiled world." Such metaphysical thinking stood in stark contrast to that of Adonis's "committed" contemporaries, Arab nationalist and Communist poets whose work hewed to a clear political line and took up realism and straight declaration as its primary tack. Not surprisingly, after the first issues of *Shi'r* appeared, he and al-Khal were accused of everything from colonialist sympathies to conspiracy to treason to sybaritic excess. Certain indignant ideologues even denounced them as "smoking pipes, having refrigerators in their houses, and drinking nothing but fine foreign beverages!" Yet far from glorifying the hermetic decadence their detractors claimed, the *Shi'r* poets were responding to what they believed ailed the Arab world at that historical moment. Al-Khal called explicitly for poetry that expressed "a lived experience in its full truth." And, refrigerators or no, they both saw "renewal in poetry as a renewal of the entire culture."

Tonally, stylistically, it was a long way from al-Khal's famously highbrow Thursday night Beirut salon to the spontaneous gatherings at Taha's messy souvenir shop on Casa Nova Street. Yet he and Michel clearly both felt an affinity for the regenerative, adventurous spirit of *Shi'r*, and on the pages of *al-Yawm* they set forth and defended this bold new poetics before the skeptical local readership. When a letter to the editor suggested that the ideas of this movement were tantamount to "heresy" and "a betrayal of the legacy of poetry," they responded patiently, by reminding their readers that "[the eighth-century Baghdad poet] Abu Nuwas and the [medieval] Andalusian poets were subjected to stinging criticism in their day and now we look to them as representing a high point in the development of our poetic legacy." Taha had still not yet begun to write his own verse, but he was in these articles already gathering his thoughts about the need for a poem to possess an "inner music," as distinct from the regular "outer music" provided by meter and rhyme.

Although the lasting critical worth of these *al-Yawm* articles may be negligible, the job did serve an important developmental purpose by exposing Taha to the literary ideas then rocking the wider Arab world. Michel would receive copies of *Shi'r* from *al-Yawm*'s editor, Nissim Rejwan, and pass them along to Taha, who read them from cover to cover. Because of its affiliation with the ruling Mapai party—and because its editors were all Jews, whether European-born and trained orientalists or Iraqi immigrants like Rejwan—*al-Yawm* was hardly considered a "threat to public security," so its writers labored under few of the restrictions imposed on their Palestinian counterparts at *al-Jadid, al-Ittihad,* and *al-Fajr.* A sobering case in point: in 1960, Rashid Hussein was arrested and imprisoned for the high crime of possessing six issues of an Egyptian newspaper and two copies of a Lebanese magazine. "The poet is the witness of his age," wrote Yusuf al-Khal, in one of the excerpts from an essay that Taha and Michel reprinted in *al-Yawm,* so smuggling in, perhaps, their own quiet critique of such repression. "And it isn't wise for us to plug his mouth or cover his eyes."

◆

Taha now enjoyed a certain local authority as a critic: he was invited to speak at the Nazareth YMCA on existentialism, on Taha Hussein, on "Realistic Literature." The latter lecture was reprinted in a 1961 issue of *al-Jadid,* and in it Taha held forth on the notion that all great writers are in some way realists, which doesn't mean that "we . . . define literature merely as a photograph of life . . . but [as a tool for] criticizing it, fixing and renewing it."

His souvenir business was also brisk. After just a few years at his Casa Nova Street location he had saved enough—in the form of gold ingots, whose value was much steadier than the ever-fluctuating lira—to invest in a plot of land near Mary's Well, where he began to oversee construction of a spacious building for offices, restaurants, and shops. And he had found at the same time real contentment in his role as husband and father—he and Yusra understood each other in some essential way, and the children were a source of joy for them both—though the basic satisfaction of those years was also sometimes shot through with pain. In 1963, Yusra gave birth to a second son, 'Isam, and when he was just a few months old, he took ill with a blockage of the urinary tract. The doctors ordered surgery, but soon after the operation was performed, the little boy died. For understandable reasons, neither Yusra nor Taha is eager to say much about their third child and his brief life. Neither is it possible for an outsider to begin to know if the many untimely deaths to which they had each already been witness made it easier or harder to bear yet another. The death of one's child may, one imagines, occupy a region of agony distinct from—and still more hellish than—the others.

But who can really say? And who can know if the death that followed, less suddenly, was any less devastating? If nothing else, Taha and the others did have the time and the awareness of what was happening to prepare themselves to say good-bye to the ailing Abu Taha.

At sixty-five he was not very old—but he had lived through so much hardship that Taha says his father seemed far more aged than his actual years. He had been slowing for some time now, and he had decelerated further after 1955, when his old friend Sheikh Saleh Salim dealt him a tremendous emotional blow by making a deal with the government. "On behalf of the refugees of Tzippori," he and the heads of a handful of other families had relinquished all rights to their property in the village, in exchange for small parcels of agricultural land near the moshav, in the old basatin, and much smaller plots in Nazareth, on which they were permitted to build houses. Sheikh Saleh had agreed to exchange his 2,500 dunams in Saffuriyya for 20 dunams on the  edge of Tzippori and 3 dunams in Nazareth. He had also agreed to help the government convince, or pressure, other Saffuriyya refugees to take compensation—and so concede all further claims to their village lands. (For his efforts he had, in addition, received an undis-

closed sum.) In 1958, his family was the first to move into a brand-new
neighborhood that looked out on the former Saffuriyya. Most of the
residents of what would later become known as Safafra were from the
village: a small fraction of them received land from the government,
but many more purchased plots there later, at their own expense.

According to files of the prime minister's adviser on Arab affairs,
"From our point of view this [deal] is a serious achievement," since it
was the first time a collective agreement had been reached with a
group of refugees, "and in this an opening has been created to persuade other villagers to accept the government's terms." According to
Abu Taha, meanwhile, Sheikh Saleh's move had been tantamount to
prostitution: not only had Sheikh Saleh lost his home, he had lost his
honor. (Taha says the former mayor of Saffuriyya even allowed coun-
terfeit papers to be drawn up in his name, declaring that he'd sold his
land to the Jewish Agency in 1944.) Abu Taha was so enraged by this
betrayal that he cut off contact with Sheikh Saleh and sunk into a depression that seems to have affected his health. By the time Abu Taha
took ill in 1965 with a kidney ailment, it was clear that his near-
legendary will to live had left him.

Often when Taha tells me stories of his past—and before I've
moved on to the next step of checking his version of events against
others' memories or the documentary evidence—I must stop him to
be sure he is not embellishing for dramatic or comic effect: indeed,
his formidable storytelling gifts tend to involve fanciful improvisation
on more-or-less true themes. This makes for great entertainment—
but poor biography, and when I do halt him (always feeling a bit of a
dullard) to ask if what I am hearing *really* happened or if he is using
me as a narrative lab rat, on which to test the effects of his newest
yarn, he will sometimes grin a bit crookedly and admit that "parts" of
what he just related took place, while "other parts" are pure fiction.
But even though the story that Taha tells of his father's final hours
sounds lifted right out of A *Thousand and One Nights*—with over-
tones of *King Lear*—this time he insists, somberly and without my asking, that "This *happened*. Believe me. It is not a made-up story." What
might sound self-congratulatory coming from another has about it, in
Taha's telling, an almost matter-of-fact humility.

"My father," says Taha, "he was dying, and I was sitting beside him. Well, the doctor came and told me, 'Taha, he has only a couple of days. Things are very serious for your father.'

"My father said: 'Taha, I am going to die.' I said, 'No!! You are okay.' He said, 'No, I am not. But you see, Taha my son, I want you to listen carefully. I have three wishes for my three children: one for you, one for Feisel, and one for Amin.' I asked him, 'Father, what is your wish for me? For Feisel? For Amin?' He said: 'I wish Amin could pay off all his debts. I wish that Feisel would find a wife. And for you— for you, I wish nothing.'

"I said, 'What? Nothing? I'm not your son?' He said, 'Taha, I cannot. I am afraid that your ambition is much greater than any wish I could make for you.' And he began to cry. . . . And I didn't want to show him that I was also crying, so I said, 'Father, it isn't fair. You don't want me to have my share?' And he just repeated himself: 'Any wish I could make, it would be so humble. . . . Your ambition is much greater.'" Taha sighs. "I remember this like it was yesterday. It is," he adds. "A true story."

NAZARETH II

◆

I've always been writing, even before I ever tried to write anything. The career of a writer doesn't begin at the moment he begins to write. The career and the writing may coincide earlier or later.

> *Jean Genet, quoted by Mohamed Choukri,*
> Jean Genet in Tangier

WHERE

♦

AND WHERE, IN THE END (or in the beginning), did Taha's first poem come from?

In attempting to unravel this mystery, one can try on oedipal explanations and say that the death of Taha's father somehow freed him from the weight of filial responsibility and allowed him to venture into the risky and basically impractical realm of verse.

Or one could turn that answer on its head and speculate that Abu Taha's stirring deathbed declaration was precisely what propelled Taha to stretch toward his highest hopes for himself: poetry had always been part of his consciousness, and his earliest memories of hearing it recited were bound up with the remembered sounds, smells, and sights of his father's Saffuriyya madafeh. Perhaps writing poetry was a way to preserve a live emotional link to the late Abu Taha and to the village itself.

One could, on the other hand, see Taha's preliminary foray into poetry in economic terms. Providing for his family had, for him, an essential moral dimension, and he considered it a value above almost all others. Only when he had figured out how to care for their material needs could he set out to indulge this private, slightly selfish desire.

Taha's initial attempt at poetry may have become possible only after he'd educated himself sufficiently and had gained a steady grasp of Arabic grammar and the classical sources and of English, only after he'd read and absorbed the work of both foreign and local, ancient and modern poets and prose writers of all stripes and sorts. Maybe before writing a single poem of his own Taha had to take in the short stories of the Egyptian master Yusuf Idris, whose exacting and often heartbreaking tales of provincial poverty and city squalor brought James Joyce's "style of scrupulous meanness" to bear on the Nile Delta and the back alleys of Cairo's dingiest quarters. In doing so they may have prompted Taha to consider writing of the humble places and people that he had himself known.

It is also possible that before setting out to write poetry rooted in his life and surroundings Taha needed to encounter novels written halfway around the globe—those, for example, by John Steinbeck, whose sprawling and affectionate portrayals of only slightly fictionalized American places spoke uncannily to his own experience. With its teeming cast of odd-lot neighbors and the warmly microcosmic view it sets forth of all the world's foibles, *Cannery Row* could be the story of Saffuriyya. Or so it seemed to him. And the Joads for their part were, according to Taha, practically Palestinian: the long, forced exodus from the Dust Bowl to California that Steinbeck conjured in *The Grapes of Wrath* might as well have been his own family's hard trek from Saffuriyya to Lebanon, so familiar did the hunger, uncertainty, fear, and homesickness they suffered seem to him.

He also needed, perhaps, to first work his way through the novels of another gifted American realist, Erskine Caldwell. Hugely popular in the 1940s and 1950s with socialists and other progressives the world over, Caldwell wrote crushing portraits of poor, "simple" Southerners that were as fierce and unforgiving as Steinbeck's could be sticky sweet. Caldwell's people were also grounded profoundly in a particular place—Georgia—and by rendering this milieu in all its cruel, stupid particularity, he managed somehow to write of the injustice and bleakness of the entire planet. Again, Taha says he saw Saffuriyya in *God's Little Acre*; he saw it in *Tobacco Road*.

One might find political explanations for what first pushed Taha toward poetry rather than prose. His horizons—like the horizons of his friends and neighbors in Nazareth—had been gradually widened by the fact that, in the years following that stormy 1958 May Day demonstration, calls to end the military government had steadily mounted. This opposition to official policy had spread and even entered the Israeli Jewish mainstream. Pragmatism compelled many: "Our enemies could find no fiercer weapon of propaganda to use against us than this continuing discrimination," wrote one army general, and various establishment "Arabists" warned that the strict controls placed on one segment of the population were counterproductive and "forc[ed] every Arab to hate the state or to become a saboteur." From Gaza and Jordan, groups of fedayeen had been staging cross-border attacks since the early 1950s, and they stepped up their activities after Fatah was founded in 1959 by several Cairo University classmates, including a young engineering student named Yasir Arafat. The thought that such forms of violent resistance might appeal to embittered Arabs inside Israel may well have startled many Jews into questioning the wisdom of the state's more repressive policies.

In December 1966, the military government was finally abolished. And though certain serious restrictions still pertained to the Palestinian citizens of Israel—and "innovative" methods were now used to monitor the actions of those viewed as troublemakers, including many of Taha's more outspoken friends—the average Arab citizen was no longer required to request permits to travel, and areas that had been considered closed military zones were ostensibly open to them. Taha was not counted among the agitators, and perhaps the newfound physical freedom he now enjoyed gave him a sense of possibility and unlocked certain closed zones *within* him as well.

The events of early summer 1967 must have added, too, to the change of emotional air pressure. Arabs everywhere viewed Israel's quick and total vanquishing of the Egyptian, Syrian, and Jordanian air forces as a second catastrophe—in some ways even more devastating than the nakba itself. In 1948, it had still been possible to blame the disaster on the neglect or mistaken priorities of the colonial powers and to believe its results were temporary, whereas this latest loss—the June or Six-Day War, known rather euphemistically in Arabic as *al-naksa*, the setback—was one for which the Arab leaders themselves were responsible and whose outcome seemed far more final. "The ancient word is dead," wrote Nizar Qabbani in perhaps his best-known political poem, "Marginalia in the Notebook of the Setback," composed in the wake of the war and subsequently banned from Cairo to Khartoum: "The ancient books are dead. / Our speech with holes like worn-out shoes is dead. / Dead is the mind that led to defeat."

Humiliation, confusion, and anger set in as Israel occupied the Sinai, West Bank, Gaza Strip, and Golan Heights and, within days of the fighting's end, annexed East Jerusalem. In less than a week, Israel had tripled its landmass and placed a million Arabs from the occupied territories under its control. (Before June 1967, Israel's total population had been just 2.6 million.) Huge waves of additional refugees had been created, as had a newly cocky Israeli mind-set. "We have returned to our holiest places, we have returned in order not to part from them ever again," gloated Defense Minister Moshe Dayan—hardly known for either his piety or his loyalty—as he first stood before the Western Wall.

Though many shared Dayan's attitude, not every Israeli Jew was ecstatic, and in fact as early as April 1968, the fiercely devout chemist and philosopher Yeshayahu Leibowitz—whose widely publicized, often scathing pronouncements about the ethical state of the Jewish state made him a figure both loathed and revered—prophesied that if Israel insisted on ruling over the Palestinian residents of the territories, the "Arabs would become the working people, and the Jews would be the bosses, the inspectors, the clerks, the policemen, and most essentially, the secret agents. The state that rules over a hostile population of . . . 1.4–2 million non-citizens will necessarily be a state of its secret police, with all that that implies for education, freedom of speech and thought, and for democratic rule. The corruption that typifies every colonial regime will spread throughout the State of Israel." He warned that the result would be nothing less than "the eradication of the State of Israel as the state of the Jewish people, the destruction of the Jewish people as a whole, and the collapse of the state's social structure and the corruption of the individual—Arab and Jew alike."

The results of the war were, meanwhile, extremely complicated for Taha and the other Arabs on the "inside." For while they, too, were swept by a sense of shock and dismay at all that had transpired, the fences and gates had suddenly fallen, and they found themselves face to face with family and friends from whom they'd been cut off for twenty long years. In a bittersweet and Pyrrhic way, it was a moment of triumph—and one with profound implications both for the way they were seen by other Arabs and how they saw themselves. For nearly two decades, they knew, they had been looked down upon by those on the "outside" who considered somehow treasonous their decision to stay on and accept Israeli citizenship and the ideological compromises that would seem to entail. "They thought the state had made us Jewish," one lawyer who lived in Nazareth at that time chuckles ruefully as he remembers. "But after 1967, they discovered we were Arabs. That we were Palestinians. That we could still speak the Arabic language. And we even knew the grammar! In 1967," he goes on, more somberly. "We discovered ourselves as Palestinians. When they discovered us, we discovered ourselves. It was like a mirror." The rhetoric changed accordingly: "Israeli Arabs" dared to call themselves Palestinians again, and the notion of being *samid,* steadfast, became central to popular Arabic parlance. Now, those Palestinians who had remained on the land were seen not as collaborators but as heroes for having stood their ground. Even in the face of Israeli oppression, it was said, they'd held fast to their language, their culture, what remained of their olive groves.

Although Taha would never use such prefab terms to account for his own person or place in the world, he does describe the flood of Arabic books that washed in from the surrounding states in the wake of the war and that seem to have affected him as much as any grand shift in self-definition. He recounts as well his initial trips to Jerusalem, Hebron, Nablus, Bethlehem, Gaza; the highlight of these adventures appears to have been his stumbling upon a bookshop on East Jerusalem's Salah al-Din Street, where he discovered many volumes he'd never seen before. Taha was not alone in viewing this complex period as, if nothing else, an excellent chance to expand his library: Emile Habiby has written of a formative post-1967 visit he made to a Nablus bookshop, where he found an Arabic translation of *Candide, or the Optimist*—which inspired him a few years later to write *The Secret Life of Saeed, the Ill-Fated Pessoptimist*. (Another—less cheerful—goad that pushed Habiby to write his first novel was a remarkable statement made by Yigal Allon when he was Israel's minister of education: "If there had been a Palestinian people in this land, it would have left behind a literature." With that, Habiby "decided in all seriousness to leave a Palestinian literature in this land that would outlive me and him." *The Pessoptimist* soon followed.)

In 1968, Yusra gave birth to another son—Usama, a sweet-tempered baby who looked just like his father had as an infant—and the fact of this brand-new human being in his life seems to have restored to Taha a wonder that had been missing since 'Isam's death. Maybe this renewed sense of promise spurred him toward poetry. . . .

Or maybe it didn't. Where *was* it that Taha's first poem came from?

None of the answers sketched above makes much sense on its own, though together they might start to form a complete picture. And perhaps there are other, less tangible factors at work as well, factors that have nothing to do with Taha's being a father or son, a shopkeeper or Palestinian. Maybe it is worth admitting that the germ that generates a true work of art is precisely what we cannot track, what we do not know.

Taha himself can't say why a particular poem came to him when it did—without fanfare—sometime in the mid-1960s. And in a much later poem, written nearly thirty-five years after his first, the aging poet still wondered "Where"?

> Poetry hides
> somewhere
> behind the night of words
> behind the clouds of hearing,
> across the dark of sight,
> and beyond the dusk of music
> that's hidden and revealed.
> But where is it concealed?
> And how could I
> possibly know
> when I am
> barely able,
> by the light of day,
> to find my pencil?

◆

His first poem, "Crack in the Skull," is dated, in its published form, August 1, 1971—a few days after he turned forty—but Taha's initial attempts to write it would seem to precede that official accounting by several years. There is no precise way to check this, since he has saved no drafts or notes from any of his work and relates that most of his poems start as oral compositions, which he memorizes before he sets a single word to paper. He tells me he places a date on a poem only when he considers it finished and that his first poem took him "some time" to write; he also says he thinks that several of his early poems may reach back as far as 1965.

A haunted dreamscape of singular sorts, "Crack in the Skull" describes how "The town shut down / the day the school's / manager died . . ."

Women's breasts went soft,
and the people went to sleep
in the late afternoon,
so great was their grief.

Although the poem wells up from a deep spring of recognizable feeling, its hallucinatory images and assemblage of grotesques seem not to derive from Taha's memory or life but from some macabre back cranny of his imagination. The poem does contain certain elements that would typify his later work, most notably its sinister humor, its startling shifts of scale and pitch, its essentially narrative approach, its sense of tragedy just past or imminent, and the gentle way it conjures a town's collective mood. But with its strongly absurdist atmosphere and bizarre array of characters, it is not really indicative of the work that would follow. Taha himself says that the poem is fundamentally nonsensical and that he conceived of it as a series of vivid, free-floating fragments, "like a piece of music." (Besides the school's "manager"—which Taha says is a make-believe position with no equivalent in the real world—the poem features "a man / with bushy eyebrows, and a fan, / who works as a drummer," a fainting "head guard," and a sobbing, Armenian graveyard attendant who vows to protect the dead man from "the crows / and the spotted hyenas.")

At the same time, "Crack in the Skull" has little to do with anything he had ever written before. The poem is in fact such a hyperbolic vault forward in Taha's literary development that it is almost impossible to believe it was written by the same man who published those melodramatic and derivative short stories just a few years before. The poem describes the effect of the manager's passing on the people of this unnamed town and lists "the primary / causes of death" as

> a crack in the Byzantine inscriptions
> lining the walls of the skull,
> tumescence in the dextral
> Latin clause,
> fatigue, hunger, vagrancy,
> debts and addiction to ruin.

The Palestinian-Israeli novelist, poet, and translator Anton Shammas was just twenty-one when, as an editor at the Jerusalem literary magazine *al-Sharq,* he first read this poem, written out in Taha's hand. He was, he says, "totally floored by it at the time, by its sheer genius and originality and dazzling tone. After reading it I felt an actual crack in my skull, a crack of epiphany."

Shammas knew Taha's name because of the introduction defending shi'r manthur that Taha had written to Michel Haddad's first book, published in 1969. (In retrospect, it seems clear that Taha was already writing his own poems as he set down these words, which celebrate a poetry "new in its thinking, new in its style, and new in that imagistic weave that links the thought to the image with rigor, freedom, and spontaneity.") As Shammas remembers it, Taha had "poems he kept in his drawer" and which he was initially reluctant to publish, even as his friends urged him on. Shammas describes Taha as "a poet against his will" and writes of Taha's "uncommon sense of humor—the best that I know." He says he thinks it was Michel Haddad who eventually persuaded Taha to send "Crack in the Skull" to the magazine.

Although it is possible that at the time Taha was playing the part of the naive amateur with no designs on public recognition, he tells the story a bit differently and says the initiative to publish was his own. He explains that for some time he had indeed been writing poems for himself or for that proverbial drawer but that after reading the work of the Syrian poet Muhammad al-Maghut, he thought that he, too, might be able to publish what he had previously believed wouldn't interest anyone else. A member of Adonis's *Shi'r* circle, al-Maghut was an autodidact like Taha whose "prose" poems—with their pellucid surfaces and relaxed register—were rife with muted black humor and stark, often menacing juxtapositions. Taha seems to have recognized something of his own sensibility and style there and felt that if the world was interested in al-Maghut, perhaps it would also want to read Muhammad Ali. He sent the poem to Shammas at *al-Sharq*—and here it seems likely that Michel did play a part in Taha's poetic debut by guiding him to the magazine, where he often published his own work, later becoming one of its editors. And so it was that the November 1971 issue included Taha's first poem, dedicated "To my brother Michel Haddad, friend on the path, comrade in the trenches."

◆

Over the next few years, Taha would publish a series of poems that were remarkable on their own terms—"Slaughter on the Acre Shore," "Postoperative Complications Following the Extraction of Memory," "Abd el-Hadi Fights a Superpower," and "Thrombosis in the Veins of Petroleum"—but even more startling was the fact that they were ostensibly the work of a beginner. The secret, though, was that Taha was no such thing: while he had waited this long to set pen to paper, he had laid the ground so carefully over the decades that when the poems emerged at last from that fertile soil, they popped up as full-grown, flowering trees.

In a brief, unsigned introduction to "Slaughter on the Acre Shore," which was the first of Taha's poems to appear in *al-Jadid* (for the subsequent twenty years he would publish much of his work there), the editor, Taha's old friend the younger poet Samih al-Qasim, described what followed as possessing an "excellent chemical balance. It has elements of Bertolt Brecht and Eliot, but it is neither one of these. . . . [It] mixes baseness and hatred with tolerance, and it is a good example of the new poetry, which is free of all trickery." (Al-Qasim seems to have felt the need to preface the poem with these comments because it marked the first time *al-Jadid* had ever published shi'r manthur, and he thought it best to praise it highly before the skeptics.) A tragicomic short story of a poem about a young man named Mahmud Mustafa Abu Eliyyan, who "left our village / at late morning / before the ripening of the figs," "Slaughter" is the first of

Taha's works in which the village appears. It is also the first that centers on an unassuming, even gullible Palestinian peasant overwhelmed
by forces far more powerful than he is. The poem's narrative unfolds
in the early 1940s, when Mahmud sets out from the village to enlist in
the British army, his head filled with dreams of a girl named Fatima
and fantasies of "dropping in a parachute." But as he stands waving
good-bye to a tank on the shore, praying to Allah and the local folk
saints "to put an end / to this war / and return every foreign tank / to
its people and country," the British believe he is sending signals to the
enemy and "surround him / from three directions / and stab him in
the back."

When I ask Taha, years later, where Mahmud Mustafa Abu Eliyyan came from—that is, how did this imaginary but very believable
historical figure surface suddenly in his consciousness, in July 1972
Nazareth—he answers without irony, "He came from Saffuri."

Indeed the notion of writing about the people of the village—or
their fictionalized cousins, sisters, neighbors, uncles—seems to have
been what catapulted Taha into this fecund new realm in his verse.
Although it is something of a saw to suggest that one must write of
what one knows, in Taha's case that familiar idea paved the way for
some of his best work, poems that twined the simple and subtle, the
gentle and stark. And though these poems speak only sometimes of
the literal village of Saffuriyya, they all embody the spirit of the people
who once lived there and so preserve their mores—not in the form-
aldehyde of nostalgia but in the dynamic present tense. "Abd el-Hadi
Fights a Superpower," for instance, published in July 1973, doesn't
mention the village by name, but it is clearly inspired by the homely
ethos of the place:

> In his life
> he neither wrote nor read.
> In his life he
> didn't cut down a single tree,
> didn't slit the throat
> of a single calf.
> In his life he did not speak
> of the *New York Times*
> behind its back,

didn't raise
his voice to a soul
except in his saying:
"Come in, please,
by God, you can't refuse."

Like Mahmud Mustafa Abu Eliyyan, Abd el-Hadi faces sinister forces he does not recognize, though the poet himself sees them closing in all too clearly. Abd el-Hadi is a mild-mannered peasant who means no harm. "Nevertheless—" Taha writes,

his case is hopeless,
his situation
desperate.
His God-given rights are a grain of salt
tossed into the sea.

And although the poet empathizes with Abd el-Hadi, it would be wrong to confuse him with his subject. As a public defender of poetic sorts, he pleads the case of this Arab everyman:

Ladies and gentlemen of the jury:
about his enemies
my client knows not a thing.
And I can assure you,
were he to encounter
the entire crew
of the aircraft carrier *Enterprise,*
he'd serve them eggs
sunny-side up,
and labneh
fresh from the bag.

Abd el-Hadi would become a recurring figure in Taha's work—at times (in the 1990 poem "Abd el-Hadi the Fool") coming to represent the innocent, vulnerable aspects of the poet's personality and at other times (as in the poem at hand) standing at a clear remove from him. Like a good screenwriter, Taha has his character's backstory straight, and he explains when asked about this made-up prototype that Abd el-Hadi is a man who was forced to leave Saffuriyya in 1948 and now lives in Nazareth; the poem was inspired by a radio report about how the USS *Enterprise* docked in the Suez Canal, and the Egyptian villagers ran to sell bottles of Coca-Cola to the American marines. "Hi! Hi!" Taha imitates them broadly. "Coca-Cola one dollar!" Taha says that when he first dreamed up Abd el-Hadi, he imagined a composite of certain fallahin he knew from Saffuriyya—and the hapless movie fat man Oliver Hardy.

Taha was clearly drawing from his experience as he conceived of representative personalities like Mahmud Mustafa Abu Eliyyan and Abd el-Hadi. However unconsciously, his quietly politicized turn to the realm of folklore was also, it seems, part of a wider movement that had taken hold among Palestinians both within Israel and outside it. Far from looking to the peasant past as some sweet yet fading and innocuous memory—a mishmash of idealized longings for an irretrievable Palestine Lost—many of those who set out to maintain and honor their humble village heritage saw the act as part of the more general struggle to assert a Palestinian presence in the here and now. (To take the most extreme example, the revolt of 1936–39 was often invoked as a historical and even sartorial model for the armed Palestinian "revolution" that had erupted around 1965 in the Lebanese and Jordanian refugee camps and along Israel's borders, with the young fedayeen adopting both the guerrilla methods and the checked kaffiyehs of their Qassamite forebears.) This defiant stance was aimed not just at an Israel that preferred to obliterate most traces of its recent Palestinian past but also at the Arab states, whose leaders often espoused a brand of blanket Arab nationalism that—despite the lip service paid to the contrary—nearly smothered the idea of a singular, independent Palestinian people. Or worse: it sometimes smothered actual Palestinians. In September 1970—to take the most notorious example—the Jordanian military launched an all-out war on the Palestinian guerrilla groups who were threatening the authority of the regime in Amman and killed an estimated three thousand Palestinians.

Taha, it should be said, was no armed fighter, and his artful, wry, and often ambiguous use of a rural setting was at once organic and distinct from that of many of his contemporaries, who saw the preservation of raw folk material in purely political terms and as an end in itself. Taha's "peasant" poems were, meanwhile, sophisticated transmogrifications of (and even knowing commentaries on) the world of the fallahin. He was driven by the sense that careful attention paid to the customs and culture of one locale might illuminate the wider human condition. Yet he shared certain concerns with other folklorically minded Palestinian intellectuals of the time; like them, Taha was propelled by a pressing need to keep the village *alive* in his work. As his friend the Communist activist and poet Tawfiq Zayyad put it, "We do not look at [folk literature] as a corpse to embalm and entomb. Rather we see [it] from the point of view of the present and future, and as part of our march toward political and social freedom."

This was, of course, far from Taha's rhetoric—though it was classic Tawfiq Zayyad. In the spring of 1967, Zayyad had published an article in *al-Jadid*, "Save Our Folk Literature from the Danger of Disappearing," in which he used his signature populist style to argue that in any culture "there are summits that no individual artist or poet has been or will be able to reach. And the inadvertent poet of these heights, the outstanding creator, is the *people*—as a *group*."

Great artists and thinkers share a secret, he writes: "their connection to the people and their ability to see their own experience as part of the general experience." Their power is, however, always limited by their personalities, circumstances, and "the scope of their historical understanding." But folk literature is superior, he argues, because of its collective and sustained nature. It has evolved over epochs, and various generations have added to it but have "preserved its essential form and content, so that it arrives in our age pure, distilled, strong, and powerfully expressive."

He goes on to issue an urgent call for the preservation of this folkloric material by any means necessary, even arguing for its "translation" from the local dialect into what he calls "proper"—that is, standard—Arabic, so that it might be read more widely. Yet as he aims to reach the Arab world at large, Zayyad makes an eloquent case for saving from neglect the various local traditions: "the songs of the Galilee and the Triangle [a largely Arab area near what was then the border with Jordan], of the fishmongers and donkey drivers, the cheers and dirges and wedding songs and stories of the struggle against the Turks and the British." These are all in danger of disappearing, he warns, since "time's passage is what gives this work its strength, but it's also its fiercest enemy."

Taha was too much of a believer in the individual artist's vision and will ever to polemicize about "the people" as Zayyad did—or to make it his task, as Zayyad also did, to spend his time traveling from village to village and transcribing the stories and popular songs he heard there from the peasants. Zayyad published several folktale collections and incorporated various lyrics into his books of poems, which also included his own "folk songs." These he wrote by taking up the standard oral forms and the heroes of popular Palestinian legend. In "Sirhan and the Pipe," for instance, he sang the praises of one Sirhan al-'Ali who blew up part of the oil pipeline to Haifa during the revolt.

Taha had great affection for the bearish, mustachioed Zayyad, who also came from a poor Muslim family and who shared Taha's earthy sense of humor and hunger for knowledge, and he relates that the two of them loved to talk—and to argue, since their differences went well beyond the subject of folklore. Zayyad was a hard-line Communist ("A Stalinist!" proclaims Taha. "Even his own brother disagreed with him!"), and he viewed poetry primarily as a political tool: after being sent by the party to study philosophy and economics for a year in Moscow, he had begun to translate from Russian and had also rendered the work of Nazim Hikmet into Arabic; the influence of the great Turkish poet on his verse and thought is clear. Like Hikmet, Zayyad wrote poems from prison, and it may well be from the Salonika-born Marxist that Zayyad evolved his ideas about the value of folk literature and the notion of writing poems that glorified past peasant rebellions. (Hikmet's last work published in Turkey was an epic about a fifteenth-century popular Ottoman uprising.) And although Zayyad's poetry never came close to approaching the grace, scope, and lyrical power of Hikmet's, he did share the Turkish exile's political convictions and his belief that poetry could, in Hikmet's words, "both . . . address just one other person and call out to millions." Zayyad's poems were largely topical—written to commemorate ("Before Lenin's Tomb," "Cuba") or to protest ("Taxes," "To the Striking Workers of Ata"); they were meant to be intoned before large crowds and to instill optimism in the masses. Taha felt close to Zayyad personally but strongly disagreed with his ideas about literature: "I always told him that direct poetry is shallow. And he said: 'No! If you want powerful poetry, the only scale is the people.'"

That said, Zayyad does seem to have exerted at least a passing

influence on Taha's poetry. Published in 1966—the year after the Israeli Communist Party split in two, fragmenting into separate Arab
and Jewish parties—the most famous and arguably the most potent
of Zayyad's poems, "Here We Remain," begins:

> Like twenty impossibles,
> in Lydda and Ramla and the Galilee
> here . . . we remain like a wall on your chests,
> in your throats,
> like a piece of glass, like a cactus thorn
> and in your eyes,
> a storm of fire.

The confrontational tone and unambiguous message of Zayyad's
poem—the accusatory use of that "you!"—are light-years from the
realm of Taha's work, though for all the differences between the two
men and their verse, it is intriguing to place Taha's poem "Thrombosis in the Veins of Petroleum," published in 1973, alongside Zayyad's.
"When I was a child," begins Taha,

> I fell into a pit
> but didn't die;
> I sank in a pond
> when I was young,
> but did not die . . .

The poem winds through a complicated meditation on who is (or
isn't) responsible for his fate, then mounts to an agitated final stanza
in which the poet declares his refusal to disappear:

> I won't die! I will not die!
> I'll linger on—a piece of shrapnel
> the size of a penknife
> lodged in the neck;
> I'll remain—
> a blood stain
> the size of a cloud
> on the shirt of this world!

On the surface at least, the poems are strikingly similar. Both include a vow by the poet to hold his—or his people's—ground against tremendous odds; both threaten to pierce the anthropomorphized peace with a set of sharp, pain-inflicting objects (glass, cactus thorns, shrapnel, penknives); both rely on the insistent repetition of key phrases. Though Taha usually prefers to duck straightforward political readings of his own poems, he admits when asked that his is "a direct poem about the Palestinians." It is an assertion of their rights as a people to exist, he says, as well as a demand for the world to take some responsibility for their plight. But looking back now, he shrugs a bit dismissively: "The poem is angry. It is too direct."

Yet even when Taha was being "angry" and "too direct," he managed a measure of tonal complexity that distinguished his poem from a deliberately emphatic crowd-rouser like Zayyad's. For all their overlap, the poems are quite distinct. While Zayyad's poem is a stirring declaration of the prerogative of the Arabs of Israel to stay on their land, Taha's evolves into a statement of something more existential and eternal: the desire of any person or people simply to *be*. It was a poem that would sound rather strange if shouted into a bullhorn.

HOMELAND AND SUITCASE

◆

FOR VARIOUS REASONS, TAHA'S EARLY POEMS did not draw much attention when they first emerged: he published little, he was not a member of a political party with its own journal and well-placed contacts abroad, and—more essentially—most of his poems were too hushed and peculiar to make themselves heard in the strident literary context that then prevailed. That they were written without meter or rhyme and in a register not generally deemed sufficiently "poetic" by many readers of Arabic also played a role. His poems lacked the incantatory rhythms and lofty tone that made other Palestinian verse popular.

Ironically enough, however, these same years brought with them the thrilled discovery by the rest of the Arab world of the poets "of the occupied homeland." In 1966, the exiled Palestinian novelist, journalist, and critic Ghassan Kanafani had published in Beirut his seminal *Literature of Resistance in Occupied Palestine*—a literary, sociological, and historical tract that was, in essence, a lionization of the political poetry of Mahmoud Darwish, Samih al-Qasim, Tawfiq Zayyad, Salem Jubran, Hanna Abu Hanna, and several others whom Kanafani considered "poet warriors" for the daring stance they had taken in their poetry and lives. All of these poets had been writing, reciting, and publishing their poems of protest for years inside Israel, but they had remained, according to Kanafani, "unknown to us [abroad] during the years of exile, despite the fact that they constitute the most brilliant aspect of the struggle." It is worth noting that they were also all Communists or poets close to the Communist Party. Although one hardly expects to find an "apolitical" poet like Michel Haddad mentioned by a radical like Kanafani, Rashid Hussein's name is a notable absence from his list. Perhaps Rashid was excluded on ideological grounds—though a more practical explanation also makes sense: Kanafani had limited access to the magazines published inside Israel and, it seems, took all of his information from *al-Jadid,* where Rashid did not publish.

The thirty-year-old Kanafani was already a star of the Lebanese literary and political scene (a few years later he would become the spokesman for the Marxist Popular Front for the Liberation of Palestine), and his book seems to have come as a revelation to the rest of the Arab world, which, because of the various physical and political barriers that had sprung up in the region since 1948, knew little if anything about the situation of the Palestinians—let alone the Palestinian writers—on the "inside." As a result, they either ignored or looked down on them. These Palestinians had generally been suspected by Arabs elsewhere for having, it was thought, "collaborated" by staying put and accepting citizenship in the Jewish state. And though Kanafani's rhetoric was fairly programmatic and hostile to Israel— "Zionist aggression" and "the enemy" are mentioned often—his book marked an important turning point in that it did not blame those Palestinians who had remained in the land. Rather, Kanafani summoned a host of convincing details to make his case for the way the difficult conditions in which the poets and the other Arabs in "occupied Palestine" had lived since 1948 had given birth to a new sort of writing, what he dubbed the "literature of resistance." The term was the same as that used to describe the violent resistance, *al-muqawama,* then being waged by the fedayeen. To Kanafani's mind, this literature had its roots in the anti-British Palestinian folk songs of the 1920s and 1930s, and it shared certain traits with the "literature of exile," written since 1948 by Palestinians elsewhere, but it also marked a bold and novel category unto itself.

Of all the poets whom Kanafani sent hurtling into international prominence with his book, the one on whom he lavished the most attention and praise was "the young man from al-Birwa," Mahmoud Darwish, aged twenty-four when Kanafani's volume appeared. It was, in particular, Darwish's third collection, *A Lover from Palestine,* written during one of the young poet's many stints in an Israeli prison, that Kanafani singled out for adulation: by fusing the ancient Arabic tradition of the *ghazal,* the love poem, with powerful (even erotic) feelings for the land, wrote Kanafani, Darwish had revolutionized the local poetry, "and all of life became a single cohesive picture that was at once particular and general."

After June 1967, all of the "resistance poets"—as they were now known in an almost card-carrying way—gained notoriety in the wider Arab world. But the celebrity of Darwish and Samih al-Qasim in particular would grow exponentially after the war, turning them into the poetic equivalent of rock stars. The primary reason for this was, of course, their poetry itself, which seems to have broken through the generalized gloom that had enveloped much of the rest of the Arab world since the naksa. "When we read their poems . . . amid the torrent of despairing poems that poured forth after that calamitous June," explained one Lebanese critic, "we felt an extraordinary power surging forth again . . . from the depths of despair and misfortune, defying despair and misfortune."

It also didn't hurt that the two best friends and roommates were strikingly handsome and photogenic—both bursting with youthful sex appeal and an all-around glow that made it easy for the masses to embrace them. (The sexual element, inter-estingly enough, seems ultimately to have trumped national concerns: Darwish wrote several of his most famous poems to his Is-raeli Jewish lover, a woman he called Rita, and to this day her Hebrew pseudonym is in-toned with longing by Palestinians every-where.) With their casual dress and unpreten-tious manner the two had the easy glamour of certain Beat poets; at the same time, their willingness to risk imprisonment for their  poems and principles—and, by extension, for their people's rights— gave them a visionary aura. They were viewed as righteous rebels with a cause. Despite the often oppressive constraints imposed on them by the authorities, they proclaimed loudly and clearly that no one could lock up their spirit. Darwish's poem "The Cell Has No Walls," published in 1969, says this directly: "As usual / my cell saved me from death / . . . / I saw on its ceiling the face of my freedom / and the orange grove," while in al-Qasim's "End of a Talk with a

Jailer," written around the same time, the prisoner-poet slyly taunts his guard: "From the narrow window of my small cell— / I can see your big cell!"

Al-Qasim and Darwish wrote poems that were memorized and set to music throughout the Arab world, though the public adoration wasn't confined to them alone; in the years immediately following 1967, the "resistance poets" became everyone's romantic heroes, and they took on a nearly mythic status. Fanciful stories are told, for instance, of a secret gathering held in Haifa in the spring of 1968, when the Nablus-born poet Fadwa Tuqan met with several of the poets she called her "brothers in the wound," those who lived within Israel. Her eyes, according to popular legend and several of Darwish's English translators, were so striking that "it is said that only two men have been able to look into them, the Italian poet Quasimodo and Mahmoud Darwish."

Such loopy lore aside, the symbolism of the encounter was manifold. Besides reuniting this West Bank Palestinian with her counterparts on the "inside," it linked the memory of Fadwa's late older brother, Ibrahim Tuqan—the first "Palestinian national poet"—with the members of the younger generation, especially Darwish. In the wake of the gathering she dedicated to "the poets of the resistance" a modern variation on a pre-Islamic qasida, first mourning the "ruins of those who departed and abandoned their homes," then vowing to weep no longer but to follow the example of her old-new friends and "set my eyes / on the road of the splendor and sun." Darwish responded with a poem of his own, certain lines of which are now so renowned as to be almost clichés: "my homeland isn't a suitcase," he wrote, "and I am not going. / I am a lover and the land is the beloved." In his poem, he addressed Fadwa Tuqan as his "sister," so creating the sense of the Palestinians both inside and outside of Israel's borders as a single family and by implication—was it deliberate?—taking up Ibrahim's mantle. (The role of national poet is, it should be said, one that Darwish would alternately reject and embrace for decades to come.)

Meanwhile, other books and numerous articles were written about the "poetry of resistance." Controversy even broke out about whether it should be termed "resistance" or "opposition" poetry, and lengthy critical arguments ensued about whether either term really applied.

Literary magazines throughout the Arab world dedicated entire issues to "Poems from Beyond the Barbed Wire" (*Shi'r*) and "Poetry after the naksa" (*al-Adab*); radio stations around the Middle East played recordings of the poets reading their work and rushed to interview them. The best-known poets abroad wrote high-flown, often fawning odes to the Palestinian poets and their work. Nizar Qabbani's 1968 "To the Poets of the Occupied Land" was perhaps the most flamboyant example. In almost parodically purple terms he describes the Palestinian poets as a glorious, single entity: "O most beautiful bird, flying from the night of captivity, / O clear-eyed sadness, pure as the dawn prayer, / O rose bush sprouting from the ember's core, / O rain falling despite the injustice and despite the defeat," and so on and on, stemming the flood tide of florid metaphors only long enough to hoist the Palestinian poets high above their versifying peers throughout the Arab world:

Our poets
if they stood before your poems
would seem the smallest of dwarves.

Not surprisingly, the backlash against such extravagant flattery wasn't long in coming; less predictable was that it issued from the pen of one of the very poets whose praises were being sung to the heavens' heights. "Save Us from This Cruel Love!" pleaded Mahmoud Darwish on the front page of *al-Jadid,* exactly two years after the June 1967 war. In an editorial subtitled "An Attempt to Put Our Poetic Movement in Its Proper Place," Darwish argued fiercely against the blind embrace of all Palestinian poetry. The veneration pouring in from afar was, he wrote, "exaggerated and irresponsible in historical terms." And it "is no excuse that this stance stems from good will and genuine excitement, and deep feelings for the circumstances of the poetic movement in our country." It's extremely dangerous to wrench this work from the context of modern Arabic poetry in general—its past and its present. The "exaggerators," as he called them, treat this verse as if it had appeared suddenly, like a bolt of lightning. But Palestinian poetry isn't, he wrote, cut off from that of the rest of the Arab world; neither is it a rival or substitute for that other poetry: it's a tributary in the larger river.

Without referring to himself as one of the poets in question—though of course all his readers would know precisely who he was talking about—Darwish went on to insist that "it's important to treat the poetry as poetry and to soften the spotlight on the characters of the young men who are writing it. And by this I don't mean to deny the link between the . . . poetry and the circumstances that surround its creation, but to call for a more balanced approach that uses an artistic scale and not just a political one." The poets come, after all, from a wider social context: they "aren't a group of palm trees planted in a dry desert" but are, as he put it, "sons of this people that educated them and that gave them roots."

The article created a small sensation when it was published—with some accusing Darwish of ingratitude and others taking his cri de coeur as a not-so-tacit critique of much of the "poetry of resistance" itself, since between the lines of his selfless-sounding statements about roots, education, and the people was the sense that Darwish viewed his work as superior and preferred not to be lumped together with so many second- and even third-rate poets. These poetasters were, he made it clear, being acclaimed merely because of their subject matter, combative tone, and geographical location. He practically said as much in later interviews and referred to one of the special Palestinian issues of a Beirut literary magazine as having "consisted of the worst poetry written in the history of Arabic literature." The magazine was, he wrote "an insult to the intelligence." Although his words may sound sharp, they seem fairly prophetic in retrospect. While the period of hero-worship passed after a few years, to this day it seems that Darwish was right and that the usual critical standards tend to evaporate where Palestinian writers are concerned. At least in popular or journalistic contexts, they are most often judged not as individual artists but as spokesmen for a cause.

As it turns out, his article was prophetic in other ways as well. Though no one aside from the author himself knew it at the time, this critical disquisition seems to have forecast Darwish's departure from the country a year later—first on a year-long Communist Party–funded scholarship to study in Moscow and then permanently, after calling a press conference in Cairo to announce his decision.

It seems he was pulled—both as a writer and as a citizen—by the promise of the wider world beyond Israel's borders. The idea of paddling beyond that tributary of Palestinian poetry that he had described in his 1969 article and swimming out into the larger river of Arabic, and even international, literature must have tempted. But he was also pushed toward this move by the increasingly harsh treatment he had suffered at the hands of the Shin Bet and Israel Police: he was arrested repeatedly, once for "traveling without a permit" but usually for no stated reason. (This was legal under the so-called Emergency Regulations.) He would be released from prison only to return to his apartment and find the police waiting with a new arrest warrant. Throughout the 1960s, he was forbidden by the authorities from leaving Haifa, and after 1967 he lived under partial but permanent house arrest, being forced to report home by sunset each evening and stay there through morning. When asked about how he viewed, in hindsight, his decision to leave, he said it wasn't easy but that he didn't feel he had a real choice. He realized that he could either spend the rest of his life writing poems about jail and jailers or he could leave. He didn't tell anyone of his plans but says he knew before he traveled to the Soviet Union that he would not return.

So it was that on February 11, 1971, in the Egyptian capital, before a bank of blinking flashbulbs and primed microphones, the twenty-nine-year-old Mahmoud Darwish declared that he belonged not to a "people who plead for mercy or beg for charity, but to a fighting people." Then he took up the most quoted line of his poetry and fiddled with it, explaining, "The homeland for me isn't a suitcase. . . . The homeland is a cause I defend wherever I am. I am not the first citizen or poet to travel far from his country in order to draw close to it."

If his "Cruel Love" article had caused controversy, Darwish's decision to leave the country—and to declare his intentions in such a theatrical way—brought on a firestorm. Though he made a point of insisting that the choice to go was personal and entirely his own, this was, in a sense, a critical juncture for all the Palestinian poets in Israel: whatever their ideological differences, they had somehow rallied around the shared value of staying put and digging in their heels, no matter the difficulties. (It's true that Rashid had left—but he'd left for a *woman,* and by quietly slipping away; he had, too, mourned the choice actively, writing after the fact: "I wish I were free / in the pris-

ons of Nazareth.") Now one of their best and brightest was setting out
for other lands, both actual and metaphoric, and even if many of
them understood his decision—and may in fact have envied it—others felt starkly betrayed.

If anything, though, Darwish clinched his position as the "national poet" only after he left and began, like so many of his people,
to wander the globe. His exit from Israel was also his first step toward
a more radical politics and a more abstract poetics: in 1973 he would
move to Lebanon and join the PLO, and the rocks and trees of his
poems would soon evolve from the tangible objects of a daily landscape into elusive, almost airborne symbols of a sort of cosmic exile.
("We have a country of words," he would write in 1986, "speak, speak,
so that we may know the end of this journey.") And while all eyes were
on him that day in Cairo, the other poets who remained behind and
in the wings were suddenly placed on the defensive. Al-Qasim says
that after Darwish left, many of the Israeli Jews he knew made snide
comments about how the Palestinians "say and don't do." He remembers a Hebrew headline from that time that also took up Darwish's
"my homeland isn't a suitcase / and I am not going" and shot back "HE
WENT ANYWAY." The article that followed called Darwish's departure
emblematic of his people's tendency to flee when the going got tough.
Meanwhile, the Palestinian public inside Israel felt burned and took
out its hurt on the writers who remained, maybe assuming that they
would *all* bolt if given the opportunity. Having been placed on a
pedestal, the resistance poets had a long way to fall.

"It was so bad," al-Qasim remembers, "that I'd be walking down
the street, in Rama [his village], or Haifa or Nazareth, and someone
would call out, 'It'll be cold for you in Moscow. Take a jacket.' Or: 'It'll
be hot in Cairo: wear something lighter.'" Though none of the writers
admits this in retrospect, one wonders if those who stayed behind
were also suddenly conscious of the condescension with which the
rest of the Arab world may have viewed them. Despite all the praise that
had come their way in recent years, they were now—with Darwish's
"graduation" to the international arena—made to feel like provincials,
frittering their personal and poetic time in a primitive backwater.

Whatever their complicated and evolving reactions, though, at
first Darwish's move simply shook them. Hanna Abu Hanna writes in
his memoir of how:

That day, at noon, the telephone rang. . . . On the line was Samih al-Qasim, saying, "turn on 'The Voice of the Arabs' right now, and we'll talk afterwards."

The voice of Mahmoud Darwish from the [radio] station "The Voice of the Arabs" from Egypt: he spoke of the Nile and Arabism, and about how changing one's place . . . wasn't changing one's stance.

Samih called again. . . . In his voice there was a blend of conflicting feelings. He said: "And us . . . we don't want to see the Nile?" And we talked about the difference between place and stance.

LANDSLIDES

◆

WHEN MAHMOUD DARWISH LEFT THE COUNTRY, Taha had not yet published a single poem. "Crack in the Skull" appeared in print some nine months after the most famous of the Palestinian poets made his much ballyhooed Cairene break. By then, Darwish had brought out six books of poetry, while al-Qasim and Zayyad had each produced seven.

Through no conscious design Taha had, for better or worse, somehow managed to bide his time and sidestep or dodge the literary zeitgeist. Though he did not receive any of the wild acclaim that came the way of his Communist poet friends after June 1967, he also suffered none of the resentment or recriminations that they sometimes endured, and he wasn't forced to defend himself, his poems, or his beliefs in any prominent public forums. Neither would he later face the difficult task that awaited his younger colleagues—of breaking free from the audience's confining expectations of "*their*" resistance poets. To this day, Darwish's blunt poem "Identity Card"—"Write it down! / I am an Arab!"—composed when he was just twenty-one years old is far better known and popularly beloved than any of the more complex and refined lines he wrote in the nearly half-century following, a fact that did not please the poet, who, by the time of his death in 2008, had for all intents and purposes turned his back on the direct political poetry of his youth.

And while most other writers might have felt slighted at being overlooked (when his poems did at last emerge, there was at first little if any reaction), Taha seems not to have paid much attention to his exclusion from the main poetic stage. His obscurity won him the freedom to write whatever he pleased.

Or not to write at all. For reasons Taha himself cannot really reconstruct, after his first burst of poetic energy, he went silent again for almost a decade. As he and his family describe it, this was a peace-

ful, prosperous time, during which Taha worked hard at his shop, putting in on average a twelve-hour day: he was usually there from nine in the morning until at least nine at night. In the middle, Yusra would send one of the children with a hot, home-cooked lunch, and later Taha would sometimes nap at the shop, sitting upright. Most of the time, though, he was wide awake—tinkering, talking, arranging, sweeping. He also continued to read and to study grammar and hold his informal salon at the shop. One local visitor from those years remembers "how surprised . . . the passing tourists would be to find a merchant like Taha . . . responding to his customers' requests like someone waking from a trance that he'd entered into through his absorption in reading some book, whose pages he'd turn with his delicate fingertips." But his business thrived: after saving up, he bought his first car, "a Black Austin, like the British officers drove," and he moved with Yusra and the children into one of the apartments over the shops and restaurants in the building he had constructed near Mary's Well.

The children were growing up, and Taha's souvenir shop had become something of a second home for them. As Taha and Yusra's alert and soft-spoken daughter, Layla, tells it now, Taha's shop was "a small place that he made somehow huge. He brought the whole world to the store." She would rush there after school—ostensibly to do her homework but really, she says, to see him and spend as much time as possible with him. As children, she and Nizar would sometimes help him with chores in the shop, and in between customers he would sit with them over their schoolwork; as Usama grew older, he, too, would come to the store to play and be with Taha. They were a good-natured, good-looking bunch, and Taha sometimes even used the en-

ergy of his young family to help rustle up business. On days when he knew that a group of Italian tourists was expected to spend the night at the Casa Nova pilgrim hostel up the street, he would send one of the children home with a message for Yusra: Bring food! Then the whole family would wile away the evening with him, making as much festive, mealtime noise as possible so that the tourists would be drawn by the sounds from the only shop on the street whose lights were still burning at that late hour.

Usama for his part describes his father as "like a child who is a genius. You bring him a toy and he doesn't just play with it. He takes it apart and puts it back together in a better way." He wasn't content to sell generic crucifixes and key chains but preferred to fiddle

with them and improve them. Once, for instance, a wholesaler offered him a large batch of simple wooden rosaries, which he bought, soaked overnight in buckets of stain, then clipped to playing-card-sized portraits of Mary and the Baby Jesus that he'd ordered from a local printing press. So, too, he would purchase sizable quantities of plain clay oil lamps and ask Yusra to fire them in the kitchen oven, thus doubling their sheen and their value.

Although Taha wasn't writing poetry during this time, it seems fair to say that he was, in his typically quirky and unself-conscious way, evolving what might be called a poetics of shopkeeping. That is, the same ingenuity, thrift, modesty, vitality, sense of proportion, and essential joy that characterize his best writing were also present in the thousand decisions and actions and interactions that made up a day's work at the store.

This was, for then, the realm that most mattered to Taha. His elderly mother's stroke, ensuing paralysis, and eventual death in 1975 also mattered. She had been, as Layla remembers, a nearly angelic figure, whose love for her grandchildren seemed boundless. She spent most of her small social security pension on ice cream and treats for them, perhaps finding a measure of peace after all that had befallen her over the years. The loss of her gentle and accepting presence was felt sharply by the whole family.

In the meantime, so many of the headline-worthy political developments of those years seemed, says Taha, far off: the Palestinian "Black September" group's kidnapping and murder of Israeli athletes at the 1972 Munich Olympics; the Mossad's car bomb assassination of Ghassan Kanafani in Beirut that same year; the October (or Yom Kippur) War of 1973; Arafat's pistol-packing address before the UN General Assembly in 1974; the 1975 outbreak of civil war in Lebanon, which pitted PLO forces against right-wing Christian militias; Syria's invasion of Lebanon the next year . . . . He registered these events in detail as they unfolded (keeping abreast was not a matter of choice so much as environment: everyone in Nazareth inhaled the news like noxious fumes from a nearby factory), and each would of course have its effect on the part of the world that Taha called home. But after a lifetime of such warring words and deeds, he had learned to preserve his sanity by focusing on the near at hand—on what he could control.

◆

One political event, closer to home, did touch Taha more directly: the sweeping 1975 election victory of the Communist-led Jabha (Front) to the municipality of Nazareth. After winning 67 percent of the vote,

eleven of seventeen city council members were now affiliated with
the Communists—and Tawfiq Zayyad was mayor, elected by a land-
slide in the first-ever direct vote for that position. But this was just
one of many firsts that Zayyad's win represented. For the first time in
the history of Israel, the Communists had triumphed in a city election; it also marked the first time that a completely Arab party, and not
an "Arab list" of one of the Jewish parties, controlled Nazareth, the
largest Arab town inside Israel—not to mention the first time a poet
had been in charge.

These last two facts were not unrelated, since the Jabha win was a
symbolic victory for Arab pride inside Israel—and Zayyad's charismatic
stance as resistance poet and all-round rabble-rouser made him much
more than an ordinary politician. He was already a Knesset member
given to passionate speeches and flamboyant outbursts while other
parliamentarians spoke. At one point he was taunted on the dais by
a Jewish Knesset member who shouted, "Where did you learn that
[faulty] Hebrew?" to which he shot back, "In your prisons!" In both
his political and poetic work Zayyad had come to represent a bold new
way of challenging the authorities: he would participate actively in
the democratic process as an Israeli citizen at the same time that he
insisted on asserting his own and his people's presence as *Palestinians.* This combination deeply disturbed many of his Jewish colleagues,
some of whom accused him of leading a fifth column and even lob-
bied to have him thrown out of the Knesset and straight into jail. But
Zayyad was defiant, and his defiance made him still more popular with
"the people" whose praises he so loved to sing. His election as mayor
also lifted the Palestinians inside Israel onto the platform of international politics—the day after his win the *New York Times* proclaimed IS-
RAEL WORRIED BY ELECTION OF ARAB RED IN NAZARETH—and only half in
jest was he often referred to as the foreign minister of that city.

Zayyad commanded a powerful physical and emotional presence.
His personality could flood a room, and watching old TV footage of
him in action, one is struck by the contrast between the fierce, almost
demagogic tone that took over as he speechified, the more stately,
decorous pitch he adopted as he intoned his poems, and the gently
avuncular, somehow mischievous way he would talk one-on-one with
an interviewer. It was, it seems, his ability to play the full xylophone-
range of these registers that made him so beloved in his hometown:

he was at once a fist-waving rebel, an eloquent mouthpiece, and an ordinary man of the people, without airs. His widow, Na'ila, describes how he refused the car and driver the city provided and instead

set out for his office on foot each morning—and though the walk should have taken him less than fifteen minutes, he would usually arrive at work some two hours later, since he liked nothing better than to stop at every shop along the route and have coffee with friends. This, too, was politics. That more approachable and conversational side of Zayyad was, it seems, what appealed to Taha, though he also understood Zayyad's public role and its demands—and knew he wanted to keep his distance. Recognizing Taha's social gifts as well as his wisdom, his work ethic, and the respect he enjoyed among Nazareth's many Saffuriyya refugees, Zayyad had tried to persuade Taha to serve as one of his deputies. Taha politely—but firmly—declined: "I told him I'm not a politician," and that was that. Taha did, though, suggest his brother Amin for the job instead. Amin was by nature a fighter and organizer, and he wound up serving for years as one of Zayyad's devoted deputies.

And so it was that—prompted by the loudspeaker calls that had echoed through the streets of Nazareth the morning and afternoon before—Taha took the highly unusual step of closing his shop for one whole day, March 30, 1976, yet another date in the long list of bloody dates that cram the Palestinian national calendar. Along with the anniversaries of the 1948 and 1956 massacres at Dayr Yasin and Kafr Qasim, what is now known as Land Day has come to represent for many Arabs in Israel the state's discrimination against them—as it also marked an audacious new way of fighting back and demonstrating the bolder brands of political awareness that had taken hold among them since 1967. In the popular imagination Land Day is not just another memorial to Palestinian defeat and passive victimhood but stands as symbol of a forward-looking struggle. It began when the government announced plans to confiscate some twenty thousand dunams of Arab-owned lands in the north of the country. Officially this was done for "security purposes," but when it became clear that the same area would soon be settled by Jews as part of a government plan to "Judaize the Galilee," Arab leaders including Zayyad called for a general strike and protest. And as had happened on May 1, 1958, demonstrators were confronted by huge, heavily armed police and border patrol forces, eager for a showdown—though this time it seemed more like war: early in the morning, masses of police surrounded Zayyad's house and wound up beating his wife and smashing the windows when she refused them entry. The mayor wasn't, as it turned out, even home. At the same time, tanks rolled into the villages all around Nazareth.

Accounts of what took place that day vary widely and typically, depending on who is describing what happened: "a day of pride, heroism, and sacrifice for the Palestinian Arab public of Israel and a day of shame, cowardice, and hostility for the rulers of Israel," as one Arab version has it, or, according to a Jewish source, "a wild attack by hundreds of inflamed young Arabs on an unsuspecting IDF convoy." But no one denies that the "security forces" wound up killing six unarmed citizens and wounding many more—some seriously. Land Day has come down in the history books as the first unabashedly pan-Palestinian protest against the state's policies; it is marked to this day inside Israel and on the West Bank and in Gaza by Arabs whom the government and army had inadvertently managed to reunite in a common cause.

As with all such dates, Land Day was not really an isolated event so much as a culmination—or violent realization—of feelings that had built up over decades. It was, in the words of a memorial "black book" published in Arabic and circulated underground after the events, "a long, cruel day in a long, cruel history . . . a day lasting twenty-nine years, during which the Arab public in our country has been absorbed in fierce battles and has resisted bloody attacks, and has offered many sacrifices, merely for the honor of staying on the land of our fathers and grandfathers." And even though Taha shrugs off the importance of this particular date to the growth of his own consciousness—he avoided the demonstrations and spent the day indoors, listening to the radio, eating and talking with several Saffuriyya friends—he clearly shared many of those long-simmering feelings of discrimination.

Just a month before the deadly events of Land Day, a top-secret memorandum about "Handling the Arabs of Israel," written by the Ministry of the Interior's chief official in the Galilee, Israel Koenig— a resident of Upper Nazareth, as it happens—was submitted to Prime Minister Yitzhak Rabin. Later that year, the now-notorious "Koenig Report" was leaked to the Hebrew media and created an uproar. Among other things, the report warned that in two years the Arabs of the Galilee would outnumber the Jews and offered several suggestions to combat this trend: "broaden and deepen Jewish settlement in areas where the contiguity of the Arab population is pronounced, and where their numbers greatly exceed that of the Jewish population; examine the possibility of thinning [that is, reducing] existing Arab population concentrations."

But this was just the tip of one very racist iceberg. "Endeavor," Koenig thoughtfully suggested, "to have important institutions give preferential treatment to Jewish organizations or individuals rather than to Arabs." And he had educational tips, too:

> Encourage the channeling of [Arab] students into technical professions, to physical and natural sciences. These studies leave less time for dabbling in nationalism and the dropout rate is higher.
>
> Make travel abroad for study easier, while making return and employment more difficult—such a policy will encourage their emigration.

And so on and on. Taha and his neighbors and friends, of course, hardly needed to read such a report to know about the bigotry that existed all around them. What is interesting to note in this context, though, is not the long-term or even systematic presence of that prejudice—but Taha's reaction to it.

From his earliest contacts with both Israeli Jews and the foreign tourists who visited his shop, Taha simply refused to accept the divisive terms dictated by others, whether chauvinistic Israeli bureaucrats or his more militant Palestinian friends. The best response to intolerance, he had decided, was tolerance. Taha often jokes about his ecumenism, calling himself "a Muslim who sells Christian trinkets to Jews," but he means it. Part of what makes him such a successful shopkeeper is also what makes him such a good man—or vice versa— his honesty and openness to all comers, whoever they are.

Which is not to say that years of living as a second-class citizen had rendered Taha a kowtowing collaborator—the bumbling "Pessoptimist" of Habiby's great novel—ready to sell out his identity to whoever wanted to buy a souvenir. Rather, it meant that he preferred to decide for himself who he was: human being, Saffuriyyan, Nazarene, Palestinian, Arab, Israeli, poet, storyteller, critic, shopkeeper, Communist, nationalist, father, husband, brother, friend. *He* would determine the order. So it was, for instance, that Taha set his sights as a young man on learning English—and not Hebrew, which to this day he is able to speak in only the most elementary fashion and does not read. Although he says he needed to be practical and had time to study just one other language besides Arabic, the choice he made was pointed, and it distinguished him from many of his peers who were more interested perhaps in communicating with Israeli Jews on their own terms. Taha figured that any Tel Avivian who wanted to speak to him could do so in English, which had, it seems, the added benefit of leveling the linguistic playing field.

He also separated his political beliefs from the way he treated individual people. That is, Taha maintained close friendships with various Arabs whose political views were quite far from his own; he could also criticize Israeli policy in the sharpest terms while welcoming Israeli Jews warmly to his shop. In May 1977, the right-wing Likud Party swept into power—so bringing to a dramatic end almost thirty years of Labor Party domination and making Greater Israel ideologue and former Irgun terrorist Menachem Begin prime minister. Like many Palestinians, Taha was strongly suspicious of Egyptian president Anwar

Sadat's negotiations with Israel and the United States, which came right on the heels of the Likud victory: "I was always waiting for peace between the Arabs and Israel," he says, but he viewed Sadat's surprise visit to Israel in November 1977 and the talks that followed as a selfish Egyptian ploy to win back the Sinai and curry favor with the Americans while in essence ignoring—or pushing aside—the Palestinians and their plight. And though it was unlike Taha to express himself in explicitly political terms, the introduction he wrote to Rashid Hussein's memorial book, dated January 30, 1978, reveals a more outspoken impulse. Addressing his late friend Rashid, who seems to stand here for all Palestinians, Taha writes that "the master of Egypt is talking now about a just and eternal peace that will allow 'everyone' to live without cares. But they've excluded you from the 'everyone' and ignored your presence, and denied your rights and impounded your desires and lowered a thick curtain over your tragedy."

Direct political writing still remained unusual for Taha—and even here he opted for metaphor rather than pronouncement: the brief essay ends with the ominous image of "ravens descending on the pyramids' heights." But the events of these same years did lead him to become involved in a more organized form of *cultural* activism. This came by way of his friendship with Mansour Kardosh, Taha's ice-block and soda supplier from his days running his first shop in Saffuriyya.

Remembered as an honest, exacting, and driven man—and as someone who wore a jacket and tie, "his pen correctly in the upper pocket of his coat," even in the strongest midsummer heat—Kardosh was an old political hand. Back in 1958, he had founded the small but influential nationalist movement al-Ard (The Land), together with the poet Habib Qahwaji, the former schoolteacher Saleh Baransi, a young Hebrew University law student named Sabri Jiryis, and a group of intellectuals of various beliefs and backgrounds. From the outset, al-Ard declared itself eager "to find a just solution for the Palestine question . . . in accordance with the wishes of the Palestinian Arab people; a solution which meets its interests and desires, restores it to its political existence, ensures its full legal rights, and regards it as the first possessor of the right to decide its own fate for itself." However mild such words may sound, they were considered nearly treasonous in context, and al-Ard was refused a license to print a newspaper, a

refusal the group dodged by exploiting a loophole in the law that allowed one-time publication without a license. So they brought out
each issue under a different editor and with a different but related
name: *News of the Land, The Call of the Land, This Land, The Essence
of the Land, The Rain of the Land, The Secret of the Land,* and so on.
Altogether some twelve numbers appeared, though the group was
eventually outlawed and the Supreme Court later upheld the ban
against the movement. When al-Ard attempted to run as a party in
the 1965 Knesset election, each of the group's leaders was banished to
a different town, far from his own and from the others; the authorities had, it seemed, finally managed to stamp out the movement. Yet
even now, some fifty years later and after the death or exile abroad of
most of its leaders, the case of al-Ard is still considered so sensitive
that at the Israel State Archive, the files about it remain sealed.

Taha himself had given al-Ard a wide berth in its day. He would
often stop by to talk and drink coffee or tamarind juice at Kardosh's
small café, and he clearly sympathized with Kardosh's feelings for his
people, but he was wary of his old friend's political approach, which
he considered too blunt and confrontational: "just slogans." Instead
of simply publishing a speech by Nasser, says Taha, al-Ard would
print a full-page picture of the Egyptian president—then considered
an archenemy of Israel—as a provocation. (Taha: "You are pro-Egypt?
Okay. But why such a big picture?") Over the years the leaders of the
movement had paid heavily for their commitment to the cause—and
for that provocation: Qahwaji was forced into exile in Cyprus, and
Jiryis in Beirut; Baransi served a ten-year prison sentence and was
tortured for "belonging to a 'Palestinian organization'" that was never
named; Kardosh moved in and out of jail.

By the late 1970s, al-Ard had been defunct for some time, and although Kardosh remained tireless in his political engagement—leading
an organization that supported the rights of Palestinian political prisoners in Israeli jails and another that fought for human rights—he
was also interested in creating a separate group that would honor and
raise awareness of Palestinian heritage in all its forms. After founding
the Society for the Commemoration of the Legacy of Rashid Hussein,
which brought out editions of Rashid's essays and poems as well as
the memorial book with Taha's introduction, he established the collective known as al-Sawt (The Voice) and invited Taha to join. Al-Sawt

was associated in the minds of many with the various nationalist movements and parties that were emerging in the north of the country at around the same time: Abna' al-Balad, the Sons of the Village, advocated a boycott of Israeli elections and a fairly radical form of Pan-Arabism, and the Progressive List for Peace was considered, in the words of one suspicious government official, "al-Ard brought back to life with a face lift." But Taha himself seems not to have cared much about the group's political pedigree. He continued to support the Communists' more conciliatory approach and, in typical, self-determining fashion, opted to sidestep the directly political implications of al-Sawt's program. He chose instead to focus on the fact that they would be producing *literature*.

The Anglican priest (now archbishop) Riyah Abu al-Assal managed to buy a printing press abroad, and together with Kardosh, Baransi, Taha's good friend the poet Jamal Qa'war, and several others, he and Taha undertook to publish books that they considered, in Taha's words, "progressive and Palestinian." Taha served as a reader for the group—offering his opinion on various manuscripts—and besides publishing collections of poetry by Qa'war and one by Rashid's younger brother, the poet Ahmed Hussein, they brought out historical and critical works, including a volume about the "life, stance, and legacy" of Khalil al-Sakakini and another about Ottoman history. And though Taha had no inkling of this when he joined the group, in 1983 al-Sawt would publish his own first book.

Before he could think of collecting his poems between two covers, however, Taha had first to write much more. And the force that would bring on his next, fairly frenzied bout of composition was less mysterious than that which had initially driven him to turn to poetry. It was, in fact, plain as the sound of Israeli jets whizzing high above his Casa Nova Street shop, bound north, for Lebanon.

THE EVENING WINE OF AGED SORROW

◆

"FROM WAR TO WAR," WROTE EMILE HABIBY, "their sense of hearing had grown ever sharper, so that in time they learned to distinguish perfectly between the rumble of one war and the rumble of the next. Send up a noise—the whistle of bullets or the roar of a cannon, a howling or anthems, or a military march—and they'll tell you which war it comes from, and the exact year in which the war broke out."

It was the summer of 1982. Taha had recently been diagnosed with a serious glandular disorder—acromegaly, a sort of gigantism that caused his hands and feet to grow, his jaw to protrude, and, most ominously but somehow fittingly, his heart to expand. After surgery to treat the condition, his doctor had ordered him to extricate himself from the traffic and pollution of downtown Nazareth, and Taha had moved with his family into the handsome two-story stone house they had built on an open plot of land in what was then the very rural quarter of Bir el-Amir, surrounded by slopes of olive groves. Although just a mile from the thick of the market and the bustle of his shop, the new house offered a peaceful refuge and, ultimately, an excellent place to write. Most of Taha's poetry would be composed while he lived in Bir el-Amir, which was, if anything, more like a village than a city neighborhood: even into the early 1990s, Bir el-Amir still had no sewage system or paved roads, and the water supply was erratic. On the other, more fragrant hand, he and Yusra had managed together to pack the front yard with what seemed a whole Saffuriyya's worth of fruit trees. In the early mornings and late nights that bookended his long workdays, Taha liked to putter between their baby trunks and fledgling branches. He also bought several goats, whose playfully curious presence soothed him.

But while he was trying to tend his flock, events in the near distance took over and flooded his imagination. For several years now, PLO guerrillas had been staging periodic attacks on Israel from Southern Lebanon, and Israel had been noisily rattling its sabers and threatening revenge, staging a ten-day-long offensive across its northern border in 1978. Now Minister of Defense Ariel Sharon was plotting a full-scale invasion of Lebanon, already tangled in the mess of a brutal and protracted civil war. Sharon's declared goal was to crush the PLO, which had been based in Lebanon since the organization's forced flight from Jordan in 1970; implied was his more grandiose desire to—in the words of one American journalist—"kill an idea, the idea of Palestinian nationality." Sharon's decidedly megalomaniacal plan also entailed the eviction from Lebanon of the Syrian army and the hoisting to power of pro-Israel Maronite Christian forces—among them the Phalangists, led by Bashir Gemayal and named after the Spanish fascist party. (Gemayal's pharmacist father, Pierre, had attended the 1936 Olympics in Berlin and been impressed by the order he witnessed in Hitler's Germany: he returned to Lebanon and founded the Phalange paramilitary, based on the Nazi Youth model.) This latter piece of the Lebanese puzzle would also affect the precarious geopolitics of many of the neighboring countries, since the Phalangists had long made clear their desire to rid Lebanon of its Palestinian population "whether by methods of persuasion or by other means of pressure," and according to one of the more reliable historians of the region, Sharon himself meant to "to transform the situation not only in Lebanon but in the whole Middle East."

Transform it Sharon and his counselors did, though perhaps not precisely as planned. At 10 am on June 6 of that year, the preposterously titled "Operation Peace for Galilee" commenced, as columns of Israeli tanks, trucks, and armored personnel carriers roared across the Lebanese border, and the massive naval bombardment of the seaside cities Tyre and Sidon began. Relentless aerial attacks of the coast and fertile Beqaa Valley started soon after, and within days, entire villages and city blocks had been pounded into mere heaps of dust and death. In theory, Israel was aiming to smash what it considered terrorist targets—but the destruction and bloodshed were wildly indiscriminate, and the definition of a "terrorist" was so vague as to be meaningless. By June 11, when the first cease-fire in what would turn out to be a summer of battles, sieges, and pseudo-cease-fires took hold, the Israeli army had already reached Beirut.

For Taha, the news was much more devastating and personal than that of any of the wars since 1948 had been. The reason for this was not complicated but lay in the simple geographical fact that the outskirts of Sidon housed the largest Palestinian refugee camp in Lebanon, 'Ain el-Hilweh, the Sweet Spring, where Amira and the rest of his extended family had lived for the past thirty years. By June 1982, 'Ain el-Hilweh was also home to some thirty-five thousand other Palestinian refugees—a large number of them from Saffuriyya and almost all from the Galilee. According to the radio reports to which Taha listened obsessively during the early weeks of the war, Israeli loudspeakers had ordered all the camp's residents to evacuate and converge at the seashore—after which a very lopsided battle ensued between the heavily equipped Israeli army and air force and the ragtag groups of RPG-toting Palestinian fighters, some of them children, who held out in the camp. Whatever the ostensible "terrorist" threat, the damage caused to 'Ain el-Hilweh was both general and total, as the Israeli bombs and artillery (and even napalm) made no distinction whatsoever between civilian and "military" targets. Although the Israelis claimed that terrorists were deliberately placing themselves among civilians, the basic assumption seems to have been that *all* Palestinian refugee camp dwellers were, at heart, really terrorists—or terrorist sympathizers, who also deserved to be punished. "The camp was systematically reduced to rubble," in the words of one *Jerusalem Post* reporter, who also wrote that "the bombs did not leave any craters here in Ain Hilweh," but rather, "they appear to have exploded just above the surface, saving all the force of their blast for the thin walls of the refugee houses. Ain Hilweh now is some two square kilometers of twisted broken rubble, putrid rubbish, and torn and shattered personal belongings."

It had been decades since Taha had received direct word from Amira and the rest of his family or from his former Saffuriyya neighbors and friends who had stayed in Lebanon, but he had never stopped thinking of them, and his mind rushed now across the border and into those mounds of rubble. He was haunted by a grotesque sense of déjà vu. Yet again these Saffuriyyans had been forced to flee their homes by Israeli planes dropping bombs; yet again those homes were flattened by Israeli bulldozers. (A few weeks after the assault, the United Nations Relief and Works Agency reported, "Ain Hilweh camp: totally destroyed.") On the other hand, they may not have survived the onslaught at all. And even if they had stumbled out toward the sea alive, their emotional, physical, and psychic state must have been disastrous. One eyewitness described the scene at the Sidon seashore, as some fifty thousand people stood, parched and panicked, in the heat: "The sun is overwhelming. The crowd becomes hysterical. Shouts, cries and screams are hurled at the guards, who prevent any movement." In an ironic twist, the author of these words and one of the Israeli commanders responsible for overseeing the immediate needs—food, water, shelter, sanitation—of the now-homeless 'Ain el-Hilweh refugees was none other than Lieutenant Colonel Dov Yermiya, who had led the invasion of Saffuriyya that black summer night thirty-four years before.

Though still wearing an IDF uniform, Dov was much more critical of Israel's military actions now than he had been as a young soldier, and the journal he kept during his call-up that June—which led to his eventual expulsion from the army—offers an unstinting account of the vast devastation and suffering that Israel was unleashing on Lebanon. "The damage," he wrote of the scene at 'Ain el-Hilweh, "is indescribable[;] a human settlement is crushed into smithereens." His diary also charts the waves of moral nausea that swept over him as he realized that Lebanon was not the only country being laid waste by this war: he was witnessing the destruction of Israel's soul as well. It was no doubt this anguished, inward-looking aspect of what he wrote and published soon after he returned home in July that so aggravated the powers that be. He describes, for instance, a scene that took place during the furious Friday night bombardment of 'Ain el-Hilweh the first week of the war:

> With this [shelling] in the background, like a surrealistic play, I discover in one of the stories of the building [which served as army headquarters] the religious soldiers from the unit all wrapped up in talitot (prayer shawls), praying the Sabbath prayer . . . and singing, with much enthusiasm, happy Sab-

bath melodies in an improvised synagogue under the sign "The Sidon Synagogue."

I flee from there, filled with anger. The air is permeated with the smell of corpses; destruction and death are continuing, and they are receiving the Sabbath queen as if nothing had happened. I hate them. I am ashamed to be a son of this nation, this arrogant, condescending, cruel nation, that sings at the edge of destruction.

Taha of course knew nothing of Dov or his involvement in the war. Neither, it seems safe to say, would the agonized jottings of one conscientious sixty-eight-year-old Israeli soldier have much mattered to him, given all that was happening on the ground. Unbeknownst to them both, the two men were, though, bound by a certain shared compulsion to react in words to the violent events of that summer. In his journal, Dov was compiling a matter-of-fact record of what he saw and experienced in Lebanon, much like evidence to be used later in a trial—while back in serene Bir el-Amir, Taha turned again to poetry to help him express the raging storm of all he imagined and felt.

Despite the urgency with which Taha responded to the situation in Lebanon, an eerie kind of timelessness hovers over the poems he wrote that year. And as always with his work, it is difficult to know exactly what lines were written when. Nearly half the poems that would make up his first book are dated February through May 1983, though he confirms that he was already writing throughout the summer of 1982—as the Israeli army besieged and bombarded Beirut by air, land, and sea; masses of Israeli Jews took to the Tel Aviv and Jerusalem streets to demonstrate their scorn or support for the war; Bashir Gemayel was elected president of Lebanon in a highly dubious vote; Begin's government rejoiced at the news; and the PLO was forced to accept an American plan to evacuate thousands of its fighters by Greek ship from Beirut. Taha's physical distance from these scenes of chaos and carnage no doubt made it easier for him to write. It is interesting to note that during this same time, Mahmoud Darwish was living bunkered in Beirut. Although he would later—from the remove of Paris and several years—describe a single 1982 summer day under siege in a book-length essay, *Memory for Forgetfulness*, when asked in the midst of the mayhem what he was writing, he proclaimed in rather French fashion: "I am writing my silence." The voice of the artillery was, he said, louder than his own.

♦

Of the poems Taha wrote during this period, several emerged in direct response to particular events. The poem "Exodus" begins:

> The street is empty
> as a monk's memory,
> and faces explode in the flames
> like acorns—
> and the dead crowd the horizon
> and doorways.
> No vein can bleed
> more than it already has,
> no scream will rise
> higher than it's already risen.
> We will not leave!

Taha insists in conversation that this is "a poem only about Beirut" and explains that he wrote it not to express his own point of view but from the perspective of the Palestinian fighters who were being told by the Americans and most of the Arab world to abandon the city that August. His own sense of his poem's narrow topicality is, however, peculiar, since in many ways "Exodus" is much more expansive and resonant than the literal, calendar-bound reading he suggests. (The poem was first published in Cyprus a full year after the siege—in a special issue of the PLO's official magazine, dedicated to the commemoration of "Another Land Day," alongside several articles on land confiscation in the Galilee.)

In fact, "Exodus" may not be "about" a single topic at all—so much as it is a vividly disturbing set of sounds, rhythms, and images, woven together to conjure a desperate mood. It succeeds as the best political poetry does by cutting across time and circumstance to apply to any number of other situations and to speak to people far removed from the context of its original composition. This is not, of course, part of its design—on the contrary. There is no possible way that Taha could have anticipated those future ages or later readings, but it seems fair to say that the poem has other subterranean trapdoors and levels—as well as present-day extensions:

> The shields of light are breaking apart
> before the rout and the siege;
> outside, everyone wants us to leave.
> But we will not leave!
> . . . .
> Outside they're blocking the exits
> and offering their blessings to the impostor,
> praying, petitioning
> Almighty God for our deaths.

Death, death, and more death: it filled the air as it filled his poems that late summer and fall. On September 14, the newly elected Lebanese president Bashir Gemayal was assassinated by a bomb planted by Syrian agents. With that, Sharon seized his chance and, under the Frankenstinian army code name Operation Iron Brain, ordered Israeli forces to occupy Muslim West Beirut immediately, "to preserve tranquility and order." This was a chilling euphemism if there ever was one, since in fact what happened the very next night was that IDF units stepped aside and waited nearby as Phalangist militiamen—dressed in uniforms provided by Israel, toting with them IDF rations, and finding their way with aerial photos supplied by the Israel Air Force—entered two small, crowded refugee camps in southern Beirut. What certain Israeli army commanders did or did not fathom might then take place would later become the subject of furious debate as well as a controversial state commission of inquiry, though there is no doubt that, in the name of "purging the terrorists," the Phalange proceeded over the next several days to butcher in the most grisly manner hundreds, perhaps thousands of Palestinian refugees and poor Lebanese. Women were brutally raped and murdered, young men lined up and shot or castrated and then killed, babies tortured to death. (When asked by an uneasy Israeli bystander why they were killing civilians, one Phalangist explained that "pregnant women will give birth to terrorists and children will grow up to be terrorists.") Accounts of the death toll range from the ghastly 700 to the unthinkable 3,500—of whom few if any were "terrorists." This sad spot, known collectively as "Sabra and Shatila," would from that day forward become nearly synonymous with "massacre." And here Taha's poem "Exodus," begun a month or so earlier, seems to have been prophetic: much like the massacre at Dayr Yasin in 1948, this slaughter was designed (by the Phalange), according to one Israeli newspaper report, "to create panic, to provoke an exodus, en masse, of Palestinians towards Syria and to convince all the Palestinians in Lebanon that they were no longer safe in that country."

The horror of this event was, it seems, too huge for Taha to face head-on. The shock of it—together with the devastating, cumulative effects of the entire war and its implications for Palestinians everywhere, who appeared more vulnerable and alone now than ever—may be what caused him to shift tonal gears. The poems that poured forth from his pen in the wake of the massacre are more doleful than defiant, and they draw inspiration from a general state of being rather than from specific historical incidents. They also mark a crucial turning point in his work, in that there, for the first time ever, he addresses his muse, Amira.

Maybe she had always been present, poised between the lines of his poems—or perhaps it took the dreadful doings of Taha's fifty-second year to stir in him the urge to write poems for his erstwhile fiancée as he imagined her now, far off in the ruins of 'Ain el-Hilweh. Either way, the Amira who appears suddenly in Taha's long, mournful poem "The Fourth Qasida" seems at once to be his actual cousin, the living, breathing love of his childhood, and a more archetypically literary stand-in for all of Saffuriyya and indeed for all that is ever lost to time, to death, and to separation:

> When our loved ones leave
> Amira,
> as you left,
> an endless migration in us begins
> and a certain sense takes hold in us
> that all of what is finest
> in and around us,

except for the sadness,
is going away—
departing, not to return.

Eighteen small pages in the original Arabic, "The Fourth Qasida" would become the title poem of Taha's first book—and it is in a way a signature work, a poem that set forth for the first time the mythic dimension of his verse, as it also blended elements of a received poetic tradition with an utterly idiosyncratic musical and visual sense. On the one (traditional) hand, the wistful opening strongly suggests the *nasib,* or erotic prelude, of the pre-Islamic qasida, in which the poet surveys the traces left at the abandoned campsite of his beloved: he remembers the time they passed there together, then weeps and mourns her leaving with her tribe. (In some classical qasidas, the poet experiences the vision of a visitation by his beloved, "whom he knows to dwell in a distant place.") So many poems in the Arabic canon quote or echo or simply imitate these motifs that it seems unlikely Taha would even have been aware of such reverberations in his own lines. After decades spent absorbing classical Arabic poetry, the conventions flowed through his blood.

On the other hand, Taha's poem took these ancient tropes and turned them on their formal ear. He had no interest in replicating the standard rhymes and meters in which all the pre-Islamic and later medieval (and even many modern) poems were composed; neither does the shape of the rest of "The Fourth Qasida" hew to the strict formulaic progression of the classical ode. Instead he relied as he always did on more intuitive sounds and structures, which allowed him to explore a meandering, gently melancholy line of feeling and thought and to create a charged poetic landscape, populated by "strange birds seeking refuge . . . / among them quails / and songbirds with colorful wings, / and also birds of prey." The poem unfolds as an extended vision of Amira, too, as a bird—"The Dove Who Traveled on the Train of Winter" as the poem's eccentric subtitle has it—who the poet imagines will one day fly with these other winged creatures from afar and alight "near / the almond tree in our garden."

The minute I see her, I'll know her,
and recognize, too, catastrophes' rings

hanging from her tender neck.
I'll know her clear, springlike glance,
her dewy gaze
like the dreams of lakes.
I'll know her shy, velvety steps,
her measured paces,
like breaths taken by seedlings of lettuce.

The poem works as both private fantasy and cosmic symphony: the images and metaphors are absolutely Taha's own (shy, velvety steps? breaths taken by seedlings of lettuce?), while the careful modulation between the "we" of the opening and the "me" of what follows allows him to alternate grand gesture and reticence. When he writes in that collective voice ("an endless migration in us begins") his words again suggest those of the pre-Islamic poets who spoke for the family or tribe. But then he'll retreat to the hush of his most intimate thoughts. And indeed the poem's title both does and doesn't refer to the tradition, since a qasida originally meant one of the pre-Islamic odes, while in modern Arabic it is—older echoes aside—simply a poem.

"The Fourth Qasida" is part of a constellation of powerful works that were composed around the same time and that all crystallize around the elusive figure of Amira. These poems may have been triggered by the Lebanese experience, but they provide a more sweeping view of the Palestinian—and indeed the human—condition than their provenance might suggest. "The Evening Wine of Aged Sorrow" takes shape as a meditation on the oppressive power of sadness itself ("At dusk a sensation / of darkness and gloom / floods the chest— / amassing like silt, /closing in / like a wall"). "Ambergris" opens with lines even more reminiscent of the ancient desert odes than what had come before ("Our traces have all been erased, / our impressions swept away— / and all the remains / have been effaced . . ."), then changes tack several times, moving eventually to a harsh vision of the land as "a whore . . ."

holding out a hand to the years,
as it manages a ballroom
on the harbor pier—
it laughs in every language

and bit by bit, with its hip,
feeds all who come to it.

As counterpoint, Amira is here, too, though not by name. In this case
she is more an essence than a living presence—and her memory offers the poet's only salvation:

> and I—if not for the lock of your hair,
> auburn as the nectar of carob,
> and soft as the scent of silk,
> if not for the camphor,
> if not for the musk and the sweet basil,
> if not for the ambergris—
> I would not know it,
> and would not love it,
> and would not go near it . . .
> *
> Your braid
> is the only thing
> linking me, like a noose, to this whore.

With "Ambergris," Taha puts forth in startling fashion the idea
that would later dominate much of his work—that the land itself is
not what's sacred. Those who dwell or have dwelled in it are. The
greatest loss was not, then, the houses, groves, and fields of Saffuriyya or of Palestine: it was the *people* of Saffuriyya, the *life* of Palestine. And of all those whose absence continued to haunt him years
later, Amira remained the epitome. So the lock of her hair is granted
here the power of a talisman that can summon an entire world.
"Where," Taha would ask in a much later poem, surveying the rubble
of the village, "is the ease of Amira's braid?"

It is, however, important to realize that by invoking his childhood
sweetheart's long-lost plait, Taha was not expressing a literal desire to
travel back in time and tug it; neither was he eager to undo his happy
marriage to Yusra, to negate the births of their children, or to close
down his shop and cancel the rich life he had experienced in Israel
since 1948. Amira's presence in Taha's poetry is a subtle, almost holo-
graphic phenomenon—a complex interplay of ideal and real dimen-

sions. To attempt to understand it, one must begin, perhaps, with her name itself.

"Amira"—the word means princess in Arabic—is the pseudonym that Taha has assigned to his Saffuriyya fiancée and which he uses both when he writes and speaks about her. In life, she is called something else. (And in fact one of the only stipulations that Taha made when he agreed to be the subject of this biography was that I refer to her in print as "Amira," since he considers it inappropriate and disrespectful to publish her true name.) It seems that some essential imaginative metamorphosis took place the moment Taha chose to turn his onetime betrothed into Amira—and in doing so performed an act of poetic alchemy that transformed her from flesh-and-blood woman into a kind of quintessence: the very human embodiment of all that was lost when Saffuriyya was lost. At the same time, she has never become *solely* a symbol or literary conceit. Since the sixth-century days of 'Antar and 'Abla, Arabic poets have addressed their love poems to specific women, some more actual than others. The real "Amira" is always there in Taha's mind and heart as poignant biographical fact.

Never was this more evident than on one early morning in the summer of 1983, when Taha found himself outfitted in the borrowed old coat of a day laborer and seated next to the driver of a large UNRWA-owned semitrailer, loaded with concrete. Neither man spoke much as the truck lumbered over the wave- and salt-hollowed boulders that form Israel's northern border crossing at Ras al-Naqura, or Rosh Hanikra, and made their way toward what remained of the camp called 'Ain el-Hilweh, the Sweet Spring. . . .

◆

For some thirty years now, Taha had stayed in touch and on good terms with Yosef Averra, the Iraqi Jewish orderly he had befriended as he ailed with TB and pined for Amira at Schneller. Averra lived in Upper Nazareth and would often travel down from the Jewish suburb on the hill to drink coffee with Taha at his shop.

Now an employee of Israel's Ministry of Agriculture, Averra had—with the Israeli occupation of Southern Lebanon—been placed in charge of regulating the health of goat and sheep herds there. An affable native Arabic speaker, he made the hour-long commute daily to

Lebanon, and he had friends throughout the Israeli civil administration, in UNRWA, and in the South Lebanon Army, Israel's mostly Christian proxy force to the north. Here was yet another irony brought on by yet another Israeli war: the invasion of Lebanon had been a catastrophe from Taha's perspective—yet one of the many chatty connections that Averra had established in the midst of the conflict had allowed him to arrange for Taha to receive a two-day pass to cross over into Lebanon and, at long last, to be reunited with Amira. Posing as a laborer, Taha would accompany the driver of a cement truck bound from Haifa to help with UN reconstruction efforts in her camp.

"The minute I see her, I'll know her," Taha had written just a few months before, and he says that when he first stood facing Amira—who had been summoned, without explanation, to her brother's recently rebuilt home on the outskirts of the camp—he recognized her, though she, for her part, did not identify him right away. (The scene was one that Taha would later reimagine in dramatic fashion in one of his most moving poems, "Meeting at an Airport": "I recognized you / but you didn't recognize me. / 'Is it you?!' / But you wouldn't believe it.") She had not been warned that he was coming, and she could hardly be blamed for not connecting this slightly hulking, probably weeping middle-aged stranger before her with the skinny, joking boy to whom she had once been engaged. It must indeed have been a shock to see how the unbothered planes of Taha's formerly young face had given way to an intricate network of deep grooves and snaking furrows. The teenaged cut-up to whom she had said good-bye some thirty-four years earlier at the bus in al-Qara'un was now a stern-looking husband and father with a broad torso, a commanding manner, and a thinning head of gray hair. The complicated life that Taha had lived was evident in his every pore. A similar transformation, it should be said, may also have obtained where Amira's face and frame were concerned—but Taha is stubbornly closemouthed about her physical bearing, as if mention of such details would make his memory of her sound too carnal. The closest he comes is to describe her hands—which were, he says, rough and cracked from the labor of rebuilding her house after the camp's destruction.

And what, after all the years of separation, did they say? "Silly things," says Taha. "How are you? How is your family?" Their meeting was, nonetheless, "very emotional," and over the course of the next forty-eight hours they "talked and talked and talked." Among other things, she recounted what had happened during the Israeli attack on the camp: her husband had been working in Libya, while several of her sons were off laboring in the Gulf states. She had been alone with a younger son and several daughters when the order came to evacuate—and they had lost everything. Their small house (more of a shack) was leveled. They lived for months in tents that UNRWA had provided. By the time Taha visited they had managed to reconstruct their very humble dwelling, two tiny rooms with a tin roof. Cement roofs—a supposed sign of permanency—were still forbidden in the several-decades-old camp, which Taha characterizes as far more dismal than the dismal refugee camps on the West Bank. Compared to 'Ain el-Hilweh, he says, "Jenin is rich."

Taha was welcomed as an honored guest in the home of Amira's brother, his cousin, and during his brief stay, he was reunited with many old friends and relatives from Saffuriyya: a steady stream of visitors poured in throughout the day and night—eager to see him and hear news of others from whom they'd had no word for so many long, hard years.

When it was time to leave the camp and to leave Amira, Taha had, he says, already resolved to see her again. Yosef Averra set about pulling a whole fistful of strings, and within several months' time he had arranged for Amira to receive a pass to come to Israel for a full forty-five days. (During this period, the Israeli government had adopted an unofficial policy of allowing certain Palestinian refugees from Lebanon—most of them older women, considered a "low security risk"—to visit in this way.) And so it was that the impossible had at long last occurred: a dove had traveled on the train of winter. Or, more precisely, a slightly nervous Palestinian refugee wearing a modest headscarf and long cotton dress and clutching a small suitcase had ridden in a taxi south from Sidon to the Israeli border in the height of the summertime heat. Taha and a driver he had hired for the day were waiting to meet her on the other side—Rosh Hanikra was about an hour from Nazareth—and as Taha tells it (laughing in slightly sinister fashion), the Israeli soldier who ferried Amira through the crossing thought that she and Taha were to be married. "Il-arus!"

he announced cheerfully in Arabic: the bride! "The bride is here!" He
had no idea of how those words must have sounded to the man who
had come to greet her that day.

But Amira was—it is crucial to note—no longer the bride in this
story. The relationship between her and Taha was by now strictly pla-
tonic: not only were they both contentedly married to others, but the
societies in which they lived and still live were and are traditional in
the extreme, and the mere suggestion of illicit or extramarital anything would be cause for serious scandal. The very idea of betrayal
upsets Taha to his core.

That said, there were questions about Taha's relationship to
Amira—and by extension, Yusra's relationship to her husband's old
flame, both in real life and in his poems—that had long hovered, unspoken, in my mind. Of all the sensitive subjects that emerged in my
research for this book, this was perhaps the most sensitive. It is, after
all, one thing to theorize about a poet's artfully allegorizing references
to his former love—and quite another to consider the possibly bruised
feelings such references might inflict on the poet's devoted wife. . . .
Given the delicacy of the subject, though, I had planned to let it slip
and had hoped that readers would—as I had—fill in the emotional
blanks for themselves.

But then one day these questions begin to answer themselves, almost without my asking.

Since that first morning when I'd arrived with my tape recorder at
Taha's house in Bir el-Amir, the process of interviewing him and indeed his whole family has widened and relaxed immeasurably. I have
been at it now for several years, and the more formal question-and-
answer sessions have given way to an extended and emphatically
irreverent conversation, punctuated by nearly nonstop rounds of cardamom coffee or fresh rosewater drink, depending on the season.
Taha's home has a bustling openness that makes it easy for others—
for me—to come and go without disturbing its basic rhythms. Like
many traditional Palestinian homes, it is shared by several generations: Nizar and his wife, Aisheh, live downstairs, while Usama has a
room on the same floor where Taha and Yusra live, and where the
large kitchen—with its industrial-sized refrigerator—sits. (As is also
customary, when Layla married, she moved out and into her in-laws'

house; she and her teenage children visit once a week, on Thursdays.) The kitchen is the house's hub, and Imm Nizar—as I call Yusra to her face—and Aisheh are almost always cooking: they prepare a large lunch every day for the family and the workers at Taha's shop, all in all between eight and twelve people. And because Taha needs to lie down and rest periodically, I often find myself seated with the women at the kitchen table, surrounded by heaps of sliced eggplant or piles of grape leaves for rolling. As a serious cook myself, I enjoy Imm Nizar's lessons—and she seems to take special pride in instructing me on the ins and outs of roasting green wheat, chopping mlukhiyyeh, and stitching sheep intestine. Sometimes (to my delight) she will even interrupt my interview with Taha to pull me into the kitchen and show me how the proper texture had been achieved in one of her burbling pots. This, too, is part of my research. Although we have never talked about it, Yusra and I seem to share the belief that to write a responsible Life and Times of Taha, I need to know about more than the wars and elections and poetic trends that defined his day: every bit as important is to understand what—over the course of the turbulent years— he has eaten.

This morning, she and I are alone. It is Aisheh's designated day to dress up and go visit her parents in Safafra. (She, too, is the daughter of Saffuriyyans and was raised in that Nazareth neighborhood, surrounded by other descendants of the village.) Taha is not feeling well and has taken himself to the doctor. After first plying me with a very large breakfast of minty eggs, labneh, tomato, olives, and sliced avocado, which I eat as she washes dishes and we discuss which kinds of squash are best for stuffing, Yusra goes about her endless chores— today is her day to tend the fruit trees, which have in the years since she and Taha first planted them grown wide and strong and seasonally heavy with their sweet-smelling yield—and I sit scribbling in my notebook on one of the living room couches.

Suddenly, she appears from outdoors, a bit pink cheeked, a few strands of hair poking from under her loose kerchief. She is smiling brightly and holding out a small sprig of chicory, gone to vivid blue flower. "See?" she says. "In Arabic when someone's eyes are very blue, we say they're the color of chicory." And almost without pausing, she continues to chatter: "Abu Nizar's fiancée—you know she came to visit us. Her eyes are exactly the color of chicory flowers." She is still smiling as she offers me the spray of pretty weeds—and, it seems, a one-time-only invitation to ask the unaskable question. . . .

"Ya, Imm Nizar—" I hesitate before plunging. "Can I ask you about that? How you felt when she came to visit?"

She laughs in her full, unflappable way and says, "Everybody wants to know about that. I love her, she's like a sister. She's such a good, dignified person, with beautiful blue eyes, and a long, long neck." She indicates "Amira's" straight posture. "She came here and we went everywhere together, to Saffuri and Jerusalem and Tiberias. When she left, I cried. And the whole time she was so emotional, like Abu Nizar, weeping. . . ."

"And you weren't—" I stall temporarily, as my spoken Arabic runs aground, "you didn't feel somehow . . . "

"No, no!" She laughs again, knowing exactly what I mean. "I wasn't jealous at all. She and Abu Nizar are almost like brother and sister. When she came she was so good and so kind, without airs, how could I possibly think bad things about her?"

By now, I've begun to think bad things about myself—for being jealous on Yusra's behalf, while she seems so wholly untroubled by this complicated emotional arrangement. But it is too late to turn back: "And what about the poems? How do you feel when he writes poems for her?"

Once again she chuckles, pushing a strand of hair back under her scarf. "The way you ask me about stuffing squash, so we'll have something to talk about? A poet needs something to write about! This is what Abu Nizar chooses to write about. It's something very personal." Saying this, she points to her breastbone, as if to indicate the depth of this feeling.

"But don't you ever wish he'd write a poem for you?"

"Who writes a poem about his wife!??" Yusra grins and then bursts into an especially gleeful gale of laughter.

FOOLING THE KILLERS

◆

IN 1175 CE, SOME FIFTEEN YEARS AFTER an earthquake devastated Syria, toppling among many things the walls of the city of
Shayzar and burying most of his family alive, the Arab poet, knight,
and chronicler of the Crusader wars Usama ibn Munqidh wrote an
introduction to an anthology of pre-Islamic lamentations that he had
assembled and titled *Campsites and Dwellings*:

> What moved me to compile the present book was the ruin
> which had visited my country and my home. Time, in all its
> arrogance, seemed to have made it its design to efface them
> by every means. Everything came to be as if it had never ex-
> isted. Those courtyards, formerly so full of life, were now
> turned desolate. When I reached home, the fury of the earth-
> quake had already passed. Thus I saw the extent of what had
> happened to that earth which was the first thing to touch me
> in my life. I did not recognize my own house, nor my father's
> or my brothers' houses. . . .
>
> My only solace I found in the compilation of this collec-
> tion, as I made it from my tears over my home and over those
> I loved. I know it is too late for help or benefit now, but all the
> same, in it goes all that I have.

Give or take eight hundred years, the words could be Taha Muhammad Ali's own. And just as the grief that Ibn Munqidh felt over the
disaster that befell him and his homeland opened out through poetry

to make room for a much wider and more general registration of loss (one eminent scholar describes how "this filtration of deep personal experience . . . seems to contain a whole people's historical reservoir of sorrow, loss, yearning"), so by the time Taha's first book, *The Fourth Qasida,* appeared in 1983, his urge to mourn the ruins of Saffuriyya had already given way in his poems to a grander impulse.

It seems to have been Mansour Kardosh's idea for Taha to collect his poems at long last in a book, to be published by al-Sawt. Taha agreed, and went about arranging the eleven poems he had written and stored on scraps of paper in a small cigar box. As with most books written in Arabic in Israel, no editing took place, though Kardosh invited Rashid's brother, Taha's friend Ahmed Hussein, to write an introduction, which he did, praising in the highest terms Taha's "singular consciousness." Hussein had known of Taha's unpublished work, he wrote, yet had tried for a long time "to restrain my great enthusiasm for this intellectual and teacher who had left occasional footprints—but strong and clear ones—on the ground of our local literature. And I could only hope that many of our intellectuals would come to know Taha as I know him." The small volume at hand represented, he declared, "a unique poetic event."

Hussein's excitement apart, *The Fourth Qasida* was treated to an extremely modest reaction, and—for the same formal and political reasons that Taha's work had not made much of a stir when it first appeared in magazines—it remained mostly off the radar of the reading public: not only was this verse written without meter and rhyme (which made it not poetry but prose in traditional Arabic terms and the minds of all but a few local readers), it did not take up the usual themes and so probably confused many of those who did bother to crack the book's thin spine. It wasn't direct protest poetry; neither was it the dreamy romanticism that usually served as an alternative. This work was jagged and personal. It had a dark sense of humor and oddly syncopated rhythms. Tragicomedy of the plainspoken sort that Taha offered in his poems may have struck certain readers as too irreverent, too disturbing, too much of a rhetorical hodgepodge. It lacked, they may have felt, a certain propriety. Although he had only tentatively begun to experiment with inserting bits and echoes of the spoken dialect into his verse, Taha was already (with his unconventional diction) threatening the classical idea of *fasaha*—purity, fluency, or eloquence—which is the rolling, luxuriant ground upon which most of the history of Arabic letters rests. And while the building blocks of his verse were profoundly Palestinian (there were olive trees, a boy named Mahmud, and the memory of a vanished village), the poet's manner of arranging these familiar elements seemed somehow strange; he didn't bow to the tonal or structural conventions that many felt a real poem needed. Even those local readers of Arabic who enjoyed Taha's work seem in large part not to have considered it poetry and to have confused the unadorned surface of the poems with a lack of sophistication: "This is poetry without technique," one critic would later claim. According to this reading, Taha's "poetics are more the poetics of the story, the poetics of a folktale-teller, and less the poetics of a poet who is an artist of the art of poetry."

But before it came to passing judgment on the work itself, there was the problem of simply making the presence of his poetry known. At first it seems some people confused his name with that of another, more widely published Palestinian short-story writer, Muhammad Ali Taha. Furthermore, only a handful of Taha's poems had appeared in journals, and he was neither a member of the Communist Party nor affiliated with the government and its cultural outlets. He was, in other words, something of a one-man show and lacked an ideological representative who would push his name out into the world, which was how publishing worked in the Palestinian context. Al-Sawt was too new and too peripheral to have helped much on this score, and "book distribution" as it is known in the West was an almost entirely alien concept: the Communist Party disseminated books by subscription and door-to-door sales, and the Ministry of Education sent its publications to teachers, libraries, and certain critics. There were but a few small Arabic bookstores in the country, and it seems unlikely that Taha's book would have been available in any of them. Meanwhile he himself was singularly uninterested in public relations. He simply gave the book to his friends. When asked why he did not sell copies in his shop, he says he considered his mercantile life and his writing life distinct. Writing was not a business.

One Hebrew literary magazine featured translations of a few of Taha's poems by the person responsible for first publishing his work in Arabic, the bilingual Anton Shammas, who also wrote a brief article there announcing the book's publication and praising this "poet of

the underground," Taha Muhammad Ali, "a name worth remembering." But other than that, little attention was paid in print to *The
Fourth Qasida*. So far as I have been able to determine, but a single
Arabic review appeared, in *al-Jadid,* praising the "truth" of Taha's
work and noting the way "his simple subject matter links up with the
larger questions." Tiptoeing around the formal conservatism of the
local audience, the critic seemed to need to defend his appreciation
for the book (and here it's worth noting that in Arabic the word "prose"
means literally that which is loose or scattered, that is, not bound by
metrics): "all the poems in the book lack poetic meters, but in this
case, we must make clear the poet's ability to convince us that this
prose is indeed poetry."

More important, *The Fourth Qasida* had convinced Taha once and
for all that he was indeed a poet. This realization had been sneaking
up on him for decades—but now, with the publication of a book, he
felt more confident and freer to declare aloud his poetic intentions.
Never mind the indifference of many readers or the grumbling of his
detractors (and there was plenty of that: even some of those close to
Taha dismissed what he'd written as "not poetry"—both to his face
and behind his back), over the next several years, he would begin to
write more steadily and to identify himself publicly as a poet, even becoming the spokesman for the Union of Arab Writers in Israel with
its founding in 1987. The union was unofficially but plainly associated
with the Communist Party—Taha's old friend the poet and party
member Samih al-Qasim was president—and though it was unlike
Taha to join organizations or to take on such functionary-like roles,
he understood, he says, that it would serve as "a bridge" for him and
would offer a way to make himself better known as a writer in the
wider Arab world. When the union was asked by the publisher Riad
el-Rayyes to send a delegation of three writers to spend a week in
London as guests of an Arabic literary festival and book fair, al-Qasim
chose as his traveling companions Taha and a third local poet. Taha's
selection did not, it should be said, mean that his work was especially
known or appreciated by his peers. Rather, it was a sign of al-Qasim's
affection for him.

Taha jumped at the chance to travel. Besides his brief, unplanned
sojourn to Lebanon as a refugee and the two days he had spent at 'Ain

el-Hilweh with Amira, he had never been abroad, and he was hungry
to see the world. (His sons Usama and Nizar were now working with
him in the shop, and they assured him that they could run the business in his absence.) So it was that he arrived in London at age fifty-
seven, a most unlikely candidate to make friends and influence people.
Although no one at the festival had ever heard of him, and although
some of the most respected, urbane, and famous writers in the Arab
world also participated—among them the by-then internationally
celebrated Darwish and al-Qasim (who had renewed their friendship), Nizar Qabbani, the Egyptian poet Muhammad 'Afifi Matar, the
Lebanese Unsi al-Hajj, the Iraqi Buland al-Haydari, and the Syrian
short-story writer Zakariyya Tamir—the trinket-selling rustic from
Nazareth was, it seems, an instant hit, both with the other poets and

with the audience. This was the
first time Taha had met Arab
writers from beyond Israel and
the West Bank, and they felt to
him like long-lost friends; he
spent much of his time in London sitting, talking, and laughing over coffee with them in the
hotel lobby. ("How is it that we
didn't even know you existed?" Buland al-Haydari is reported to have
exclaimed to Taha, with a mixture of wonder and regret.) And the audience responded in the most visceral way to his unvarnished presence and his potent poems.

In the wake of the festival, the Egyptian literary critic and journalist Ghali Shukri offered what is perhaps the first recorded account
of what might be called the Taha Effect. Describing him—a bit oddly,
given Taha's birth date and relative robustness—as an "aged man from
Palestine," Shukri registered a brand of awe that would come to typify so many enchanted first brushes with Taha. "You can read his entire story-poem in his face," he wrote. "He has educated and trained
himself and with that knowledge could have become an excellent
fighter, as his friends say, or a poet, as he says. [He is] a tall, wide man,
who nearly stoops; his hair is white; his gaze never stills. He wears a
simple shirt and pants—believing that the London summer is just

like the summer in Nazareth." He goes on to describe Taha's international debut as a comedy of endearing errors:

> He rose and almost tripped over his briefcase, which wouldn't let him go. He left the briefcase behind and at the distance of a meter, returned to take it with him. The clapping pursued him like a whip. No sooner had he reached the stage than he started searching for the papers on which he had written. He rifled through them several times—and the applause chased after him as Samih al-Qasim helped him. Finally he found "Abd el-Hadi Fights a Superpower" and stopped the crowd—temporarily—from applauding . . . .
>
> The effect on the audience of the [poem's] simple words and the even simpler structure was to increase its applause for the Palestinian elder whose poetry takes up the path of directness . . . which suits the simplicity and spontaneity of his speech.

The London crowds were, it is clear, primed to embrace the Palestinian poets not just as individual writers but as representatives of a cause. The intifada, or uprising, had broken out eight months before in the West Bank and Gaza, as the pent-up frustrations of Palestinians forced to live for twenty years under a cruel and humiliating occupation flared spontaneously into the most heated, widespread, and sustained revolt against Israeli rule that the territories had yet known. And the Israelis, for their part, had responded with unprecedented ferocity against the tire-burning, flag-waving Palestinians, with Minister of Defense Yitzhak Rabin famously ordering his troops to "break their bones." The intifada and the umpteen David-and-Goliath newspaper and television images it inevitably spawned—as small children armed with nothing but slingshots faced down rows of tanks—had, meanwhile, seized the imagination of the world at large. Other Arabs in particular rallied around the Palestinian people, and many poets throughout the region offered impassioned tributes to the "children of the stones," as those young rock-throwers were known. At the festival in London, attended mostly by well-heeled expatriate Arabs now living in Europe, Qabbani won ovations by reciting poems from his *Trilogy of the Children of the Stones,* and al-Qasim stirred the crowd mightily by declaiming his "Poem of the Intifada," an extended, defiant indictment of, as he called them, "Occupiers Who Do Not Read."

Given this backdrop, the warm embrace that Taha received in London is in some ways even more surprising, since he refused in his poetry to take up current events. None of the poems he read contained a single direct reference to the uprising, to the "struggle," to children or to stones. The closest he came to that was in "Empty Words," a tricky Chinese box of a poem he wrote that year (and, one assumes, did not recite at the festival), in which he chastises his own "little notebook, / yellow as a spike of wheat," for *not* containing such incendiary stuff: "And where is the passage / whose tenor is this: / I wish I could be / a rock on a hill / which the young men / from Hebron explode / and offer as a gift to Jerusalem's children, / ammunition for their palms and slings!"

In a later interview, Taha would make his critique of placardlike poetry more explicit: "The poetry of the stones," he declared, "is fleeting, and the true poetry that lasts is that which depicts what's behind the stones and what's behind the intifada, which shows life brimming with feeling and sensation and pain."

Taha had spent years in relative isolation, carving out a literary nook for himself that was deliberately removed from the spotlight. And yet, once that bright beam was finally trained on him, he found that his hard-earned words had a peculiar way of burrowing straight into the hearts of his listeners. It seems the audience reacted in the overwhelming way it did because of his ability to address simultaneously his Ibn Munqidh–like grief—at once particular and general—even as he somehow conveyed the most profound and infectious joy. Since the Lebanon War, sorrow itself had become one of his primary themes, as he wrote, for instance, "The Falcon," an extended 1984 meditation on his sadness, and how he would, in a sense, be lost if it ever left him: "For without my sorrow, / at the end of the day, / rivers will only be water, / and the flower / merely a plant— / without my grief." Yet for all the pathos of such lines, an unmistakable zest bursts through. Taha's words are too keen, too spiked with wit and vigor ever to slide into the languorous zone of mere melancholy. And when Taha read a poem in his granular baritone, his feet planted widely, as though he were planning a sudden standing broad jump, the force of his personality was what came through: his relish at simply *being*. Taha had turned his own gusto into a kind of protest and so had in a sense reinvented for himself the very notion of resistance poetry.

But that may sound loftier than is quite right. As Ghali Shukri's description attests, Taha's slightly slapstick stage presence was a far cry from the more formal bearing of those poets whose long-term public role had made them polished performers—and whose metered poems gave their appearances a certain incantatory gravitas. One Palestinian critic has described with admiration how Darwish, for instance, "prefer[red] the way a poet has always addressed his audience in the Arab world: facing them like a prophet and delivering his poetry like an oracular pronouncement while the spellbound audience hangs on every word and, relating to the message of the poem, erupts periodically in sudden, emotional bursts of acclaim that provide a much-needed catharsis." Taha offered a gruffer, less studied show. And though as a performer he was a natural, he was a natural of a more disarming sort. One of the poems he read to the most torrential applause in London was a bittersweet ode to the village—and to the memory of a beloved cow, Sabha, who swallowed a rope and had to be slaughtered, so bringing the neighbors together in mournful solidarity.

> Imm Hashem
> sent up her wailing,
> as the knives sliced
> away at Sabha,
> and her daughters wept.
> Everyone grieved,
> and everyone lent a hand,
> insisting,
> "We'll share the burden.
> We'll manage."

The poem has about it the dramatic air of a stage play—a kind of Arabic-language, Galilean *Our Town*—and centers on a conversation between an elderly Palestinian peasant couple, reminiscing in dialect. As he read, Taha acted their parts. ("Do you remember—" the wife chides her husband, Abu Muhammad, at one point, "or have you fallen asleep?") Then he modulated into the more elegiac pitch of his own narratorial voice: "For a while, / the village was choked / in a muted sort of grief, / like Abu Hashem's hoarse voice, / and green as Sabha's eyes." Such a tender description of bovine beauty must have startled audience members accustomed to the strictly cadenced panegyrics of al-Mutanabbi and Qabbani—but they loved it and seem, too, not to have cared whether this was "prose" or poetry that they were hearing: they knew that it moved them.

◆

Although the gap between the lukewarm reception to which he'd been treated at home and the adulation abroad was yawning, Taha insists that he "was not too surprised" by the reaction of the crowds in London. He knew the value of his work, and since it was his natural tendency to accentuate the positive, he simply chose to ignore the scowls and focus on the applause.

Whether or not he expected such a glowing reaction, though, the contact with readers beyond his small circle clearly spurred him to get to work, and in the wake of this first taste of public acclaim, Taha seems to have been propelled as if by jet fuel to publish another book. He returned from London in the middle of August and began obsessively setting down on paper, revising, and finishing poems he had composed in his head over the last several years. The month that followed was intense: fifteen of the eighteen poems that make up his next collection are dated between August 20 and September 28 of that year.

Taha spent the autumn eagerly waiting for the book to be printed. The Union of Arab Writers was publishing it, along with a new edition of *The Fourth Qasida,* both at Taha's own expense—a phenomenon common in the ragtag world of Palestinian letters, where most books are funded out of the writers' pockets and where such a notion does not carry the stigma of "vanity publication" that it does in the West. The humble economics of the local literary scene are such that there is rarely another option.

Those same months were eventful ones for the Arab world at large. In October, Naguib Mahfouz was awarded the Nobel Prize for Literature. It was the first—and to date the only—time in the history of the then-eighty-seven-year-old prize that an Arab writer had won. The Swedish Academy cited Mahfouz for "works rich in nuance, now clearsightedly realistic, now evocatively ambiguous," and the Egyptian novelist responded by telling reporters that "clarity is valuable, but ambiguity sometimes has its values, too." The reaction of the Western world, meanwhile, seems to have been mixed—or perhaps confused by this unfamiliar Arabic name and the almost entirely unknown and untranslated literature it represented. The *New York Times* correspondent in Stockholm for one reported on the response of those who had gathered in that city's historic Stock Exchange building to hear the declaration of the prizewinner, "There was a jubilant reaction to last year's announcement that the winner was Joseph Brodsky, the exiled Soviet-born poet now living in New York City, but today publishers and literary critics dispersed quietly and quickly." The Arab world, too, had a complicated reaction to Mahfouz's win: many considered him one of their greatest novelists and were proud that such an honor had at long last been bestowed—not just on an Arab writer but on the Arabic language. Politics, however, inevitably entered the conversation, since there were those who believed that Mahfouz had received the prize not for literary reasons but as a reward for having criticized Nasser and supported Sadat, normalization with Israel, and the peace talks at Camp David.

Another symbolic Middle Eastern landmark was reached when, a month later, in Algiers, the PLO's legislature, the Palestinian National Council, adopted the Palestinian Declaration of Independence, written—"in the name of God, the Compassionate, the Merciful"—in Arabic by Mahmoud Darwish and in English by Edward Said. Proclaiming as it did the "establishment of the State of Palestine on our Palestinian territory with its capital Jerusalem," the declaration was of solely ritual importance, since the PNC had no real authority or ability to act on these words, which also announced "the State of Palestine . . . the state of Palestinians wherever they may be." But it did mark an important turning point in that—while lambasting "the mind of official Israel, which has for too long relied exclusively upon myth and terror to deny Palestinian existence altogether"—it pointed to the 1947 UN partition resolution as the document that would "ensure the right of the Palestinian Arab people to sovereignty" and so, by implication, recognized the right of Israel to exist.

Taha himself describes the declaration of independence as having had exactly zero effect on him and the other Palestinian Israelis around him. (Whether this was the case for the West Bank, Gaza, and diaspora Palestinians is probably a more complex question; the Israeli government under the leadership of Yitzhak Shamir was, for its part, predictably quick to denounce the PLO's recognition of Israel as "a deceptive propaganda exercise.") In the meantime, Taha was busy issuing what might be considered his own private declaration of poetic independence. If his first book had been considered by some a fluky aberration from the local poetic norms, his second announced without flinching that his absolutely individual and assured voice was here to stay. Whether or not readers approved of that voice, no one could deny that it was Taha's own. *Fooling the Killers* appeared in the summer of 1989, and it opened with a "Warning."

Lovers of hunting,
and beginners seeking your prey:
Don't aim your rifles
at my happiness,
which isn't worth
the price of the bullet
(you'd waste on it).
What seems to you
so nimble and fine,
like a fawn,
and flees
every which way,
like a partridge,
isn't happiness.
Trust me:
my happiness bears
no relation to happiness.

It was now four decades since Taha had set foot in Saffuriyya, and *Fooling the Killers* stood as a tribute both to the memory of the village and to the poet's own present-tense resiliency: the title poem is one of those classic Taha creations that both refers to something (and someone) specific even as it opens out into other, more enigmatic and

all-inclusive realms. It takes shape as a ruminative speculation on the
fate of his long-lost childhood best friend:

> Qasim,
> I wonder now
> where you are . . .
> I haven't forgotten you
> after all these years,
> long as the graveyard
> wall is long.

While he tries to imagine Qasim as an old man "with your poise, / your
cane, and memories," he also considers the possibility of death ("Did
you make it to Mecca? / Or did they kill you / at the foot of the Hill of
Tin?").

Qasim, in Taha's imaginative scheme, seems to have eluded his
opponents by means of wit and wile:

> But even if they did it,
> Qasim,
> if, shamelessly,
> they killed you,
> I'm certain
> you fooled your killers,
> just as you managed
> to fool the years.
> For they never discovered
> your body at the edge of the road,
> and didn't find it
> where the rivers spill,
> or on the shelves
> at the morgue,
> and not on the way to Mecca,
> and not beneath the rubble.

Although Taha himself had not vanished as Qasim did in 1948, his
friend's disappearing act seems to have offered a model for how to
wiggle out of all kinds of torments, how to live (and even die) on one's

own terms—without leaving tracks. Could Taha be writing about himself? The thought had first occurred to me as I rummaged through the Israeli archives and found references to almost all of his writer friends—left and right, rebel and Rotary Club member alike—but became conscious quickly of the absence of his name there. It is possible that some passing mention of him does exist in files I did not see, yet I found not a trace of him in any of the documents I examined—not in the lists of Nazareth shopkeepers who bolted their doors on strike days, not in the reports on Arabic-language writers' gatherings, but neither in the files (like the ones where Michel Haddad's name appears) about the provision of government support for certain cultural endeavors or the encouragement of "positive" contributions from "the Minorities."

This silence becomes still more intriguing when one realizes that all sorts of ordinary people—not just intellectuals and activists— were also being closely watched during this time. I read documents about Arab men who had been observed sitting in cafés or lounging on beaches with Jewish women. Details about their dating habits and even sex lives are now a matter of public record. And one need not have done anything particularly scandalous to have found one's way into a police file: the name of Taha's crippled father appears in a 1958 report about the confiscation of excess amounts of foreign cigarette-rolling paper, of all things, and both of Taha's younger brothers turn up in police documents as well. Amin was accused of having supplied his father with that forbidden paper, and in 1957 Feisel "aged 22 [sic], born in Tzippori and a resident of Nazareth, a Muslim bachelor with a basic education and a peddler of [sewing] notions," was arrested for blocking sidewalk traffic with his vending cart. ("The family of the accused," notes the police report, "are known to be nationalists.") Yet for all the invasive and pervasive surveillance around him, Taha somehow slipped through the cracks. And anyone trying to catch and pin him down ideologically would also have had a hard time: he was close to Communists, nationalists, and establishment figures alike and had, over the years, carefully avoided aligning himself officially with any of them.

But Taha's absence was more than just bureaucratic, legal, or political. It was literary as well. Perhaps because he was mute for so long, maybe because he didn't match the description of what a Palestinian poet "should" be, or possibly because he came into his own in print well after the Palestinian poetic canon had been fixed in the minds of many—Taha escaped notice as a writer for many years. This must not, it's true, have been a situation he either planned or enjoyed. Taha thrives on attention and would have been happy had his poetry been celebrated from the beginning—but he never expected a large readership, and even after his big London debut, his books barely circulated in the Arab world. He is not alone in this sense. Most Arabic work that is published in Israel and not reprinted abroad by a political party or the PLO has met a similar fate, and even today, long after most of the old ideological certainties have washed away, these books—Taha's books—remain largely unknown to most readers of poetry in his own language. And though Taha does have articulate Arabic-speaking champions closer to home, the formal and thematic innovations of his work still mark it, on the whole, too eccentric and original to please local tastes, which are on the whole quite conservative.

Yet he had resolved from the outset to write what he needed to write, no matter what—or how limited—the reaction. While Taha has, late in life and through both translation and the much wider distribution of his Arabic in the West (by means of bilingual editions and readings), become an internationally celebrated literary figure—his work is acclaimed the world over, and the American essayist Eliot Weinberger recently dubbed him "perhaps the most accessible and delightful poet alive today"—open most textbooks about Palestinian poetry and, even now, his name barely appears. . . .

> As no one saw you
> concealing your corpse,
> so no one will ever set eyes on you,
> and no earthly breeze
> encounter a bone of your body,
> a finger of your hand,
> or even a single shoe
> that might fit you.
> Qasim, you fooled them.

The poem winds back, as so many of Taha's do, to the fields of a Saffuriyya at once mythic and actual:

I always envied you, Qasim,
your skill at hiding
in the games of hide-and-seek we played—
barefoot at dusk—forty years ago—
when we were little boys.

It is, in fact, almost dusk when he and I get around to talking
about this poem. We are sitting under the large pecan tree that shades
his small Bir el-Amir back courtyard, and Taha is clearly tired—
whether of this particular day or of my constant questions, I can't say.
But when I ask him if he himself might be Qasim—a survivor skilled
at shaking off his pursuers, he straightens and answers quickly, almost spryly: "No. Qasim was a real person. I am just the narrator here."

INSIDE OUT

◆

BY THE TIME TAHA SET ABOUT WRITING the poems that would form his third book, *Fire in the Convent Garden,* he had already given vent in a variety of ways to the anger and sadness brought on by Saffuriyya's demolition—and, indeed, by the demolition of an entire way of life. In "The Bell at Forty: The Destruction of a Village," for instance, composed in the summer of 1988 to mark the four decades that had passed since the demise of Saffuriyya—he had written that "bitterness follows me, / as chicks trail / after the mother hen."

But in a new poem, dated May 1990, these feelings emerged more forcefully than ever, and according to a much more complex choreography. Evolving a dramatic, dialectical structure, Taha managed, with "Abd el-Hadi the Fool," to articulate the furthest emotional extremes that coexisted inside him. The poem begins in the caustically retrospective first person:

> Before the dough of my skull was ravaged
> by the buzzards of the world,
> I was a fool!
> I was naïve . . .
> and wanted to fly.

After describing his former dream ("of a meal / that would last forever," out of *A Thousand and One Nights*), he shifts gears, and the poem takes on a much harsher tack—albeit one that avoids the literal transcription of experience and instead relies on an especially unsettling battery of metaphors:

> But after the rape
> of the light of morning's laughter,
> suddenly,
> hatred filled me.
> After the springs were buried alive,
> after the watercourses' destruction,
> the flame swept through me.
> After the pillaging of the shadow
> and the sundering of the spikes of wheat . . .
> after the murder of the doves . . .
> I was charged with a sharpened hatred,
> blue as the edge of death itself!

And with that he lets loose a litany of all the ways his hatred drove him to thirst for revenge. There is, in this section, the sense of the poem as punching bag, into which the speaker is pounding his imaginative fists:

> I wanted to burn down the world!
> Wanted to stab it
> in its soft belly,
> and see it dismembered
> after I'd drowned it.

And so on and on—even to the point of "lower[ing his] eyelashes / on the raging" and "dreaming of bombers! / However," he says, his

> great apostasy
> is this:
> no sooner does the laughter
> of a child reach me,
> or I happen upon
> a sobbing stream,
> no sooner do I see

a flower wilting,
or notice a fine-looking woman,
than I'm stunned
and abandoned by everything,
and nothing of me remains
except
Abd el-Hadi the fool!

Although the poem again pivots here—and the rage gives way in an instant to tenderness—the sudden, anger-dissipating appearance of the poet's illiterate alter ego does not come as a simple relief. If anything, the presence within himself of the naive Abd el-Hadi seems to disturb the poet almost as much as does the vengeful destroyer inside him: "Abd el Hadi" writes Taha, "who gets on my anger's nerves / and lights the fuse of my folly, / as he unfurls his warm smile, / embracing that very same world!" Yet he is helpless to stop this sunny, trusting fallah from welcoming his loved ones and enemies with the same open arms.

He shakes hands with creatures of various sorts,
embraces the righteous and wicked alike,
greets the victim and hangman as one.
The fool!

By the end, and through Abd el-Hadi, Taha has in a sense resigned himself (with no small measure of irony) to synthesis: he is at once poet and fool. Although the poem gives powerful expression to the nearly impossible—and, once again, pessoptimistic—position in which Taha found himself, it seems also to have provided him with a necessary catharsis. By articulating the most brutal and mawkish impulses that haunted him, he had also mostly rid himself of them in poetic terms, and he was—his poetry was—now free to move on.

In much of the rest of the work that would make up his third book, he seemed to be concentrating his verse into an essence and, by zeroing in so tightly on the wisdom he'd acquired from his own particular, provincial existence, breaking through to a still more universal level. In a series of short poems, called "Twigs," written between

July 1989 and September 1991, Taha took up subjects as basic and common as love, music, pain, and death and presented in the process a "vision of experience" that one American-born Israeli critic would later describe as "equally applicable to Arabs and Jews, kings and paupers, the quarter of the world's population that is Chinese and the other three-quarters as well." It was, in other words, human. One of these "Twigs" stands, in a sense, as Taha's poetic creed. It is dated July 27, 1991—his birthday:

And so
it has taken me
all of sixty years
to understand
that water is the finest drink,
and bread the most delicious food,
and that art is worthless
unless it plants
a measure of splendor in people's hearts.

Plain surface aside, such homespun-sounding common sense had taken a long and very complicated life—and intense poetic labor—to achieve. And while Taha had managed to whittle his worldview down to this sage maxim, he had never betrayed or sought to leave behind the very specific situation of his life as a Saffuriyya-born Bir el-Amir dweller and seller of souvenirs. He remained intensely grounded in the soil, language, and mores of his own small patch of earth. It is telling that, for all its wide-ranging humanism, *Fire in the Convent Garden* was published in the village of Tayba by the nationalist activist Saleh Baransi, as part of his Center for the Renewal of Arab Heritage series. After working with al-Sawt, Baransi had opened this center in his hometown and begun to plan cultural activities and publish Palestinian literature—organizing, for instance, several festivals and bringing out a memorial volume in honor of the poet 'Abd al-Rahim Mahmud, killed in battle just days before Saffuriyya's fall.

The center's 1992 publication of *Fire in the Convent Garden*, wrote Baransi on the back of the book, "expresses its profound concern with the dissemination of genuine and exceptional works of Palestinian

culture." At once rooted and branching outward, this was poetry that
Baransi must have realized had the ability to speak for Taha's own
people—and to people everywhere.

◆

It was, in fact, around this same time that Taha began to speak literally to all sorts of others. Although he had, at his store, always maintained friendly contact with foreign pilgrims and day-tripping Israeli
Jews, the roles that he played as shopkeeper and they played as
tourists had naturally limited the terms of the exchange.

But in the years to come, Taha would begin to look outward in a
more literary way: this was, it seems, both a function of his desire to
widen his poetic horizons and because of the warm new breezes that
were blowing all around him in the wake of the signing of the Oslo
Accords on the South Lawn of the White House on September 13, 1993.

It wasn't just Yasir Arafat and Yitzhak Rabin who were shaking
hands and agreeing to try and live side by side in peace—but Palestinian and Israeli writers and artists as well. In his usual idiosyncratic
and roundabout fashion, Taha would eventually become involved in
this cross-cultural give-and-take, though the more high-profile act of
forging ties and issuing conciliatory declarations was largely the work
of his old friend Emile Habiby, who (true to his own public fashion)
played a central—almost presidential—role in this process of artistic
rapprochement.

That process had, it should be said, started well before Oslo and
even the Madrid Talks that had preceded it, and might best be dated
to the period, from 1977 to 1980, which Habiby spent in Prague as an
emissary of the Israeli Communist Party. He was no longer a Knesset
member, but he was still a profoundly political creature, and while he
was in Europe, he met and spent hours deep in conversation, and
often argument, with a range of Palestinian political figures—from
Arafat to Abu Jihad to leaders from the more extreme "rejectionist
front," like George Habash and Naif Hawatmeh. From these exchanges he realized, he later said, that peace would indeed be possible between the warring peoples—and that as both a Palestinian
and an Israeli, he could serve as an ideal bridge between the two.

When he returned to Israel from his stint in Czechoslovakia, he made a point of forging ties with various Jewish artists and intellectuals, and as early as June 1988, after almost a year of intensive negotiations, a group of some 150 Israeli and Palestinian writers, painters, performers, and academics signed a trilingual (Arabic-Hebrew-English) peace treaty, based on the establishment of a Palestinian state on all the lands that Israel had occupied after the war in 1967 and Jerusalem as an open city, the capital of both states. Habiby was the first to sign, and he would later reveal that before the press conference announcing the treaty he had flown to Paris for the express purpose of calling Arafat and reading him the agreement: Arafat had offered to sign it himself, as had Abu Jihad.

In fact it took the politicians several years to catch up—though to judge from the literary laurels heaped on Habiby's head during that

time, his thinking must not have been considered so outré by those in power: in 1990 he received the highest Palestinian honor, the al-Quds Prize, and in 1992, Israel's most prestigious award, the Israel Prize. His acceptance of the latter caused an uproar and furious debate throughout the Middle East, as right-wing Jews created a fracas at the awards ceremony and others decried the decision to grant an Arab the prize ("garbage, garbage," a crowd of Likud supporters hooted at Habiby at a Haifa evening in his honor), while Habiby was both lauded and vilified throughout the Arab world, with some proclaiming his prize "a victory for Arab culture" and others calling it "poisonous." Habiby, for his part, dismissed his denouncers and stated that "a dialogue of prizes is better than a dialogue of stones and bullets." He later also explained that "together with the whole Arab population of Israel, I feared for many years for our continued presence in our land." One of his primary reasons for accepting the Israel Prize, "despite the opposition of many of my very closest Arab friends," had been, he says, "that I was convinced that into my hands had fallen an additional tool with which to fight the threat of expulsion."

Habiby continued to speak out in favor of dialogue and reconciliation as the Oslo Accords themselves came under fire throughout the Arab world. Although Oslo signified the first time that the legitimate political rights of both peoples were mutually recognized, diaspora intellectuals like Edward Said decried Arafat as having sold out the Palestinian people and their history, and Mahmoud Darwish resigned from the PLO Executive Committee in rather equivocal protest against the agreement. ("I said that I could not accept it, nor would I be able to reject it, for that would be a historic gamble.") Yet Habiby continued to insist that Oslo was the best—and perhaps only— option. "Over the years," he said, "I have become increasingly convinced of the rightness of the philosophy of pessoptimism, which maintains that one must distinguish between bad and worse."

Other local intellectuals seem to have agreed, and just a month after the signing of the Oslo Accords, a group of Arab and Jewish writers were invited to Mishkenot Sha'ananim, the Jerusalem guesthouse and cultural center, to participate in a gathering of those whom one newspaper report described as "committed to literature and coexistence." The meeting was, in a way, testimony to how much—and how little—had changed in the thirty-five years since Rashid Hussein had first arranged to bring Arabic- and Hebrew-language Israeli writers together to talk over sweet black coffee in Tel Aviv. While the 1993 proceedings were much more like official diplomatic talks than that more organic, scrappy, and confrontational writers-only gathering had been, this latter-day assembly was far friendlier, and there seems to have been much more goodwill all around. According to that same newspaper report, Samih al-Qasim took the floor and reminisced in perfect Hebrew about much earlier meetings between Arab and Jewish writers "and claimed that they defused the hostility between Jews and Arabs, leading the way for politicians." On the other hand, one of the Jewish writers pointed out what a long way there still was to go toward true cross-cultural understanding, noting that "even in the novels of an outspoken political advocate of peace like Amos Oz, Arabs are often threatening, nightmarish figures." So, too, one of the Arab poets offered the same complaint that had been made at that first Tel

Aviv 1958 meeting, namely: "Israeli Arabs know Hebrew and they have access to Israeli literature in translation, but Israeli Jews don't know Arabic, and very little Arabic literature is translated."

Taha was present at this event, and as was his wont, he mostly remained outside this earnest and occasionally grandstanding conversation; he was waiting for the later part of the program, when he would have a chance to read his poetry and tell a few of the short, funny, prefatory stories he called his "Mickey Mouses," for the comic trailers that used to precede the feature films at the Empire Cinema in Nazareth. And when he did at last stand up to read and talk, the audience was delighted. It seems he managed in one fell swoop to topple any preconceived ideas that the Jews in the room might have held about the nature of the "other." One Israeli Jewish participant who had never heard of Taha before that evening remembers the powerful impression he made. He was, she says, "so different looking and sounding" from everyone else on the stage. She was struck by his face, "like a George Grosz painting," and his enormous hands. Minus the apt Grosz image, her words are repeated almost verbatim by the poet and translator Gabriel Levin, who was taken with the way Taha commanded the room.

Levin had first heard Taha's name a short while before from Roger Tavor, a Lebanese-born Israeli Jewish acquaintance who worked for the Arabic service of Israel TV, and who had suggested that together they attempt to translate a few of Taha's poems into English for a special Palestinian issue of a literary magazine that Tavor was editing. "Taha's like nobody else," he promised, and explained (incorrectly, as it happened) that Taha wrote in the Palestinian dialect and sold antiquities. Since Levin had no Arabic, he and Tavor worked together—through the veils of Hebrew and French—on two preliminary translations, and when Levin arrived at Mishkenot that evening (walking in late, he remembers, and finding a packed house), he had come to meet Taha and to arrange to visit him in Nazareth: he says he was immediately struck by Taha's bearing and by the crowd's rapt reaction.

Without fanfare, Taha had broken or was breaking through to the other side, and as a result of this performance, he was invited back to take part in a series of more involved meetings between Israeli and Palestinian intellectuals held at Mishkenot between June 1994 and December 1995. Habiby was again a major force at these weekend-long gatherings. One participant remembers him as having been a domineering though good-natured presence and of having held most of his interlocutors in a kind of awestruck silence. But a wide range of other Israeli, East Jerusalem, West Bank, and Gaza writers, artists, and thinkers did eventually speak up and came to engage in what was reportedly a very free and open exchange—made possible, as someone present would later put it, "at least in part by the fact that the press and the general public were not invited." Various lectures, movies, readings, gallery tours, and conversations took place in this context, and at the first session, Taha recited his poetry in Arabic, offering an impromptu translation into broken English. A later weekend-long meeting ended with a lecture by the archaeologist Zeev Weiss about the recent archaeological excavations at Tzippori and Taha telling stories about Saffuriyya.

Doors were opening all around, and it was through this Jerusalem portal that Taha stepped through to the International Poets' Festival held at Mishkenot Sha'ananim in the spring of 1995.

Maybe for a more cosmopolitan or well-traveled poet, such a festival wouldn't have much mattered; it would have been just one more station that dotted the winding way of a long and varied public career. But to Taha, who rarely left Nazareth and was only slowly inching his way out into the literary world, it was the ultimate sign that he had at long last arrived as a poet. In some sense it was more important to him to be recognized here, at home, than it had been to be celebrated by those huge foreign crowds in London. The Czech poet Miroslav Holub and the American Galway Kinnell were probably the two best-known participants in the Jerusalem festival—though Taha had, it seems safe to say, never heard of either of them or of the other foreign writers who attended, whether Japanese, Irish, Bengali, or Russian. He was most excited to have his poems appear in the festival catalogue alongside those of two Israeli Jewish poets, Yehuda Amichai and Natan Zach—not, it seems, because he knew their work but because of their local luster.

It is hard—in retrospect and in general—to gauge the complex effect that Taha may have had on the mostly Ashkenazi Jewish audiences who attended the festival; that people were charmed by him there is little doubt. He won tremendous applause and was lavishly praised for his "entertaining" performances. ("During the festival," wrote *Haaretz,* in a lengthy feature story about Taha, "everyone was interested in the blue-eyed sixty-four-year-old." The reporter dubbed him "a kind of discovery" and described the crowd as having received him "with appreciation and warmth.") The very fact that he read his poems in Arabic to such acclaim in the heart of strictly Jewish West Jerusalem was, in its way, a modest victory and may have been a sign that many of those who filled the theater seats felt the time for peace between Arabs and Jews, Palestinians and Israelis had at long last come; maybe when they clapped for Taha they were really clapping for that idea. That said, there was more than a touch of condescension in the attitude of some of the Jewish audience members toward Taha: his wizened countenance, his tendency to joke and tell stories that had what seemed to them a nostalgic ring, and the fact that his poems rarely approached political subjects head-on also made it easy for certain Jewish Israelis to look on him as a harmless old grandfather and folksy raconteur. Although few would have used the term— the festival audience was, on the whole, quite "liberal" and its members considered themselves very open and progressive—he seemed every bit the "good Arab." It would, one imagines, have been much harder for these same crowds to have embraced in this adoring way a more confrontational figure like Samih al-Qasim or Emile Habiby.

The possibility that Taha *knew* this and was deliberately playing the part of the court jester (Abd el-Hadi?) is not to be dismissed: for all his seeming naïveté, Taha was—after a certain backwoods fashion—in fact quite worldly wise. ("A peasant . . . / the son of a peasant," he would later write, "there lies within me / a mother's sincerity / and a fishmonger's guile.") It is altogether likely that he understood that the best way to get his words across to this particular audience was first to set them at their ease by making them laugh. Perhaps a more serious appreciation for all the complicated humanity, culture, and history his words represented would follow.

The festival also marked the moment when Taha's Arabic and presence first came to the attention of my husband, Peter—who would soon become not only Taha's primary English translator but his voice in the world beyond Israel/Palestine. Taha's performance itself left him, he confesses, with a "mixed impression." The scramble of English, Arabic, and broken Hebrew—all of it slurred through toothless gums—in which Taha recounted his stories seemed almost as bumbling as it was appealing. But Peter, a poet and translator from medieval and modern Hebrew, was intrigued by the cunning ways in which Taha, with the artistry of his levity, was playing off of—or with—the expectations of his audience.

But much more compelling than what he saw onstage was what Peter found on the pages of the festival catalogue. There, alongside the Arabic, were the strong, unsentimental Hebrew translations of a handful of Taha's poems by Anton Shammas and the poet Salman Masalha.

Perhaps because the Palestinian village setting wasn't exotic to either Shammas or Masalha—or maybe because their accomplished Hebrew was deeply grounded in the Arabic—their translations had bite and did much more than any previous renderings had to convey the intensity of Taha's poetry *as poetry*, and not as mere entertainment. Reading the Arabic and then those Hebrew versions, Peter knew that he wanted to translate this work. It was, he says, like "hearing a tuning fork sounded."

DIFFICULT SIMPLICITY

◆

MEMORY AND THE HISTORY BOOKS AGREE that the next few years were tumultuous ones for the whole Middle East: the details of Yitzhak Rabin's assassination, of suicide bombings, West Bank closures, rocket attacks, military campaigns, massive expansion of settlements, and stalled peace talks do not need repeating here. Taha, meanwhile, was concerned during this time with matters both professional and existential. On the former front, he returned in 1996 to short-story writing and throughout the period gave multiple poetry readings (in France, Spain, Gaza, Hebron, Jordan, Jerusalem, and France again and Spain again). On the latter score, these same years marked the deaths in close succession of several of his friends.

In 1994, as Tawfiq Zayyad was driving himself back to the Knesset from a Jericho reception in honor of Yasir Arafat's arrival in the Palestinian territories, he was killed in a head-on car crash. In 1996, Emile Habiby succumbed to cancer and was buried under a tombstone engraved with the words "I stayed in Haifa." In 1997, Michel Haddad—perhaps Taha's closest companion—passed away, after an illness, in Nazareth. At a memorial gathering in his honor, Taha described with emotion the conversation between them that had lasted some forty years. Until the very end of his life, Michel had still been coming to sit in Taha's shop every day.

At around the same time, Taha himself took seriously ill, and there were once again real fears for his life: his glandular condition had worsened, and for a year he rarely left the house.

If Haddad's and Habiby's deaths hit Taha hard, Zayyad's passing also registered on him strongly—in ways at once private and public. In the wake of the poet-mayor's death, the atmosphere in Nazareth changed, and not for the better. Zayyad had been a Muslim Communist married to a Christian, and his popularity and impeccable ecumenical credentials had somehow kept interreligious strife in the city at bay. Now the job of mayor fell to one of his deputies, a mild young Communist and Orthodox Christian named Ramez Jeraysi, who threw himself into the ambitious development project that Zayyad and the Israeli authorities had outlined for the upcoming millennium and the anticipated visit to Nazareth of the pope and millions of pilgrims. But as these $100 million preparations began and Jeraysi set plans in motion to build a large plaza to welcome the hoped-for hordes of Christian tourists, local Islamists felt compelled to assert their presence.

Unfortunately for all involved, the site of the projected plaza also happened to house a small, neglected Muslim tomb—believed to contain the remains of Shihab al-Din, whom local tradition holds to be Saladin's nephew, killed at the 1187 Battle of Hittin. Although the tomb was slated to remain untouched in the renovation, activists from the Qur'an-thumping organization known as the Islamic Movement saw the construction of the plaza—by a Christian mayor, for Christian pilgrims—as a provocation. And so it was that four days before Christmas 1997, they offered their very own provocation and stormed the site, beat up several municipal workers, and effectively took over, soon erecting a huge green protest tent and massive loudspeaker system—all within inches of Taha's shop.

Although the Islamists' campaign was ostensibly religious in character, it was more immediately political, and it marked the start of a nasty, noisy struggle for power—a bid to upstage the nearby Church of the Annunciation and the festivities known as Nazareth 2000 and so assert religious Muslim control over once predominantly Christian, once left-leaning Nazareth. (Muslims now constituted 70 percent of the population, and the Communist Party had lost much of its clout after the fall of the Soviet Union.) The activists had plans—and money from the Gulf states—to erect over the tomb an enormous mosque with a 325-foot minaret topped by a laser crescent moon, but for now the green tent would serve as a fine substitute. Large banners inscribed with Qur'anic sayings were plastered all over the area, the loudspeaker volume was cranked up at prayer time, and hundreds of bearded activists, some connected to Hamas, poured in from across Israel and the West Bank, especially on Fridays at noontime, when furious sermons—about the evil of the "new crusaders" and "Salman Rushdie," as the protesters dubbed the beleaguered mayor Jeraysi—were blasted throughout downtown. "On any given day," according to an American journalist, "one could see Western tourists cringing at the spectacle and scuttling away from the gift shops to the security of their air-conditioned tour buses."

By 1998, the Islamic Movement had exploited the Shihab al-Din controversy to win a majority in the Nazareth city council, and in 1999, with a national election looming on the horizon and the various Jewish candidates cynically playing one Arab voting bloc against the other, the situation turned bloody. On Easter weekend that year, militant Muslims rampaged through the streets, burning cars, beating anyone (Christian or Muslim) who defied them, and smashing the windows of Christian-owned stores. Meanwhile, the television news showed Israeli police in riot gear literally standing by and doing nothing as the town—and years of relative harmony—imploded.

It was the sort of dirty political fight from which Taha usually took pains to keep a real distance, and his shaky health gave him further cause to stay away. Now, however, he had no choice but to act, and by the time later that month that the Israeli cabinet put forth a plan granting the Islamic Movement the right to build the mosque directly over the area that included his shop, he had already arranged to rent a much bigger store up the street, alongside the church, and out of harm's way. As a secular Muslim with no patience for violence or the self-serving manipulations of religious or political leaders—whatever their tribe—Taha was scornful of the way the whole affair had been handled. And although his business suffered badly because of the unrest, his quick thinking had, it seemed, saved his livelihood in the longer run. Whether it could save the larger cultural forces to which he felt himself most strongly connected was another matter. "The more mosques," he has been known to say, "the less poetry."

◆

Like Peter, I had first encountered Taha at the Jerusalem festival in 1995 and had been struck by his offbeat presence and his stories—though I cannot say that I had any sense at that time of how much he or his poetry would later come to matter to us both. My memory of our first conversation with him is surprisingly blurry. It was June 1997, at another poetry festival, in the tiny, toylike town of Metulla, on Israel's border with Lebanon, and I seem to have registered little about him besides his phenomenal wrinkles. I also recall being struck by a palpable sense of his *peasantness*: despite the warm, early summer air, he wore a pancake cap and heavy peacoat, and his bundled-up bearing somehow suggested (absurdly, in retrospect) that of a turn-of-the-last-century Russian Jew who'd just stepped off the boat at Ellis Island.

Although we had never spoken with Taha before this Metulla encounter, we were already involved with his work. Since that revelatory first encounter with the Hebrew versions of Taha's poems in the 1995 Jerusalem festival catalogue, Peter had begun translating them into English. Because his Arabic was still somewhat new, he consulted periodically with a Palestinian friend, Yahya Hijazi, whose sense of poetry and people Peter greatly admired. At first he asked questions about specific lines and words, but Yahya's answers, which filled in the endlessly intricate cultural background that lay behind those particular lines and words, convinced Peter that Yahya should be a partner in the translation project. Raised in the Old City of Jerusalem in a large, working-class Muslim family, Yahya was now an educational counselor and college lecturer (on, among other things, "coexistence") who navigated between Arab and Jewish, traditional and modern, Eastern and Western worlds with remarkable grace; as such he served as an excellent guide to both the social force field of Taha's poetry and to his language. Peter did not know this when he started working with Yahya on the poems, but the small-world nature of Palestinian life and letters was driven home—literally—by the fact that Yahya's social-worker wife, Ahlam, comes from a Nazareth family originally from Saffuriyya.

Since Gabriel Levin had first met Taha, he had enthused to us about the man. He, Peter, and Yahya had been talking of late about the possibility of gathering the existing translations and expanding them into a full-fledged book. Now, in the cypress-shaded courtyard of Metulla's incongruously named Alaska Inn, Gabriel introduced us, and we sat and discussed the idea of our newly founded press, Ibis Editions, publishing a collection of Taha's poems in English.

Taha was, not surprisingly, pleased by the prospect, so over the next several months Peter and Yahya set about reading through all of his poems and making a selection, which they kept adjusting as they worked. Peter then continued to ford his way from the Arabic and into the English, with Yahya checking and unpacking especially difficult phrases and cultural concepts. They also hashed out numerous idioms, Arabic literary references, and historical allusions over our dining room table. Gabriel weighed in regularly as he began to write the book's introduction. In my role as one of the Ibis editors, I combed through and commented on the translations and that introduction, which went through multiple drafts. Then Taha himself read over the English versions, suggesting the addition of one poem, "Meeting at an Airport," and approving the selection as a whole.

His initial sense of Taha's singular narrative abilities also made Peter want to include one story in the volume: Taha nominated for this honor his 1996 story "So What," about the barefoot boy who may or may not be an earlier incarnation of the author. And, for use in the introduction, Taha transcribed by hand in Arabic one of the stories he had related at the Jerusalem festival—about the way he became what he calls "a real poet." Set on the sidewalk in front of a slightly fictionalized version of his souvenir shop, this is a wily, apocryphal tale about how he used to bribe a friend with "small wooden camels" to sit still on a low straw stool and listen to his poems.

Peter's decision to undertake the translations may have come in one spontaneous flash, but the process of rendering them was much more protracted and deliberate. Although the surface of Taha's Arabic was ostensibly "simple," conveying the subtle music and wry tenor of his poems in another language was as complex an operation as transposing the ornate formal elements of the most outwardly sophisticated odes. (In attempting to account for this challenge, Peter has described how Taha's work embodies the classical Arabic notion of *al-sahil al-mumtaniʿa*, "a difficult, elusive, or even inscrutable simplicity.") Meanwhile, the further he, Gabriel, and Yahya entered into Taha's poetry, the more urgent—in literary, political, and human terms—became their need to give this work life in English.

The same month that the al-Aqsa intifada broke out in the autumn of 2000, we printed the first copies of *Never Mind: Twenty Poems and a Story*. Produced in the modest, pocket-sized format that we use for all the Ibis books, it was greeted warmly but quietly when it came out. Taha's name and poems were unfamiliar to English-language readers, though it was clear from the responses that began to trickle in that his work struck a deep chord among readers of all sorts. "I have been anhedonic for something like thirty years now," one veteran American poet wrote us in a letter whose arc would prove typical of others to come, "and it is truly magical when a poetry manages to inject a shot of joy into my old bones. It happens with frightening rarity, but it has happened here."

WORK HARD, FLY RIGHT

◆

THE DYING ABU TAHA HAD BEEN RIGHT. His eldest son had long harbored ambitions that were greater than any wish the old man could possibly have made for him—though even the very imaginative Taha himself could not, it seems, have anticipated the trajectory of the reception he would one day receive abroad.

The years that followed the publication of *Never Mind* brought him a growing and widening international readership. And while the world was starting to discover Taha, he was also beginning to discover the world, a process Peter and I had the fortune to witness up close. On Taha's first trip to the United States in 2002, we found ourselves in a rental car and his alert company, bound for various readings up and down the East Coast. It was our first extended experience of being with him, eating three meals a day together and spending most of our waking hours side by side—and it was startling.

Both onstage and off, Taha maintained a joy and poise at once ready and relaxed: his "readings" (the word doesn't quite do these performances justice) were a Thelonious Monk–like blend of inspired invention and careful choreography, and the often-comic riffs he offered up during these appearances and throughout the day derived from his improvisational sense of the world's kaleidoscopic possibility. As soon became clear, Taha is both a storyteller with an uncommon structural sense and—at heart—a lover of odds and ends. Traveling with him and listening to his running narrative, we came to see the way he picked each incident up, turned it, studied it, prodded it, and devised its most appropriate use.

At the same time, audiences of all sorts seemed mesmerized by his presence. No matter the variations of setting or mood, when Taha read in Arabic from a small black date book issued by Egged, Israel's national bus carrier, and into which he had copied all his poems longhand, these American listeners, most of whom spoke not a word of that language—and who, given the raw memory of September 11, might have been made anxious by it—seemed electrified by the sheer shape of his vowels, the modulations of his gravelly Eastern music. Then, as Peter read the English translation, Taha would step to the side, cock his elaborately wrinkled brow, thrust his jaw forward as if to taste the poem, and take turns beaming, nodding, and looking like the world's most melancholy ventriloquist. His bearing cast a kind of spell—though it was clear from the often ecstatic response of these crowds that the poems themselves were what stirred them. An unconventional stage presence alone would not be enough to elicit such a response. Neither would plain politics, since many of his auditors had only the sketchiest idea of Middle Eastern history or Taha's place in it.

That said, the many native Arabic speakers who also attended Taha's appearances seemed just as swept up by his poems, and—it became a poignant ritual—nearly every reading was followed by an emotional encounter, or three, with transplanted natives of Bethlehem, Damascus, or the village of Reina: like long-lost cousins, they approached Taha with their eyes shining (whether with pleasure or tears), and he greeted them in kind, often seeming most overwhelmed by this late-breaking response to his poems—in his mother tongue.

◆

Held in a colonial era New Jersey village called Waterloo, the Geraldine R. Dodge Poetry Festival is the largest such gathering in the English-speaking world, and for one long weekend that fall, more than sixteen thousand people came to hear poets reading and talking under the tents that lay scattered over the pastoral grounds. It was a singularly festive and profoundly American event, something of a cross between the Ringling Brothers circus and a (democratic, non-denominational) revival meeting. Soon after Taha made his American debut, he and Peter were invited to be guests of the festival, and although Taha was listed as a "featured poet" alongside five U.S. poets laureate and a host of other distinguished poets—including Robert Bly, Adam Zagejewski, Edward Hirsch, Gerald Stern, Coleman Barks, Amiri Baraka, Naomi Shihab Nye, and Grace Paley—he was, it seems safe to say, an unknown quantity to most everyone who attended this biennial blowout. The festival's big-hearted director, Jim Haba, was, though, one of Taha's ardent new fans, and he didn't care much about name recognition. He had heard about Taha from a range of people, and as soon as he read the poetry in *Never Mind* he had resolved to invite him, with Peter, to Dodge. It was a decision that would snowball, as Haba's enthusiasm would draw others to Taha, and the momentum of this rolling, speeding sphere of interest would mount in the course of just a few full days.

Numerous events took place simultaneously at the festival, and on the damp first morning—a Thursday, when the audience was made up mostly of high school students—Taha and Peter found themselves in the gray drizzle, facing a group of fewer than a dozen drowsy teenagers. Peter says that at that moment, he felt terrible for having dragged the slightly frail Taha all the way across the ocean to appear before such a small, scraggly crew. But they began to read, with Taha stopping periodically to tell a story in his usual animated tones—sometimes, in his jet lag or simply out of habit, veering off into upbeat Arabic from which Peter needed to yank him back to English—and even at one point fishing from his peacoat pocket a crumpled piece of paper on which he had copied in his exacting hand a lengthy quotation from a letter by Walt Whitman about Kaiser Wilhelm and his expansionist ways. That Taha had been preparing this measured little poetic-political riff (an indirect yet perfectly pitched commentary on the Bush administration's recent invasion of Afghanistan and its planned war in Iraq) came as a surprise—though it was hard, at this stage, to know just what effect Taha's, and Whitman's, words were having on this sleepy-looking adolescent bunch. No one reacted strongly, but neither did anyone get up to leave, and by the end of the session, some twenty people were sitting quietly in the tent.

Taha and Peter had just an hour to rest before their next appearance—and when they arrived at the designated tent, they found, to Peter's amazement, many of the same twenty people waiting for them, along with a few dozen others. Although he was worried that he and Taha might repeat themselves, the audience seemed wholly unconcerned at this prospect, and in fact they turned out to be right. Taha demonstrated that morning what we would soon recognize as his rather Bob Dylanesque—or Heraclitus-like—refusal to play the same song, or step into the same river, twice. That is, he would often launch into a tale that we had in theory heard many times before, but the slight variations he would bring to bear on the story—whether in terms of cadence, rhythm, structure, or the deployment of a host of small comic asides—were transformative, and they seemed in many ways to hold the secret to his sly art.

By the middle of the four-day festival, Taha's anonymity had been swallowed up completely by the audience's curiosity about the man and excitement about his work. The high point came when he and Peter read before a crowd of some three thousand people, who then rose in sustained ovation. Meanwhile, the other featured poets—all of them a good deal more prominent and experienced at appearing onstage than Taha—demonstrated an admirable openness to this latecoming outsider. Their generosity of spirit was best exemplified perhaps by what noted poet and Guggenheim Foundation president Edward Hirsch would write in the *Washington Post* a few weeks after encountering Taha and *Never Mind* at Dodge. He called the book "a deeply humane collection" and described Taha's style as "both ancient and new, deceptively simple and movingly direct. . . . I am," wrote Hirsch, "grateful for [the book's] large embrace."

◆

Taha's literary star had clearly begun a steep and fairly rapid ascent, but the reaction of all these strangers to his work was also significant in that it extended outward and implied as well a response to something *beyond* himself. He would of course never claim to be speaking for anyone besides Taha Muhammad Ali of Saffuriyya—and if forced to play on a team in some cosmic soccer match, Taha would, I'd wager, prefer to represent "poetry" rather than "Palestine." He certainly didn't aim with his writing to change minds or persuade anyone of a particular position. Yet it was plain to us that by reckoning with Taha's exceptional personality and poems, many of these American audiences were also reckoning for the first time with a Palestinian—not as a menacing or pitiable abstract concept but as a complex, individual human being and a genuine artist who was, of all things, speaking directly to their hearts.

The weeks that followed Taha's appearance at Dodge emphasized the ripple effect of his work, as we were joined on the road by the Israeli Jewish poet Aharon Shabtai (whom Peter also translates), and the three of them set about appearing together—with Taha reading in Arabic, Shabtai in Hebrew, and Peter from his English translations of both. It was, on the face of it, an unlikely meeting of the minds, since it is hard to think of a writer farther from Taha in sensibility and style than Shabtai. An outspoken poetic provocateur and modern Hebrew's most important translator from the classical Greek, Shabtai is at once wild man and rationalist, Hellenist and Hebrew, European intellectual and no-nonsense Israeli, a poet who has described his work as hewing to the classical Greek imperative—to praise and to scorn. His verse had taken on drastically different forms over the decades, though most recently he had emerged in his poetry as a fierce critic not just of the state's policies but also of the wholesale demolition of the ethics, language, sense of proportion, and humanistic ideals that he remembers from his Tel Aviv youth. For several years he had been writing in a scathing prophetic mode about the destruction of Israel from within: "The pure words I suckled from my mother's breasts: Man, Child, Justice, Mercy, and so on, / are dispossessed before our eyes, imprisoned in ghettos, murdered at checkpoints," he writes, in "The Reason to Live Here."

Taha and Shabtai had met several times before and liked each other, but they were not close, and it might, we realized, take a while for the two to grow used to performing as a duo. The initial dynamic between them was respectful but a touch awkward: What language should they speak with one another? (English.) What should they talk about? It was somehow easier for Peter and me to move in and out of both their worlds than it was for the two to cross over. But they were, it was clear from the faintly stiff, first-date air that crept into their voices when they spoke to each other, trying.

And over the course of the trip what emerged was a strangely moving compound of their different approaches to poetry and life. As anyone could see from watching them together, Taha and Shabtai were discovering in the most concrete terms not so much their differences as all that they shared: a birthplace, a love of poetry, a translator, a bedrock belief in the possibility of coexistence and the essential humanity of the so-called other, and a political fate. The welcoming crowds before whom they read—from Providence to Asheville to Albany to Middlebury, Vermont—seemed inspired both by their poetry and by the complicated bond that existed between the two gray-haired poets and between them and their younger translator. And though none of us deluded ourselves into thinking that our little road trip could change the bloody course of world events, these joint appearances did at least offer a shard of hope—to ourselves as much as to the audiences we encountered on our travels.

Meanwhile, behind the scenes, the journey seemed to be filling Taha and Shabtai with a childlike trust in each other. Sometimes

we would find them sitting in their underwear and T-shirts on the edge of their hotel-room beds, immersed in talk about Coleridge or Shakespeare, their families, Shabtai's sweet tooth, Taha's anise tea. During a long van ride toward Albany, Taha announced plaintively that he'd gone twelve days now without music. With equal gravity Shabtai offered up his precious headphones, and Bach.

On the plane to North Carolina, Taha sat beside me in his weathered New York Giants ski cap and, after chuckling to himself at the slogan on the napkin the flight attendant had placed under his plastic cup of milk—"Work hard. Fly right."—and which he and Peter had already analyzed at length on the transatlantic flight (after Taha had asked him, "Peter, what do you think this *means?*"), he grew suddenly serious and announced in a stage whisper that he considered Shabtai "a good man . . . a brave man." Shabtai's political poems in particular were "very important." Although Taha himself would never use Shabtai's full-frontal approach to current events and preferred when dealing with politics to play his rhetorical games of *bill-i-ar-des*—aiming *here* to reach *there*—he needed, it seems, to put his cards on the airplane tray table. But perhaps his comment about Shabtai itself was meant as a kind of social pool cue: I sensed that Taha was telling *me* what he thought so that *I* would tell Shabtai. Before I could ask him, he closed his eyes, leaned his head on his arms, shifted into what he called "neutral," and promptly went to sleep.

◆

After his own admittedly eccentric fashion, Taha was finding a way to balance the role of fledgling international literary celebrity with that of Saffuriyyan shopkeeper. The next few years brought further trips and more readings—held everywhere from Iowa City to Berlin to Niskayuna, New York, and invitations to read in places as far-flung as Taipei, Bucharest, and Mumbai had begun to pile up; his poem "Twigs" would soon appear in a Prentice Hall textbook called *World Masterpieces,* alongside work by Virgil, Dante, Lorca, and Camus. Meanwhile, Taha had returned from his first few American trips intent mainly on replicating some of the catchy advertising slogans he'd seen while traveling there and arranged to have similar signs made for his large new store by the church. (The Islamic Movement's grandiose mosque-building project had, in the wake of various shady political maneuvers by the Israeli authorities, fizzled, so Taha now found himself the proud proprietor of *two* Casa Nova Street shops: Nizar 1 and Nizar 2, like twin spaceships. The competition, he said, was good for business.) A European journalist had once written of Taha that he was the owner of "a prominent Nazareth souvenir shop," a phrase that Taha then soon adapted, erecting a large shingle announcing:

THE PROMINENT SOUVENIR CENTER OF NAZARETH.

"Work Hard, Fly Right" had also made its mark—though in typical fashion, Taha had tinkered with it, arranging for another, smaller sign to be printed and framed for his shop:

Then he dreamed up others of his own:

and

He rounded off this collection with a jingle by that great Madison Avenue adman, John Keats:

Usama now ran the store in a morning-to-night way, while Taha spent several hours a day there, keeping the books, overseeing orders, paying bills, greeting customers and friends, eating. (The hot lunch that Yusra and Aisheh cooked every day was ferried at midday from Bir el-Amir and eaten at both shops.) He also had more time to spend at home, devising various practical yet inspired contraptions. So he poured hours into designing and overseeing the construction of a waist-high, tiltable olive oil jug, padded in quilting and suspended from a heavy iron frame. Over the next several years, he also built a thickly insulated stainless steel outdoor oven, fired with olive wood and especially intended for the long, slow baking of his breakfast broad beans; next came a walk-in chicken coop and dovecote outfitted with self-serving grain troughs. He called this his "Hen Hotel," and a bit later it was followed by an elevated, revolving, multiroom hutch for another set of favorite animals. This he dubbed his "Rabbit Palace."

At the same time, he continued to write and to publish in Arabic— bringing out a fourth collection of poems in 2002 and a book of short stories the next year. The poems were prefaced with a good-natured defense of shi'r manthur but, more essentially, of his own artistic method. Though he never once refers to himself or his work in this short essay, he appears to be facing down those who would relegate him to the role of mere naïf. There is, he seems to be saying, more to his poetics than meets the eye—and ear. To illustrate this, he quotes Alexander Pope, in English: "True Ease in Writing comes from Art,

not Chance, / As those move easiest who have learn'd to dance." Taha
appears throughout the book to be searching for new forms and subjects, as he tests a frothier tone. Much of the collection is turned out
to face the wider world and was written when he was abroad—like
the ode composed in honor of Nabil, a Yemenite cashier whom Taha
had befriended at the Manhattan bagel shop where we'd eaten breakfast one day (and the next, at Taha's insistence), and "Michelle," a
beautifully modulated wisp of a poem about Taha's time in Marseille,
where "the marvelous woman / in whose house I stayed / for a week /
was called—Michelle." Yet for all his newfound wanderlust, Taha experimented more freely than ever before in this book with
the most local device imaginable—the Galilean dialect. His increasing poetic confidence and sense of adventure were obvious in this
gesture—for if composing unmetered poems is still considered dubious in Palestinian circles, the written use of the vernacular is beyond
the pale. A long tradition of dialect poetry does exist in Arabic (dating
back to medieval Spain), and in Egypt and other countries throughout the Arab world, certain modern poets had evolved throughout
the twentieth century a popular body of colloquial verse—much of
it grounded in radical left-wing politics. But Naguib Mahfouz was
speaking for many Arab writers when he famously declared colloquial
Arabic "one of the diseases from which the people are suffering." He
dubbed it "one of the failings of our society, exactly like ignorance,
poverty, and disease."

Taha, though, had other ideas. Despite his reverence for the classical language and his abiding love for the novels of Mahfouz, he also
heard in the colloquial the voice of his mother, his father, his Saffuriyya neighbors, and saw in that no shame. To write about their world
meant to let them speak for themselves, while to "translate" their
words into "pure" Arabic would be, he felt, a violation of their spirit
as well as a mimetic failure. That said, he continued to write most of
his poems in standard Arabic, reserving the vernacular for conversations between his characters. (This is not, to put it otherwise, the
unadulterated demotic in which most "dialect poets" write.) But by
threading a casual, often semicomic colloquial strand through his
standard Arabic—onto which he also sometimes "grafted" a colloquial construction or turn of phrase—he was attempting to make the
registers more flexible and the surface of his poems truer to his own

fluid, happily hybrid experience of the world. Taha had never been one to segregate high and low, and he describes his use of the various Arabic modes as being akin to the way a painter uses the different colors on his palette: certain lines require one hue, others another; sometimes the colors are mixed.

And beyond the question of registers, the very homegrown nature of Taha's project found expression in the most powerful poem in his fourth book, which returns him to his beginnings, and the invocation of "Jamil, / my father's cousin, / our neighbor in Saffuriyya," who

> married three wives
> but had from them
> neither a son to inherit his name
> nor a daughter to refresh his heart.

This same "Jamil, my father's cousin, / our neighbor in Saffuriyya,"

> owned a wide-eyed,
> long-haired,
> blond Damascene she-goat
> that gave birth to six wooly kid goats
> two days after he returned from Mecca;
> their silken breath reminded you
> of the childhood
> of the world!

The most musical—and exuberant—of Taha's poems to date, "The Kid Goats of Jamil" takes shape as an extended description of the frisking baby goats whose "craziness simply goes crazy / on evenings when the almonds go green." They "leap out of the windows of their skin. / They sway, pounce, and dance / in the silvery fullness of the world, / like dangling lamps of mercury / being tugged at by puppy-sized jinn." But as with all of Taha's best work, the poem runs deeper than it may first seem: this is and is not a poem about goats. In some ways its true subject is *motion*—but it also embodies so profoundly the affection and excitement it describes that it becomes, in a sense, a poem about what a poem can do. That said, "The Kid Goats of Jamil" is no dryly self-reflexive exercise in postmodern poetics but

a poem fairly bursting with the most kinetic and infectious human
longing and glee. Its climax comes as the poem shifts into the rhap-
sodic past tense and the memory of how the goats brought with them
a "rare, buoyant splendor" that filled the "hearts of Jamil and his
wives" and "spilled soft as velvet / into their home, / into the goat shed
and onto the path, / perfuming the storeroom." And then in almost
cinematic fashion, it begins to pull back, and the view widens to take
in the broader expanse:

> That pleasure was never limited
> to the three wives;
> the gladness was never restricted
> to the blond, wide-eyed,
> long-haired,
> golden-hearted Damascene she-goat;
> the happiness was never confined to Jamil,
> my father's cousin, our neighbor in Saffuriyya.
> A bright hopeful joy
>   spread out over the people,
>   over the village,
>   like the joy of the year's first rain.

The poem set the tone for the book. Delight was a crucial ingredient in the composition of all this new work, as was an almost mani-
acal sense of purpose. When we were on the road we often watched
as Taha went about the compulsive labor of writing a poem. Whether
on a plane, in a car, restaurant, train, or hotel room, he blocked out
whatever was around him and lifted his steno pad up near his face.
Alone with the words, he scribbled, crossed out, mumbled a line to
himself—testing, or tasting, the sound—then scribbled something
else. This process seemed a natural extension of his playful yet intent
approach to building his various contraptions: in both cases, he
would conceive of the grand design as if gripped by a fever. (The usually uncomplaining Imm Nizar had been known to curse Taha's stubborn obsessions on this front.) Then he'd spend weeks cheerfully ignoring everything else—possessed by the work of soldering iron,
twining wire, replacing a word, cutting a stanza. A poem or a rabbit
hutch—it came from the same place.

THE PLACE ITSELF

◆

And so I come to the place itself,
but the place is not
its dust and stones and open space. . . .

—TAHA MUHAMMAD ALI

IT IS MID-AUGUST AND OPPRESSIVELY HOT. The latest war has
just ended, and so I've taken to the road, renting a car and wending
my now habitual way north and back to Bir el-Amir, where the fruit
trees have grown a few years thicker since I arrived that first chill February day but where the derelict construction site across the street
from Taha's house remains as untouched and ghostly as ever.

Increased olive and pomegranate yield aside, the neighborhood
landscape looks much as it did when I began to write this book. Yet
dozens of other changes—most invisible to the naked eye—have
taken place here in that time. Most recently, the so-called Second
Lebanon War brought with it a battery of old-new fears and frustrations. It is 2006, and for the last month, Taha, Imm Nizar, and the
other people of Nazareth have been living an impossible paradox,
both huddling in dread as Hezbollah fired rockets in their direction
from Southern Lebanon and helplessly watching the television news
as, yet again, Israeli jets bombarded the homes of their family, friends,
and former neighbors across the northern border. The ironies of this
situation were almost too much to take in. "No vein can bleed / more

than it already has," Taha had written during the first Lebanon War almost twenty-five years earlier, and unfortunately he was wrong.

In the course of the fighting—carried out under the perverse operational name "Change of Direction" and with the enthusiastic support of the vast majority of the Israeli Jewish public—the IDF had reduced to rubble the Lebanese town of Bint Jbeyl, where Taha and his family had once found shelter from other Israeli planes dropping bombs. As the Israeli air force laid waste to numerous other Shiite and Christian villages in the same region—as well as large swaths of Beirut, its airport, and much of the country's infrastructure, including bridges, roads, ports, sewage- and water-treatment facilities, schools, hospitals, and some fifteen thousand homes—thousands of fleeing Southern Lebanese villagers had taken refuge among the refugees in the 'Ain el-Hilweh camp, on which Israeli army gunships did not hesitate to fire, killing several people and sending one shell slamming into the Sidon amusement park, "an obvious hotbed of terrorism," as one American commentator quipped. Altogether the IDF killed more than a thousand Lebanese civilians during the war, nearly a third of them children. When its planes bombed the Jiyyeh power plant near Beirut, they also caused what is likely the worst environmental disaster the Mediterranean has ever known: the attack sent more than four million gallons of crude oil gushing out into the sea. Meanwhile Hezbollah fired Katyushas that burned thousands of acres of Israeli forests and damaged a hospital, a railroad depot, and the historic Haifa offices of *al-Ittihad*, where Emile Habiby, Mahmoud Darwish, and Samih al-Qasim had all once worked. They also killed forty-four Israeli civilians—nearly half of them Arab. The dead included two small Nazareth brothers, aged three and nine, who were outside playing when the rocket hit and whose family comes from Saffuriyya.

The war had been hard on many Israelis, but it was especially difficult for the Palestinian citizens of the north, who were not only torn emotionally by what was happening on both sides of the border but—if they dared question the government's or army's actions—were subject to harsh denunciations and the usual accusations of being a fifth column. At the same time, they were much more vulnerable to rocket attack than Israeli Jews in even the poorest and most neglected communities. Like most other Arab towns throughout the

Galilee, Nazareth has not a single bomb shelter. (Mostly Jewish Upper Nazareth, by contrast, boasts 523.) Neither had the government provided emergency instructions in Arabic or outfitted the town with air raid sirens, which meant that there was no warning before a Katyusha fell—and nowhere to take cover. All one could do to protect oneself was stay inside and pray.

Not surprisingly, the tension brought on by protracted periods of waiting and worrying indoors also exacerbated tensions that had nothing whatsoever to do with the war. Never mind the UN Security Council's declaration of an official cease-fire, a heavy sadness hovers over the kitchen table today, and as I sit talking with Imm Nizar, who looks drawn and vaguely miserable, she pours me coffee and a whole bathtub of woes—which range from how skittish and sleepless she has been throughout this last month to her dismay at the fact that the thirty-eight-year-old Usama isn't married and seems thoroughly unbothered by this fact. She is near tears as she describes the death of those two little Nazareth boys by Katyusha: they were, she says, so young, just babies, with their whole lives before them. . . . And she does not need to say what she is thinking for me to understand what, and who, she is also describing.

In February 2005—on the eve of yet another American reading tour that had been scheduled for Taha but that we had, abruptly, to cancel—Layla's only son, Taha and Yusra's only grandson, the fifteen-year-old Basel, was diagnosed with liver cancer. A small, serious boy with wire-framed glasses and an uncannily adult air, he knew that he was dying, and Taha—who had in his day seen far too many children ail and die—knew it, too. Imm Nizar had also suffered the untimely loss of a father, a sister, a brother, a child, but she and Layla were desperate to believe that Basel would somehow live. Layla closed down the nursery school she ran in her house and devoted herself to shuttling Basel from hospital to hospital, doctor to doctor; she also donned the *hijab,* began to pray five times a day, and arranged for exotic folk remedies to be smuggled from Syria by way of Jordan. . . . To no avail. Basel died within six months, and the weight of his absence was crushing. As Taha tells it, none of their other losses had prepared them for this death. It was as if the world was ending, and for months, they were plunged in a cavernous depression. Imm Nizar would burst into tears at the slightest provocation. Layla cried most of the time and was now a strictly religious Muslim, since she believed her fasting, prayer, and charity would help Basel in paradise. Taha, for his part, remained calm and secular as ever—but he would later somberly admit that of all the difficult experiences through which he had lived, Basel's dying and death were the hardest.

It had been a year now since his passing, and the family had begun slowly to recover. ("Life," says Taha, "is very strong.") But the war had, it seems, churned up in Imm Nizar many of the same feelings of defenselessness and despair that she had experienced during the boy's illness, and she is almost beside herself again as she lets it all spill out. Tourist traffic in Nazareth—and with it Taha's business—has also dried up because of the war, and this has only added to her worries. It is just six weeks since I saw her last, but she appears to have aged several years in that time.

Taha, for his part, is subdued when he finally emerges, loping, from the bedroom—but he seems still to be himself, offering me his usual crooked grin and extended hand, from which a gold snake coiled on his pinkie ring glints. "HOW are you?" he demands to know, half stern, half joking. "And HOW is he?" meaning Peter. We sit on adjacent couches under the unblinking gaze of the Mona Lisa as Imm Nizar wipes her eyes, adjusts her kerchief, and hustles off to get us a plate of fruit and yet another round of potent coffee.

It is a bittersweet time for Taha. As painful as the past few years have been, they have also marked his greatest public success as a writer: word of his work has continued to spread in unexpected, almost airborne ways. When the American-born Jerusalem poet Shirley Kaufman, for instance, included in her 2003 collection *Threshold* a poem that mentions in passing how "Taha Muhammad Ali begins / his poem / *what makes me love / being alive . . .* ," her editor, Michael Wiegers, was instantly curious. He had never heard of Taha Muhammad Ali and had no particular interest in Palestinian poetry—but, remarkably, and in fact somewhat inexplicably, all it took were these six, sporelike words, and far off in Port Townsend, Washington, he bought a copy of *Never Mind* and was, he says, "transfixed" by what he found there. (The infectious effect of Taha's work on all kinds of readers was by now familiar, but Wiegers's intuition about this off-hand snippet suggested a preternaturally keen sensitivity.) As the executive editor of Copper Canyon Press—one of the liveliest and most distinguished publishers of poetry in the United States—he felt "rejuvenated" by these poems and knew that he "wanted to be a part of bringing them to the world," recognizing immediately that he was in the presence of "a Neruda or a Merwin or some other great poet who defined an era." Since Ibis had published that book, Peter had continued to translate Taha's newer poems, and with Wiegers's encouragement, the idea of an expanded volume published in a bilingual edition by Copper Canyon had sprouted. Not only would such a book bring Taha's work in translation to a whole new world of American readers, it would at long last make his Arabic available beyond Bir el-Amir.

Plans were soon under way for another, more extensive American tour, which would follow the new book's publication and bring Taha and Peter back to the Dodge Poetry Festival as well as to New York, Washington, DC, and the West Coast—San Francisco, Seattle, Port Townsend. Closer to home, meanwhile, Taha's poetry was also making its mark: in the winter of 2006, a Hebrew collection of his poems, translated by Anton Shammas, was published in Israel to extremely warm reviews in the major daily papers. Taha began to appear regularly before Jewish groups around the country, and it was (not coincidentally) during this period of steady exposure to these enthusiastic Israeli audiences that he wrote the poem, "Revenge," which would eventually meet with widespread acclaim in both English and Hebrew translations.

Written too late to be included in the Copper Canyon volume, "Revenge" is in some ways the "simplest" of Taha's poems, as it is the sparest in its imagery and most streamlined in its design. Its seeming directness is, though, possibly an illusion—and part and parcel of its quiet drama. It begins with a stanza that subtly plays off many readers' conviction that Palestinians "only understand force."

> At times . . . I wish
> I could meet in a duel
> the man who killed my father
> and razed our home,
> expelling me
> into
> a narrow country.

And if he killed me,
I'd rest at last,
and if I were ready—
I would take my revenge!

Having established the musical and emotional pitch of his poem, and
having given expression to frustrations common to most Palestinians
but also to anyone who has ever suffered at the hands of another, he
then modulates:

But if it came to light,
when my rival appeared,
that he had a mother
waiting for him,
or a father who'd put
his right hand over
the heart's place in his chest
whenever his son was late
even by just a quarter-hour
for a meeting they'd set—
then I would not kill him,
even if I could.

"Likewise . . . ," he goes on, incrementally raising the level of complication as he fleshes out the human scene that surrounds his antagonist—
brothers, sisters, wife, and children, friends, and neighbors, "allies from
prison / or a hospital room, / or classmates from his school"—all of
whom would make his murder untenable.

   "But if he turned / out to be on his own— / cut off like a branch
from a tree—" writes Taha, anticipating what his readers are anticipating, as he then stretches like a bow over the course of five lines our
growing sense of dread:

without a mother or father,
with neither a brother nor sister,
wifeless, without a child,
and without kin or neighbors or friends,
colleagues or companions . . .

He releases the arrow:

> then I'd add not a thing to his pain
> within that aloneness—
> not the torment of death,
> and not the sorrow of passing away.

"Instead," he writes, drawing on a lifetime's worth of sorrows and scores to settle, of quarrels and wars and grandly staged sulhas:

> I'd be content
> to ignore him when I passed him by
> on the street—as I
> convinced myself
> that paying him no attention
> in itself was a kind of revenge.

"Revenge" is without doubt among the most effective of Taha's poems—audiences of all sorts respond almost instinctively to its suspenseful torque and turn-the-other-cheek "message," and he would soon come to consider it his poetic calling card. The poem also sometimes brought about unlikely, almost surreal shifts of perspective—as the time Taha read "Revenge" before a hugely appreciative all-Jewish Israeli crowd, and afterward a middle-aged woman in sensible sandals and a sun hat approached and announced she had something to tell him. "Your reading was marvelous," she declared, "and that last poem you read, about revenge, was very beautiful. You know, the Jews felt the same way for many years." Then she leaned close and peered at Taha over her glasses. "But I'm sorry to tell you, *it doesn't work!*" Then she threw her arms up in the air, smiled, and walked off.

◆

Now that this latest war is over, I've traveled to Nazareth for another round of interviews and in order to bring Taha a brand-new copy of the Copper Canyon volume, *So What: New & Selected Poems, 1971– 2005*. A remarkable portrait of the artist as an old man stares out from the cover. Shot by the New York photographer Nina Subin at her studio during a spontaneous and uproarious session that took place between trips to the flea market and Macy's on Taha's first American tour, the picture captures perfectly the knowing and utterly unflappable dimensions of his gaze—at once defiant *and* tender. When I pull *So What* from my bag and present it to him, he fumbles for his reading glasses and then—facing off with his own face and the bold yet quizzical question/statement that is the book's title—offers the highest praise possible, a barely audible, catch-all "Abayyyeehhhh!!" Then, "Yusra, Yusra, come quick!" and soon Imm Nizar is standing at his side, dishtowel in hand. Taha lifts the book to show her. "*See?*" She sees, and her face lights up with a full-wattage smile.

This calls, clearly, for a celebration, and the next day that takes place, rather inadvertently. After I've finished my other interviews in and around the Nazareth suq, I return to Taha's shop and find him sitting outside amid the crèches, menorahs, stuffed animals, keffiyehs, and sequined belly-dancing outfits. Looking especially spiffed up, in clean khakis and a black cotton shirt, with a different (bright red stone) pinkie ring and his best wristwatch, he is waiting for Sharif, a longtime worker at his shop and close friend of the family, who seems to be running late today. "He's taking me to Saffuri," Taha explains.

"Let me take you," I suggest. "I'll drive."

"Okay," he says, with no further discussion and pulls himself to standing as he grasps his favorite tote bag—which serves him as both businessman's briefcase and peddler's sack.

Although I know why Taha wants to go to Saffuriyya, I was not expecting a pilgrimage today. A few years earlier, in fact, when I'd ask Taha if he would take me to see what was left of the village, he'd begged off—insisting that every time he visited it he had a headache for three days. At that point, he had volunteered his brother Amin to accompany me instead—and had, in the end, written a poem called "The Place Itself, or I Hope You Can't Digest It," explaining his reluctance to return to the literal location of Saffuriyya, which is nothing but "dust and stones" when emptied of the lives and life that gave it meaning: "For where are the red-tailed birds / and the almonds' green? / Where are the bleating lambs / and pomegranates of evening— / the smell of bread / and the grouse?" It is hard to believe he's had a sudden change of heart—and indeed the site of the de-stroyed village is not our destination now. He orders me to keep driv-ing as we pass the turnoff to Moshav Tzippori and the national park, where the only trace of Saffuriyya is the Qal'a, surrounded by a veri-table army of Jewish National Fund pines.

Further along, Taha suddenly points at a tiny, unmarked opening on the other side of the road—"Here!"—and we are soon bouncing along a narrow, winding, and exceedingly bumpy dirt path and into what once were the farthest outskirts of the Saffuriyya basatin. When Sheikh Saleh made his 1955 deal with the authorities to establish Nazareth's Safafra quarter, several village families received small par-cels of agricultural land here. And though that compromise had once been the source of fierce controversy and of Abu Taha's lancing anger, such debates have long ago faded. The village families have contin-ued to tend their miniature plots, and Taha for one does most of his vegetable shopping in "Saffuriyya"—convinced as he has always been of the superiority of its soil and water. Visiting this area, it seems, does not make his head hurt as trips to the moshav or JNF forest do, since this is not a ruin, and the basatin fields have remained more or less as they were since he was a child—farmland owned and worked by Palestinians.

The midday heat is stifling—but he is in an excellent mood and seems unbothered by the strong sun. In booming tones, he com-mands me to stop beside a rickety tin lean-to, where he gives firm but friendly orders to the young man working at the stand: "khayyeh," he calls him, a Galilean endearment for which there is no precise English equivalent. "Brother," "friend," "neighbor," it works to establish an immediate, affectionate bond with even a stranger—the idea being, I suppose, that no one in this context is really a total stranger. The young man smiles faintly as Taha pokes and squeezes the merchandise, makes his selection—a cardboard crate of tomatoes, ten pounds of green peppers, four heads of cauliflower, five eggplants, a large heap of mlukhiyyeh, still on the stalk—then pulls with a flourish several bills off the large wad he keeps wedged in his back pocket. The young man loads our pungent purchases into the car and Taha buckles in again, directing me to drive forward.

The bumpy path grows still bumpier as we make our cautious way over the rocks and into the heart of a dry-looking field where a larger lean-to sits. This is the source of Taha's family's lunchmeat—and as soon as we get out of the car, we can hear it clucking. Taha greets the mustachioed farmer grandly, then gives his order for eight of his noisy chickens. After a brief conversation about which size birds Taha would prefer and whether the feathers should be left on or taken off, he reaches into his tote bag and without any warning or segue pulls out his copy of *So What*, which he brandishes before the farmer as a peacock might suddenly show off its feathers. As the chickens squawk and peck at the ground around his rubber boots, the farmer stands there, half bewildered, half charmed, holding the shiny American book that Taha has just thrust into his weathered hands; he is not entirely sure what to do. Taha laughs a bit mysteriously, then snatches it back and stuffs it into his bag. The man ushers us into the makeshift courtyard behind the lean-to, where his kerchiefed wife is washing clothes in a plastic basin. She nods and welcomes us, as do the two young men—grandsons of other Saffuriyya refugees—who are resting from their fieldwork and smoking on the battered couches that, together with a lush grape arbor, make up this ramshackle outdoor living room. As Taha and I sit down beside them, waiting for the chickens to be slaughtered and plucked, we are offered black coffee and orange soda, and Taha again fishes out his book and offers it up. With a blend of courtesy and wonder, the young men pass it back and forth, flipping it open, reading a few lines, and peering into its bright cover. The vine's shade is a relief from the heat, and the dense smell

of the summertime fields mixes headily with that of the boiling coffee. Taha, meanwhile, leans back on the couch. Lacing his fingers
over his chest and closing his eyes, he lets out a sigh of—it seems—
contentment, as he breathes in what remains of the Saffuriyya air.

ILLUSTRATIONS

Captions appear here as they do in the original albums and collections.

Unless otherwise noted, all photographs of Taha Muhammad Ali and his family are courtesy of Yusra Qablawi and Taha Muhammad Ali.

20: Document with fingerprints. ISA 27/2665/NZ77, "Saffuria Village—General Correspondence"

23: Saffuriyya, c. 1940. Eric Matson Collection, Library of Congress

23: "Saffuria, School boys happy at their Dabkeh, a fine native dance that should be preserved," 1932. From the (Humphrey) Bowman Album 3, MEC Archive, St. Antony's College, picture 42

24: "Monolithic column and a capital from the Basilica." From Leroy Waterman, *Preliminary Report of the University of Michigan Excavations at Sepphoris, Palestine, in 1931*

25: "Medieval fort variously restored; now used as school building." From Leroy Waterman, *Preliminary Report of the University of Michigan Excavations at Sepphoris, Palestine, in 1931*

27: Ordnance Survey map of Saffuriyya, serial number T/51/4. Courtesy of the Saffuriyya Heritage Society, with the author's notations

29: Saffuriyya, Kelsey archive, neg. nos. 13 and 14. By permission of the Kelsey Museum of Archaeology, University of Michigan

30: Saffuriyya, c. 1940. Eric Matson Collection, Library of Congress

35: "Expedition staff, August 15, 1931," Kelsey archive, neg. no. 60. By permission of the Kelsey Museum of Archaeology, University of Michigan

36: "Excavating the Theater, July 23, 1931," Kelsey archive, neg. no. 18. By permission of the Kelsey Museum of Archaeology, University of Michigan

44: "Water supply and distribution station at Saffuriyya." Eric Matson Collection, Library of Congress

68: Saffuriyya children. Unknown photographer

78: The "cinema substitute" (no caption on the original). Khalil Ra'ad Collection, by permission of the Center for Information and Documentation, the Institute for Palestine Studies, Beirut

NOTES

Research for this book has entailed extensive use of both written and oral material. While I have mined archives, books, magazines, and newspapers for any relevant information, it would (for all the reasons described in the chapter "Map of a Vanished Town") have been impossible to reconstruct the various worlds that are rendered here without relying heavily on interviews. The notes that follow are, then, partial in that they account only for written sources, with occasional reference to interviews. Taha Muhammad Ali, Amin Muhammad Ali, and Yusra Ibrahim Qablawi all very patiently agreed to sit through an interview that lasted some four years; their answers to my endless questions form the basis for much of this book, as do the remembrances and descriptions of Feisel Muhammad Ali, Usama, Nizar, and Aisheh 'Abd el-Mo'ti, and Layla 'Abd el-Mo'ti Zaydani. Other interviews were also crucial. I conducted these in English, Arabic, or Hebrew, depending on the situation. In each case, I taped the conversation and transcribed its contents myself: all quotations in the book are direct quotes.

The Interviewees

DAOUD BADER, coordinator, the Association for the Rights of Internally Displaced Persons, Nazareth, May 10, 2004

ZIYAD AWASIE, physiotherapist, activist in the Saffuriyya Heritage Society, Nazareth, May 10, 2004

JAMAL QA'WAR, poet, Nazareth May 11, 2004

'AFAF SROUJI, lifelong Nazareth resident, volunteer at the Sisters of Nazareth convent, Nazareth, May 11, 2004

HADRA HUSSEIN, scholar, Ahmed Qablawi's oldest daughter, Berlin, Sept. 24–25, 2004

RIAD KAMEL, scholar, high school principal, author of a book in Arabic about Taha's poetic language, Nazareth, Nov. 30, 2004

ISHADI MISLIH, former Saffuriyya villager, Nazareth, Dec. 1, 2004

'UMAR HAMUDI (ABU FILASTIN), folk poet, former 'Illut villager, Nazareth, Dec. 1, 2004

JAMIL 'ARAFAT, educator, historian of Palestine's destroyed villages, Nazareth, Dec. 2, 2004

NISSIM REJWAN, writer, historian, former editor of *al-Yawm,* Jerusalem, Dec. 21, 2004

SASSON SOMEKH, scholar of Arabic literature, translator, Tel Aviv, Jan. 10, 2005

ANIS AL-'AFIFI, businessman, Taha's former business partner, Nazareth, Jan. 25, 2005

KHALIL HADDAD, high school teacher, Nazareth, Jan. 25, 2005

YUSUF BANNA, shopkeeper, Nazareth, Jan. 26, 2005

HILLEL COHEN, writer, scholar, Jerusalem, Feb. 2, 2005

DOV YIRMIYA, see the chapter "What Happened," Nahariya, May 23, 2005

DR. NAKHLE BISHARA, medical director, Nazareth Hospital, historian, Nazareth, Oct. 27, 2005

TUVIA RUEBNER, poet, Kibbutz Merchavia, Oct. 27, 2005

MAHMUD YASIN, pharmacist, former political prisoner, Nazareth, Nov. 20, 2005

WALID AL-FAHUM, writer, former human rights lawyer, Nazareth, Nov. 20, 2005

ROBERTA BELL-KLIGLER, educator, member of Moshav Tzippori, Moshav Tzippori, Feb. 19, 2006

NA'ILA ZAYYAD, board member, Tawfiq Zayyad Association, widow of Tawfiq Zayyad, Nazareth, Feb. 20, 2006

SAMIR KHOURI, engraver, former Communist Party activist, Nazareth, Feb. 20, 2006

HANNA ABU HANNA, poet, teacher, Haifa, Feb. 21, 2006

'ABDULLAH 'UTHMAN (ABU GHANEM), restaurant owner, former Saffuriyya villager, Nazareth, Feb. 22, 2006

SIHAM DAOUD, poet, editor, Haifa, Mar. 22, 2006; Metulla, May 23, 2007

DR. ELIAS SROUJI, pediatrician, one-time head of the Schneller smallpox hospital, Nazareth, July 3, 2006

SAMIH AL-QASIM, poet, Rama, July 4, 2006

YOCHAI ADLER, tour guide, member of Moshav Tzippori, Moshav Tzippori, Aug. 16, 2006

DINA and NATAN CARMELI, farmers, members of Moshav Tzippori, Moshav Tzippori, Aug. 16, 2006

HIND (IMM ADIB) and ADIB HADDAD, the widow and eldest son of Michel Haddad, Nazareth, Aug. 16, 2006

SALEM JUBRAN, poet, journalist, Nazareth, Aug. 16, 2006

MAHMOUD DARWISH, poet, Ramallah, Aug. 19, 2006

ANN LAVEE HUSSEIN, professor of management, former wife of Rashid Hussein, Philadelphia, Dec. 19, 2006,

AHARON AMIR, editor, Metulla, May 23, 2007

SALMAN MASALHA, poet, translator, Metulla, May 24, 2007

Archival Abbreviations

CZA   Central Zionist Archive, Jerusalem
HA   Haganah Archive, Tel Aviv
IDFA   IDF Archive, Tel Aviv
ISA   Israel State Archive, Jerusalem
      17   Palestine Police
      27   Galilee District Commissioner (pre-1948)
      49   Ministry of Minority Affairs
      57   Ministry of Health
      79   Israel Police
      102   Prime Minister's Adviser on Arab Affairs
      130   Foreign Ministry
Kelsey   Kelsey Museum of Archaeology, Ann Arbor, MI
MEC   Middle East Centre Archive, St. Antony's College, Oxford
NA   National Archives, Kew
      CO   Colonial Office
      FO   Foreign Office
      WO   War Office

Transliteration and Translation

Throughout the book and these notes I have, for the most part, used a simplified version of the *International Journal of Middle East Studies* transliteration system for standard Arabic. The letter *ayin* appears as ' and *hamza* as '. The aspirated *ha'* is written as an *h* and the harder *kha'* (as in Bach) as a *kh*. Exceptions to this system are made for writers and public figures like Mikhail Naimy, Mansour Kardosh, Mahmoud Darwish, and Taha Muhammad Ali himself, who have chosen to transliterate their names a certain way in English. In these cases, I have maintained their preferred spellings. (In the interest of something like consistency, I've rendered related names—like Muhammad Ali, that is, Abu Taha—the same way.) Names that appear in previously published English translations follow the original transliterations (i.e., Abd el-Hadi, not 'Abd el-Hadi). Words in dialect are written as they sound when spoken. While *Umm*, for instance, is "mother" in standard Arabic, it is *Imm* in Palestinian dialect and in this book; the standard Arabic article "al-" is transcribed as the colloquial "il-" or "el-"; and so on. Certain personal names—Nijmeh, Ghazaleh, Saleh— are also written in dialect. The names of Palestinian villages are set down here in their standard Arabic forms, though colloquial variations (el-Birweh for al-Birwa, for instance) do exist. Hebrew words use ' for *ayin, ch* for *chet,* and *kh* for *khaf.* Unless otherwise noted, all translations are my own.

3, "Feasts would be declared": A. J. Arberry, *The Seven Odes: The First Chapter in Arabic Literature* (Macmillan, 1957), 14.

4, "In his life": Taha Muhammad Ali, "Abd el-Hadi Fights a Superpower," *So What: New & Selected Poems, 1971–2005,* trans. Peter Cole, Yahya Hijazi, and Gabriel Levin (Copper Canyon, 2006), 3.

8, "a recent survey": Eli Ashkenazi, "Most Jews Would Refuse to Live in a Building with Arabs," *Haaretz,* Mar. 23, 2006.

9, "In my poetry": Interview with Jeffrey Brown, *The NewsHour with Jim Lehrer,* first broadcast Mar. 22, 2007 on PBS.

Saffuriyya I
MAP OF A VANISHED TOWN

13, "418 Palestinian villages": This is Khalidi's figure. Other scholars cite other numbers, which range from 383 to 472. See Walid Khalidi, ed., *All That Remains: The Palestinian Villages Occupied and Depopulated by Israel in 1948* (Institute for Palestine Studies, 1992), 585–86.

13, "Now and then a few": Khalidi, ed., *All That Remains,* xv.

14, "Almost every plot": *Saffuriyya: huquq wa-mazalim* (Jam'iyya Turath Saffuriyya, n.d.), 8.

16, "recently a former villager": Muhammad Amin Bashar-Saffuri, *Saffuriyya: tarikh, hadara, wa-turath,* 2 vols. (Maktab al-Nauras li-l-Nama' al-Tarbawi, 2000).

16, "another slender memorial": Tawfiq Isma'il and Salih Muwassi, *Saffuriyya: 'arus al-jalil* (Dar al-Watha'iq, 2001).

16, "burned some": Edward Horne, *A Job Well Done: A History of the Palestine Police Force, 1920–1948* (Anchor, 1982), 478.

17, "The strict legalism": See, e.g., ISA 17/1201/5. (Note: All ISA documents are listed according to their record group, box, and file numbers. The Mandatory files have not all been catalogued by the archive yet and so sometimes contain their original British numbers and letters. Citations are provided here as they appear in the ISA listings.)

17, "In one case": ISA 17/1200/4, charge dated May 29, 1942.

17, "Other loaded interactions": ISA 27/2656/N117, "Saffuria Roads."

19, "on behalf of prisoners": ISA 27/2671/NZ410, "Prisoner Ahmad Mohdi Tobi of Safouria Village."

19, "the desperate letter of a father": ISA 27/2665/NZ77, "Saffuria Village—General Correspondence."

19, "files called Maronite Monks": These are all the actual names of files in ISA 27.

19, "Once in hand": ISA 27/2665/NZ77.

21, "fine wolf": *Palestine Post,* Oct. 4, 1943.

21, "Saffuriyya flour mill": *Palestine Post,* May 5, 1944.

21, "one Jewish historian": He was Ben-Tzion Luria. See Shimri Solomon, "Sherut hayidiot ha'aravi shel hahaganah u-proyekt skirot hayishuvim ha'aravim b'Eretz

Yisrael, 1940–1948," *Daf mi-haslik,* no. 9–10, December 2001, 30. Solomon quotes Luria, "Yiliday haaretz u-benei chul," *Davar,* Oct. 3, 1937.

21, "Saffuriyya was one of the villages": HA 105/134, 105/135.

22, "an Arab collaborator": Solomon, "Sherut hayidiot," 12; Hillel Cohen, *Army of Shadows: Palestinian Collaboration with Zionism, 1917–1948,* trans. Haim Watzman (University of California Press, 2007), 188.

23, "Between 1898 and 1946 ": George S. Hobart, introduction to G. Eric Matson, *The Middle East in Pictures,* vol. 1 (Arno, 1980). See also Mia Gröndahl, *The Dream of Jerusalem: Lewis Larsson and the American Colony Photographers* (Journal, 2005).

23, "a group of educational inspectors": Sarah Graham-Brown, *Palestinians and Their Society, 1880–1946* (Quartet, 1980), 35; MEC, Bowman Album 3, nos. 42–48.

24, "Fadeel Sabba": See Leroy Waterman, *Preliminary Report of the University of Michigan Excavations at Sepphoris, Palestine, in 1931* (University of Michigan Press, 1937); and Elias S. Srouji, *Cyclamens from Galilee: Memoirs of a Physician from Nazareth* (iUniverse, 2003), 18.

PREHISTORY

28, Information about the village comes from numerous interviews, as well as *Saffuriyya: huquq wa-mazalim* and *Saffuriyya aidan,* both published by the Jam'iyya Turath Saffuriyya; Bashar-Saffuri, *Saffuriyya: tarikh;* Isma'il and Muwassi, *Saffuriyya: 'arus;* Mustafa Murad al-Dabbagh, *Biladuna Filastin* (Dar al-Huda, 2002); Taha Muhammad Ali, *Ma yakun wa-qissas uchra* (Dar al-Mashriq, 2003); and Khalidi, ed., *All That Remains,* 350–53. About Palestinian village life in general, see Suad Amiry and Vera Tamari, *The Palestinian Village Home* (British Museum Publications, 1989); Tawfik Canaan, *The Palestinian Arab House: Its Architecture and Folklore* (Syrian Orphanage Press, 1933); Florence Mary Fitch, *The Daughter of Abd Salam: The Story of a Peasant Woman of Palestine* (Bruce Humphries, 1930); Elihu Grant, *The People of Palestine* (J. B. Lippincott, 1921); Hilma Granqvist, *Marriage Conditions in a Palestinian Village,* 2 vols. (Helsingfors, 1931, 1935), and Granqvist, *Birth and Childhood among the Arabs: Studies in a Muhammadean Village in Palestine* (Helsingfors, 1947); Karen Seger, *Portrait of a Palestinian Village: The Photographs of Hilma Granqvist* (Third World Centre for Research and Publishing, 1981); Shukri 'Araf, *al-Qarya al-'arabiyya al-filastiniyya* (Jami'yyat al-Dirasat al-'Arabiyya, 1985); Nimr Sirhan, *Mausu'at al-folklor al-filastini,* 3 vols. (al-Bayader, 1989); and Graham-Brown, *Palestinians and Their Society.*

29, "Sepphoris, Tzippori, and Le Sephorie": Khalidi, ed., *All That Remains,* 350.

29, Information about ancient Sepphoris comes from Rebecca Martin Nagy et al., eds., *Sepphoris in Galilee: Crosscurrents of Culture* (North Carolina Museum of Art, 1996); Stuart S. Miller, *Studies in the History and Traditions of Sepphoris* (Brill, 1984); Lee I. Levine and Zeev Weiss, eds., *From Dura to Sepphoris: Studies in Jewish Art and Society in Late Antiquity* (Journal of Roman Archaeology, 2000); and Tzvika Tzuk, *Tzippori u-svivata* (Ariel, 1995).

31, "In Palestine": Fitch, *Daughter of Abd Salam*, 19.

32, "Nijmeh couldn't read": *A Survey of Palestine*, 3 vols. (Government Printer, 1945–1946), 3:table 7, 1174.

33, "Life ceases": Fitch, *Daughter of Abd Salam*, 39.

34, "smokeless fire": *The Koran*, trans. N. J. Dawood, 55:16 (Penguin, 1956).

34, "Leroy Waterman": Elise A. Friedland, "Leroy Waterman: Portrait of a Scholar," in *The Scientific Test of the Spade: Leroy Waterman and the University of Michigan Excavations at Sepphoris, 1931*, ed. Elaine K. Gazda and Elise A. Friedland (Kelsey Museum of Archaeology, 1997), 3–6.

35, "the site of the city": Waterman, *Preliminary Report*, v–vii. (Unless otherwise noted, all quotations from Waterman are from his preface to the *Preliminary Report*.)

35, "A detailed examination": Waterman, *Preliminary Report*, vi.

36, "Had 14 dishes": Leroy Waterman, Sepphoris excavation diary, July 8, 1931, Kelsey.

36, "The workmen": Waterman, diary, July 9, 1931.

36, "the first": *New York Times*, Sept. 6, 1931.

36, "a stone amulet": S. Yeivin, "Historical and Archaeological Notes," in Waterman, *Preliminary Report*, 17–34; "Checklist of Artifacts," in *Scientific Test*, ed. Gazda and Friedland, 17–21.

37, "*New York Times*": *New York Times*, Oct. 29, 1931.

37, "an editorial": *New York Times*, Oct. 30, 1931.

37, "several contingents": Josephine Shaya, "An Archeologist's Vision of the Holy Land: Sepphoris 1931," in *Scientific Test*, ed. Gazda and Friedland, 14.

37, "Some four thousand clerks": Reported in *Palestine Bulletin*, July 15, 1931.

38, "population of Palestine": Census, 1931, *Survey of Palestine*, 1:30.

IF NOT CAMELS

41, "The Templars": Alex Carmel, "The German Settlers in Palestine and Their Relations with the Local Arab Population and the Jewish Community," in *Studies on Palestine during the Ottoman Period*, ed. Moshe Ma'oz (Magnes, 1975); Tsahar Rotem, "Street on Wheels," *Haaretz*, Feb. 6, 2005. See also S. Turel, ed., *Chronicle of a Utopia: The Templers [sic] in the Holy Land, 1868–1948* (Land of Israel Museum, 2006).

43, "If not camels": Imru' al-Qays, trans. Peter Cole.

44, "modern stone structure": Tzuk, *Tzippori*, 98–99; *Palestine Post*, Dec. 18, 1935.

45, "In his diary": Waterman, diary, Sept. 2, 1931.

48, "As a precautionary measure": Bertha Spafford Vester, *Our Jerusalem: An American Family in the Holy City, 1881–1949* (Ariel, 1988), 246; Tom Segev, *One Palestine, Complete: Jews and Arabs under the British Mandate*, trans. Haim Watzman (Metropolitan, 2000), 18–19.

49, "British Empire": *Filastin*, quoted in CZA S25/22741, April 1936.

50, "nothing shall be done": Walter Laqueur and Barry Rubin, eds., *The Israel-Arab Reader: A Documentary History of the Middle East Conflict* (Penguin, 1984), 18.

See also Erskine B. Childers, "The Wordless Wish: From Citizens to Refugees," in *The Transformation of Palestine: Essays on the Origin and Development of the Arab-Israeli Conflict,* ed. Ibrahim Abu-Lughod (Northwestern University Press, 1971), 170–74. Also Rashid Khalidi, "The Palestinians and 1948: The Underlying Causes of Failure," in *The War for Palestine: Rewriting the History of 1948,* ed. Eugene L. Rogan and Avi Shlaim (Cambridge University Press, 2001), 19.

50, "By 1935": Yehoshua Porath, *The Palestinian Arab National Movement, 1929–1939: From Riots to Rebellion* (Frank Cass, 1977), 129.

BLACK HAND, WHITE PAPER

52, "al-Qassam liked": Ted Swedenburg, *Memories of Revolt: The 1936–1939 Rebellion and the Palestinian National Past* (University of Arkansas Press, 2003), 2.

52, "a night school": Abdullah Schleifer, "The Life and Thought of 'Izz-id-Din al-Qassam," *Islamic Quarterly* 23, no. 2 (1979); May Seikaly, *Haifa: Transformation of an Arab Society, 1918–1939* (Tauris, 2002), 243; A. W. Kayyali, *Palestine: A Modern History* (Third World Centre for Research and Publishing, 1981), 180.

52, "al-Qassam wanted": Philip Mattar, *The Mufti of Jerusalem: Al-Hajj Amin Al-Husayni and the Palestinian National Movement* (Columbia University Press, 1988), 29–30, 67; Yehoshua Porath, *The Emergence of the Palestinian Arab National Movement, 1918–1929* (Frank Cass, 1974), 205–6.

52, "secretive bands": Subhi Yasin, *al-Thawra al-'arabiyya al-kubra fi Filastin, 1936–1939* (Dar al-Hana l'l-Tiba'a, 1959), 21.

52, "dignified, charismatic": Seikaly, *Haifa,* 242.

52, "Another historian": Meron Benvenisti, *Sacred Landscape: The Buried History of the Holy Land since 1948,* trans. Maxine Kaufman-Lacusta (University of California Press, 2000), 204.

53, "Israeli military account": Anaf historia b'matei haclali, *Toldot milchemet hakomemiut* (M'arakhot, 1959), 249.

53, "a brutal people": Uriel Ben-Ami, *Shaga achrona b'Metulla* (Misrad Habitachon, 1990), 68.

53, "secret military drills": Porath, *Palestinian Arab National Movement,* 134.

53, "an outrage": *Palestine Post,* Dec. 25, 1932.

53, "two were condemned": *Palestine Post,* Oct. 6, 1933; HA 8/clali/2.

53, "There has been": *Palestine Post,* Feb. 22, 1934.

54, "In accordance": *Palestine Post,* Feb. 28, 1934.

54, "Saffuriyya YMMA": Porath, *Palestinian Arab National Movement,* 134; Shai Lachman, "Arab Rebellion and Terrorism in Palestine, 1929–39: The Case of Sheikh Izz al-Din al-Qassam and His Movement," in *Zionism and Arabism in Palestine and Israel,* ed. Elie Kedourie and Sylvia G. Haim (Frank Cass, 1982), 64; *Palestine Post,* July 27, 1933.

54, "his testimony": *Palestine Post,* July 28, 1933; HA 8/clali/2, "The Nahalal Murder."

54, "Palestinian history book": Yasin, *al-Thawra al-'arabiyya,* 26.

54, "Mustafa 'Ali Ahmed": MEC, Sir Charles Tegart papers, box 2, file 3.

54, "The magistrate": *Palestine Post,* Jan. 7, 1934.

55, "indications that a branch": NA CO 733/370/9; MEC, Tegart papers, box 2, file 3; Porath, *Palestinian Arab National Movement,* 136–37.

55, "The people of Saffuriyya": HA 8/clali/68, dated Mar. 20, 1933.

55, "Still another": HA 8/clali/67, "Concerning the Murder in Nahalal."

55, "Die as martyrs!": Ghassan Kanafani, *The 1936–1939 Revolt in Palestine* (Committee for a Democratic Palestine, 1972).

55, "series of bloody clashes": CZA S25/22741.

56, "The strike paralyzed": Mattar, *Mufti of Jerusalem,* 79.

56, "According to one veteran": Porath, *Palestinian Arab National Movement,* app. B, "Officers of the Revolt."

57, "It is a quick": CZA S25/22741.

57, "more peaceful note": *Survey of Palestine,* 1:36.

57, "the government dumped": CZA S25/22741.

57, "offers a prospect": *Palestine Royal Commission Report* (His Majesty's Stationery Office, 1937), 395.

57, "walking to evensong": CZA S25/22763.

57, "so gay in life": *Palestine Post,* Sept. 28, 1937.

58, "at close range": NA CO 733/332/10.

58, "two strikes against him": Cohen, *Army of Shadows,* 96.

58, "an unprecedentedly huge reward": *Palestine Post,* Sept. 29, 1937.

58, "fled to Lebanon": Porath, *Palestinian Arab National Movement,* 236; Mattar, *Mufti of Jerusalem,* 83; *Survey of Palestine,* 1:42–43. Edward Horne says that the mufti escaped dressed as a woman (*Job Well Done,* 222–23).

58, "a party of police": ISA 27/2542/C697, "Murder of LY Andrews."

58, "A letter written": NA CO 733/332/10, "1937 Situation."

58, "Hebrew-language intelligence report": CZA S25/3292, Sept. 27, 1937.

58, "political undesirables": CZA S25/22763; NA FO 371/45406; NA CO 733/332/10.

58, "640 men, all told": MEC, Tegart papers, box 2, file 3.

58, "a cell with 780 cubic yards": NA CO 733/328/10, "Prisoners at the Central Prison, Acre, 1937."

59, "There was really little": MEC, Tegart papers, box 2, file 3.

59, "Although the killing": The archives do contain a confession, but there is no sign that the accused ever stood trial (MEC, Tegart papers, box 1, file 3c, "Statement of Mohamed Niji Abu Rub").

59, "permanent British army": MEC, Tegart papers, box 2, file 3; NA WO 32/9401, "Palestine Disturbances"; ISA 17/4212/8.

59, "Until 1940": A. J. Sherman, *Mandate Days: British Lives in Palestine, 1918–1948* (Thames and Hudson, 1997), 106.

59, "Some six thousand": Walid Khalidi, *Before Their Diaspora: A Photographic History of the Palestinians, 1876–1948* (Institute for Palestine Studies, 1984), 226.

60, "The human toll": W. Khalidi, *From Haven to Conquest: Readings in Zionism and the Palestine Problem until 1948* (Institute for Palestine Studies, 1971), app. 4, 846–49.

60, "white paper": Laqueur and Rubin, eds., *Israel-Arab Reader*, 69.

60, "charge logs": ISA 17/1201/5; 17/1200/7; 17/2457/5785.

61, "another police document": ISA 27/2659/N283, "Collective Punishment Saffuriyya."

61, "backhanded compliment": Waterman, *Preliminary Report*, viii.

61, "a 1938 plan was hatched": CZA S25/22762; MEC, Tegart papers, box 2, file 3; NA CO 733/383/1, "Sir Charles Tegart's Mission in Palestine."

61, "They shoot": CZA S25/22732.

62, "Hebrew-language intelligence reports": HA 105/134, 105/135.

62, "a series of letters": ISA 27/4310/14.

62, "Their front doors": Stories of such searches are common. See Swedenburg, *Memories of Revolt*, 13; and NA CO 733/370/9, which includes two pamphlets by Frances Newton, "Punitive Measures in Palestine" and "Searchlight on Palestine," as well as frantic attempts by British government officials to dismiss her charges as "Arab propaganda."

64, "There is no god": *The Koran*, trans. A. J. Arberry (Oxford, 1983), 2:255–65.

Saffuriyya II
THE WINDOW IS OPEN

67, "I went barefoot": Taha Muhammad Ali, *So What*, 179.

67, "the late great": Guy Davenport to Peter Cole, Mar. 5, 2003.

71, "The files": ISA 27/ 2662/N524, "Saffouria Village School."

72, "*The Garden*": Muhammad Is'af al-Nashashibi, *al-Bustan: kitab al-istizhar* (Matb'at al-Ma'arif, 1927), 4. Poems, trans. Peter Cole. Information about al-Nashashibi comes from Radi Saduq, *Shu'ara' Filastin fi al-qarn al-'ishrin* (al-Muassasa al-'Arabiyya li-l-Dirasat w-al-Nashr, 2000), 93–94; Nasser Eddin Nashashibi, *Jerusalem's Other Voice: Ragheb Nashashibi and Moderation in Palestinian Politics, 1920–1948* (Ithaca, 1990), 3, 8.

73, "transmit to students": Khalil al-Sakakini, *Yawmiyyat Khalil al-Sakakini, al-kitab al-thalith, 1919–1922* (Khalil Sakakini Center/Institute of Jerusalem Studies, 2004), 44.

73, "the number of students": A. L. Tibawi, *Arab Education in Mandatory Palestine: A Study of Three Decades of British Administration* (Luzac, 1956), 49.

73, "classes that reached": NA CO 733/282/11, "Rural Education."

73, "just 14 percent": Ami Ayalon, *Reading Palestine: Printing and Literacy, 1900–1948* (University of Texas Press, 2004), 16–17.

73, "Like an engine": Ayalon, *Reading Palestine*, 1.

74, "'Antara ibn Shaddad": For background about 'Antar, see *Antar: A Bedoueen Romance*, trans. Terrick Hamilton (J. Murray, 1819); H. T. Norris, *The Adventures of Antar* (Aris and Phillips, 1980); Peter Heath, *The Thirsty Sword: Sirat 'Antar and the Arabic Popular Epic* (University of Utah Press, 1996); Robert Irwin, ed., *Night and the Horses and the Desert: An Anthology of Classical Arabic Literature* (Overlook, 1999); A. J. Arberry, *Seven Odes.*

75, "When a camel": Hamilton, *Antar,* 30.

77, "Egyptian preachers": *Saffuriyya: huquq,* 18.

81, "field-worker's daily wage": *Statistical Abstract of Palestine* (Government Printing Press, 1942), 68.

HOME FRONT

85, "Even word of the Italian": *Survey of Palestine,* 1:60.

85, "These broadcasts": Baruch Kimmerling and Joel S. Migdal, *The Palestinian People: A History* (Harvard University Press, 2003), 142.

86, "for Palestinians to disagree": *Filastin,* Sept. 9, 1939, front-page editorial by Yusuf Hanna.

86, "One of the characters": Taha Muhammad Ali, "Madhbaha 'ala shawati' 'Akka," *al-Qasida al-rabi'a* (al-Sawt, 1983), 31–36.

87, "The archives contain": ISA 27/2665/NZ77, "Saffuria Village."

88, "illegal to slaughter": *Survey of Palestine,* 2:1000–1001.

89, "head of the Saffuriyya": HA 8/clali/3.

89, "prisoners of war": MEC, Klingeman papers; NA CO 537/2619, "Return of Alien Missionaries." In Turel, ed., *Chronicle of a Utopia,* Yaron Perry writes that they were deported on the *Queen Elizabeth.*

WHAT IF

96, "Anglo-American Committee": Khalidi, *Before Their Diaspora,* 242; Laqueur and Rubin, eds., *Arab-Israel Reader,* 89–90.

96, "binational option": Laqueur and Rubin, eds., *Arab-Israel Reader,* 104–5.

96, "Arab League": Khalidi, *Before Their Diaspora,* 242.

97, "President Truman": Michael J. Cohen, *Palestine to Israel: From Mandate to Independence* (Frank Cass, 1988), 203–6; Khalidi, *Before Their Diaspora,* 242–43; Sherman, *Mandate Days,* 188–89.

98, "The Poet of Palestine": Information about Ibrahim Tuqan comes from Fadwa Tuqan, *Akhi Ibrahim* (al-Maktaba al-'Asriyya, 1946); Saduq, *Shu'ara' Filastin,* 36–38; Salma Khadra Jayyusi, *Trends and Movements in Modern Arabic Poetry,* 2 vols. (Brill, 1977), 1:284–95.

98, "Angels of Mercy": "Mala'ikat al-rahma," Ibrahim Tuqan, *al-A'mal al-kamila* (Riad el-Rayyes, 1993), 49–50; Tuqan, *Akhi Ibrahim,* 19–22; Jayyusi, *Trends,* 1:290–91.

98, "brokers of the land": "al-Samasira . . !" Tuqan, *al-A'mal,* 212; Khalid A. Suleiman, *Palestine and Modern Arab Poetry* (Zed, 1984), 4; Jayyusi, *Trends,* 1:288.

98, "contrapuntal elegy": "al-Thulatha' al-hamra'," Tuqan, *al-A'mal,* 140–43; Tuqan,

Akhi Ibrahim, 34–43; Suleiman, *Palestine and Modern Arab Poetry,* 27–29; Jayyusi, *Trends,* 1:294–95.

98, "The Freedom Fighter": "al-Fida'i," Tuqan, *al-A'mal,* 136–37; Suleiman, *Palestine and Modern Arab Poetry,* 30–1; Jayyusi, *Trends,* 1:287–88; Susan Slyomovics, *The Object of Memory: Arab and Jew Narrate the Palestinian Village* (University of Pennsylvania Press, 1998), 183–84.

98, "People!": "Ya qawm . . !" Tuqan, *al-A'mal,* 209; Jayyusi, *Trends,* 1:287; Suleiman, *Palestine and Modern Arab Poetry,* 37–38, trans. Peter Cole.

99, "generations of 'committed'": Hanna Abu Hanna, "Jawla fi al-shi'r al-'arabi al-filastini," *al-Jadid,* July 1961; Tawfiq Zayyad, *'An al-adab w'al-adab al-sha'abi fi Filastin* (Dar al-'Awda, 1970), 77; Saduq, *Shu'ara' Filastin,* 36–37.

99, "number of British troops": Sherman, *Mandate Days,* 190.

99, "The nerves": Sherman, *Mandate Days,* 190–91.

100, "asked rhetorically": Sherman, *Mandate Days,* 192.

100, "General Assembly endorsed": Laqueur and Rubin, eds., *Arab-Israel Reader,* 113–22.

100, "The vote was": Khalidi, *Before Their Diaspora,* 305.

BATTLE DAYS

101, "landgrab": Nafez Nazzal, *The Palestinian Exodus from Galilee, 1948* (Institute for Palestine Studies, 1978), 8; Khalidi, "Palestinians and 1948," 12, 32; Khalidi, *Before Their Diaspora,* 305.

101, "40 percent": Khalidi, "The Arab Perspective," in *The End of the Palestine Mandate,* ed. Wm. Roger Louis and Robert W. Stookey (University of Texas Press, 1986), 121.

101, "To be the victim": Edward W. Said, "On Palestinian Identity: A Conversation with Salman Rushdie," in Said, *The Politics of Dispossession: The Struggle for Palestinian Self-Determination, 1969–1994* (Vintage, 1995), 121.

101, "the day after the UN vote": Benny Morris, *The Birth of the Palestinian Refugee Problem Revisited* (Cambridge University Press, 2004), 65; Khalidi, "Arab Perspective," 121.

102, "*eleventh*": Khalidi, *Before Their Diaspora,* 244.

103, "drastically underestimated": Rashid Khalidi, *The Iron Cage: The Story of the Palestinian Struggle for Statehood* (Beacon, 2006), 12–22, 125–39; Mattar, *Mufti of Jerusalem,* 110–11; Nazzal, *Palestinian Exodus,* 10.

103, "'Abd al-Qadir al-Husayni": 'Arif al-'Arif, *al-Nakba,* vol. 1 (Manshurat al-Maktaba al-'Asriyya li-l-Tiba'a w-al-Nashr, 1956), 41; Rosemary Sayigh, *Palestinians: From Peasants to Revolutionaries* (Zed, 1979), 77–81.

104, "remained curiously unwilling": Avi Shlaim, "Israel and the Arab Coalition in 1948," in *War for Palestine,* ed. Rogan and Shlaim, 82.

104, "The mufti urged": Simha Flapan, *Zionism and the Palestinians* (Croom Helm, 1979), 300.

104, "the moderate majority": Morris, *Birth*, 32.

104, "issued a warning": Kimmerling and Migdal, *Palestinian People*, 153–54.

104, "the Jews nearby": Morris, *Birth*, 33; Nazzal, *Palestinian Exodus*, 11; Khalidi, "Palestinians and 1948," 15.

104, "man named Nimr": Taha told me about Nimr, but his name (along with that of Abu Mahmud) also appears in the account of the local militias given by Muhammad Nimr al-Hawari, *Sirr al-nakba* (al-Hakim, 1955), 183.

105, "Abu Mahmud al-Saffuri": Porath, *Palestinian Arab National Movement*, app. B; Walid Khalidi says Abu Mahmud was head of the Western Galilee rural fighting force, with about 140 rifles under his control (*From Haven*, app. 8, 859).

105, "irregulars from Syria": Morris, *Birth*, 66; 'Arif, *al-Nakba*, 1:38–42. The numbers of ALA soldiers range in different accounts from three thousand (Laila Parsons, *The Druze between Palestine and Israel, 1947–49* [St. Martin's/St. Antony's, 2000], 77) to five thousand (Morris, *Birth*, 34).

105, "more-than-slightly disdainful": quoted in the *Palestine Post*, Mar. 24, 1948.

106, "tens of thousands": Morris, *Birth*, 67.

106, "In Haifa, car bombs": Morris, *Birth*, 99–109.

106, "In Jaffa": Morris, *Birth*, 109–16.

106, "Rumors began": Benvenisti, *Sacred Landscape*, 103; Morris, *Birth*, 79; Khalidi, ed., *All That Remains*, 465.

106, "Balad al-Sheikh": Morris, *Birth*, 101; Khalidi, ed., *All That Remains*, 152–54; Benvenisti, *Sacred Landscape*, 297–99.

107, "But by April": Morris, *Birth*, 237–40; Benvenisti, *Sacred Landscape*, 114–17; Khalidi, ed., *All That Remains*, 290–91.

107, "mortar fire": Kimmerling and Migdal, *Palestinian People*, 161.

107, "hundreds of civilians": For a discussion of the number of people killed at Dayr Yasin, see Sharif Kana'na, "Madhbahat Dayr Yasin: qira'a jadida," in *al-Shatat al-falistini: hijra am tahjir?* (SHAML, 2000); and Benny Morris, "The Historiography of Deir Yassin," *Journal of Israeli History* 24, no. 1 (2005). I have written "hundreds" because it is clear that this is what the people of Saffuriyya believed at the time.

108, "the British had evacuated": See Turel, ed., *Chronicle of a Utopia*, 29, 48, 121.

108, "Ramat Yochanan": Details about this battle come from Sha'ul Avigur et al., *Sefer toldot hahaganah*, vol. 3 ('Am Oved, 1973), 1567; Moshe Carmel, *M'arakhot tzafon* (M'arakhot /Hakibbutz Hameuchad, 1949), 61–72; Parsons, *Druze*; Parsons, "The Palestinian Druze in the 1947–1949 Arab-Israeli War," *Israel Studies* 2, no. 1 (1997): 72–93; Parsons, "The Druze and the Birth of Israel," in *War for Palestine*, ed. Rogan and Shlaim; Anaf historia b'matei haclali, *Toldot milchemet*, 121–22; Nabih al-Qasim, *Waqi' al-Duruz fi Isra'il* (Dar al-Itam al-Islamiyya al-Sina'iyya, 1976), 24–27; Shabtai Teveth, *Moshe Dayan: The Soldier, the Man, the Legend*, trans. Leah and David Zinder (Weidenfeld and Nicholson, 1972), 133–34; Moshe Dayan, *Story of My Life* (Warner, 1976), 101–4; al-Hawari, *Sirr*, 182–83; Cohen, *Army of Shadows*, 247; 'Arif, *al-Nakba*, 1:223–25; and Swedenburg, *Memories of Revolt*, 91–93.

109, "Wahab's figure": IDFA 10001/S7/118.

109, "Moshe Carmel's count": Carmel, *M'arakhot*, 72.

109, "A contemporary estimate": Parsons (*Druze*, 159) quotes different sources, which put the Druze death count at 110, 30, or 100. Al-Qasim says 200. 'Arif says 30 and quotes a Jewish source as saying 106.

109, "Before leaving": Parsons, *Druze*, 70.

110, "Our resistance": Parsons, *Druze*, 72.

WHAT HAPPENED

112, "Exiled by force": David Ben-Gurion, *Israel: A Personal History* (Sabra, 1972), 79.

112, "al-Birwa fell": Nazzal, *Palestinian Exodus*, 65–70.

113, "On July 13": Information about 'Abd al-Rahim Mahmud comes from Hanna Abu Hanna, ed., *Ruhi 'ala rahati: diwan 'Abd al-Rahim Mahmud* (Markaz Ihya' al-Turath, 1985), 25–43; Adib Rafiq Mahmud and Tariq 'Abd al-Karim Mahmud, *'Abd al-Rahim Mahmud: bayn al-wafa' w'al-zikra* (Markaz Ihya' al-Turath, 1990); Jayyusi, *Trends*, 1:295–98; Saduq, *Shu'ara' Filastin*, 384–89; Suleiman, *Palestine and Modern Arab Poetry*, 31–32; Slyomovics, *Object*, 184–85; and 'Arif, *al-Nakba*, 3:621–27.

114, "I bear my soul": Mahmud, *Ruhi*, 101, trans. Peter Cole.

114, "village of Shafa 'Amr": Nazzal, *Palestinian Exodus*, 75.

114, "some of the young men": Nazzal, *Palestinian Exodus*, 75; Imad Mouaid, "Tilka al-layla" (www.palestineremembered.com).

114, "Unbeknownst to Abu Mahmud": Cohen, *Army of Shadows*, 253; al-Hawari, *Sirr*, 194–95.

116, "not a narrative": Edward W. Said, *After the Last Sky: Palestinian Lives* (Pantheon, 1986), 38.

117, "The Jewish, Israeli soldier": Dov Yermiya, *My War Diary: Lebanon, June 5–July 1, 1982*, trans. Hillel Schenker (South End, 1983), 80–81.

118, "A gentle, good-looking": Teveth, *Moshe Dayan*, 47.

118, "In a very painful": Teveth, *Moshe Dayan*, 292.

119, "we must create": A. D. Gordon, "Our Tasks Ahead," in *The Zionist Idea: A Historical Analysis and Reader*, ed. Arthur Hertzberg (Atheneum, 1969), 381.

120, "the night of July 15, 1948": This account is drawn from Dov's recollections; his unpublished memoir; Ben Dunkelman, *Dual Allegiance: An Autobiography* (Signet, 1976), 212–15; Carmel, *M'arakhot*, 206–7; Tzadok Eshel, *Chativat Carmeli b'milchemet hakomemiut* (M'arakhot, 1973), 214–18; and Anaf historia b'matei haclali, *Toldot milchemet*, 249. ·

121, "bringing charges": Dov related this to me in person; see also Morris, *Birth*, 481, 501–2.

122, "Dunkelman tells": Dunkelman, *Dual Allegiance*, 212–15.

123, "Three Jewish planes": Nazzal, *Palestinian Exodus*, 75.

124, "a Saffuriyyan character": Elias Khoury, *Gate of the Sun*, trans. Humphrey Davies (Archipelago, 2005), 90.

124, "a documentary film": *1948,* dir. Muhammad Bakri (1999).

127, "flabby, pampered boy": Dunkelman, *Dual Allegiance,* 36.

127, "All my life": Dunkelman, *Dual Allegiance,* 16.

127, "2,400 served": Natanel Lorch, *The Edge of the Sword* (Putnam's, 1961), 325.

127, "gifted ghostwriter": Peretz Kidron, "Truth Whereby Nations Live," in *Blaming the Victims: Spurious Scholarship and the Palestinian Question,* ed. Edward W. Said and Christopher Hitchens (Verso, 1988), 85–96.

127, "extremely unorthodox": For Dunkelman's descriptions of the attack, see Dunkelman, *Dual Allegiance,* 213–15.

128, "The attack": Carmel, *M'arakhot,* 206–7.

128, "Mass and surprise attack": Lorch, *Edge,* 274.

129, "Said himself once noted": Edward W. Said, "Permission to Narrate," in Said, *Politics of Dispossession,* 258.

130, "Benny Morris explains": Morris, *Birth,* 4.

130, "young American anthropologist": Swedenburg, *Memories of Revolt,* xxvi.

132, "most incriminating": See Guy Erlich, "Not Only Dayr Yasin," *Ha'ir,* May 6, 1992; Aryeh Dayan, "How Did Jewish Settlements Begin? It's a Secret," *Haaretz,* Apr. 1, 2005.

132, "guidelines for Operation Dekel": IDFA 721/72/310.

132, "Hebrew code words": IDFA 7249/49/115.

133, "name of the pilot": IDFA 2900137/51/83

133, "further communication": IDFA 922/75/550.

133, "one chronicle": Brian Cull with Shlomo Aloni and David Nicolle, *Spitfires over Israel* (Grub Street, 1994), 198.

134, "poor coordination": See Cull, Aloni, and Nicolle, *Spitfires,* 198; and Maj. Avi Cohen, *Toldot chayl haavir b'milchemet ha'atzmaut,* vol. 1 (Misrad Habitachon, 2004), 630, 633.

Lebanon

GOING

139, "In a poem written": "There Was No Farewell," Taha Muhammad Ali, *So What,* 60–61.

140, "ordered by their leaders": See Walid Khalidi, *Why Did the Palestinians Leave?* (Arab Information Center, n.d.); Benny Morris, *1948 and After: Israel and the Palestinians* (Oxford, 2003), 17–18; Erskine Childers, *The Other Exodus* (National Publications House, n.d.); Simha Flapan, *The Birth of Israel: Myths and Realities* (Croom and Helm, 1987), 83–118.

140, "several pamphleteers": Sayigh, *Palestinians,* 92–93. See also Childers, "Wordless Wish."

140, "drinking from cattle pools": Sayigh, *Palestinians,* 104.

141, "Bint Jbeyl, 'Adayssa": I would like to thank Jihane Sfeir-Khayat for generously providing me with information about the refugees in Lebanon during this period.

141, "Constantine Zurayk": Constantine K. Zurayk, *The Meaning of the Disaster*, trans. R. Bayly Winder (Khayat's College Book Cooperative, 1956), 2.

141, "By July 18": Morris, *Birth*, 67, 262, 448, 602–4; Kimmerling and Migdal, *Palestinian People*, 156, 162; Khalidi, *Iron Cage*, 1–3; Janet L. Abu-Lughod, "The Demographic Transformation of Palestine," in *Transformation of Palestine*, ed. Abu-Lughod.

142, "Difficulties and hardships": Zurayk, *Meaning*, 47.

142, "Just two miles": Information about Bint Jbeyl comes from Dr. Mustafa Bazzi, *Bint Jbeyl: hadarat Jabal 'Amil* (Dar al-'Amir li-l-Thaqafa w-al-'Ulum, 1998), 19–30, 404–5.

144, "Matterhorn of memos": See, e.g., the UN Information System on the Question of Palestine, or UNISPAL (http://domino.un.org/unispal.nsf) and the International Federation of Red Cross and Red Crescent Society archives (Geneva). The Jerusalem and East Mission files, housed in the MEC Archive (boxes 72–74) contain valuable records about the refugees. See also Salim Tamari and Elia Zureik, eds., *Reinterpreting the Historical Record: The Uses of Palestinian Refugee Archives for Social Science Research and Policy Analysis* (Institute for Palestine Studies/ Institute for Jerusalem Studies, 2001).

144, "One recent study": Tamari and Zureik, eds., *Reinterpreting the Historical Record*, 6.

145, "a public health": *Palestine Post*, Oct. 13, 1949.

145, "64 per cent": UNISPAL, press release Aug. 16, 1948, "Mediator's Plan for Aid to Palestine Refugees."

145, "the Quakers wrote": For a fine account of the Quakers' relief efforts, see Julie Peteet, *Landscape of Hope and Despair: Palestinian Refugee Camps* (University of Pennsylvania Press, 2005), 57–61; and Peteet, "The AFSC Refugee Archives on Palestine, 1948–1950," in *Reinterpreting the Historical Record*, ed. Tamari and Zureik, 109–28.

145, "few Arabs used banks": MEC JEM papers, box 73/1, letter dated June 16, 1948. The missionary's name was Winifred A. Coate: she was the former headmistress of the Jerusalem Girls' College. (I am grateful to Vanessa Wells of the Jerusalem and the Middle East Church Association for permission to quote from the association's papers.)

145, "I have made": Folke Bernadotte, *To Jerusalem* (Hodder and Stoughton, 1951), 200.

146, "one Red Cross official": W. de St. Aubin, "Peace and Refugees in the Middle East," *Middle East Journal*, July 1949, 250–51.

146, "An Anglican priest": Rev. Eric Bishop, in MEC JEM papers, box 73/1, "Memorandum on Arab refugees."

146, "While I was in Beirut": MEC JEM papers, box 73/1, letter dated Jan. 7, 1949.

147, "The Lebanese government": St. Aubin, "Peace and Refugees," 253; Peteet, *Landscape*, 55.

148, "historical sources": Rosemary Sayigh, *Too Many Enemies: The Palestinian Experience in Lebanon* (Zed, 1994), 24.

148, "the Lebanese army": In "'Bab al-Shams' qissat hubb, wa-fi al-akhir, al-hubb ahamm min kul shai'," a conversation between Anton Shammas and Elias Khoury (*Masharef* 17, 2002), Khoury talks about the tractors (221). In his Nakba Oral History Project interview, 'Ali Muhammad al-Hassan Nijim describes how his family was put on a bus and moved from Bint Jbeyl to al-Qara'un.

149, "It was difficult": MEC JEM papers, box 73/1, letter dated July 30, 1948.

151, "ugly-looking conflict": Bernadotte, *To Jerusalem*, 1.

151, "his mediation efforts": UNISPAL, press release, Sept. 15, 1948, "Mediator Leaves for Middle East Tour."

151, "COUNT FOLKE BERNADOTTE": UNISPAL, cablegram, Sept. 18, 1948, "Cablegram from R. Bunche."

151, "debonair career humanitarian": Information about Bernadotte comes from Kati Marton, *A Death in Jerusalem* (Pantheon, 1994); Amitzur Ilan, *Bernadotte in Palestine: A Study in Contemporary Humanitarian Knight-Errantry* (Macmillan/ St. Antony's, 1989); Sune O. Perrson, *Mediation and Assassination: Count Bernadotte's Mission to Palestine, 1948* (Ithaca, 1979); Ted Schwarz, *Walking with the Damned: The Shocking Murder of the Man Who Freed Thirty Thousand Prisoners from the Nazis* (Paragon, 1992); Ilan Pappé, *The Making of the Arab-Israeli Conflict, 1947–51* (Tauris, 1992); and Bernadotte's own *To Jerusalem*.

151, "these innocent victims": UNISPAL, "Cablegram Dated 1 August 1948 from the United Nations Mediator to the Secretary-General Concerning Arab Refugees."

152, "A simple man": Schwarz, *Walking with the Damned*, 309.

152, "crusading Don Quixote": Ilan, *Bernadotte in Palestine*, 4.

152, "rather ignorant": Ilan, *Bernadotte in Palestine*, 4.

152, "lacked the suppleness": Marton, *Death in Jerusalem*, 226.

152, "not a brilliant man": Ben-Gurion, *Israel: A Personal History*, 279.

152, "Rabbi Judah Magnes": *New York Times*, Sept. 24, 1948.

152, "the Jewish State": Bernadotte, *To Jerusalem*, 243–44.

152, "one American diplomat": Quoted in Morris, *Birth*, 326.

152, "gone to their heads": Bernadotte, *To Jerusalem*, 199.

153, "destruction of villages": Morris, *1948*, 121.

153, "transfer committee": Morris, *Birth*, 328–29; Morris, *1948*, 141–58; Nur Masalha, *The Politics of Denial: Israel and the Palestinian Refugee Problem* (Pluto, 2003), 38–40.

153, "Moshe Shertok": Quoted in Morris, *Birth*, 317–18.

153, "orders went out": Morris, *Birth*, 329.

153, "an anomaly": Quoted in Morris, *Birth*, 326.

153, "UNSPEAKABLE VIOLATION": UNISPAL, "Cablegram dated 17 September 1948 addressed by Ralph Bunch . . . to Mr. M. Shertok."

153, "DESPERADOES AND OUTLAWS": UNISPAL, "Cablegram from Foreign Minister of Provisional Government of Israel Dated 17 September 1948."

154, "It is very easy": *New York Times*, Sept. 24, 1948.

154, "Jewish National Fund forest": *Tarshomet yishivot hamemshalah harishonah*, vol. 10, meeting Aug. 17, 1949, 2–4.

154, "Everywhere you see": "Aid to Arab Refugees from Palestine," published by UNRWA, n.d.

155, "One historian quotes": Sayigh, *Palestinians*, 107.

155, "the most tragic": MEC JEM papers, box 73/2, "The Arab Refugees: Extracts from the diary of Archer Cust."

156, "Emergency Regulations": Information about the regulations and Absentee Property Law comes from Sabri Jiryis, *The Arabs in Israel*, trans. Inea Bushnaq (Monthly Review, 1976), 82–88; Morris, *Birth*, 364, 510; Masalha, *Politics*, 39–40, 152–58; Shira Robinson, "Occupied Citizens in a Liberal State: Palestinians under Military Rule and the Colonial Formation of Israeli Society, 1948–1966" (Ph.D. diss., Stanford University, 2005); Hillel Cohen, *Hanifkadim hanokhachim* (Institute for Israeli Arab Studies, 2000), 66–72; and Dan Rabinowitz and Khawla Abu-Baker, *Coffins on Our Shoulders: The Experience of the Palestinian Citizens of Israel* (University of California Press, 2005), 46–47.

157, "350 of the 370": Don Peretz, *Israel and the Palestine Arabs* (Middle East Institute, 1958), 143.

157, "a census": Charles S. Kamen, "After the Catastrophe, I: The Arabs in Israel, 1948–51," and "After the Catastrophe, II: The Arabs in Israel, 1948–51," *Middle Eastern Studies* 23, no. 4 (1987); 24, no. 1 (1988).

157, "350,000 arrived": Tom Segev, *1949: The First Israelis* (Free Press, 1986), 95.

157, "to liberate": Quoted in Robinson, "Occupied Citizens," 124–25.

LEAVINGS

158, "On the hot May day": Details about Ruebner come from my interview with him; from his memoir, *Chayyim arukim ketzarim: zikhronot ve'od* (Keshev l'Shira, 2006); and from Dalia Karpel, "Poetry Became My Homeland," *Haaretz*, May 20, 2005.

162, "several hundred": The precise number varies in different accounts: IDFA 6309/49/3 states that 397 villagers were issued ID cards. In *Sacred Landscape*, Meron Benvenisti says 200 remained, while documents from the Ministry of Minority Affairs say that only 80 people originally stayed in the village (ISA 49/297/58).

162, "Dov Yermiya remembers": This information comes from my interview with Dov and from his unpublished memoir.

163, "capitulation signing ceremony": *New York Times*, July 19, 1948.

163, "In October and November": Morris, *Birth*, 510; Benvenisti, *Sacred Landscape*, 204–5.

163, "British emergency regulations": Jiryis, *Arabs in Israel*, 9.

164, "The people of Saffuriyya": ISA 49/58/297.

164, "Next to Nazareth": Quoted in Morris, *Birth*, 517.

164, "On the morning": IDFA 1012/49/72; Benvenisti, *Sacred Landscape*, 205.

164, "550 people": IDFA 6309/49/3.

164, "RE: Saffuriyya": ISA 49/302/94.

164, "One Palestinian account": 'Ali al-Azhari, *Maariv*, Oct. 15, 1995, trans. Yael Lotan, reprinted in *Palestine-Israel: Journal of Politics, Economics and Culture* 3, no. 1 (1996).

165, "Kibbutz Sde Nachum": Morris, *Birth*, 517.

165, "A Zionist historian": Arieh Avneri, *Hachalutzim haalmonim*, vol. 1 (Peleg, 1981), 265–69; Benvenisti, *Sacred Landscape*, 216.

165, "the Arab town": Shmuel Dayan, *K'cholmim* (Masada, 1955), 115–16; Benvenisti, *Sacred Landscape*, 216–17.

166, "the Supreme Court": Benvenisti, *Sacred Landscape*, 205; Jam'iyya Turath Saffuriyya's *Saffuriyya: huquq*, 24–25, contains a partial list of those villagers who appealed to the court. See also ISA 102/17038/18.

Reina
PRESENT, ABSENT

174, "Some Egyptian soldiers": Interviews with Yusra Qablawi, Hadra Hussein, and ISA 17/2647/7, charge register entry from Aug. 1, 1943, "Premeditated murder."

176, "According to the story": Chad F. Emmett, *Beyond the Basilica: Christians and Muslims in Nazareth* (University of Chicago Press, 1995), 154.

176, "headless body": Yehoshua Palmon, quoted in Ian Lustick, *Arabs in the Jewish State: Israel's Control of a National Minority* (University of Texas Press, 1980), 48.

176, "By doling out": As'ad Ghanem, *The Palestinian-Arab Minority in Israel, 1948–2000* (SUNY Press, 2001), 18–21; Jiryis, *Arabs in Israel*, 161–77; Rabinowitz and Abu-Baker, *Coffins on Our Shoulders*, 51–55.

177, "Even in Nazi Germany": Quoted in Jiryis, *Arabs in Israel*, 12.

177, "Yet after 1948": Quotations from the regulations come from Jiryis, *Arabs in Israel*, 16–23. Further information about the emergency regulations and military government comes from Fouzi El-Asmar, *To Be an Arab in Israel* (Frances Pinter, 1975); Segev, *1949*, 49–51; and Robinson, "Occupied Citizens."

178, "The moral support": Jiryis, *Arabs in Israel*, 167–68.

178, "One Hebrew document": ISA 49/51/308.

Nazareth I
AFTER THE FLOOD

189, "untainted harmony": Titus Tobler, quoted in Emmett, *Beyond the Basilica*, 25.

189, "Even as": Information about (and descriptions of) pre-1948 Nazareth come from Emmett, *Beyond the Basilica*; Nakhle Bishara, *al-Nasira, suwar wa-basamat min al-tarikh* (n.p., 2005); As'ad Mansur, *Tarikh al-Nasira* (Matba' al-Hilal, 1924); Mahmud 'Abd al-Qadir Kan'ana, *Tarikh al-Nasira* (al-Hakim, 1964); Nahi Za'rab Qa'war, *Tarikh al-Nasira: masirat 'abr al-'usur* (Venus, 2000); Srouji, *Cyclamens*; Jean Said Makdisi, *Teta, Mother, and Me: An Arab Woman's Memoir* (Saqi, 2005);

Hanna Abu Hanna, *Zil al-ghayma* (Ministry of Education and Culture, 1997); and Michel Haddad, *Min dhikrayati* (Rubata al-Kutab w'al-Udaba' al-Filastiniyyin fi Isra'il, 1991).

191, "a large number": Srouji, *Cyclamens*, 136.

191, "public school": Hanna Abu Hanna, *Mahr al-buma* (Maktabat Kul Shai', 2004), 100.

191, "according to the presiding judge": ISA 49/308/44, "Report on the Visit of the Minister of Minority Affairs in Nazareth, 19.7.48"; Srouji, *Cyclamens*, 138–40.

191, "by 6:15 on the evening": Lorch, *Edge*, 275.

191, "resistance would end": Nazzal, *Palestinian Exodus*, 79.

191, "sixteen thousand permanent residents": ISA 49/308/44, "Report on the Visit of the Minister of Minority Affairs."

192, "thirty-five people": Marion Sigaut, *Mansour Kardosh: rajul salah min al-Nasira*, trans. Fayruz 'Abud, Jidalla Shehadah (al-Muassasa al-'Arabiyya li-l-Huquq al-Insan, 2001), 44.

192, "from 2 pm": ISA 49/308/44, "Report on the Visit of the Minister . . . 19.7.48"; ISA 130/2564/11, "Report of the Military Government in Nazareth and the District, 17.7–17.10.48."

192, "the public relations problem": Kamen, "After the Catastrophe, II," 77.

193, "with machine-guns, mercilessly": Morris, *Birth*, 418.

193, "importance to the Christian world": Morris, *Birth*, 418–19.

193, "The orders handed down": Eshel, *Chativat Carmeli*, 218.

193, "shocked and horrified": Kidron, in Said and Hitchens, *Blaming the Victims*, 87.

193, "Why so many Arabs?": Michael Bar-Zohar, *Ben-Gurion*, vol. 2, Hebrew ed. (Zmora Bitan, 1987), 775–76.

193, "satisfaction": ISA 49/308/44.

193, "the first 'Israel'": Dorothy Bar Adon, *Palestine Post*, July 26, 1948.

194, "Mrs. Zelda Popkin": "Shocked into Zionism," *Palestine Post*, Dec. 17, 1948.

194, "there are a large number": ISA 130/2564/11, "Report of the Military Government in Nazareth and the District, 17.7–17.10.48."

195, "The Baptists": Information about the aid provided to the Nazareth refugees comes from Cohen, *Hanifkadim*, 53–56; Srouji, *Cyclamens*, 137–40; Kamen, "After the Catastrophe, II," 80; Bishara, *al-Nasira*, 243–44; and ISA 49/309/15, "Report by a Welfare Worker."

195, "deplorable": ISA 57/147/5, "Monthly Medical Report, October 1948, Nazareth Town and District."

195, "Sami Jeraysi wrote": ISA 49/309/15.

195, "A Jerusalemite": Srouji, *Cyclamens*, 183.

195, "Although [the refugees'] places": ISA 57/147/5, "Monthly Medical Report, October 1948."

196, "Here": ISA 49/308/38, "A Visit of the UN Delegation to Nazareth, 6.8.48."

196, "a Jewish official": He was Max Vardi. ISA 49/308/38, letter dated Sept. 3, 1948, to the minister of religions.

196, "the military governor himself wrote": ISA 49/308/38, "Re: Refugees," Jan. 11, 1949.

197, "Various high-ranking": See the minutes of the meetings in ISA 102/17112/8. See also Kamen, "After the Catastrophe, II," 82–83; and Cohen, *Hanifkadim,* 47–52.

197, "a quarter of the town's population": Kamen, "After the Catastrophe, I," 475.

198, "mealtime bribery": Robinson, "Occupied Citizens," 153–58.

200, "Since May 1949": Information about the Austerity Plan and the black market comes from Dov Yosef, *Yonah ve-cherev* (Masada, 1975), 228–61; Segev, *1949,* 296–323; "Austerity Serves State and Citizen," *Palestine Post,* May 13, 1949; "Hakitzuv—macah u-trufah?" *Ha'olam hazeh,* Aug. 10, 1950; ISA 102/17097/49, "Supply to Arabs"; and ISA 79/2170/27, "War on the Black Market."

200, "a small nation": Yosef, *Yonah,* 231.

200, "Pioneer Poverty": Quoted in Segev, *1949,* 298.

200, "sweet potatoes": *Palestine Post,* May 13, 1949.

201, "an illness": "Shuk shachor—madua?" *Ha'olam hazeh,* Oct. 12, 1950.

202, "small fry": Quoted in Segev, *1949,* 312.

202, "a search was conducted": ISA 79/2170/27, letter from the legal adviser to the Goods and Inventory Branch.

LIKE WATER AND AIR

203, "Galilee-born journalist": Atallah Mansour, "Arab Literature and Writers in Israel," *New Outlook* 7, no. 4 (1964): 54–56.

203, "charismatic local poets": Rashid Hussein, "Arab Writers in Israel," *New Outlook* 5, no. 3 (1962): 49–53.

203, "Another novelist": Anton Shammas, "Diary," in *Every Sixth Israeli,* ed. Alouph Hareven (Van Leer, 1983), 43.

203, "greatest Palestinian prose writer": Emile Habiby, *Ihtayyeh* (reprint; 'Arabesque, 2006), 87.

203, "In objective terms": Information about the Arabic cultural scene in Israel, post-1948, comes from Ghassan Kanafani, *Adab al-muqawama fi Filastin al-muhtalla* (Muassasat al-Abhath al-'Arabiyya, 1966); Habib Qahwaji, *al-'Arab fi zil al-ihtilal al-isra'ili mundhu 1948* (PLO Research Center, 1982); S. Moreh, "Arabic Literature in Israel," *Middle Eastern Studies* 3, no. 3 (1967); Reuven Snir, "'Petza' ehad mi-petzav'—Hasifrut ha'aravit hafalastinit b'Yisrael," *Alpayim* 2 (1990); Hanna Abu Hanna, "Shi'runa fi al-hamsinat," in *Rihla al-bahth 'an al-turath* (al-Wadi, 1994); Abu Hanna, *Khamirat al-rumad* (Maktabat Kul-Shai', 2004); Abu Hanna, *Mahr al-buma;* Mahmoud Darwish, *Yawmiyyat al-huzn al-'adi* (Dar al-'Awda, 1977); Darwish, *Shai' 'an al-watan* (Dar al-'Awda, 1981); Joel Beinin, *Was the Red Flag Flying There? Marxist Politics and the Arab-Israeli Conflict in Egypt and Israel, 1948–1958* (University of California Press, 1990); Walter Schwarz, *The Arabs in Israel* (Faber and Faber, 1959); Ori Stendel, *The Arabs in Israel* (Sussex, 1996); and Jacob Landau, *The Arabs in Israel: A Political Study* (Oxford, 1969). See also

Jiryis, *Arabs in Israel*; El-Asmar, *To Be an Arab in Israel*; Robinson, "Occupied Citizens"; Kimmerling and Migdal, *Palestinian People*; and Cohen, *Hanifkadim.*

203, "one outside observer": Schwarz, *Arabs in Israel,* 59.

203, "not a single inhabitant": Atallah Mansour, *Waiting for the Dawn* (Secker and Warburg, 1975), 62.

204, "One scholar": Fahad Abu Hadara, "al-Bunya al-shakliyya fi al-shi'r al-mahalli, al-marhala al-ula," in *Maraya fi al-naqd,* ed. Mahmud Ghanayim (Dar al-Huda, 2000).

204, "a small paper": Mansour, *Waiting,* 65.

204, "a mouthpiece": *al-Ittihad,* June 11, 1968, quoted in Jiryis, *Arabs in Israel,* 271.

204, "laughingstock": Nissim Rejwan, *Outsider in the Promised Land: An Iraqi Jew in Israel* (University of Texas Press, 2006), 66.

204, "a news item": The items mentioned appear in *al-Yawm,* Jan. 28, Feb. 2, 1953, and on Independence Day of that year.

204, "Anton Shammas calls": Hareven, ed., *Every Sixth Israel,* 43.

206, "well-appointed houses": El-Asmar, *To Be an Arab in Israel,* 22.

206, "al-Sahib ibn 'Abbad": This is Reynold A. Nicholson (*A Literary History of the Arabs* [Cambridge, 1941]), quoting Ibn Khallikan, 347–48; E. K. Rowson, "al-Sahib Ibn 'Abbad," in *Encyclopedia of Arabic Literature,* ed. Julie Scott Meisami and Paul Starkey, 2 vols. (Routledge, 1998), 2:675.

207, "[Abu al-Faraj] used to go": Quoted in Irwin, *Night and Horses,* 155 (no source cited).

207, "not from Zionist motives'": Sasson Somekh, *Baghdad, Yesterday* (Ibis, 2007), 183. Information about his arrival in Israel and his connection to various Iraqi poets comes from his memoir; Reuven Snir, "We Were Like Those Who Dream: Iraqi-Jewish Writers in Israel in the 1950s," *Prooftexts* 11, no. 2 (1991); *al-Anba',* Dec. 10, 1982; *Iton 77,* January–February 1988; and multiple conversations with the author.

207, "Arabic poetry had": S. Moreh, *Modern Arabic Poetry, 1800–1970: The Development of Its Forms and Themes under the Influence of Western Literature* (Brill, 1976); Salma Khadra Jayyusi, *Modern Arabic Poetry: An Anthology* (Columbia University Press, 1987), 1–26; Terri DeYoung, *Placing the Poet: Badr Shakir al-Sayyab and Postcolonial Iraq* (SUNY Press, 1998), 187–220.

208, "New circumstances": Issa J. Boullata, trans., *Modern Arab Poets, 1950–1975* (Heinemann, 1976), vii–xii; Jayyusi, *Trends,* 2:557–58; Roger Allen, *An Introduction to Arabic Literature* (Cambridge University Press, 2000), 122–23; Starkey, "Nahda" in *Encyclopedia of Arabic Literature,* ed. Meisami and Starkey, 2:573–74.

208, "al-Jadid": Mahmud Ghanayim, *al-Jadid fi nisf qarn* (Dar al-Huda, 2004); Nabih al-Qasim, *al-Haraka al-shi'riyya al-filastiniyya fi biladina* (Dar al-Huda, 2003); Sasson Somekh, "Chayyav u-moto shel yerichon sifruti," *Haaretz,* May 13, 2005.

209, "match the rhythm": Abu Hanna, *Mahr,* 153–55.

210, "the trailblazing critics": Information about Taha Hussein, al-'Aqqad, Mandur, and *al-Risala* comes from Taha Hussein, *The Days* (American University in Cairo, 1997); David Semah, *Four Egyptian Literary Critics* (Brill, 1974); Albert Hourani,

Arabic Thought in the Liberal Age, 1798–1939 (Cambridge University Press, 1984), 324–39; Jayussi, *Trends,* 1:144–75, 2:522–29; P. Cachia, "Taha Husayn," R. Allen, "Abbas Mahmud al-'Aqqad," and A. N. Staif, "Muhammad Mandur," all in *Encyclopedia of Arabic Literature,* ed. Meisami and Starkey, 2:97–99, 296–97, 505; Fadwa Tuqan, *A Mountainous Journey: A Poet's Autobiography,* trans. Olive Kenny (Graywolf, 1990), 74, 90–99; and Ayalon, *Reading Palestine,* 51–57.

211, "poetry of personality": Quoted in Semah, *Four Egyptian Critics,* 14–15 (as are the quotations from al-'Aqqad that follow).

211, "Knowledge": Quoted in Mona El-Zayyat's introduction to Taha Hussein, *The Sufferers: Stories and Polemics* (American University in Cairo, 1993), ix.

211, "Western techniques and ideas": Taha Hussein, *The Future of Culture in Egypt,* trans. S. Glazer (Octagon, 1975), 20.

211, "We must follow the path": Quoted in Hourani, *Arabic Thought,* 330.

212, "Give us a poet": Quoted in Semah, *Four Egyptian Critics,* 11.

212, "the declamatory tone": This is Semah, *Four Egyptian Critics,* 188.

212, "sees poetry": Quoted in Jayyusi, *Trends,* 1:165.

213, "Time": E. M. Forster, *Aspects of the Novel* (Harcourt, 1927), 9.

215, "Help came": Information about the 'Afifis' Nazareth Bus Company comes from my interview with Anis al-'Afifi; Dan Rabinowitz, *Overlooking Nazareth: The Ethnography of Exclusion in Galilee* (Cambridge University Press, 1997), 112–14; ISA 49/309/22.

217, "The concert was the first": *New York Times,* May 11, 1953.

218, "At 2:35 pm": The first reference to these broadcasts that I have found is listed in *al-Yawm,* Feb. 25, 1953.

219, "On the radio": Mahmoud Darwish, "Risala min al-manfa," *Diwan,* 2 vols. (Dar al-'Awda, 1994), 1:33–39.

SPARKS

222, "carried cigarettes": Interview with Michel Haddad, *al-Yawm,* Mar. 14, 1960.

222, "A Greek Orthodox Christian": Biographical information about Haddad comes from his memoir, *Min dhikrayati;* Saduq, *Shu'ara' Filastin,* 641–42; Samih al-Qasim, "Michel Haddad sha'iran wa-insanan," in Michel Haddad, *Ila ayna ayyuha al-farah* (Dar al-Aswar, 1979); Mahmud Ghanayim, Taha Muhammad Ali, et al., in *al-Mawakib* 14, nos. 3–4 (1997); Sasson Somekh, "Le'ever hamashmaut hamurkevet: al Michel Haddad ve-shirato," in Michel Haddad, *Hitztabrut* (Hakibbutz Hameuchad, 1979); Qa'war, *Tarikh al-Nasira,* 617–18; Mansour, *Waiting;* Moreh, "Arabic Literature"; al-Qasim, *al-Haraka,* 71–79; and interviews.

223, "a platform": "Hadith al-shahr," *al-Jadid,* November 1953.

224, "Ironically—": Information about *al-Adab* and Idris comes from *al-Adab,* January 1953; Starkey, "Commitment," and I. J. Boullata, "Suhayl Idris," in *Encyclopedia of Arabic Literature,* ed. Meisami and Starkey, 1:175–76, 388–89; Jayyusi, *Trends,* 2:574–83; M. M. Badawi, *Modern Arabic Literature: The Cambridge History of Arabic Literature* (Cambridge University Press, 1992), 207–9.

224, "Letter from Tel Aviv": See, e.g., *al-Jadid*, September 1954 and March 1955.

225, "respected readers": *al-Mujtama'*, September 1954.

226, "We know": "Majallat al-Mujtama'," *al-Jadid*, September 1954.

226, "Emile Touma": "al-Thaqafa al-qawmiyya al-'arabiyya fi Isra'il," *al-Jadid*, September 1956.

226, "the Ministry of Education": ISA 102/17020/5, letter dated July 26, 1958.

226, "The poet Samih al-Qasim": al-Qasim, "Michel Haddad," 8.

227, "When applying": ISA 79/164/6, "Al-Mujtama' Magazine" (date not legible).

227, "Through cooperation": Trans. Reuven Snir, from "We Were Like Those," 160.

227, "Is there any hope": Eliahu Agassi, "Literary Production . . . ," *al-Mujtama'*, August 1956.

228, "individualistic, personal poets": Hanan Ashrawi, "The Contemporary Palestinian Poetry of Occupation," *Journal of Palestine Studies* 7, no. 3 (1978): 84–85.

228, "one critic has called": Ahmed al-Tami, "Arabic 'Free Verse': The Problem of Terminology," *Journal of Arabic Literature* 24, no. 2 (1993): 185. For more on these terms, see Moreh, *Modern*, 289–311; Jayyusi, *Trends*, 1:89–90; and Mounah A. Khouri, "Prose Poetry: A Radical Transformation in Contemporary Arabic Poetry," *Edebiyat* 1, no. 2 (1976).

229, "the Arabic type of rhyme": Quoted in M. M. Badawi, *A Critical Introduction to Modern Arabic Poetry* (Cambridge University Press, 1975), 186. Further information about the Mahjar poets comes from R. C. Ostle, "The Romantic Poets," in *Modern Arabic Literature*, ed. Badawi; Moreh, *Modern Arabic Poetry*, 82–122; and Jayyusi, *Trends*, 1:85–123.

229, "revolutionized literary art": Jayyusi, *Trends*, 1:96.

230, "didn't pay any attention": Haddad, *Min dhikrayati*, 65.

230, "Haddad's book": Taha Muhammad Ali, "Hadhihi al-majmua'," in Haddad, *al-Daraj al-mu'adi ila aghwarina* (al-Hakim, 1969).

230, "According to Haddad's own account": Haddad, *Min dhikrayati*, 11.

232, "And now whoever": Samih al-Qasim, "Bisat al-rih," *al-Mujtama'*, February–March 1959.

COMPENSATION, CONTAGION, CONSUMPTION

235, "Once a Lutheran": Information about the smallpox epidemic and Schneller comes from Srouji, *Cyclamens*, 177–85; ISA 49/308/47, "The Medical Situation in Nazareth"; ISA 57/155/3 and 57/155/5, both titled "Medical Supervision"; and interviews with Dr. Elias Srouji and Dr. Nakhle Bishara.

235, "By 1954": Information about the TB hospital at Schneller comes from ISA 57/5140/15, "The TB Hospital in Nazareth"; ISA 57/155/4, "Medical Supervision of the Arab Population of Nazareth"; and "Mustashfa al-amrad al-ri'awiyya fi al-Nasira," *al-Mujtama'*, November 1957.

236, "We desire wholeheartedly": ISA 102/17038/18, letter dated Oct. 17, 1949.

237, "I ask that you": ISA 102/17038/18, letter dated Mar. 4, 1952.

237, "We are former residents": ISA 102/17038/18, letter dated Apr. 25, 1954.

238, "Regarding the problem": ISA 102/17038/18, letter dated Sept. 26, 1954. Information about the Feder murders comes from ISA 79/2334/10; ISA 102/17058/18; and interviews with the people of Moshav Tzippori.

238, "ARAB REVENGE GANG": *Yediot Achronot*, Apr. 1, 1953, front page.

238, "The police": *Yediot*, Apr. 2, 1953.

239, "inciting the two": *Yediot*, Jan. 6, 1954.

239, "everyone in the know": "Gan hamirivah haparsi b'Tzippori," *Zmanim*, February 1955 (date unclear, from ISA 102/17038/18).

239, "Another article recounted": "Mi garam et haretzach b'Tzippori," *Zmanim*, n.d. (ISA 102/17038/18).

240, "PLEASE," ISA 79/2334/10. That Marcel Feder had been a Kapo is stated explicitly in an article in *Yediot*, Apr. 2, 1953.

241, "Town Is Terra Incognita": *Jerusalem Post*, Sept. 8, 1955.

241, "It happened in early April": Information about the murder of Ahmed Qablawi comes from ISA 102/17038; interviews; and especially ISA 79/148/8. Descriptions of the sulha are drawn from this last file—for which I am grateful to Hillel Cohen for having first shown me.

243, "a traditional Arab": Information about the sulha ritual comes from Sharon Lang, "Sulha Peacemaking and the Politics of Persuasion," *Journal of Palestine Studies* 31, no. 3 (2002): 52–66; and Sharon D. Lang, *Sharaf Politics: Honor and Peacemaking in Israeli-Palestinian Society* (Routledge, 2005).

TWO FRIENDS

247, "In June 1955": "The Two Friends," "al-Sadiqayn," *al-Mujtama'*, June 1955.

250, "Wither Literature?": "al-Adab ila ayna?" *al-Mujtama'*, October 1955.

252, "The literature": Emile Habiby, *al-Jadid*, March 1954, quoted in al-Qasim, *al-Haraka*, 66.

252, "Mandelbaum Gate": "Bawwabat Mandelbaum," in Emile Habiby, *Sudasiyyat al-ayyam al-sitta wa-qissas ukhra* (reprint; 'Arabesque, 2006), 97–105.

LIVES OF THE POETS

255, "two watermelons": See, e.g., Habiby, *Saraya, the Ogre's Daughter*, trans. Peter Theroux (Ibis, 2006), 8. Habiby used this image often.

255, "He would also": "Ana mani'a al-sawa'iq al-filastini," *Masharef* 17 (1996).

255, "You'll need this now": Abu Hanna, *Mahr*, 138.

256, "One British journalist": Schwarz, *Arabs in Israel*, 142.

256, "Maki will continue": The references to Habiby's speeches come from multiple police files, including ISA 79/2161/16, 79/29/15, 102/17109/45, and 79/29/12.

257, "didn't blaze": Abu Hanna, *Mahr*, 152–53; e-mail to the author, Nov. 26, 2006.

257, "an extraordinary new phenomenon": Information about the festivals comes from Abu Hanna, *Mahr*, 155–56; Qahwaji, *al-'Arab fi zil al-ihtilal*, 284–85;

Kanafani, *Adab al-muqawama,* 69; Suleiman, *Palestine and Modern Arab Poetry,* 204; Hussein, "Arab Writers"; and interviews with Samih al-Qasim, Mahmoud Darwish, Salem Jubran, Hanna Abu Hanna, Sasson Somekh, and Na'ila Zayyad.

259, "oratory stress": Qahwaji, *al-'Arab fi zil al-ihtilal,* 285.

260, "the village of Kafr Qasim": Information about the massacre comes from Jiryis, *Arabs in Israel,* 140–53; Habiby, *Kafr Qasim* ('Arabesque, 1986); Robinson, "Occupied Citizens"; and Darwish, *Yawmiyyat,* 107–27.

260, "shocking incident": Quoted in Jiryis, *Arabs in Israel,* 148.

260, "One must write": Natan Alterman, "Tchum hamishulash," *Hator hashvi'i,* vol. 3 (Hakibbutz Hameuchad, 1972), 355.

260, "misfortune": Boaz Evron, quoted in Jiryis, *Arabs in Israel,* 149.

261, "There is no monument": Samih al-Qasim, "Kafr Qasim," trans. Nazih Kassis, in *Sadder Than Water* (Ibis, 2006), 15.

262, "tremendous influence": Qahwaji, *al-'Arab fi zil al-ihtilal,* 275.

262, "true happiness": Darwish, *Shai',* 278–79.

262, "Still later": Interview with Mahmoud Darwish, Aug. 19, 2006.

263, "He also comments": Interview with Salem Jubran, Aug. 16, 2006.

263, "popular passive resistance": Interview with Samih al-Qasim, July 4, 2006.

264, "Between the vote": Jiryis, *Arabs in Israel,* appendix, table 8, 299.

264, "Communism was a label": Schwarz, *Arabs in Israel,* 18.

264, "nailed": Abu Hanna, *Khamirat,* 26.

264, "One gathering in particular": Police accounts come from ISA 79/136/4 and 79/164/9.

265, "Rashid Hussein": Information about Rashid comes from *The World of Rashid Hussein,* ed. Kamal Boullata and Mirène Ghossein (Association of Arab-American University Graduates, 1979); *Kitab al-ta'bin,* 2 vols. (Lajnat Ihya' Turath Rashid Hussein, 1978); Samih al-Qasim, *Rimad al-ward dukhan al-ughniyya* (Maktabat Kul Shai', 1990); Sasson Somekh, "Rashid," *Masharef* 15 (1997); Somekh, "'Reconciling Two Great Loves': The First Jewish-Arab Literary Encounter in Israel," *Israel Studies* 4, no. 1 (1999); Emile Marmorstein, "Rashid Hussein: Portrait of an Angry Young Man," *Middle Eastern Studies* 1, no. 1 (1964); El-Asmar, *To Be an Arab in Israel;* Rashid Hussein, *al-A'mal al-shi'ri* (Maktabat Kul Shai', 2004), *Kalam mawzun,* 2 vols. (Lajnat Jam' Turath Rashid Hussein, 1982); interviews with Taha, Ann Lavee Hussein, Darwish, al-Qasim, Jubran, Abu Hanna, Somekh, Qa'war, Rejwan, and others. All quotations come from my interviews above unless noted otherwise.

266, "whoever denies us": Hussein, *al-Fajr,* November 1958, 11.

267, "set all hearts afire": Uri Avnery in *The World,* 94.

267, "the model of the patriotic": *Kitab al-ta'bin,* 1:89–90.

269, "That October": Information about the gathering comes from Somekh, "Reconciling" (quotations and translations regarding the meeting are his unless otherwise noted); Abu Hanna, *Khamirat,* 40–43; Kanafani, *Adab al-muqawama,* 34–35; articles in *Haaretz,* Oct. 3, 24, Dec. 26, 1958; *Massa,* Oct. 17, Nov. 14, 1958; *Davar,* Nov. 28, 1958; and *al-Fajr,* November 1958.

269, "The Locked Door": "al-Bab al-mughlaq," Hussein, *al-A'mal*, 205–6. My translation.

271, "The greatest obstacle": Abu Hanna, *Khamirat*, 41.

271, "Nazareth": Taha told me this story. It is repeated in Abu Hanna, *Khamirat*, 43.

271, "no relation to literature": Gabriel Moked, "Hapgishah 'im hasofrim ha'aravim," *Massa*, Oct. 17, 1958. My translation.

271, "What is the literature": Hussein, "Hasofrim hayehudim ve-ha'aravim," *Massa*, Nov. 14, 1958. My translation.

273, "If I were a Jewish youth," Hussein, *Kalam mawzun*, 1:98.

274, "not because I love": Hussein in al-Qasim, *Rimad*, 55.

274, "Why don't you": Hussein in al-Qasim, *Rimad*, 47

274, "As regards my writing": Hussein in al-Qasim, *Rimad*, 56.

274, "He bought all": Fouzi El-Asmar in *The World*, 79–80.

275, "expelled by the occupation": 'Izz al-Din al-Munasara, "Rashid Hussein: shajara 'arabiyya fi New York," in Hussein, *al-A'mal*, 425.

275, "The Israeli peace activist": Avnery in *The World*, 90–92.

276, "died of homelessness": I. F. Stone in *The World*, 131.

277, "the tragedy": Hussein, "I Am an Israeli Arab," *New Outlook*, December 1961, 35.

277, "Without a Passport": Hussein, "Bidun jawaz safar," *al-A'mal*, 440. My translation.

277, "state of living anarchy": Edward Said in *The World*, 83.

278, "Dear Ann": I am extremely grateful to Ann Lavee Hussein for showing me—and allowing me to quote from—this letter.

279, "The question wasn't": Edward Said in *The World*, 84.

A LEAP OUTSIDE

280, "including the large hill": Rabinowitz, *Overlooking*, 3–31; Geremy Forman, "Military Rule, Political Manipulation, and Jewish Settlement: Israeli Mechanisms for Controlling Nazareth in the 1950s," *Journal of Israeli History* 25, no. 2 (2006): 335–59.

280, "Exhibition of the Folklore": See Robinson, "Occupied Citizens."

280, "Anticipating trouble": Beinin, *Was the Red Flag Flying There?* 202; Schwartz, *The Arabs in Israel*, 15–18; ISA 79/166/18, "Maki Disturbances in Nazareth," "List of participants," dated Apr. 29, 1958; *al-Ittihad*, May 3, 1958.

281, "riot": *New York Times*, May 3, 1958.

281, "used the excuse": *Haaretz*, May 2, 1958.

281, "At a cabinet meeting": *Tarshomet yishivot hamemshalah hashminit*, vol. 7, meeting May 4, 1958, 2.

281, "truncheons and vicious abuse": Abu Hanna, *Khamirat*, 71–72.

281, "the word does more": Kanafani, *Adab al-muqawama*, 23.

281, "Arna Khamis": Abu Ghanem's account is confirmed in *Haaretz*, May 2, 1958, which reports that the pregnant Arna Khamis was one of most vocal demonstrators.

286, "construction had begun": ISA 102/7111/11, "Nazareth"; Eugenio Alliata, *Art and History of Nazareth* (Bonechi and Steimatzky, 1995), 4, 24.

287, "a narrow window": *al-Yawm,* Dec. 16, 1960.

288, "And they were off": The "Window" appeared regularly in *al-Yawm* through Apr. 28, 1962.

288, "radical modernist poetics": Information about Adonis, al-Khal, and *Shi'r* comes from Adonis, *Ha anta ayyuha al-waqt* (Dar al-Adab, 1993); *Shi'r*; Jayussi, *Trends,* 2:569–73, 599–604; and Moreh, *Modern Arabic Poetry,* 278–88.

289, "the music of poetry": T. S. Eliot, *Selected Prose of T. S. Eliot* (Harcourt Brace Jovanovich, 1975), 112.

289, "a vision": Adonis, "Muhawala fi ta'rif al-shi'r al-hadith" *Shi'r* 3, no. 11 (1959): 79.

289, "he and al-Khal were accused": Adonis, *Ha anta,* 41.

289, "smoking pipes": Adonis, *Ha anta,* 146.

289, "a lived experience": Quoted in Jayyusi, *Trends,* 2:570.

289, "renewal in poetry": Adonis, *Ha anta,* 53.

289, "heresy": "al-Tahrir w-al-tajdid fi al-shi'r al-hadith," *al-Yawm,* July 31, 1961.

290, "Rashid Hussein was arrested": Hussein, *Kalam,* 1:73.

290, "The poet is the witness": Al-Khal, quoted in "Mabda' al-tahrir . . . ," *al-Yawm,* Mar. 23, 1962.

290, "we . . . define literature": Taha Muhammad Ali, "Fi al-adab al-waqi'i," *al-Jadid,* June 1961.

291, "On behalf of the refugees": Emmett, *Beyond the Basilica,* 154–55; Cohen, *'Aravim tovim* ('Ivrit, Keter, 2006), 133; ISA 102/17038/18, memo dated Apr. 15, 1960.

292, "From our point of view": ISA 102/17038/18, memo dated Nov. 18, 1957.

Nazareth II
WHERE

298, "Our enemies": Advertisement in *Ma'ariv,* Feb. 19, 1963.

299, "forc[ed] every Arab": Jiryis, *Arabs in Israel,* 47.

299, "The ancient word": Nizar Qabbani, "Footnotes to the Book of the Setback," in *Modern Poetry of the Arab World,* ed. and trans. Abdullah al-Udhari (Penguin, 1986).

300, "We have returned": Quoted in Avi Shlaim, *The Iron Wall: Israel and the Arab World* (Penguin, 2000), 244–45.

300, "Arabs would become": Yeshayahu Leibowitz, "Hashtachim," in *Yahadut, 'am yehudi u-medinat Yisrael* (Schocken, 1979), 420.

301, "an Arabic translation": Emile Habiby, "Safha min mufakkarati," *al-Jadid,* September 1969, 20–21.

301, "If there had been": Quoted in Dalia Karpel, "Emile ve-hamashmitzim," *Kol Ha'ir,* May 1, 1992.

302, "Where"?: Muhammad Ali, *So What,* 154–55.

303, "Crack in the Skull": Muhammad Ali, *So What,* 34–37.

304, "totally floored": Anton Shammas, e-mail to the author, Oct. 18, 2006.

304, "new in its thinking": Muhammad Ali, in Haddad, *al-Daraj.*

304, "poems he kept": Shammas e-mail, Oct. 18, 2006.

304, "poet against his will": Shammas, back flap, Taha Muhammad Ali, *Shirim*, trans. Shammas (Andalus, 2006); Shammas, "Taha Muhammad Ali: mishorer machteret," *Iton 77*, October 1984, 17.

305, "Slaughter on the Acre Shore": "Madhbaha 'ala shawati 'Akka," *al-Jadid*, July–August 1972.

305, "Al-Qasim seems": al-Qasim, *al-Haraka*, 232.

306, "Abd el-Hadi Fights a Superpower": Muhammad Ali, *So What*, 2–5.

309, "We do not look": Tawfiq Zayyad, "Linunqidh adabna al-sha'abi min khatar al-daya'," *al-Jadid*, April 1967. (The following quotations are all from the same article.) Information about Zayyad comes from *al-Sira al-dhatia* and *al-Faris* (no author listed, both published by Muwasasat Tawfiq Zayyad); "A Communist View of the Middle East," MERIP Reports, no. 55, March 1977, 18–20; Avraham Yinon, "Tawfiq Zayyad: Anachnu kan harov," in *Ha'aravim b'Yisrael*, ed. Aharon Lish (Magnes, 1981); Saduq, *Shu'ara' Filastin*, 135–36; and interviews with Na'ila Zayyad and others.

310, "both . . . address": Nazim Hikmet, quoted by Mutlu Konuk in her introduction to *Poems of Nazim Hikmet*, trans. Randy Blasing and Mutlu Konuk (Persea, 2002), xvii.

311, "Here We Remain": Zayyad, "Hona baquna," in *Diwan Tawfiq Zayyad* (Dar al-'Awda, 2000), 197.

311, "Thrombosis in the Veins of Petroleum": Muhammad Ali, *So What*, 12–17.

HOMELAND AND SUITCASE

313, "poet warriors": Kanafani, *Adab al-muqawama*, 59.

313, "unknown to us": Kanafani, *Adab al-muqawama*, 11.

314, "the young man": Kanafani, *Adab al-muqawama*, 30.

315, "and all of life": Kanafani, *Adab al-muqawama*, 49–50.

315, "When we read": Muhammad Dakrub, in Samih al-Qasim, *'An al-mawkif w-al-fan* (Dar al-'Awda, 1970), 33.

315, "The Cell Has No Walls": Mahmoud Darwish, "La jidran li-l-zinzana," *Diwan*, 1:300–301.

315, "End of a Talk": Samih al-Qasim, "End of a Talk with a Jailer," in *Sadder*, 5

316, "brothers in the wound": Fadwa Tuqan, "Lan abki," *al-Adab*, April 1968.

316, "it is said that only": Ian Wedde and Fawwaz Tuqan, *Selected Poems of Mahmoud Darwish* (Carcanet, 1973), 88.

316, "ruins of those": Tuqan, "Lan abki."

316, "my homeland isn't a suitcase": Darwish, "Yawmiyyat jurh filastini," *Diwan*, 1:347.

316, "Controversy even broke out": Suleiman, *Palestine and Modern Arab Poetry*, 195.

317, "To the Poets of the Occupied Land": Nizar Qabbani, "Ila shu'ara' al-ard al-muhtalla," *al-Adab*, April 1968.

317, "Save Us from This Cruel Love!": Mahmoud Darwish, "Anqidhuna min hadha al-hubb al-qasi," *al-Jadid*, June 1969.

318, "consisted of the worst poetry": Darwish, *Shai'*, 317.

319, "When asked": Adam Shatz, "A Love Story between an Arab Poet and His Land," *Journal of Palestine Studies* 31, no. 3 (2002): 74. Darwish repeated this to me in our interview.

319, "people who plead": Darwish, *Shai'*, 350.

319, "I wish I were free": Quoted in Darwish, al-Qasim, *Rasa'il* ('Arabesque, 1989), 77. Darwish would later use this line in his poem "Kana ma sawfa yakunu," his elegy for Rashid.

320, "We have a country": Darwish, "Nusafiru k-al-nas," *Diwan*, 2:331.

321, "That day, at noon": Abu Hanna, *Khamirat*, 49.

LANDSLIDES

322, "direct political poetry": In our interview, Darwish spoke contemptuously of his own early work, and especially "Identity Card."

323, "how surprised": Mahmud 'Abbasi, "al-Hanin ila al-salon al-adabi l-Taha Muhammad Ali al-Saffuri fi al-Casanova," *al-Sharq* 33, no. 2: (2003).

325, "After winning 67 percent": *al-Sira al-dhatia*, 15–16; Emmett, *Beyond the Basilica*, 260–61.

326, "Where did you learn": Emile Habiby, "Nisharti yichidi," *Haaretz,* July 7, 1994.

326, "ISRAEL WORRIED": *New York Times,* Dec. 11, 1975.

327, "And so it was": Information about Land Day comes from Kimmerling and Migdal, *Palestinian People*, 195–96; Rabinowitz and Abu-Baker, *Coffins on Our Shoulders*, 82–83; al-Lajna al-qatariyya li-l-difa' 'an al-aradi al-'arabiyya fi-Filastin, *al-Kitab al-aswad 'an yawm al-ard* (Dar al-Jalil li-l-Nashr, 1985); and interviews with Na'ila Zayyad, Amin, and others.

328, "smashing the windows": "Five Israeli Arabs Killed in Protest Riots," *New York Times,* Mar. 31, 1976.

328, "a day of pride": *al-Kitab al-aswad,* 8.

328, "a wild attack": Yosef Goell, *Jerusalem Post,* Mar. 26, 2001.

329, "a long, cruel day": *al-Kitab al-aswad,* 8.

329, "Koenig Report": *Al hamishmar,* Sept. 7, 1976; *Journal of Palestine Studies* 6, no. 1 (1976). See also *New York Times,* Sept. 9, 29, Nov. 2, 1976.

331, "the master of Egypt": *Kitab al-ta'bin*, 1:8.

331, "his pen correctly": El-Asmar, *To Be an Arab in Israel*, 66.

331, "to find a just solution": Jiryis, *Arabs in Israel,* 190. Further information about al-Ard comes from Jiryis, *Arabs in Israel*, 187–97; Habib Qahwaji, *al-Qissa al-kamila li-harakat al-ard* (Manshurat al-'Arabi, 1978); El-Asmar, *To Be an Arab in Israel,* 65–75; Landau, *Arabs in Israel,* 92–107; Zureik, *The Palestinians in Israel* (Routledge and Kegan Paul, 1979), 172–75; Sigaut, *Mansour Kardosh,* 59–70; and Ghanem, *Palestinian-Arab Minority,* 98–100.

332, "Baransi served": Saleh Baransi, "The Story of a Palestinian under Occupation," *Journal of Palestine Studies* 11, no. 1 (1981): 9; Hisham Sharabi, *Saleh Baransi: al-nidal al-samit* (Dar al-Tali'a w-al-Nashr, 1981), 31–32.

333, "al-Ard brought": Stendel, *Arabs in Israel,* 125.

THE EVENING WINE OF AGED SORROW

334, "From war to war": Habiby, *Saraya,* 15.

334, "no sewage system": Emmett, *Beyond the Basilica,* 220.

335, "PLO guerrillas": Information about the Lebanon War and the Sabra and Shatila massacre comes from Robert Fisk, *Pity the Nation: The Abduction of Lebanon* (Touchstone, 1990); Ze'ev Schiff and Ehud Ya'ari, *Israel's Lebanon War* (Simon and Schuster, 1984); Michael Jansen, *The Battle of Beirut: Why Israel Invaded Lebanon* (South End, 1982); Yermiya, *My War Diary;* Shlaim, *Iron Wall,* 384–423; Sayigh, *Too Many,* 15–31; and *The Beirut Massacre: The Complete Kahan Commission Report* (Karz-Cohl, 1983).

335, "kill an idea": Flora Lewis, *International Herald Tribune,* Aug. 7–8, 1982, quoted in Jansen, *Battle of Beirut,* 48.

335, "whether by methods": *Beirut Massacre,* 9.

335, "to transform the situation": Shlaim, *Iron Wall,* 396.

336, "The camp was": David Richardson, *Jerusalem Post,* July 9, 1982, quoted in Jansen, *Battle of Beirut,* 19.

337, "Ain Hilweh camp": Quoted in Jansen, *Battle of Beirut,* 19.

337, "The sun is overwhelming": Yermiya, *My War Diary,* 16.

337, "The damage": Yermiya, *My War Diary,* 41.

337, "With this [shelling]": Yermiya, *My War Diary,* 26.

339, "I am writing my silence": Darwish, "Mahmoud Darwish: hamil ja'izat Lenin li-l-salam," *al-Jadid,* June 5, 1983. He repeats this exchange in *Memory for Forgetfulness: August, Beirut, 1982,* trans. Ibrahim Muhawi (University of California Press, 1995), 61.

339, "The poem 'Exodus'": "Exodus," Muhammad Ali, *So What,* 30–33. See *So What* for all of Taha Muhammad Ali's poems mentioned hereafter.

339, "The poem was first": *Filastin al-thawra,* July 9, 1983.

340, "to preserve tranquility and order": Jansen, *Battle of Beirut,* 95.

340, "pregnant women": *Beirut Massacre,* 35.

341, "to create panic": *Haaretz,* Sept. 28, 1982, quoted in Jansen, *Battle of Beirut,* 107.

FOOLING THE KILLERS

351, "What moved me": Jeroslav Stetkevych, *The Zephyrs of Najd: The Poetics of Nostalgia in the Classical Arabic Nasib* (University of Chicago Press, 1993), 51–55 (trans. Stetkevych). Information about the earthquake and Ibn Munqidh comes from Amin Maalouf, *The Crusades through Arab Eyes* (Saqi, 1984), 154–55.

352, "one eminent scholar": Stetkevych, *Zephyrs,* 55.

352, "singular consciousness": Ahmed Hussein, "Marthiyya al-wa'y al-mutafarid," in *al-Qasida al-rabi'a,* 14.

353, "This is poetry": Salman Masalha, "Ain navi b'iro," *Keshet* 17 (2006): 175–76.

353, "poet of the underground": Shammas, *Iton 77,* 17.

354, "his simple subject matter": Atallah Jaber, "al-Sadiq al-hadari fi 'al-qasida al-rabi'a," *al-Jadid,* May 1984.

354, "When the union": "Nishatat thaqafiyya," *al-Jadid,* July 1988.

355, "Although no one at the festival": Information about the festival comes from Taha; Ghali Shukri, *Burj Babel* (Riad el-Rayyes, 1989), 159–73; and "Wafd ittihad al-kitab . . . ," *al-Jadid,* August 1988.

355, "aged man from Palestine": (and subsequent quotations) Shukri, *Burj Babel,* 171–73.

356, "impassioned tributes": Ami Elad Bouskilla, *Modern Palestinian Literature and Culture* (Frank Cass, 1999), 85–111.

357, "Poem of the Intifada": al-Qasim, "Qasidat al-intifada," *al-A'mal al-kamila,* vol. 4 (Dar Su'ad al-Sabah, 1993), 405.

357, "The poetry of stones": Riad Baydas, "al-Wail lana idha kabara al-tifl fi dakhilna," *al-Sharq* 33, no. 2 (2003): 101.

358, "prefer[red] the way a poet": Salma Khadra Jayyusi, *Anthology of Modern Palestinian Literature* (Columbia University Press, 1992), 64.

360, "works rich in nuance," "Mahfouz: Clarity Is Good, But So Is Ambiguity," *New York Times,* Oct. 14, 1988.

360, "There was a jubilant reaction": Sheila Rule, "Nobel Prize in Literature Awarded to an Arabic Writer for First Time," *New York Times,* Oct. 14, 1988.

360, "Politics, however": Sasson Somekh, "I Dream of the Day When," *Dissent,* Winter 2004.

360, "establishment of the State of Palestine": *The Israeli-Palestinian Conflict: A Documentary Record, 1967–1990,* ed. Yehuda Lukacs (Cambridge University Press, 1992), 413.

361, "a deceptive propaganda exercise": Quoted in Shlaim, *Iron Wall,* 466.

361, "*Fooling the Killers* appeared": *Dahik 'ala dhuqun al-qatala* (Ittihad al-Kutab al-'Arab, 1989).

363, "Taha's crippled father": ISA 79/148/15, document dated Feb. 21, 1958.

363, "aged 22": ISA 79/136/8, document dated May 26, 1957.

364, "perhaps the most accessible": Eliot Weinberger, "Books of the Year 2006 Symposium," www.readysteadybook.com.

INSIDE OUT

369, "vision of experience": Vivian Eden, "Home in the Poems," *Haaretz,* English ed., Oct. 27, 2000.

369, "*Fire in the Convent Garden*": *Hariq fi maqbarat al-dayr* (Markaz al-Ihya' al-Turath al-'Arabi, 1992).

370, "process of artistic rapprochement": Information about Habiby's time in Prague and the artists' peace treaty comes from Yosef Algazy, "Gesher beyn shtai sfinot," *Haaretz,* Apr. 12, 1996; Naomi Gal, "Yotzrim yisraelim ve-falastinayim kvar chatmu heskem shalom," *Yediot,* June 14, 1988; and "Heskem shalom k'akt simli," *Yediot,* June 17, 1988.

371, "right-wing Jews": "Rak yehudim ve-aravim yodim . . . ," *Yediot,* May 10, 1992.

371, "garbage, garbage": "'Zevel, zevel,' tza'aku pi'ilai halikud . . . ," *Yediot,* May 19, 1992.

371, "a victory for Arab culture": Abdullah al-Suhayl, *al-Sharq al-awsat,* Mar. 23, 1992.

371, "poisonous": *Filastin al-thawra,* June 21, 1992.

371, "a dialogue of prizes": Joel Greenberg, "To a Novelist of Nazareth, Laurels and Loud Boos," *New York Times,* May 7, 1992.

371, "together with the whole Arab population": Algazy, "Gesher."

372, "I said that I could not": Quoted in Sinan Antoon, "Mahmud Darwish's Allegorical Critique of Oslo," *Journal of Palestine Studies* 31, no. 2 (2002): 76.

372, "Over the years": Algazy, "Gesher."

372, "committed to literature and coexistence": Jeffrey Green, "Writers Created Scenario for the Peace Process," *Jerusalem Post,* Oct. 25, 1993.

374, "During the festival": Dalia Karpel, "Ve-al af hacol, matzavo no'esh," *Haaretz,* Mar. 31, 1995.

DIFFICULT SIMPLICITY

377, "If Haddad's": Information about the Shihab al-Din controversy comes from Charles M. Sennott, *The Body and the Blood: The Middle East's Vanishing Christians and the Possibility for Peace* (PublicAffairs, 2001), 203–31; Raphael Israeli, *Green Crescent over Nazareth: The Displacement of Christians by Muslims in the Holy Land* (Frank Cass, 2002); Atallah Mansour, *Narrow Gate Churches: The Christian Presence in the Holy Land under Muslim and Jewish Rule* (Hope, 2004); 280–84; Deborah Sontag, "God's Half Acre, But Whose God? A Town Is Torn," *New York Times,* Apr. 13, 1999; Sontag, "Defiant Muslims Begin Building Nazareth Mosque," *New York Times,* Nov. 24, 1999; and Hany Abu-Assad, dir., *Nazareth 2000.*

379, "On any given day": Sennott, *Body,* 210.

381, "a difficult, elusive, or even inscrutable simplicity": Peter Cole, "A Note on the Translation," in *So What,* xxiii.

WORK HARD, FLY RIGHT

386, "a deeply humane collection": Edward Hirsch, "Poet's Choice," *Washington Post,* Oct. 13, 2002.

387, "The pure words": "The Reason to Live Here," Aharon Shabtai, *J'accuse,* trans. Peter Cole (New Directions, 2003), 5.

391, "fourth collection": *Ilah, khalifa, wa-sabi farashat mulawanat* (Venus, 2002).

391, "book of short stories": *Ma yakun wa-qissas uchra.*

392, "one of the diseases": Quoted in Gabriel Levin's introduction to *So What,* xvii–xviii.

THE PLACE ITSELF

396, "Lebanese town of Bint Jbeyl": Omayna Abdel-Latif, "Hail Bint Jbeil," *al-Ahram,* July 27–Aug. 2, 2006; Richard A. Oppel, Jr., "Largely Empty, Stronghold of Militia Is Still Perilous," *New York Times,* Aug. 14, 2006.

396, "thousands of fleeing": UN General Assembly, Human Rights Council, "Written Statement Submitted by BADIL Resource Center . . . ,"Aug. 11, 2006.

396, "an obvious hotbed": Juan Cole, "Informed Comment," www.juancole.com, Aug. 10, 2006.

396, "more than a thousand": BBC News, "PM Says Israel Pre-Planned War," Aug. 3, 2007; "Timeline of the July War 2006," www.dailystar.com/lb/July_War06.asp.

396, "Jiyyeh power plant": Matthew Weaver, "Oil Slick Threatens Mediterranean Beaches," *Guardian*, Aug. 1, 2006; Bassem Mroue, "Lebanon Sees Environmental Devastation," AP, Aug. 1, 2006.

396, "offices of *al-Ittihad*": Assaf Carmel, "The Rocket Hit the Struggle for Peace," *Haaretz*, Aug. 8, 2006.

396, "family comes from Saffuriyya": Nazir Majali, "Torn between Both Sides," *Haaretz*, July 21, 2006; Sharon Roffe-Ophir, "No One Told Us, the Arabs, to Take Shelter," Ynet, July 19, 2006.

397, "Nazareth has not a single bomb shelter": "Arab Community Stands for Peace during War in Lebanon," *Mossawah News*, May 2007; Yariv Oppenheimer, "No Sirens in Arabic," Ynet, July 20, 2006; Shelly Paz, "Most Arab Communities in North Have No Bomb Shelters," *Jerusalem Post*, May 7, 2007.

398, "transfixed": Michael Wiegers, e-mail to the author, Mar. 12, 2008.

ACKNOWLEDGMENTS

In ways huge and small, dozens of people have contributed to the making of this book. Taha Muhammad Ali has spoiled me completely for future biographies by being the most honest, delightful, and unassuming subject conceivable. Yusra Qablawi and the rest of Taha's immediate family—Aisheh, Nizar, and Usama 'Abd el-Mo'ti—have allowed me into their home and their lives in the warmest and least neurotic manner. Their kindness and quiet understanding, along with their willingness to trust the head of their household to my biographical (and sometimes physical) care, have made this book possible. Amin Muhammad Ali, meanwhile, has been more than a remarkable interview subject: he has been a thoroughly munificent guide to both the Saffuriyya of his childhood and the Nazareth of today, arranging introductions, plying me with hard-to-find Arabic books, and traipsing across any number of thorny fields in my company. Layla 'Abd el-Mo'ti Zaydani has been a poised and gentle presence, while Feisel Muhammad Ali has provided me with both several marvelous photographs and some valuable perspective. Others in Nazareth have also made me feel at home there. In particular I would like to thank Ala'a Jabari and the Sisters of Nazareth, Faryal 'Abd el-Mo'ti, and Naseem Awwad—who has offered so many different kinds of help, and with such good-natured modesty, it's impossible to thank him enough.

To all of my interview subjects—in Nazareth and elsewhere—I owe a tremendous debt. (Their names appear on pp. 409–10.) I am especially beholden to Siham Daoud, who has proven a wonderfully candid and compelling font of insight and information, while Anton

Shammas and Hanna Abu Hanna have been gracious and patient in response to my volleys of questions. From the start of my work on this book, Sasson Somekh has been unflagging in his support and generous with his unmatched knowledge.

I am also indebted to scholars in various fields, who might easily have been reluctant to share their considerable learning but who were, to a one, open and eager to help: Hillel Cohen, Elliott Colla, Mahmud Ghanayim, Asher Kaufman, Linda Kerber, John Knight, Jackson Lears, Julie Peteet, Shira Robinson, Orit Rozin, Rosemary Sayigh, Sherene Seikaly, Jihane Sfeir-Khayat, and Avi Shlaim. A. J. Sherman belongs high on this list—as he does on several others. I am thankful to him in ways too numerous to account for here. Robert Schine, too, has spurred me on both with friendship and intellectual engagement. "Boundless" hardly conveys the scope of my gratitude to Michael Sells, whose erudition is as broad as his enthusiasm is wide: his "heart can take on / any form"—hardly a given where the modern Middle East is concerned.

Lauren Sobel, Richard Laster, and Ariella Grinberg clarified several important legal points, while Sinan Antoon, Roberta Bell-Kligler, Rob Blecher, Kamal Boullata, David Caligiuri, Yael Cohen, Vivian Eden, Elise Friedland, Gali Gamliel-Fleischer, Lisa Grant, Moin Halloun, Violette Khoury, Michal Krumer-Nevo, Gidi Nevo, Cathy Nichols, Rina Ofek, Marita Schine, Jawad Siyam, Jakov Spichko, Azza Tzvi, Assia Vilenkin, and Jeremy Zwelling all made important contributions to my research. So, too, I would like to thank the staffs of the archives where I conducted research and the librarians of the Oriental and General Reading Rooms at the Jewish National and University Library in Jerusalem, who went well out of their way to fish journals, books, and old newspapers out of their basement labyrinth.

Miriam Altshuler and Ileene Smith have been steadfast in their belief in this book; I am enormously lucky to work with them both, and feel very fortunate as well for the gifted and punctilious staff of Yale University Press, who made the book's complex production possible.

William Kennedy deserves special thanks for having first urged me to write about Taha. Barbara Surk, Mary Taylor Simeti, and Phyllis Rose offered words of wisdom at important early stages of the project. Rosellen Brown, Joyce Chopra, Robert Cohen, Tom Cole,

Claudia Cooper, Yahya Hijazi, Marvin Hoffman, Gabriel Levin, María Rosa Menocal, Corey Robin, Nina Subin, Peter Theroux, Eliot Weinberger, and Michael Wiegers helped in various crucial ways later on. I am grateful beyond these words for their encouragement and their friendship, as I am for the companionship of many others, near and far.

Nearest of all, Peter Cole is everywhere in these lines, and between them. This book would be unimaginable without him.

Index